CARNET DE VOYAGE

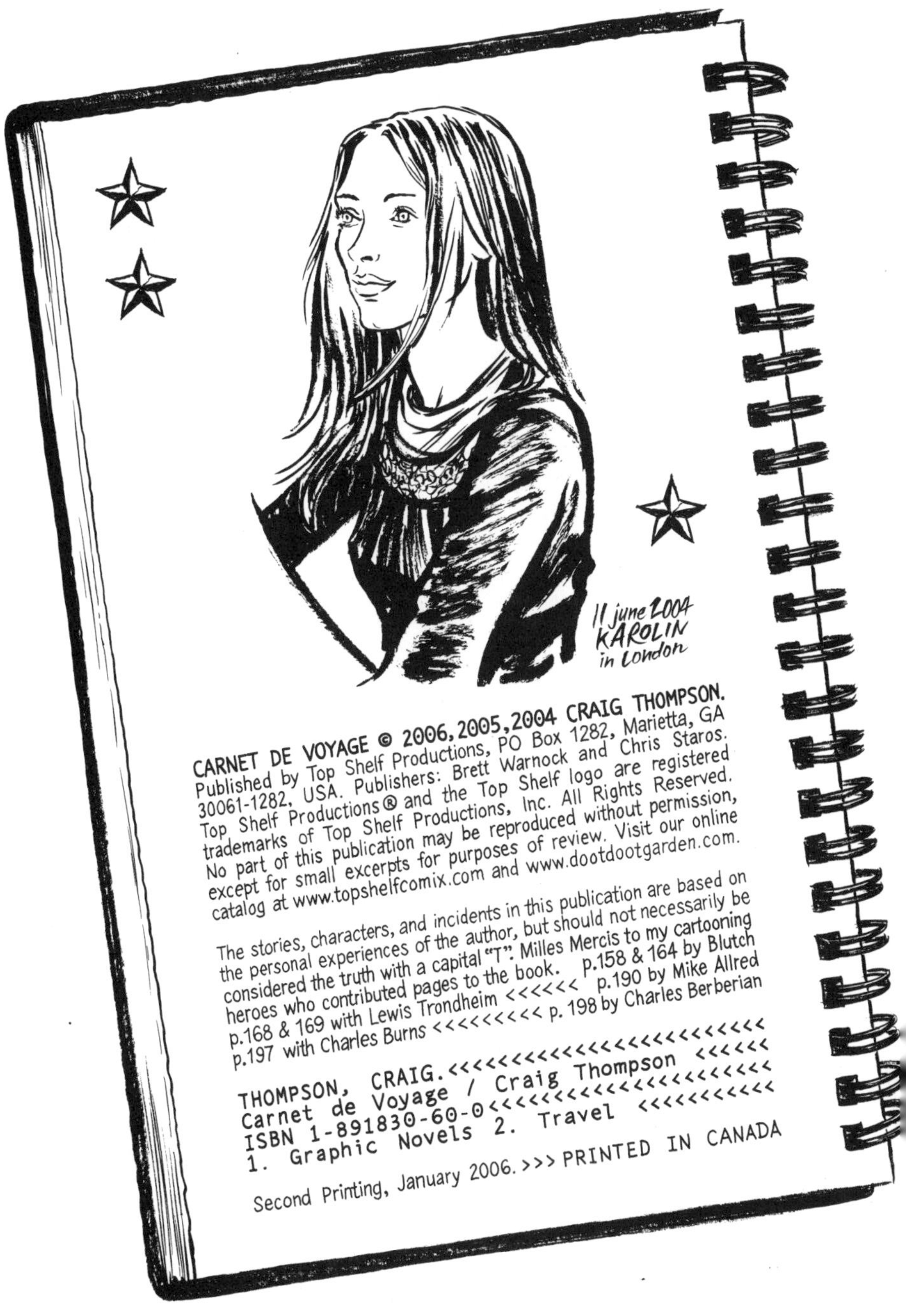
11 june 2004
KAROLIN
in London

Published by Top Shelf Productions, PO Box 1282, Marietta, GA 30061-1282, USA. Publishers: Brett Warnock and Chris Staros.
 Visit our online catalog at www.topshelfcomix.com and www.dootdootgarden.com.

The stories, characters, and incidents in this publication are based on the personal experiences of the author, but should not necessarily be considered the truth with a capital "T". Milles Mercis to my cartooning heroes who contributed pages to the book. p.158 & 164 by Blutch
p.168 & 169 with Lewis Trondheim <<<<<< p.190 by Mike Allred
p.197 with Charles Burns <<<<<<<<< p. 198 by Charles Berberian <<<<<<<<<<<<<<<<<<<<<<<<

THOMPSON, CRAIG. <<<<<<<<<<<<<<<<<<<<<<<<<
Carnet de Voyage / Craig Thompson <<<<<<
ISBN 1-891830-60-0<<<<<<<<<<<<<<<<<<<<<<<
1. Graphic Novels 2. Travel <<<<<<<<<<< PRINTED IN CANADA

Second Printing, January 2006. >>>

CARNET DE VOYAGE

Travel Journal Volume One >>>>> CRAIG THOMPSON

TOP SHELF PRODUCTIONS <<<<< Marietta, Georgia, USA

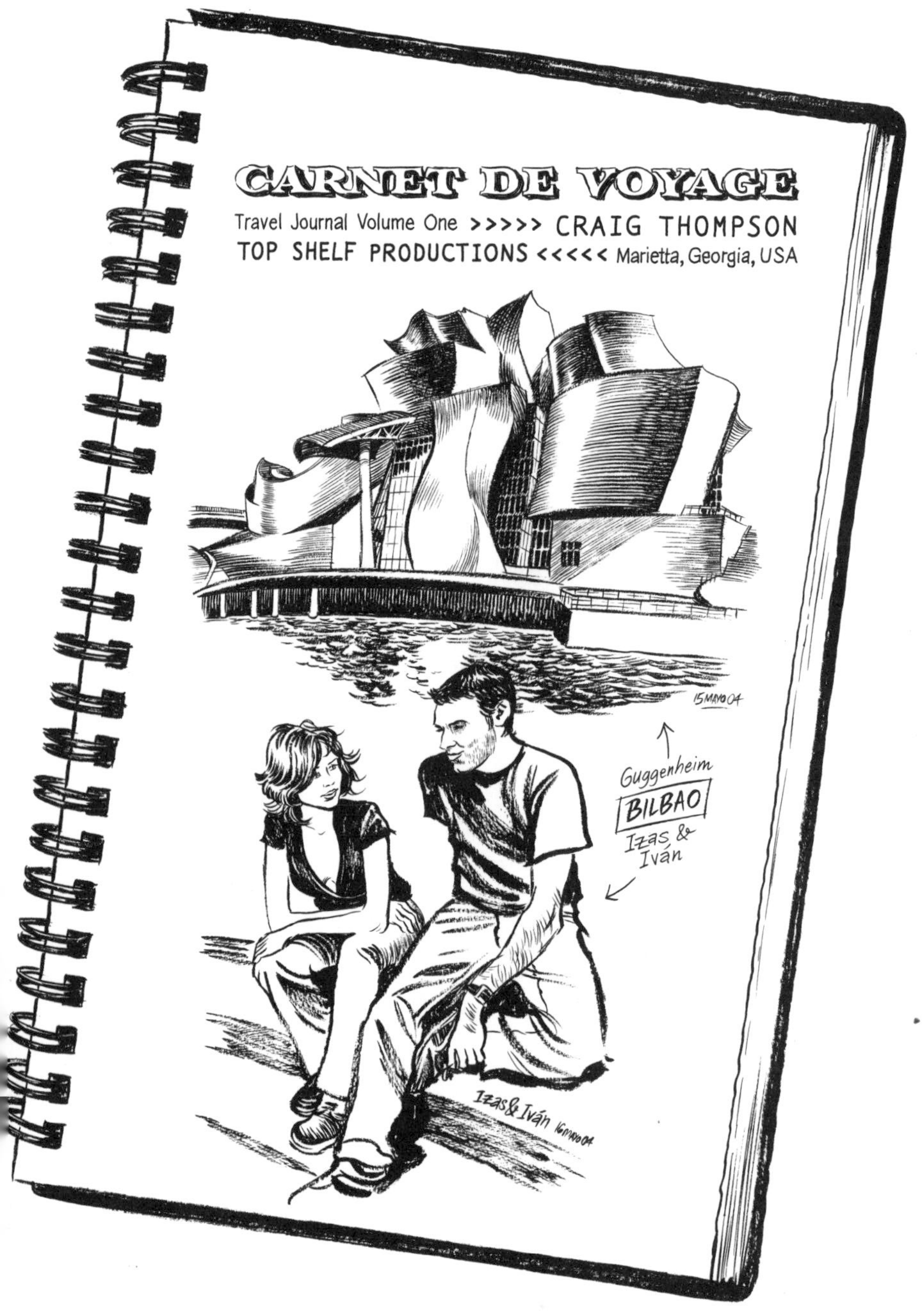
15 MAYO 04
Guggenheim
BILBAO
Izas &
Iván
Izas & Iván 16 MAYO 04

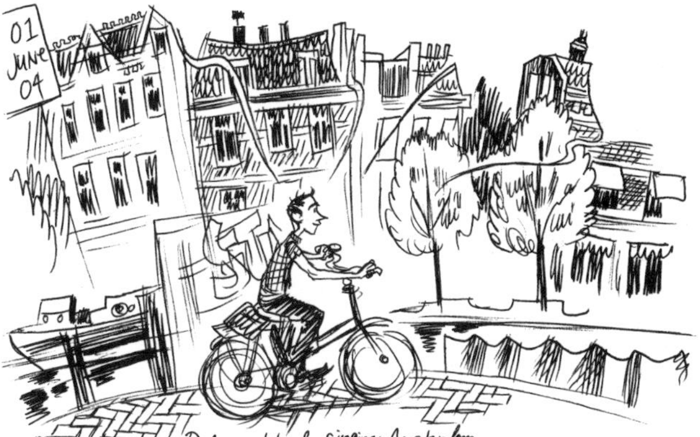
01
JUNE
04
Riding a bike & singing: Amsterdam

DISCLAIMER:

This is not "the Next Book", but rather a self-indulgent side-project --a simple travel diary drawn while I was traveling through Europe & Morocco from March 5th to May 14th, 2004.

It stirred people's interest - suggesting it could see print - so I copped the example of French publisher L'ASSOCIATION who published casual carnets with matching dimensions in their COLLECTION CÔTELETTE.

Perhaps it's ill-advised to release such off-the-cuff material... Feel free to tell me if you think so, but know you've been warned.

As for my loyal readers, this is a little snack - à la airline pretzels - while you're waiting for "the Next Book". Hopefully, it's more agreeable than a slideshow.

GROSSES BISES,
CRAIG (Lyon, France 22 mai 04)

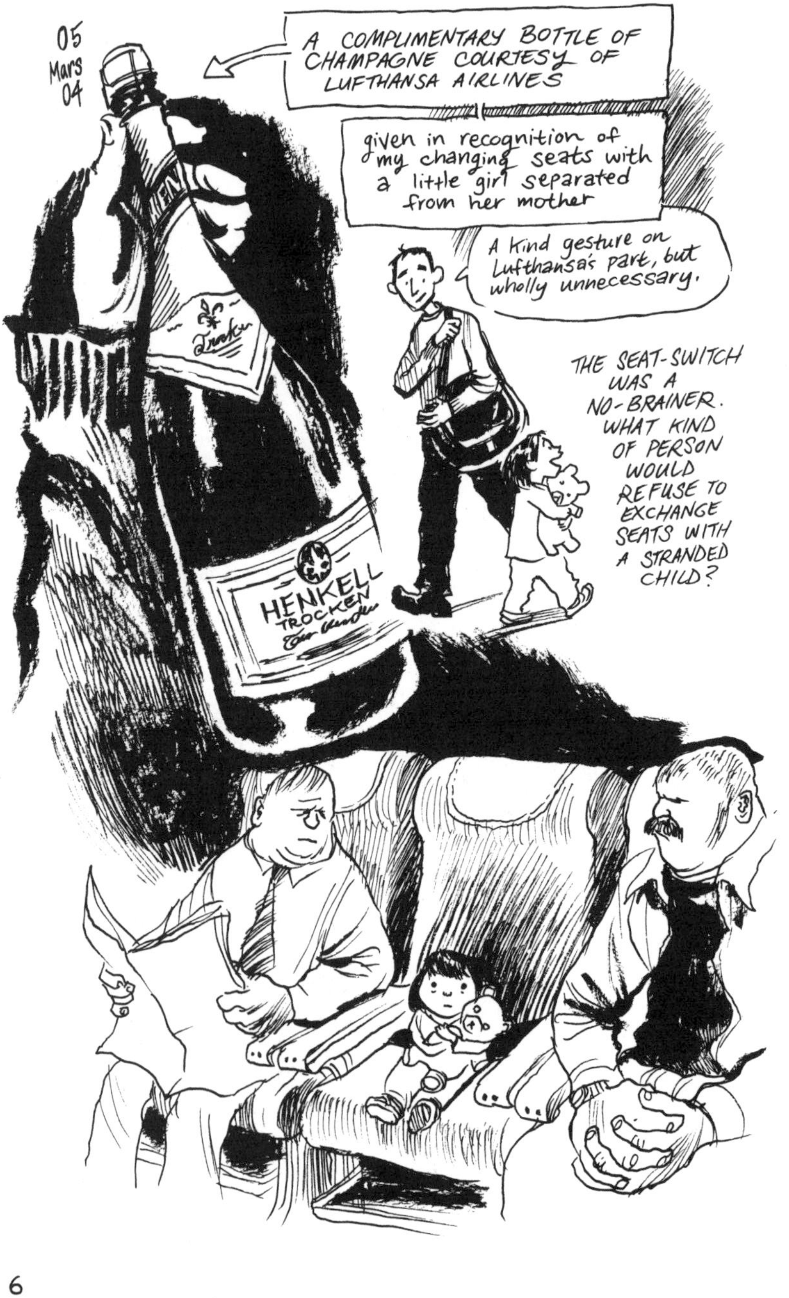
05
Mars
04
A COMPLIMENTARY BOTTLE OF CHAMPAGNE COURTESY OF LUFTHANSA AIRLINES
given in recognition of my changing seats with a little girl separated from her mother
A kind gesture on Lufthansa's part, but wholly unnecessary.
THE SEAT-SWITCH WAS A NO-BRAINER. WHAT KIND OF PERSON WOULD REFUSE TO EXCHANGE SEATS WITH A STRANDED CHILD?
HENKELL
TROCKEN

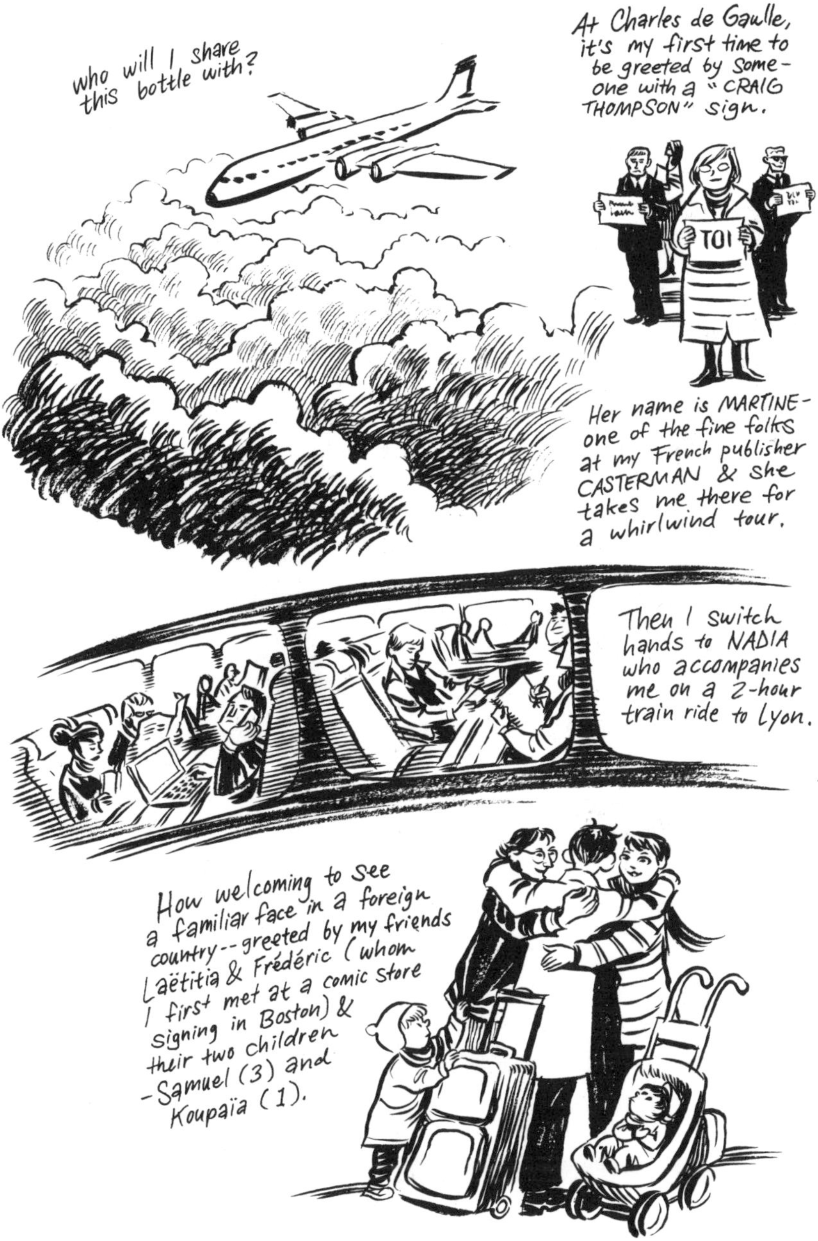
who will I share this bottle with?
At Charles de Gaulle, it's my first time to be greeted by some-one with a "CRAIG THOMPSON" sign.
TOI
Her name is MARTINE-one of the fine folks at my French publisher CASTERMAN & she takes me there for a whirlwind tour.
Then I switch hands to NADIA who accompanies me on a 2-hour train ride to Lyon.
How welcoming to see a familiar face in a foreign country--greeted by my friends Laëtitia & Frédéric (whom I first met at a comic store signing in Boston) & their two children -Samuel (3) and Koupaïa (1).

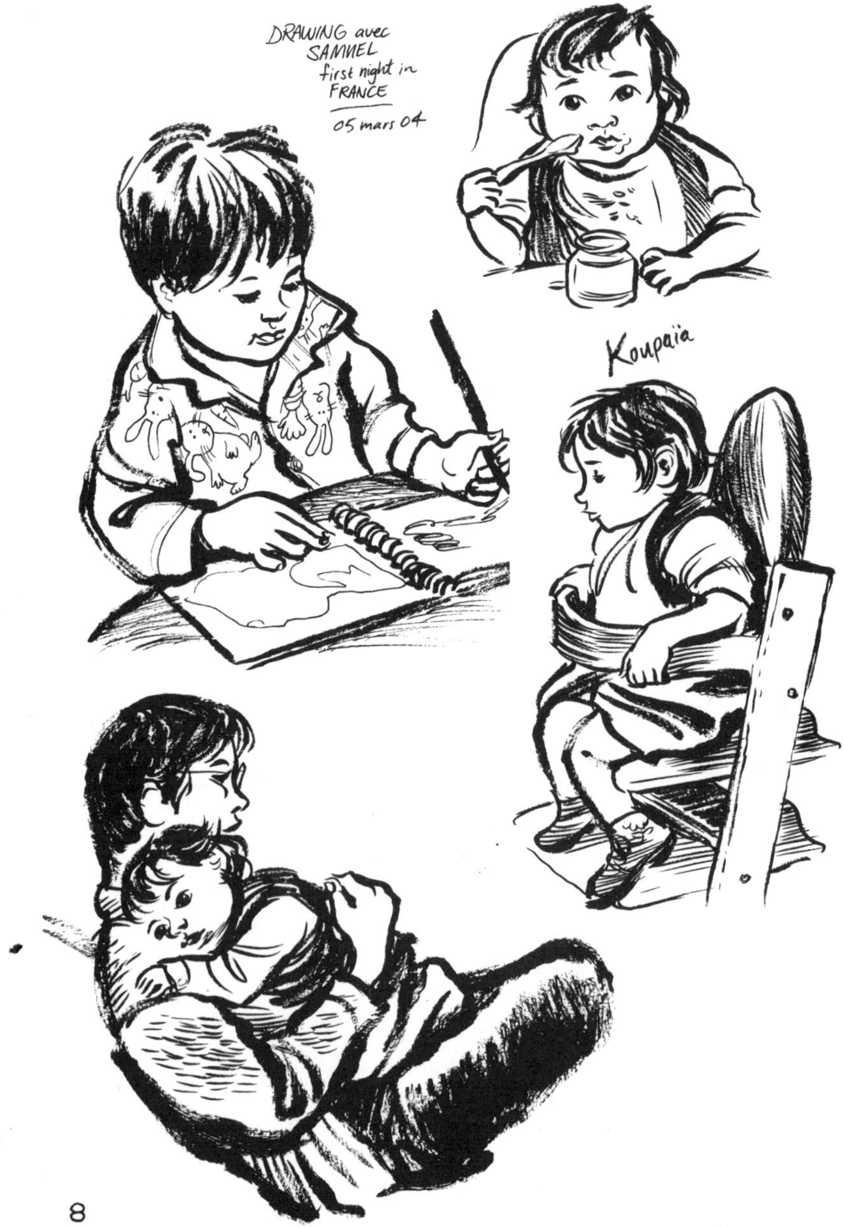
DRAWING avec
SAMUEL
first night in
FRANCE
05 mars 04
Koupaia

06 mars 04

Woke to the clamor of kids and sun pouring in an unshuddered window. My body trashed & eyes pasted shut, I waited until the house was peaceful (children to preschool) before getting up. Then, basic French breakfast: bread, butter, honey, and caramel tea sipped from a bowl. Parfait. Frédéric and I took the subway to L'EXPÉRIENCE — an amazing comic shop

hosting a signing for me on my first official day in France. First, lunch with Nadia and nine journalists and cute Agathe who works at the store. Round-table interviews between bites of food. Frédéric translated. At the shop, drew in 50 plus books and then a magic marker sketch for the ceiling. Most abstract request was to draw "HOPE". I managed something like this.

CLICHÉ

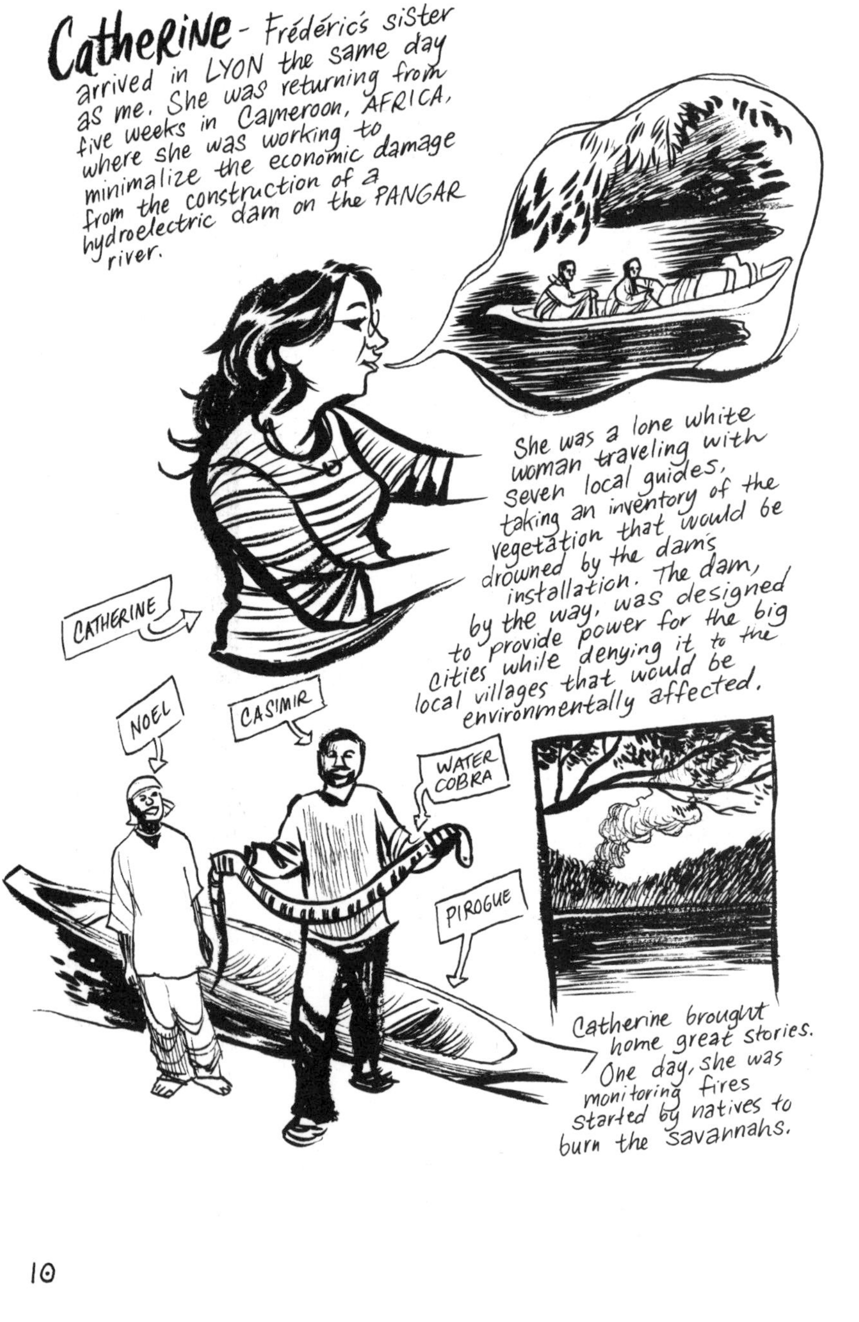
Catherine - Frédéric's sister arrived in LYON the same day as me. She was returning from five weeks in Cameroon, AFRICA, where she was working to minimalize the economic damage from the construction of a hydroelectric dam on the PANGAR river.
She was a lone white woman traveling with seven local guides, taking an inventory of the vegetation that would be drowned by the dam's installation. The dam, by the way, was designed to provide power for the big cities while denying it to the local villages that would be environmentally affected.
CATHERINE
NOEL
CASIMIR
WATER COBRA
PIROGUE
Catherine brought home great stories. One day, she was monitoring fires started by natives to burn the savannahs.

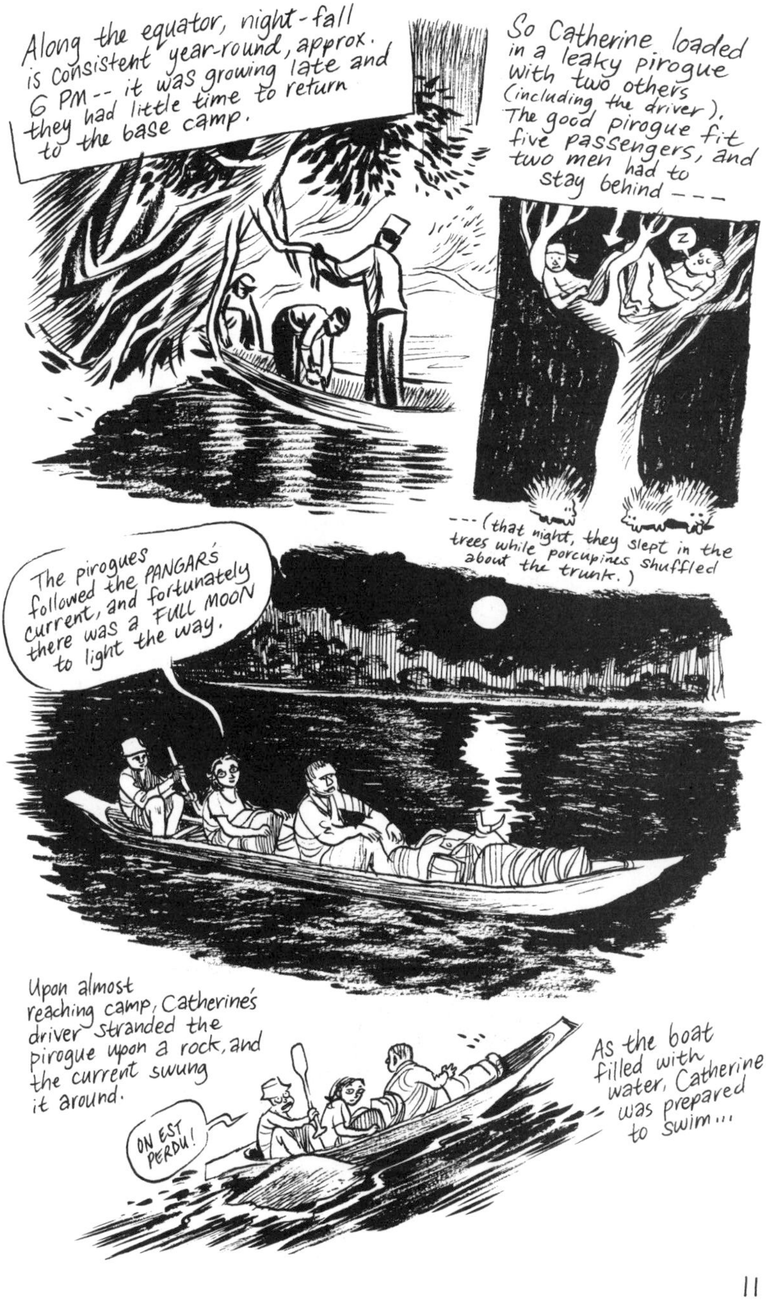
Along the equator, night-fall is consistent year-round, approx. 6 PM -- it was growing late and they had little time to return to the base camp.
So Catherine loaded in a leaky pirogue with two others (including the driver). The good pirogue fit five passengers, and two men had to stay behind ---
Z
---(that night, they slept in the trees while porcupines shuffled about the trunk.)
The pirogues followed the PANGAR'S current, and fortunately there was a FULL MOON to light the way.
Upon almost reaching camp, Catherine's driver stranded the pirogue upon a rock, and the current swung it around.
ON EST PERDU!
As the boat filled with water, Catherine was prepared to swim...

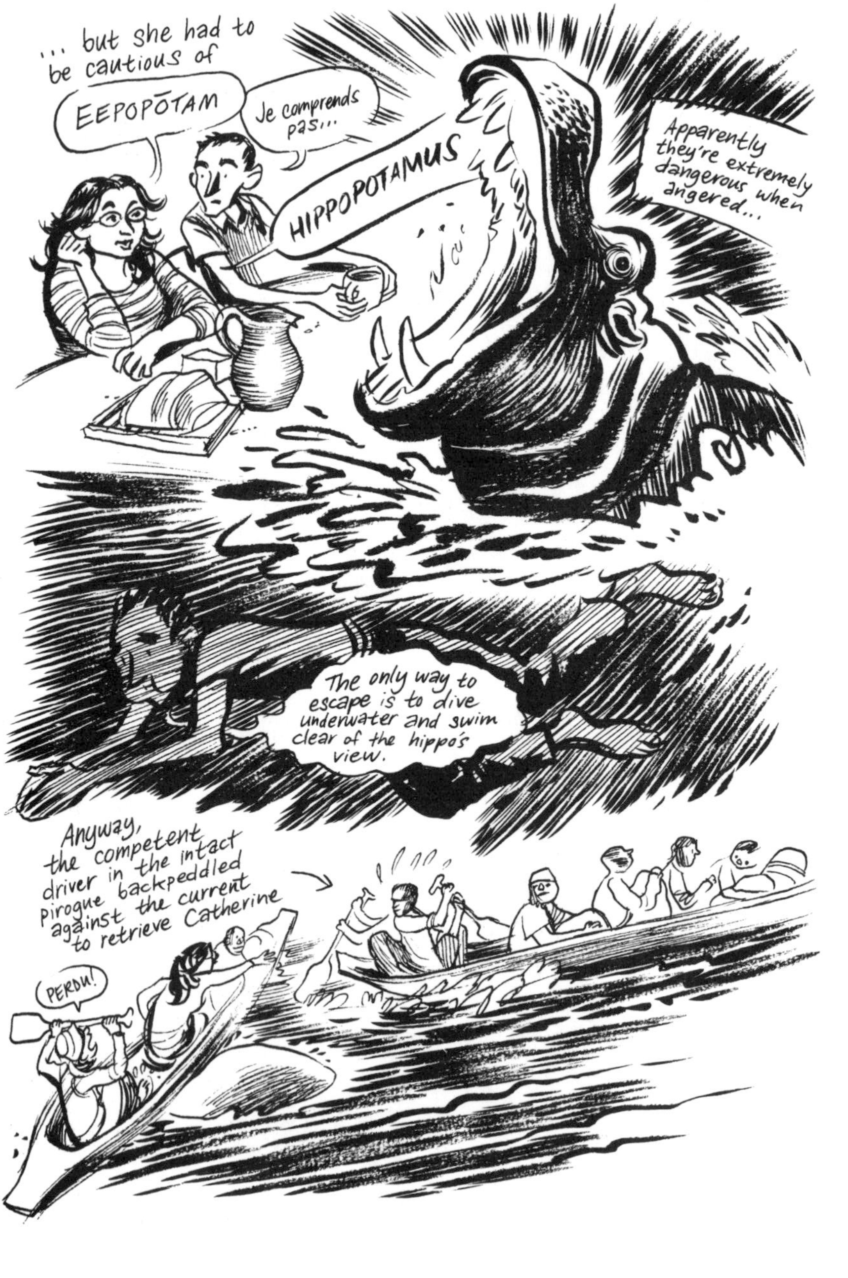
... but she had to be cautious of
EEPOPŌTAM
Je comprends pas...
HIPPOPOTAMUS
Apparently they're extremely dangerous when angered...
The only way to escape is to dive underwater and swim clear of the hippo's view.
Anyway, the competent driver in the intact pirogue backpeddled against the current to retrieve Catherine
PERDU!

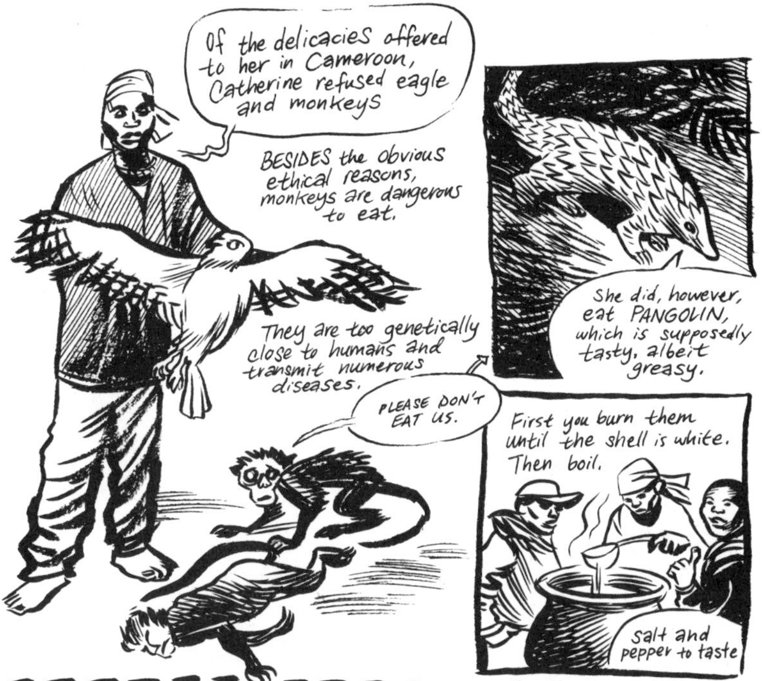
Of the delicacies offered to her in Cameroon, Catherine refused eagle and monkeys
BESIDES the obvious ethical reasons, monkeys are dangerous to eat.
They are too genetically close to humans and transmit numerous diseases.
PLEASE DON'T EAT US.
She did, however, eat PANGOLIN, which is supposedly tasty, albeit greasy.
First you burn them until the shell is white. Then boil.
salt and pepper to taste

And here I am in France taking on my own culinary adventures:

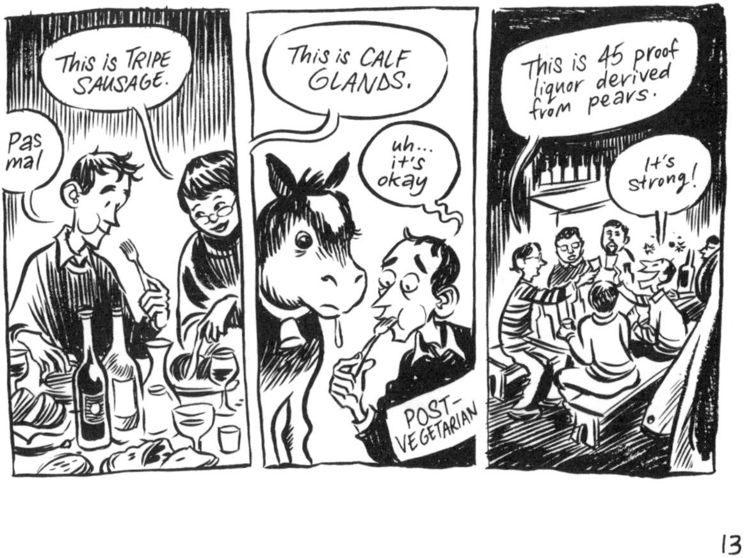
This is TRIPE SAUSAGE.
Pas mal
This is CALF GLANDS.
uh... it's okay
POST-VEGETARIAN
This is 45 proof liquor derived from pears.
It's strong!

08 mars 04

I was interviewed at RCF - French Christian radio - by a man with a white beard and gentle blue eyes. We sat in a sound room with Laëtitia at my right translating the bearded man's questions, and Frédéric at my left, translating my answers.

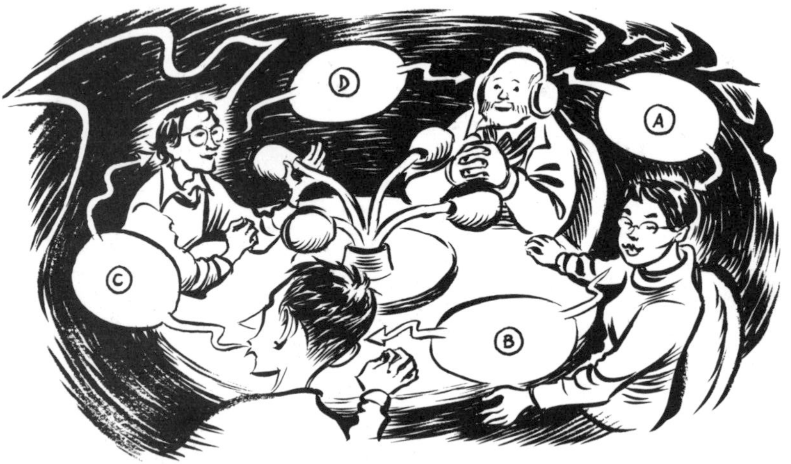
D
A
C
B

The radio station was stuffy, as you'd imagine French Christian radio to be, but it was decorated with amazing photos of developmentally disabled persons painting, dancing, playing music. The French Minister of Agriculture shook my hand as he walked by.

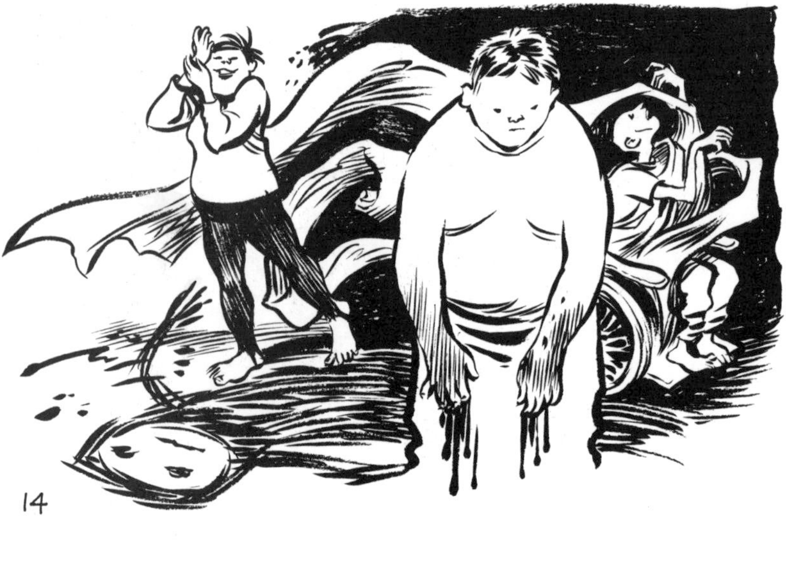

Frédéric, Laëtitia and I continued on with the religious theme, visiting the two major churches in Lyon--Basilique Notre-Dame de Fourvière and Cathédrale Saint-Jean. The former is gaudy, saturated in decoration, but brought me to tears as I stared up at Mary encircled by angels. I thought not of Jesus, but of my own MOM & my last girlfriend and how we'd taken care of each other and how abandoned we all felt.

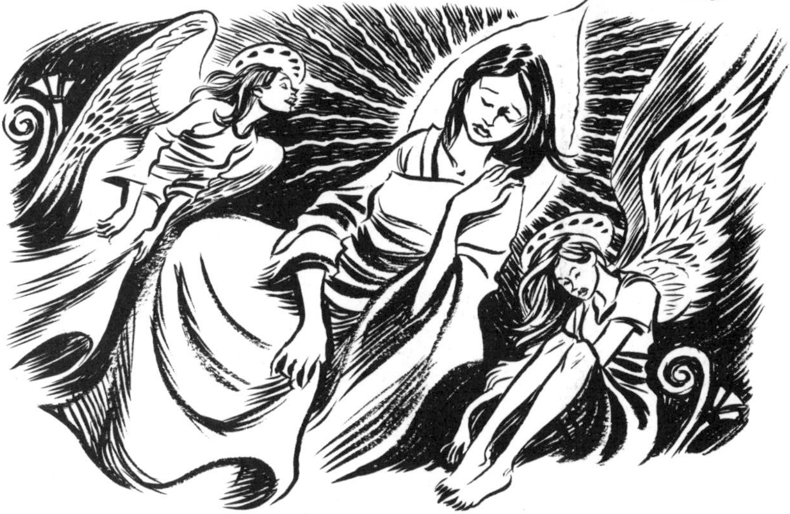

All evening, Laëtitia and I looked after Samuel & Koupaïa. (Frédéric was at a meeting.) My legs became a slide, and my belly a trampoline.

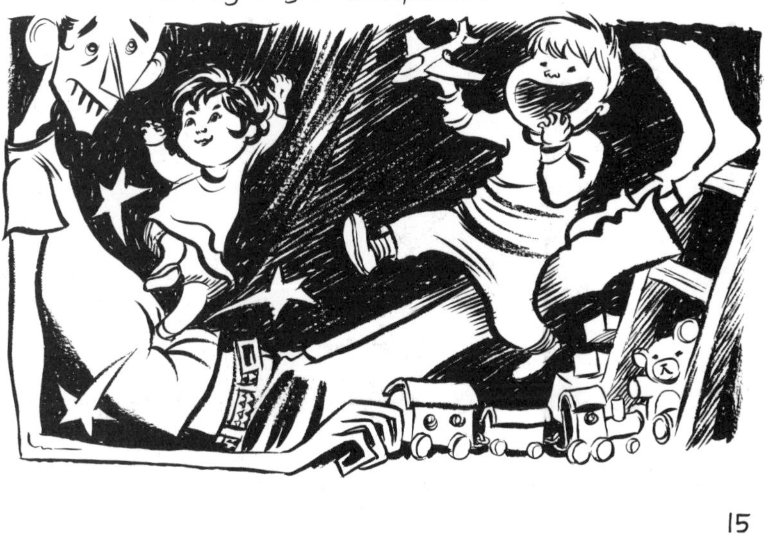

09 mars 04

Today is the day of being spoiled by my French publisher-CASTERMAN. They paid for my train ride from Lyon to Paris, then lunch, then a cab ride (accompanied by a cute girl, no less) to a SPACIOUS APARTMENT (all mine for the week) and finally a cell phone (my first ever) for European communication.

(like Femme Nikita!)

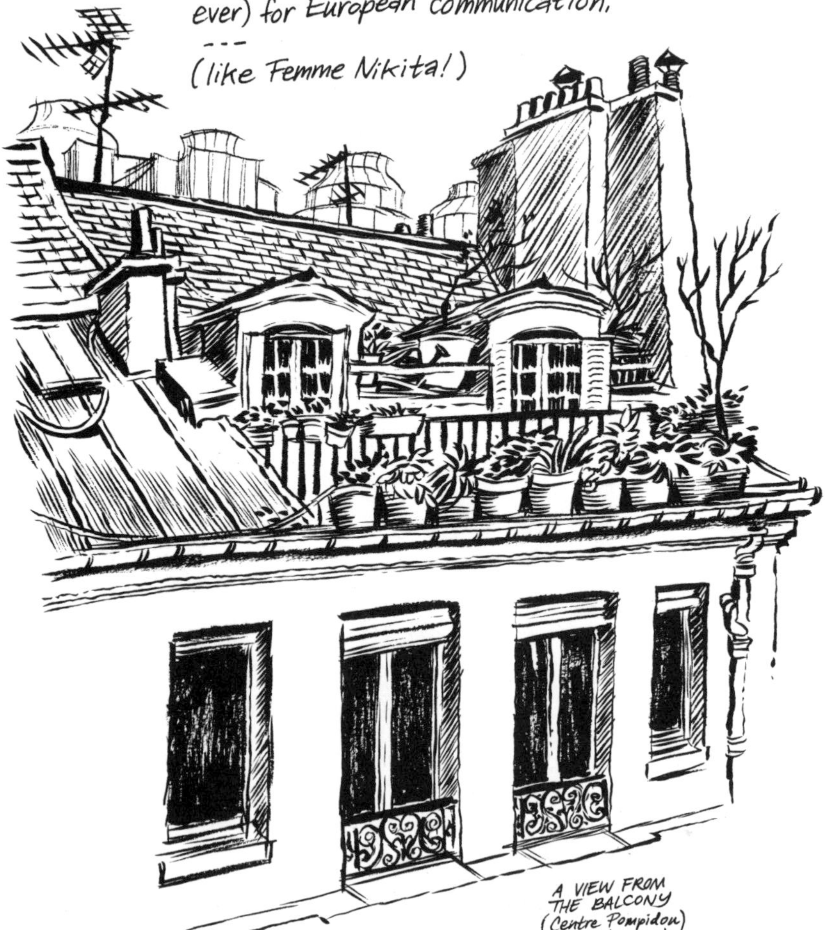

A VIEW FROM THE BALCONY (Centre Pompidou in background)

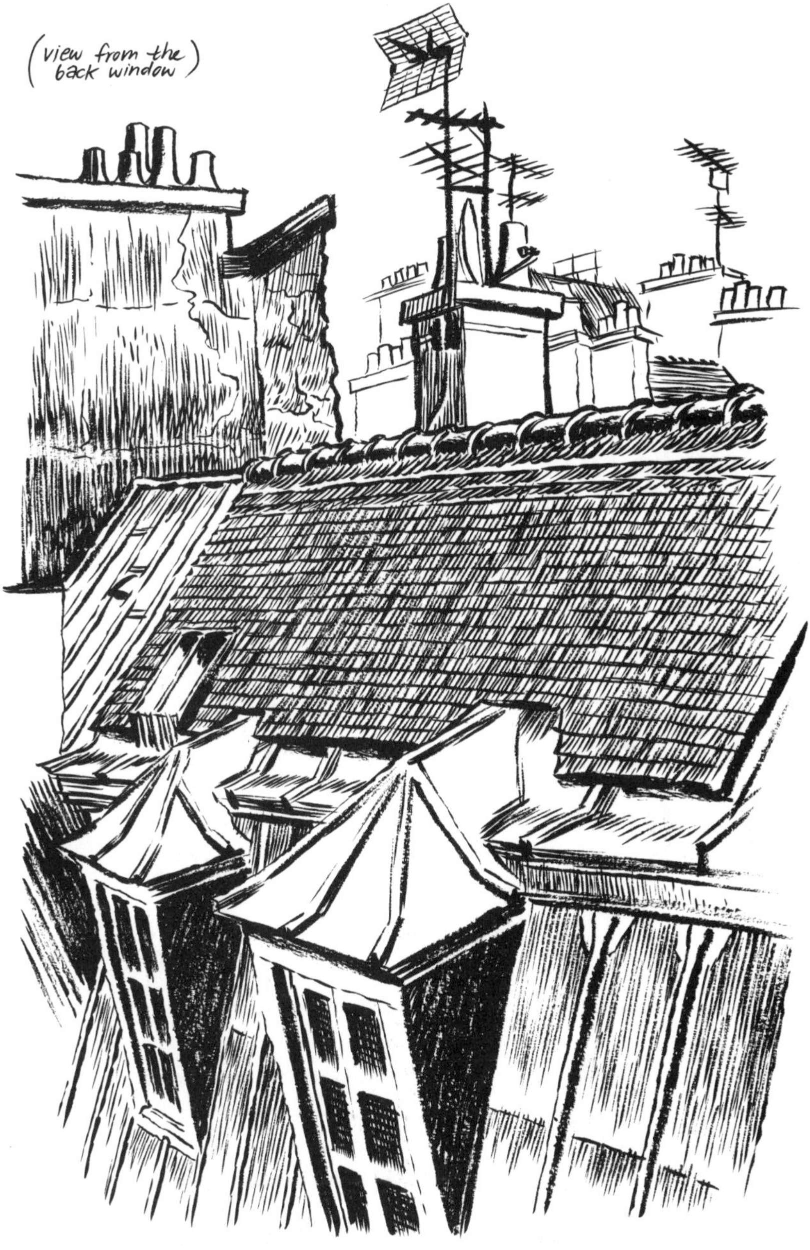
(view from the back window)

The cute girl (Marie) then accompanied me by cab to LA COMETE de CARTHAGE-- a comic shop/gallery run by my friend Valéry. They were in the midst of setting up an exhibition of BLANKETS original art. In the basement, I was overwhelmed by gorgeous Baudoin (my favorite French cartoonist) originals. His brush lines are bold, then delicate, always confident, and his women are beautiful. Valéry says he prefers drawings of women to photos, because photographs can be insincere/intrusive-- --they steal an image, while a drawing is an active interaction and interpretation. You can look at a Baudoin drawing and know he cares for the girl. "The drawings don't lie," Valéry says.

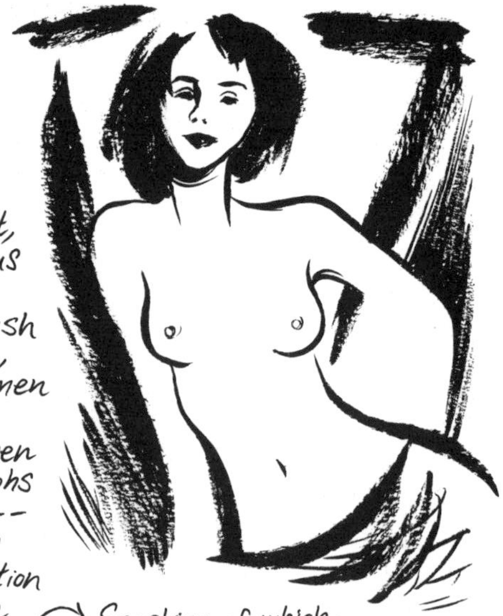

Speaking of which, the serigraphs of my Melissa drawings arrive. I sign/number beaucoup until my hand is numb. For dinner, Valéry and I go out for sushi, and I am so grateful to be eating non-French food. My stomach can't handle any more sausage, duck or veal.

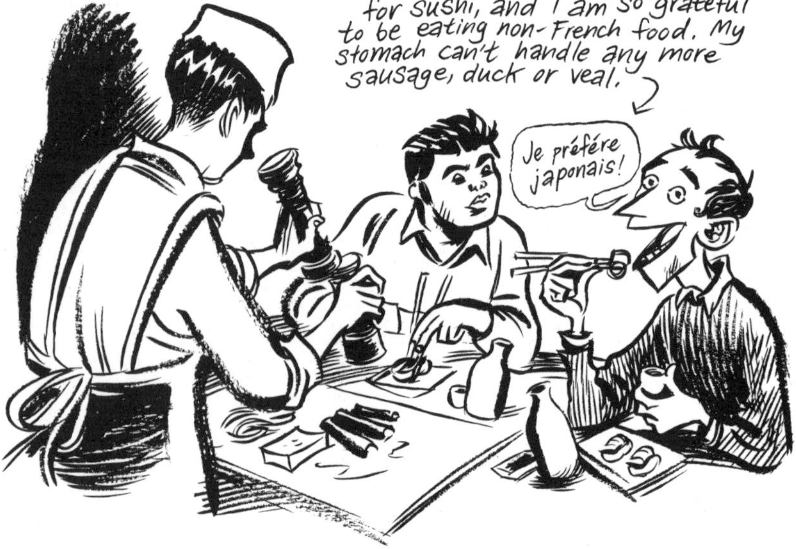
Je préfére japonais!

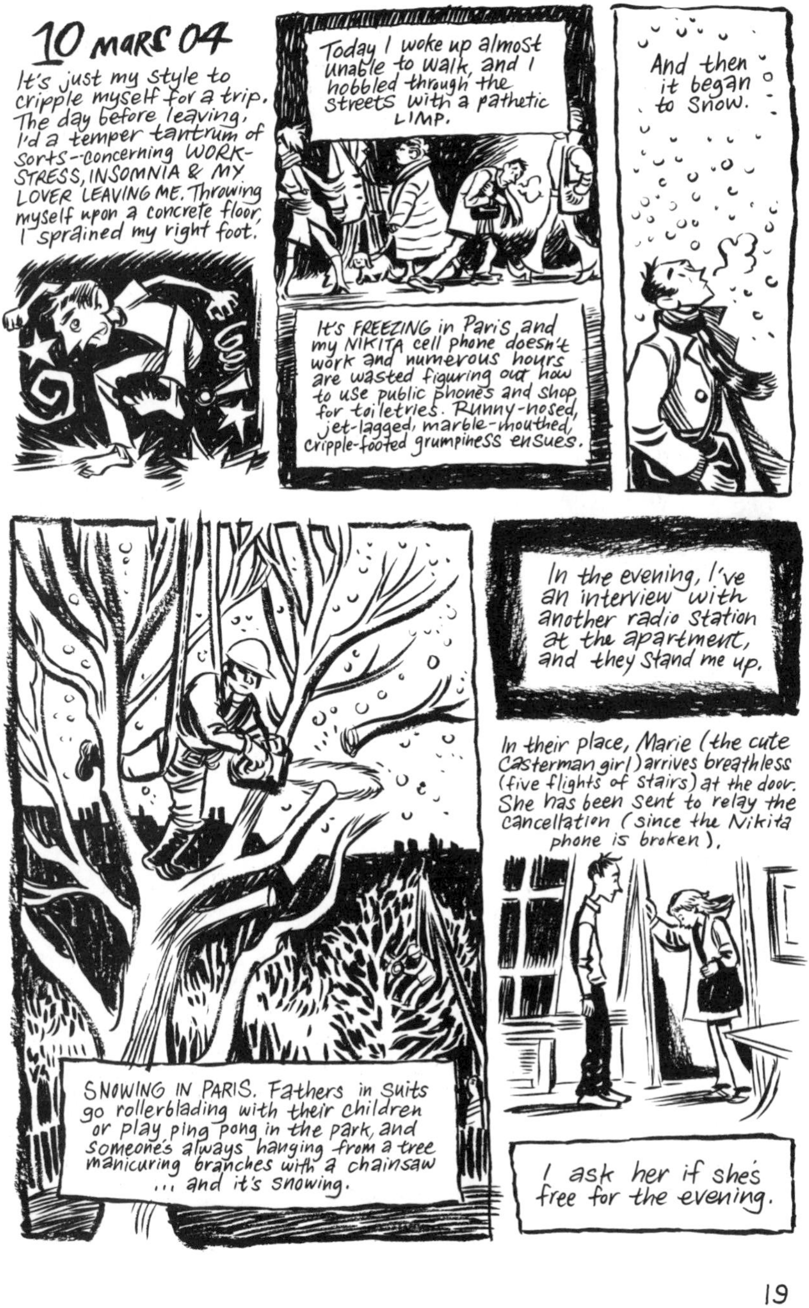
10 MARS 04
It's just my style to cripple myself for a trip. The day before leaving, I'd a temper tantrum of sorts--concerning WORK-STRESS, INSOMNIA & MY LOVER LEAVING ME. Throwing myself upon a concrete floor, I sprained my right foot.
Today I woke up almost unable to walk, and I hobbled through the streets with a pathetic LIMP.
It's FREEZING in Paris and my NIKITA cell phone doesn't work and numerous hours are wasted figuring out how to use public phones and shop for toiletries. Runny-nosed, jet-lagged, marble-mouthed, cripple-footed grumpiness ensues.
And then it began to snow.
SNOWING IN PARIS. Fathers in suits go rollerblading with their children or play ping pong in the park, and someone's always hanging from a tree manicuring branches with a chainsaw ... and it's snowing.
In the evening, I've an interview with another radio station at the apartment, and they stand me up.
In their place, Marie (the cute Casterman girl) arrives breathless (five flights of stairs) at the door. She has been sent to relay the cancellation (since the Nikita phone is broken).
I ask her if she's free for the evening.

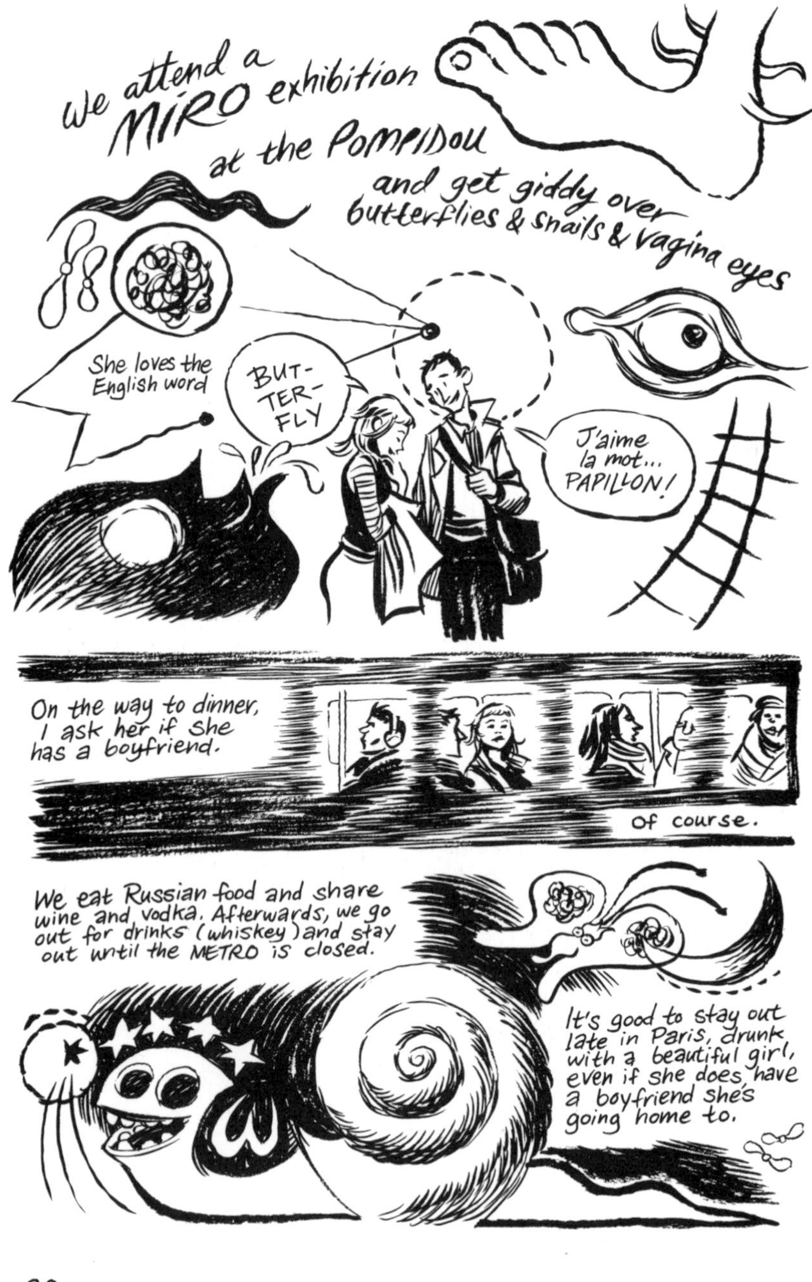
We attend a MIRO exhibition at the POMPIDOU
and get giddy over butterflies & snails & vagina eyes
She loves the English word
BUT-TER-FLY
J'aime la mot... PAPILLON!
On the way to dinner, I ask her if she has a boyfriend.
Of course.
We eat Russian food and share wine and vodka. Afterwards, we go out for drinks (whiskey) and stay out until the METRO is closed.
It's good to stay out late in Paris, drunk with a beautiful girl, even if she does have a boyfriend she's going home to.

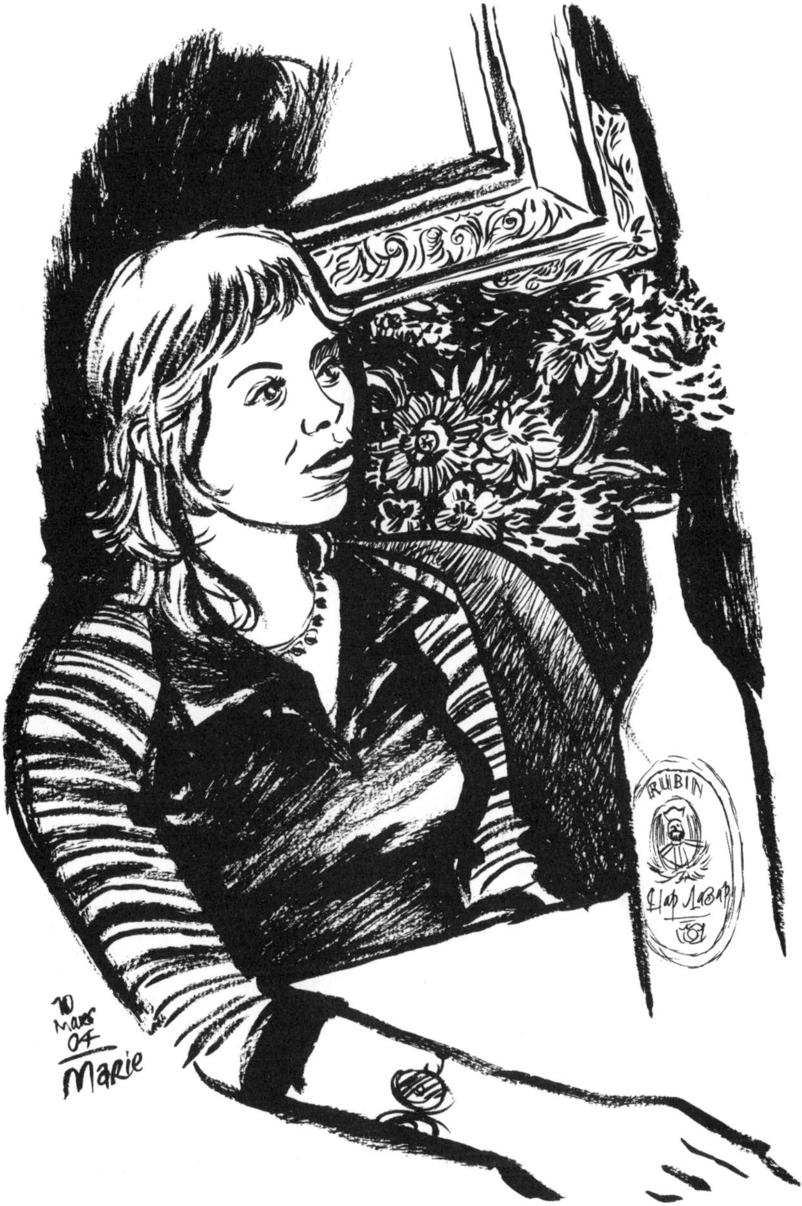
RUBIN
Цар Лазар
10 Mars 04
Marie

11 MARS 04 Woke up from a "Raina" dream. We were at church and the congregation was singing "Head On" by Jesus & Mary Chain as a hymn. My little hangover feels no different than the JETLAG.

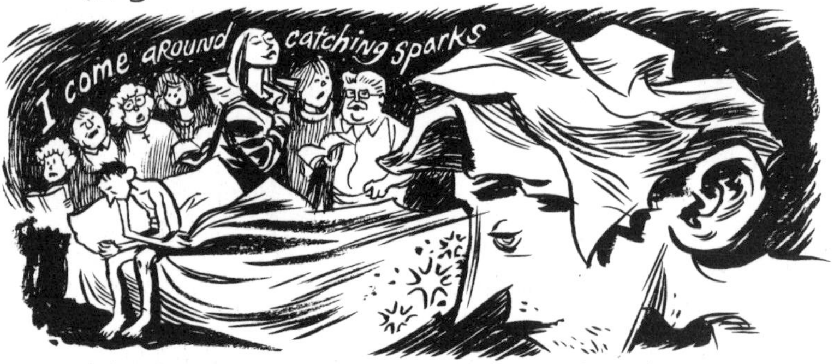
I come around catching sparks

Three interviews use up most of the day (1. Chronic art 2. les INROCKUPTIBLES 3. France Culture), but most amusing is an extensive photo shoot for Casterman publicity.

How ridiculous & surreal for a simple Wisconsin country bumpkin lad to pose for a hundred "glamor shots" in the streets of PARIS.

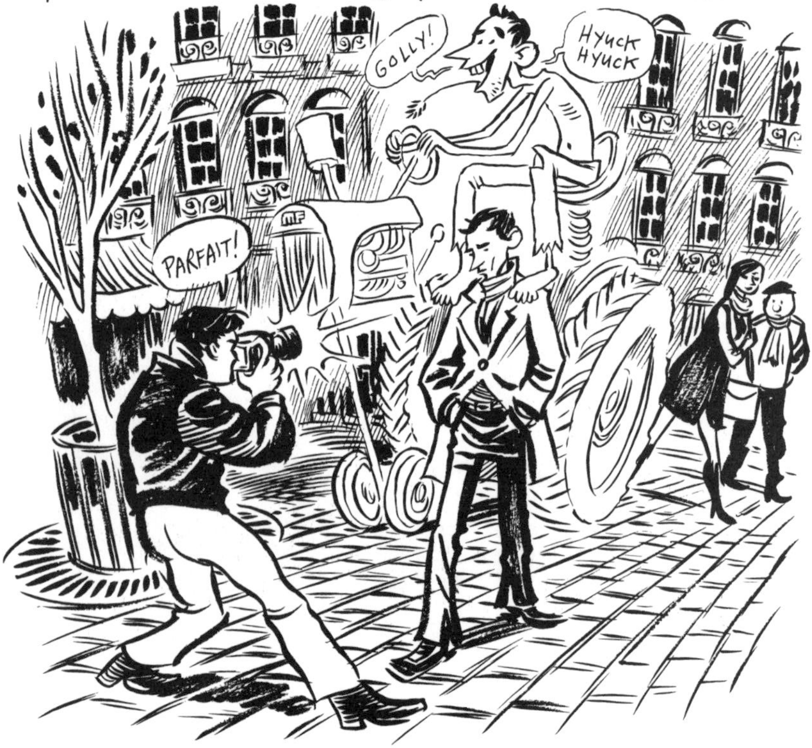
GOLLY!
HYUCK HYUCK
PARFAIT!

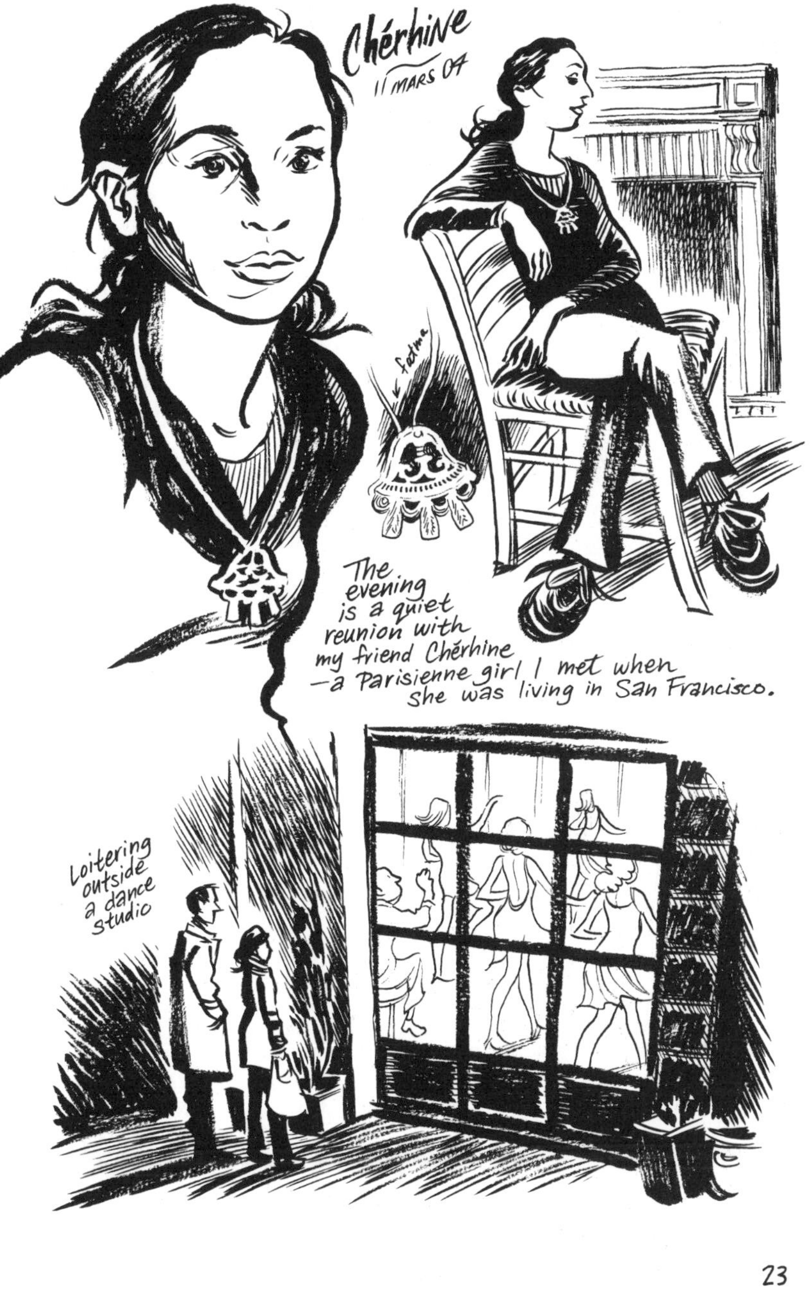
Chérhine
11 MARS 04
fatma
The evening is a quiet reunion with my friend Chérhine —a Parisienne girl I met when she was living in San Francisco.
Loitering outside a dance studio

12 MARS 07

FRICKIN' BUSY ALL DAY.

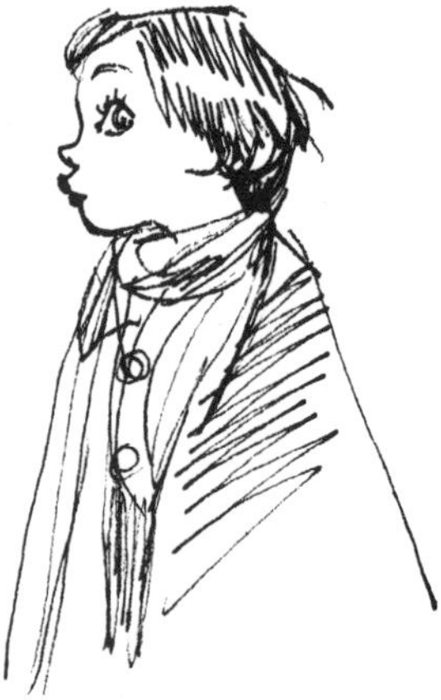

① Another radio interview -- this time at France's premiere station RTL by a beautiful Lebanese woman named Monique. (translated by Julia)

② Embellished "ex-libre" books at CASTERMAN.

③ Signed/numbered prints at LA COMETE DE CARTHAGE.

④ My press representative from CASTERMAN- Kathy- drove me to the Paris suburbs for another in-store signing, accompanied by her 5-year old daughter Fanny. Fanny seemed a bit disturbed by my crappy language skills and kept her distance with suspicious eyes. Then, once she saw me drawing in people's books, she draped by my side, and upon leaving, kept repeatedly kissing me on the cheek. Now if I could only get that method to work on girls my own age.

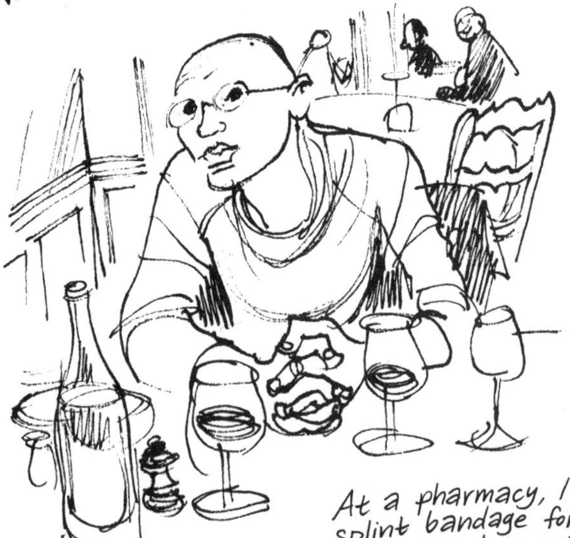

At a pharmacy, I purchase a splint bandage for my foot, then proceed to cripple my hand -- from drawing all day (!) but none of it is for my carnet. Dinner with another interviewer continues until one in the morning.

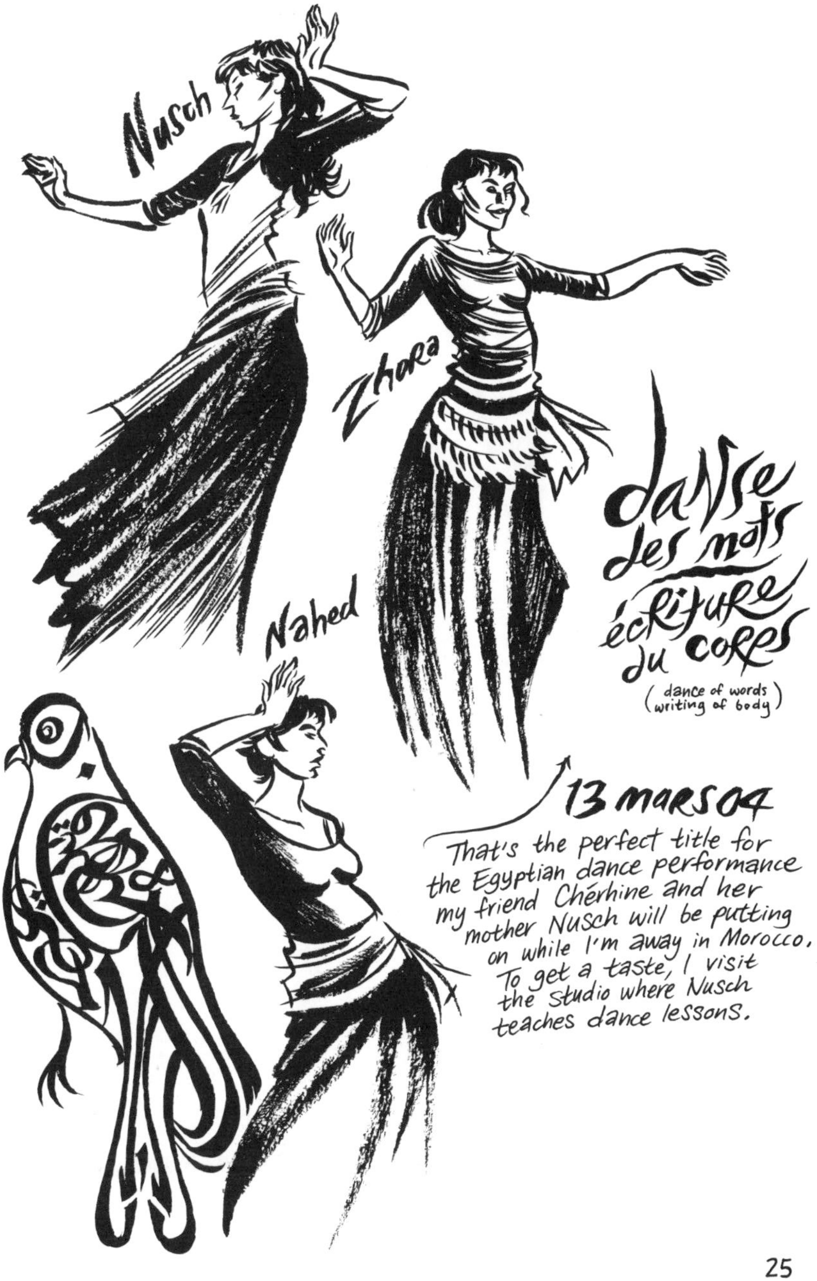
Nusch
Zhora
Nahed
danse des mots
écriture du corps
(dance of words
writing of body)
13 mars 04
That's the perfect title for the Egyptian dance performance my friend Chérhine and her mother Nusch will be putting on while I'm away in Morocco. To get a taste, I visit the studio where Nusch teaches dance lessons.

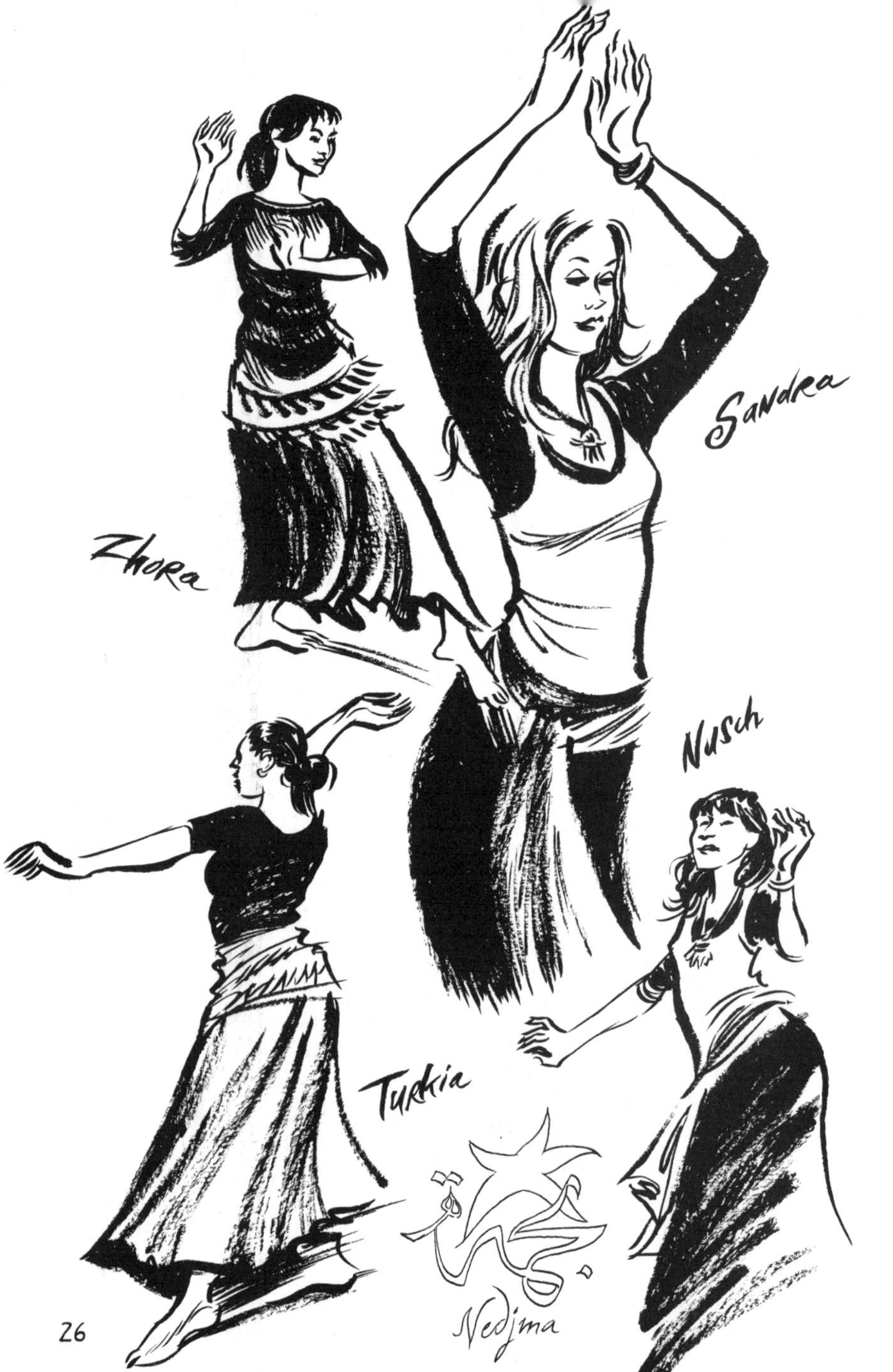
Sandra
Zhora
Nusch
Turkia
نجمة
Nedjma

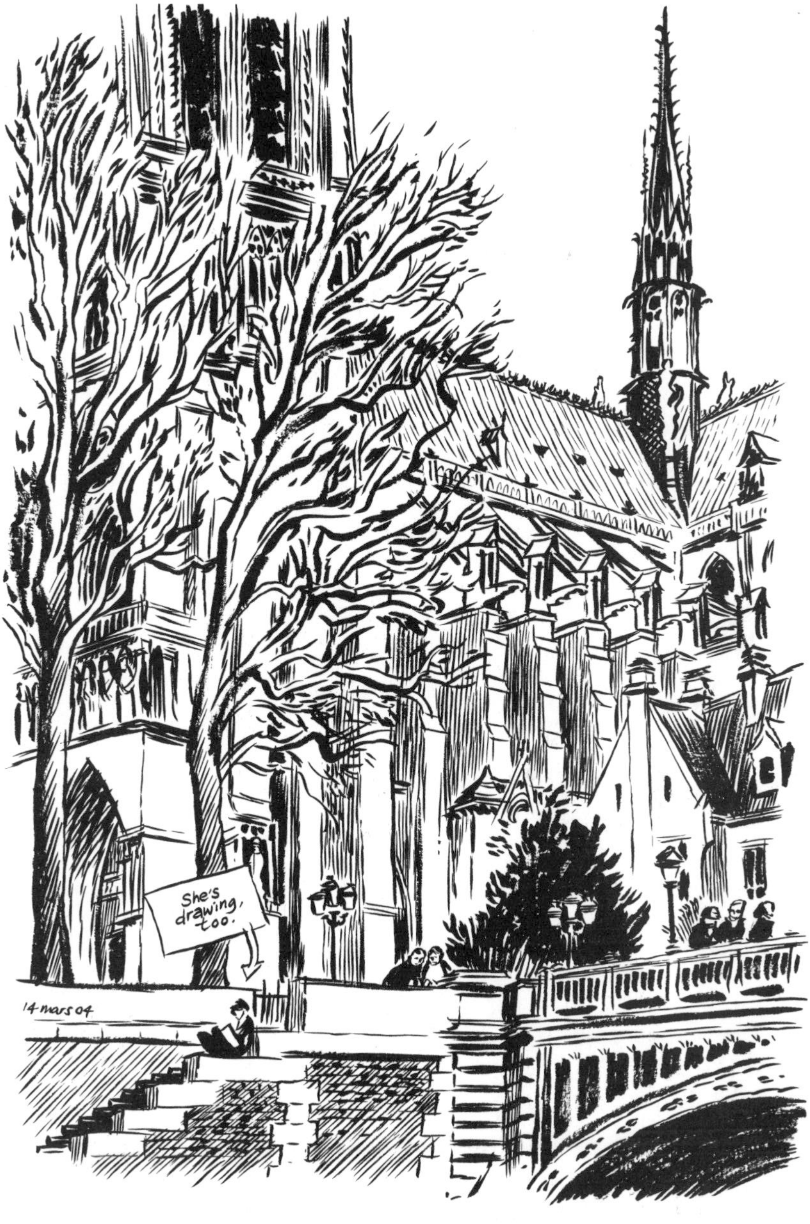
She's drawing, too.
14 mars 04

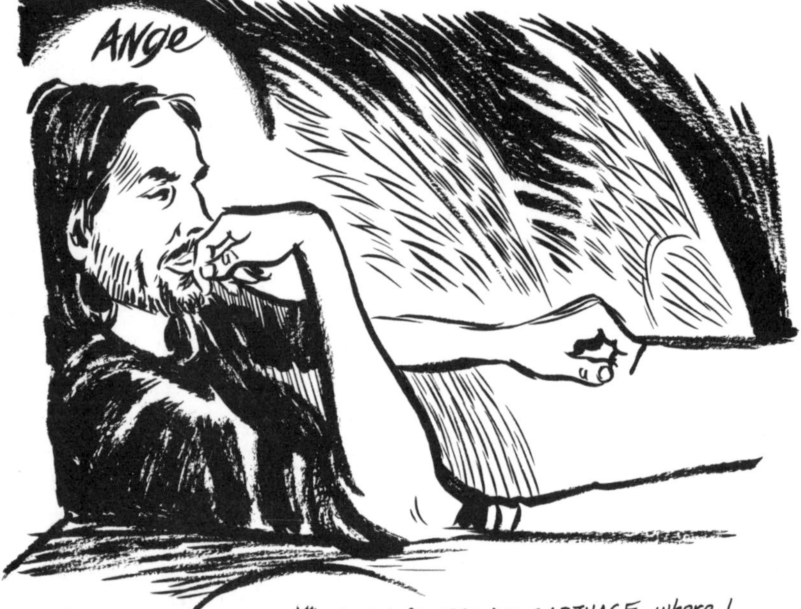
ANGE

14 MARS 04: Sunday in Paris in a sour mood --lonely & broken-footed.

At LA COMETE DE CARTHAGE, where I signed for another four hours, Valéry's mom examined my foot and diagnosed a TORN LIGAMENT.

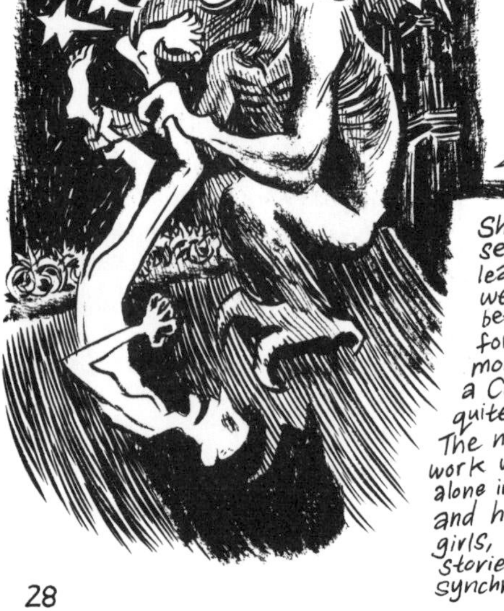

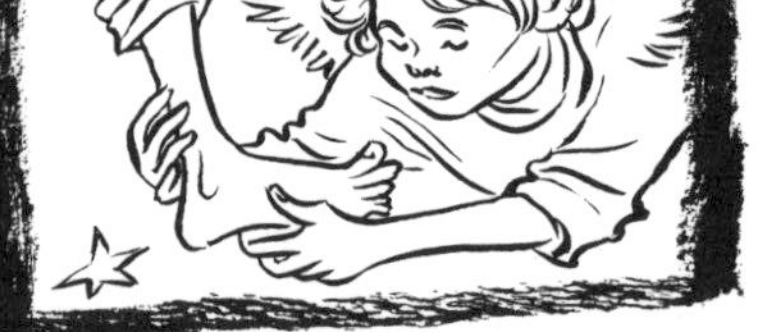

She said I shouldn't walk for several days ... tomorrow I leave for Morocco. The streets were cold. I managed one drawing before returning to the shop for warmth. Signed/numbered more prints (over 1000!) and then a Corsican/Iranian man showed up quite surprised/delighted to see me. The night before he had discussed my work with Slovakian friends. Well, I was alone in Paris, so we shared dinner, and he reassured me about travel, girls, life. His name is ANGE and his stories are blessed with luck and synchronicity. Hopefully it's contagious.

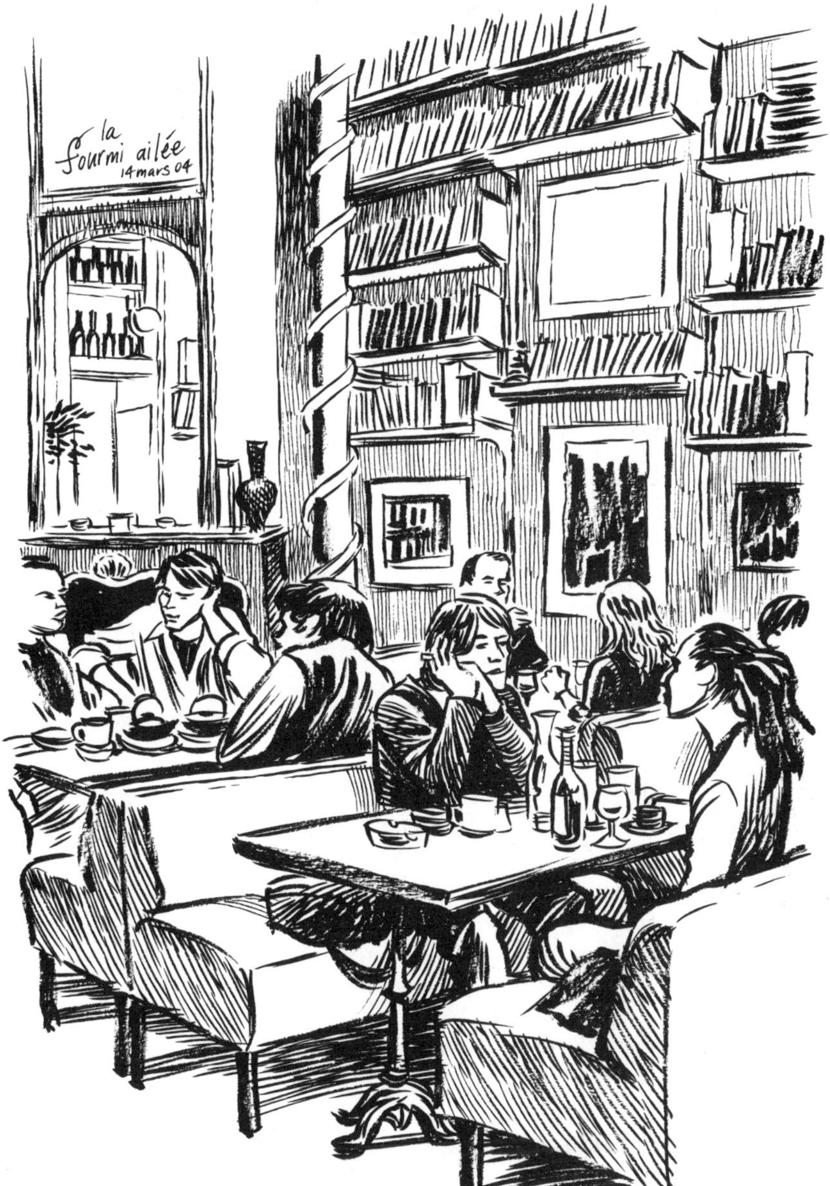
la
fourmi ailée
14 mars 04

15 mars 04 Arrived in the central medina of Marrakesh just at dusk, and checked in to the first hotel I found that was listed in the guide book. Looks like a good one.

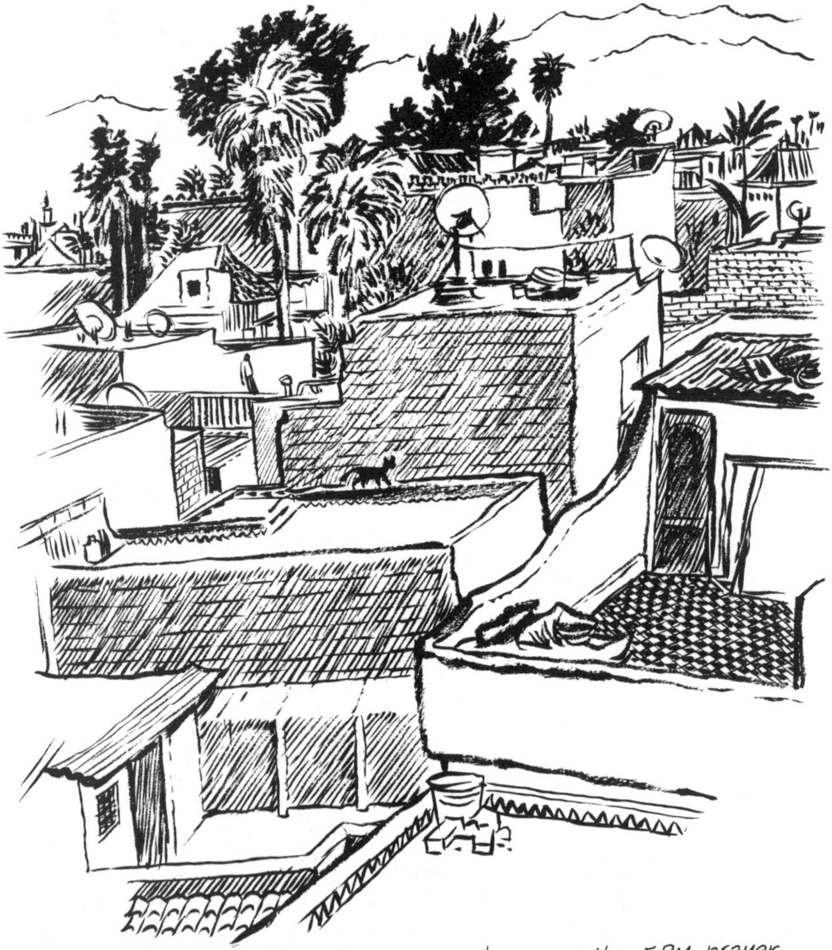

Here's the view from the terrace, drawn as the 5PM prayer call echoed throughout the city. (I thought they were recordings, but a chant from the west included coughing.)

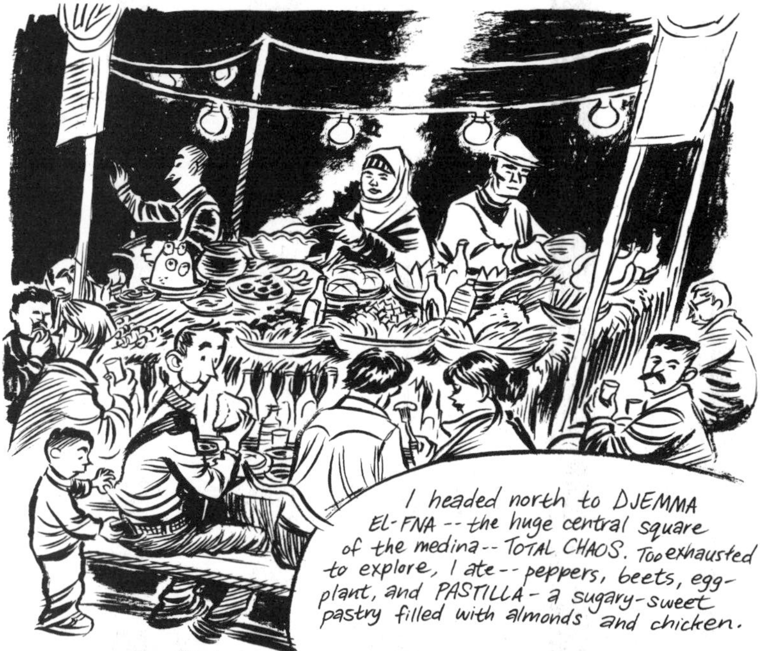
I headed north to DJEMMA EL-FNA -- the huge central square of the medina -- TOTAL CHAOS. Too exhausted to explore, I ate -- peppers, beets, eggplant, and PASTILLA - a sugary-sweet pastry filled with almonds and chicken.

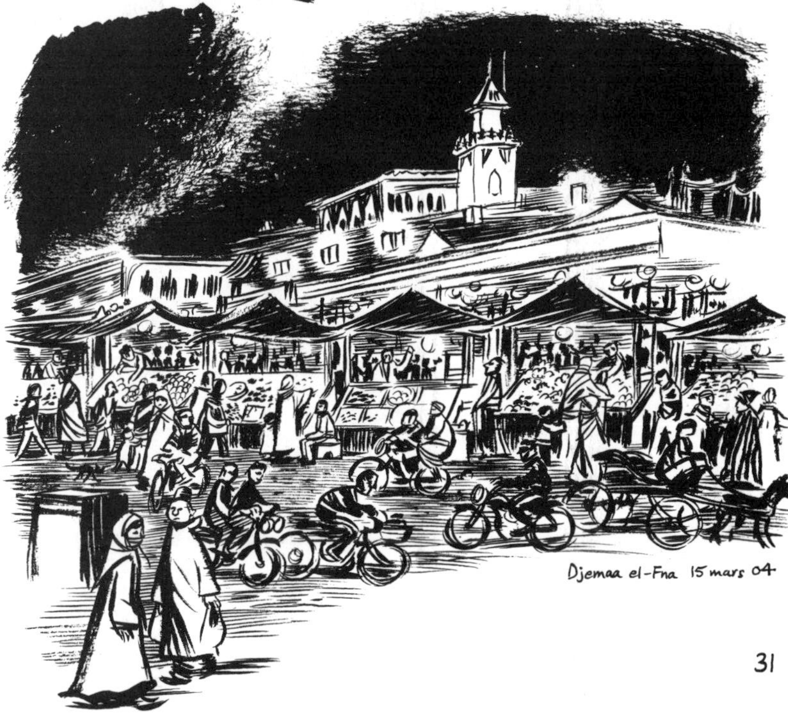
Djemaa el-Fna 15 mars 04

Marrakesh is overwhelming. The entire city has a built-in alarm clock -- 5 AM PRAYER CALL -- and from there on it's churning with music, noise, flies, dung, fragrant food, and POOR POOR people. I felt like such a wussy, ignorant American (though I said I was Canadian) and stupidly drew more attention to my awkwardness by sketching in the street. Children swarmed around asking for pens and sketchbooks. Beggars wove empty hands in my face.

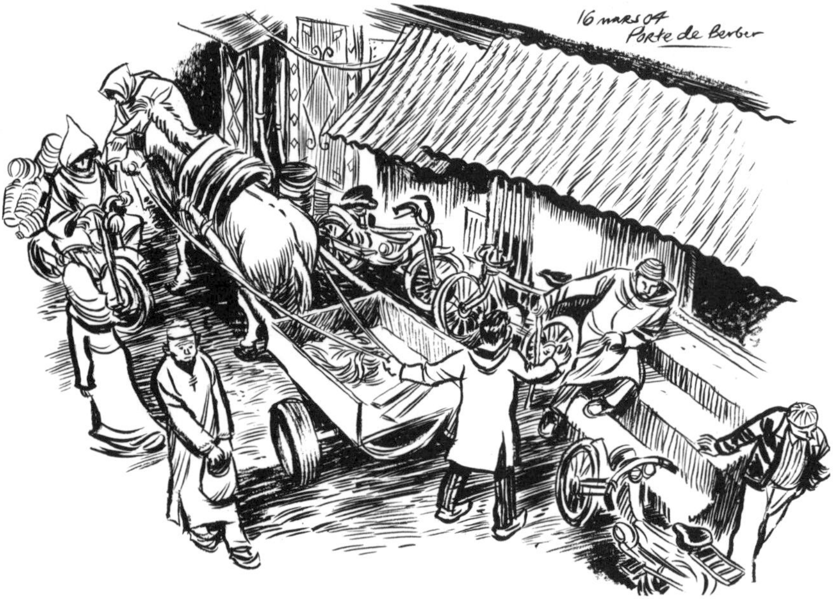
16 mars 04
Porte de Berber

One man lingered by my side for a long time watching me draw. Then he offered me a free tour of the Berber tannery where he worked. Suspicious, I told him I had no money, then followed... The tannery was fascinating & disgusting as you'd imagine it to be.

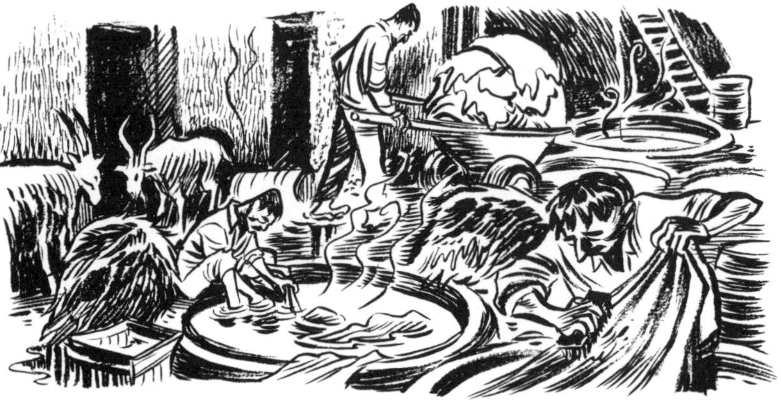

The tour was followed by the MANDATORY HARD SELL--leather products, rugs, shoes, antiques, etc. Wanting nothing, I did get suckered into an antique ink well. And I tried on a jallab and a Tuareg head wrap like a true tourist. Actually, the big Sucker part was forking over 100 dirham as a tip. (They wanted 250.)

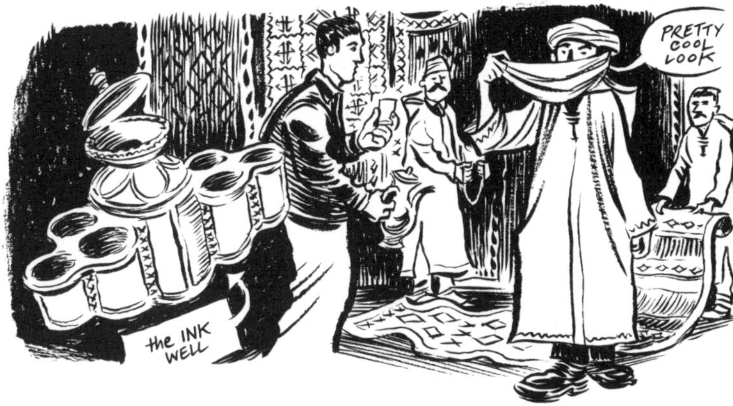
PRETTY COOL LOOK
the INK WELL

Afterwards, I was lost, stinky, and still cripple-footed. A small boy led me back to the central Medina, but I had no money left to offer in return.

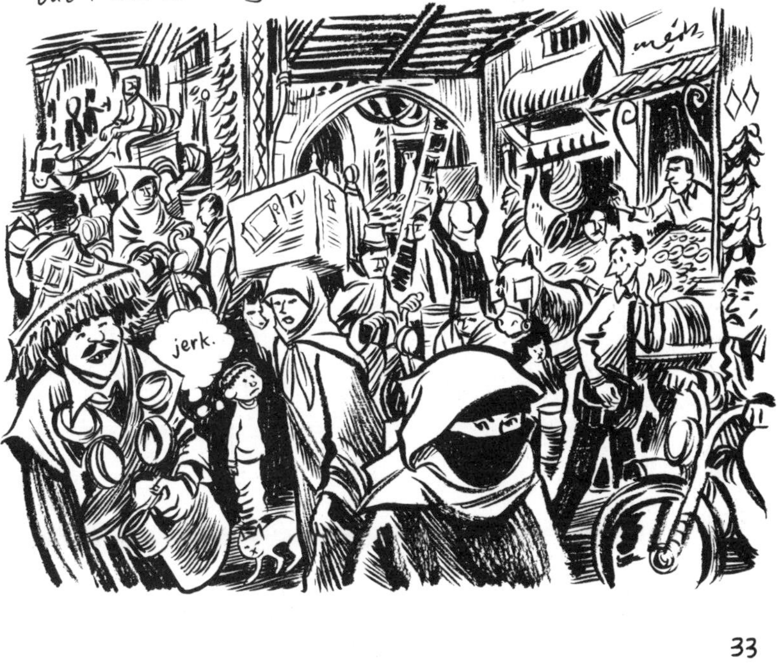
TV
jerk.

16 mars 04
Les Terasses de L'Alhambra

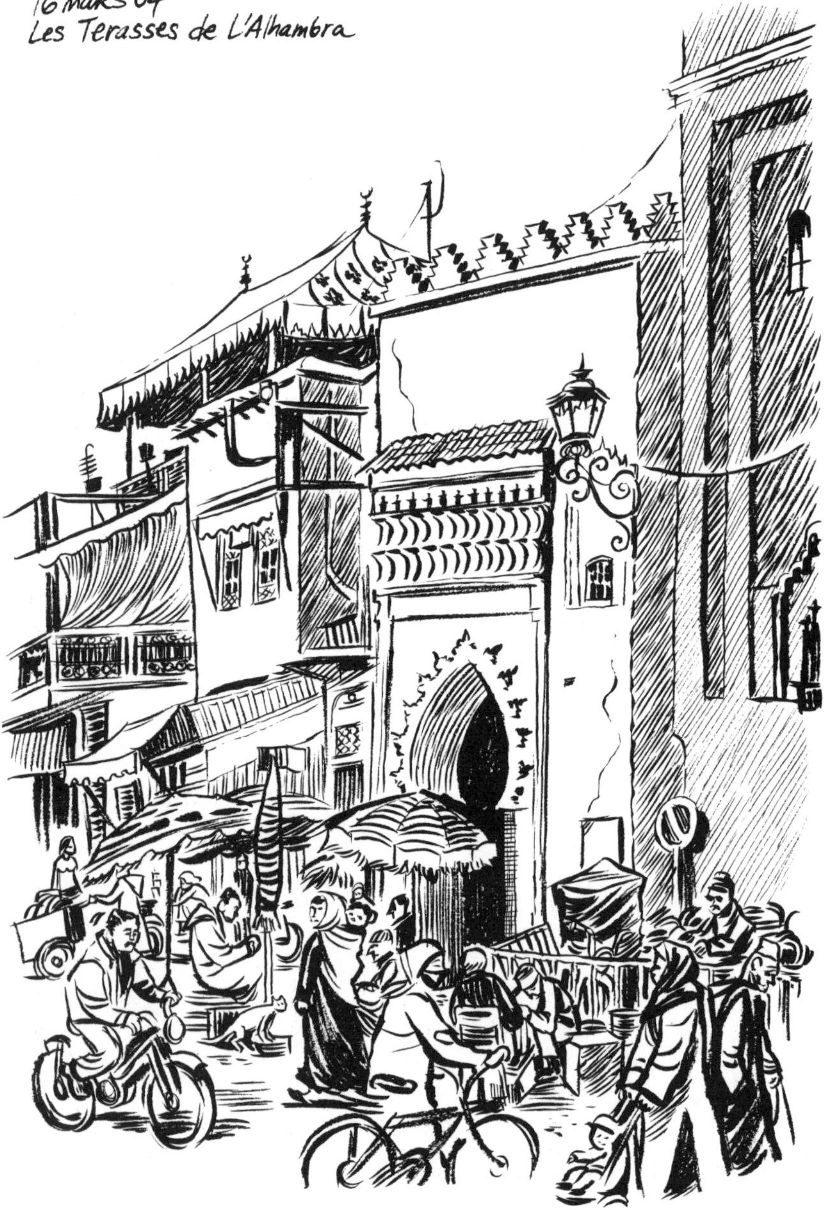

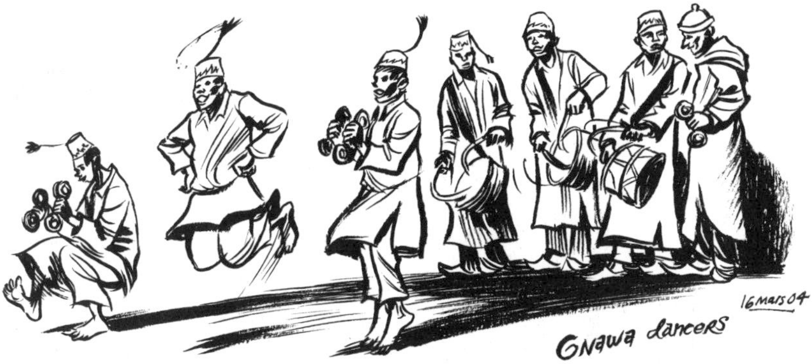
16 mars 04
Gnawa dancers

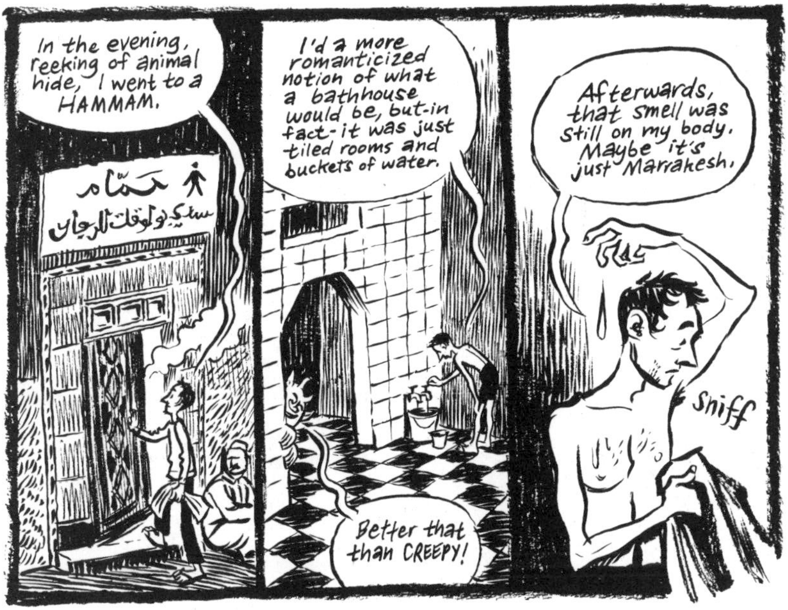
In the evening, reeking of animal hide, I went to a HAMMAM.
حمّام
I'd a more romanticized notion of what a bathhouse would be, but-in fact-it was just tiled rooms and buckets of water.
Better that than CREEPY!
Afterwards, that smell was still on my body. Maybe it's just Marrakesh.
Sniff

16 mars

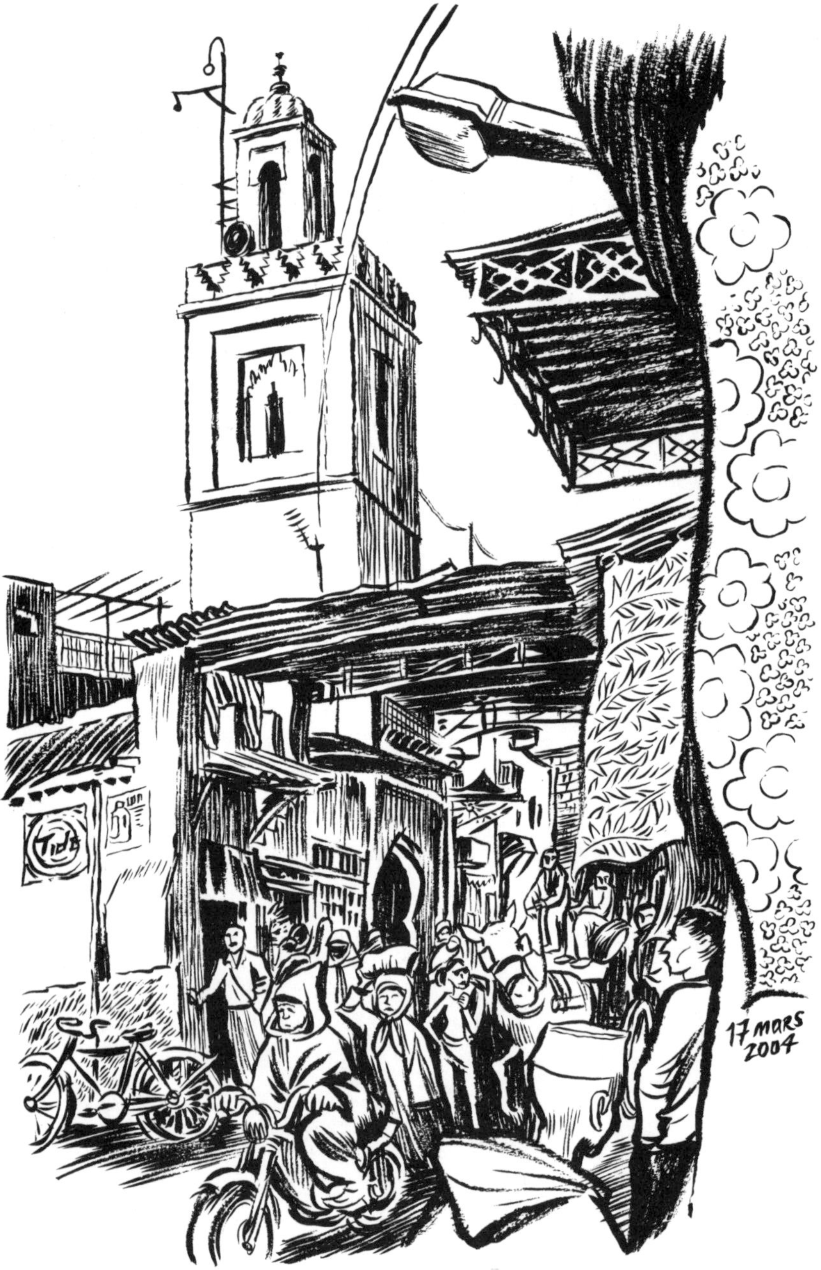
17 mars 2004

HASSAN
SHIHO
ABDUL
Nº 6
HUSSEIN
MEGUMI
17 MARS 04
juice stand no. 6

It was 3:30 before I touched a bite of food, but I dropped by the same juice stand twice. The second time around, there were two cute Japanese girls there, and I ventured they might speak English. They didn't, but they didn't speak French or Arabic either, so it felt good to meet someone else clunky with communication. They were tickled over my sketchbook, taking photos and all, and thanks to them the Arabic fellows who run the stand chimed in with introductions. Shiho & Megumi from Osaka. Hussein, Abdul & Hassan- born & raised in Marrakesh.

From there on, it was my most social day--dined with a charming couple from the south of France & lounged on the terrace with a British couple (always couples). Most importantly, I began interacting with the locals. Some adolescent boys tried to teach me basic Arabic words, but I just made them laugh. Presumably, because my pronunciation was lousy, but maybe because they were CUSS WORDS.

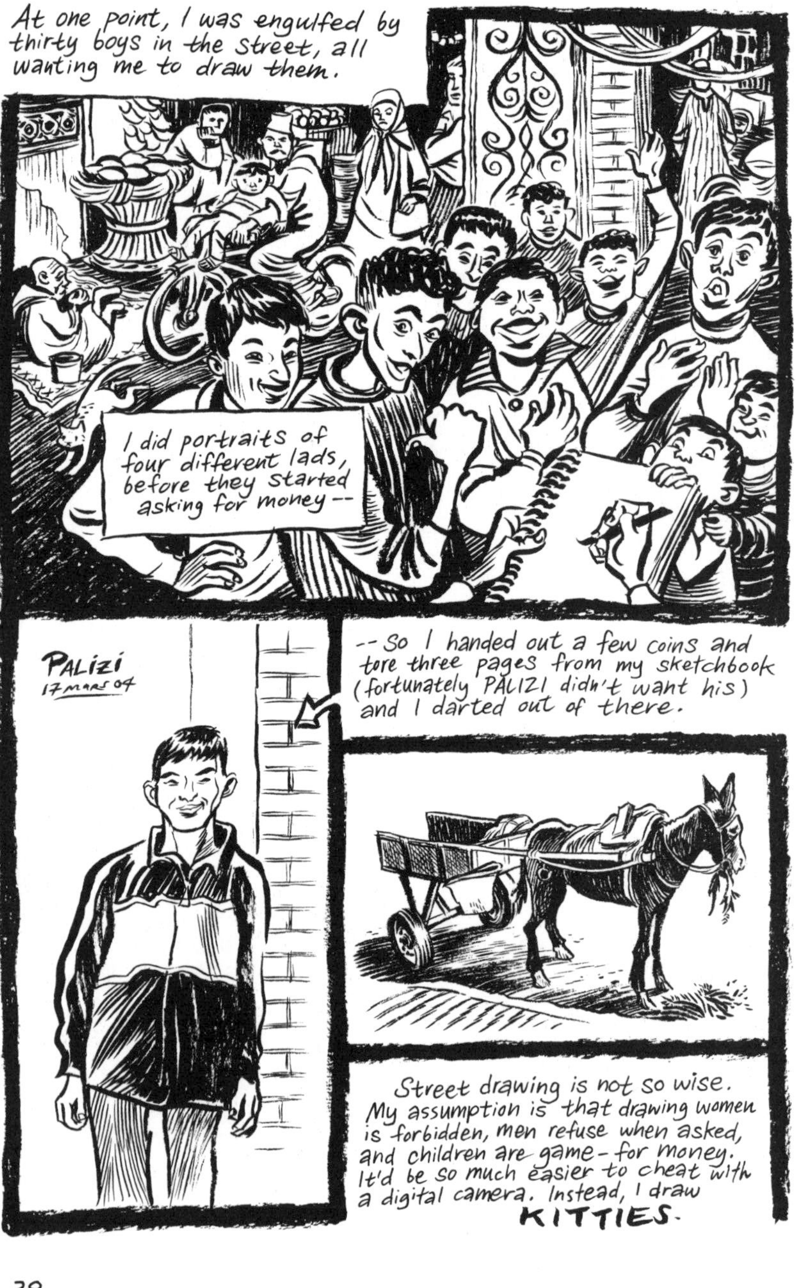

At one point, I was engulfed by thirty boys in the street, all wanting me to draw them.
I did portraits of four different lads, before they started asking for money--
PALIZI 17 MARS 04
--So I handed out a few coins and tore three pages from my sketchbook (fortunately PALIZI didn't want his) and I darted out of there.
Street drawing is not so wise. My assumption is that drawing women is forbidden, men refuse when asked, and children are game- for money. It'd be so much easier to cheat with a digital camera. Instead, I draw KITTIES.

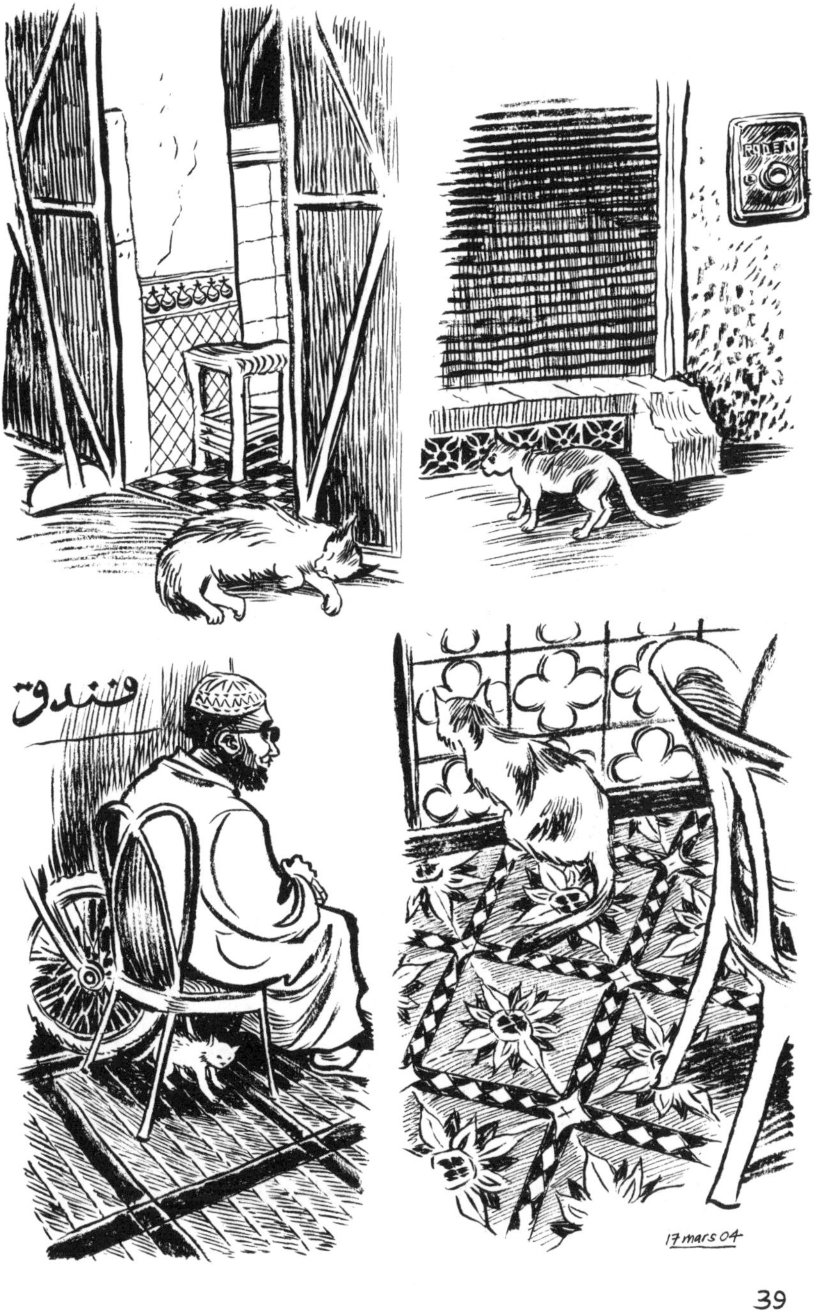
فندق
17 mars 04

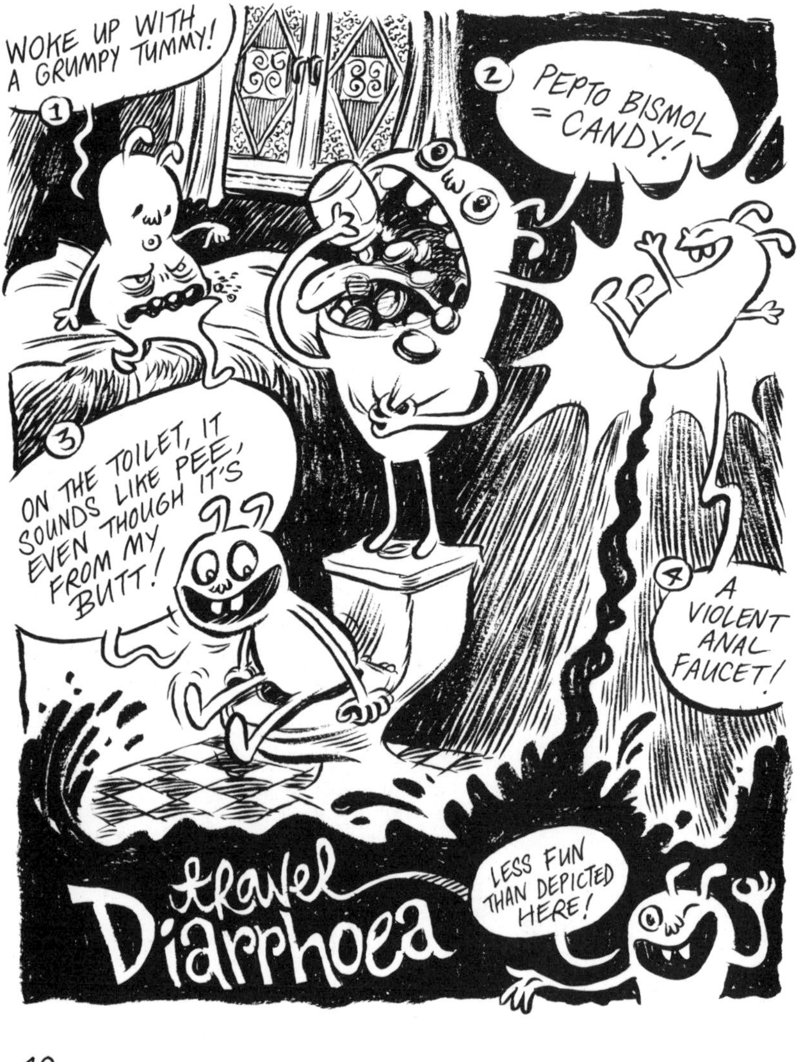
WOKE UP WITH A GRUMPY TUMMY!
1
2
PEPTO BISMOL = CANDY!
3
ON THE TOILET, IT SOUNDS LIKE PEE, EVEN THOUGH IT'S FROM MY BUTT!
4
A VIOLENT ANAL FAUCET!
travel Diarrhoea
LESS FUN THAN DEPICTED HERE!

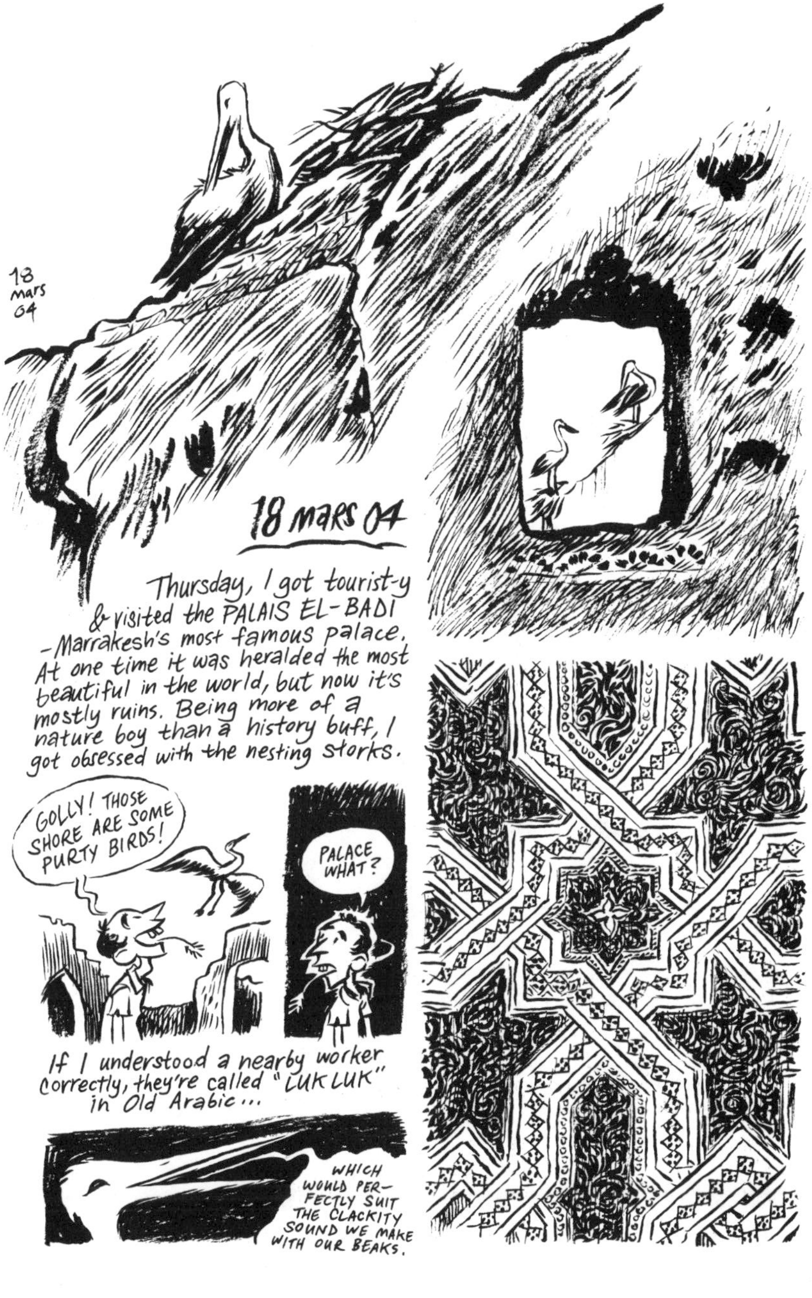
18 mars 04
18 mars 04
Thursday, I got tourist-y & visited the PALAIS EL-BADI - Marrakesh's most famous palace. At one time it was heralded the most beautiful in the world, but now it's mostly ruins. Being more of a nature boy than a history buff, I got obsessed with the nesting storks.
GOLLY! THOSE SHORE ARE SOME PURTY BIRDS!
PALACE WHAT?
If I understood a nearby worker correctly, they're called "LUK LUK" in Old Arabic...
WHICH WOULD PERFECTLY SUIT THE CLACKITY SOUND WE MAKE WITH OUR BEAKS.

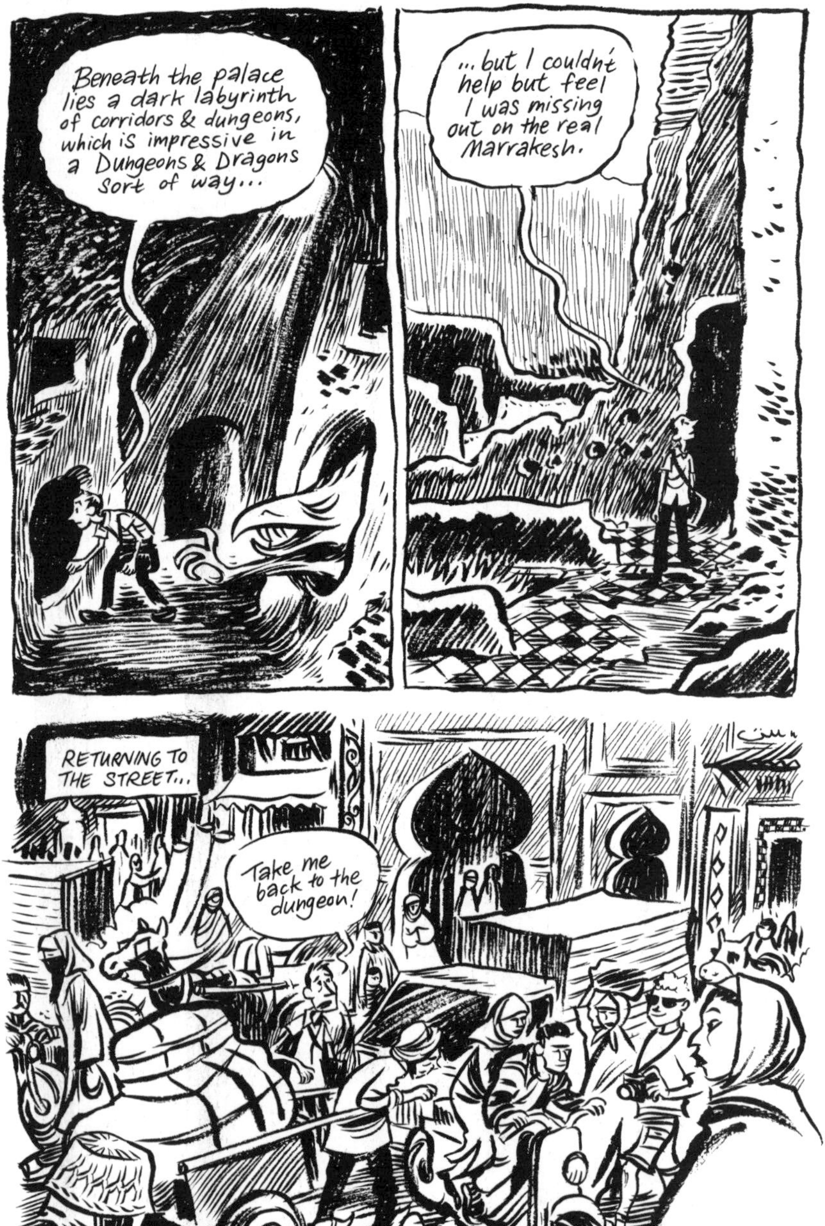
Beneath the palace lies a dark labyrinth of corridors & dungeons, which is impressive in a Dungeons & Dragons sort of way...
...but I couldn't help but feel I was missing out on the real Marrakesh.
RETURNING TO THE STREET...
Take me back to the dungeon!
18 mars 04

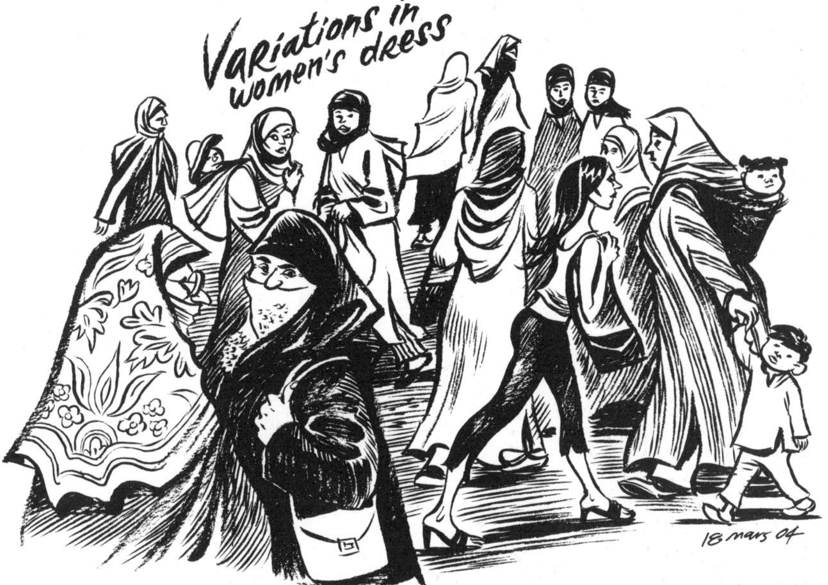
Variations in women's dress
18 mars 04

I'm sick from the belly outward, but resisting the idea. Running into the couple from the South of France again, they mock my American immune system -so conditioned to sterility that I can't handle a little bacteria in food. It's true. And I'm conditioned to ample breathing space, too-- the claustrophobia turns me woozy. My vision is blurry with snake charmers & sad little monkeys & more Gnawa dancers, and I'm dreaming of my friends back home.

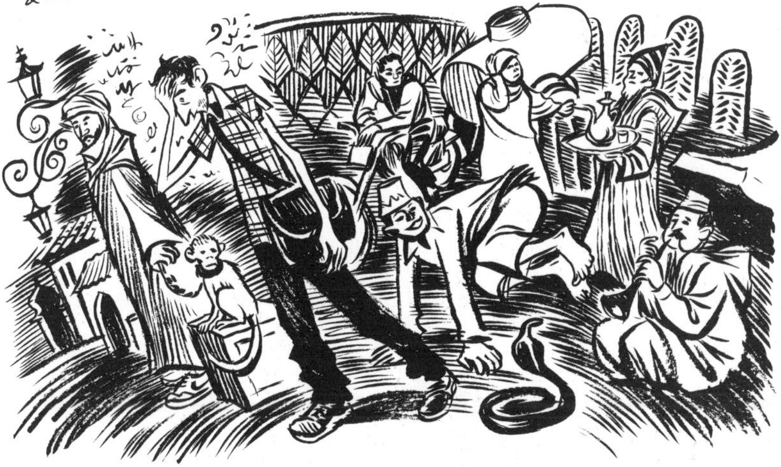

19 mars 04

They say "WHEREVER YOU GO, THERE YOU ARE"... I thought with Morocco, I'd be setting out on some exotic adventure, but it turns out I'm just a simple, quiet fellow. For some time, I'm fixated on a tiny finch sipping from a fountain.

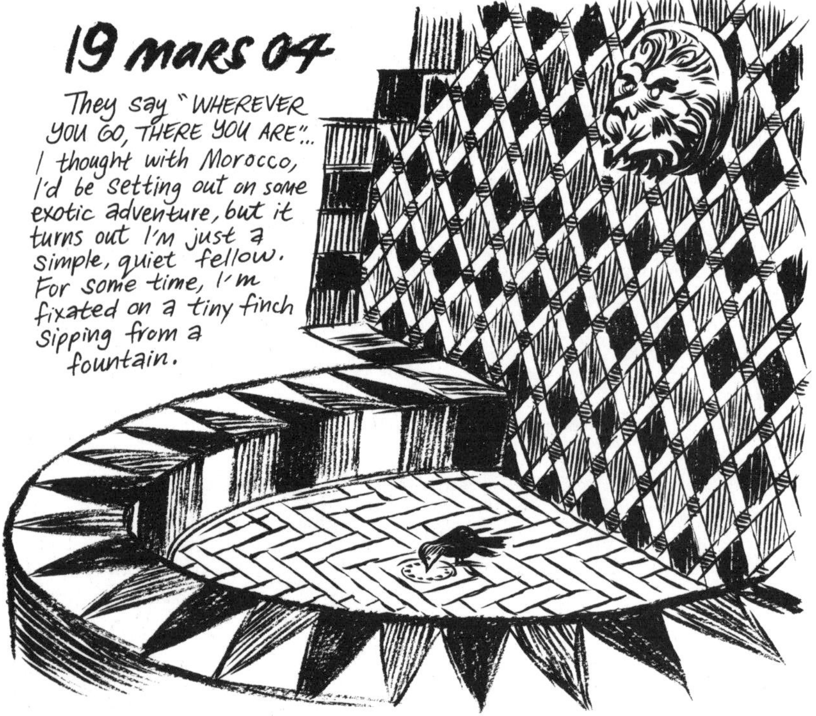

I stayed in bed all morning, recovering from crappy illness. In the afternoon, the redundancy of the souqs washes over me, which-of course- is an oxymoron. I've barely nibbled at what there is to see, but somehow it all looks the same. My own loneliness takes precedent.

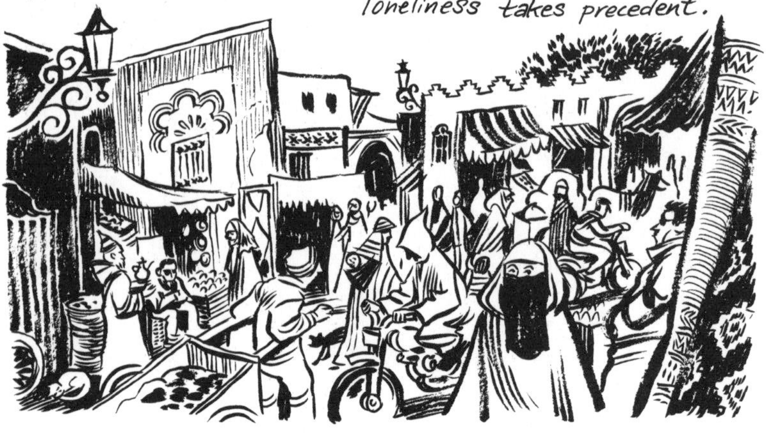

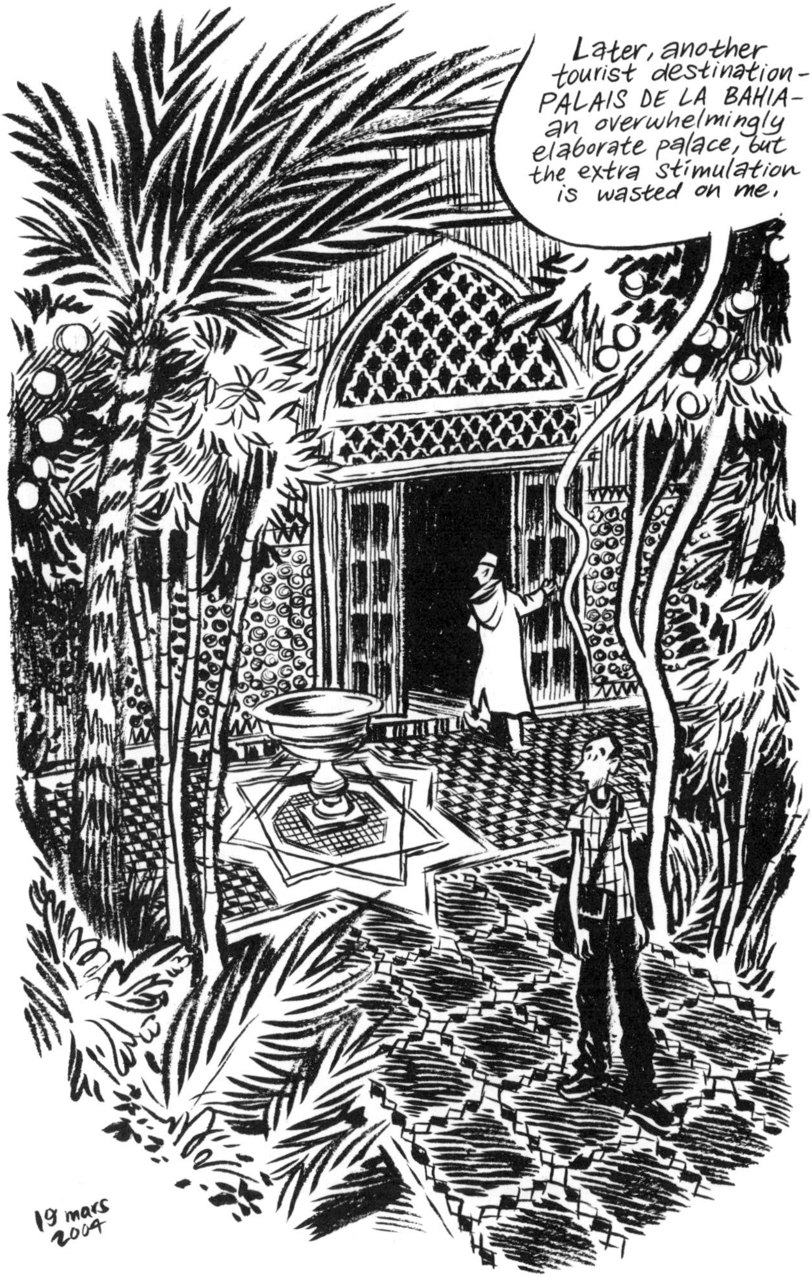
Later, another tourist destination- PALAIS DE LA BAHIA- an overwhelmingly elaborate palace, but the extra stimulation is wasted on me.
19 mars 2004

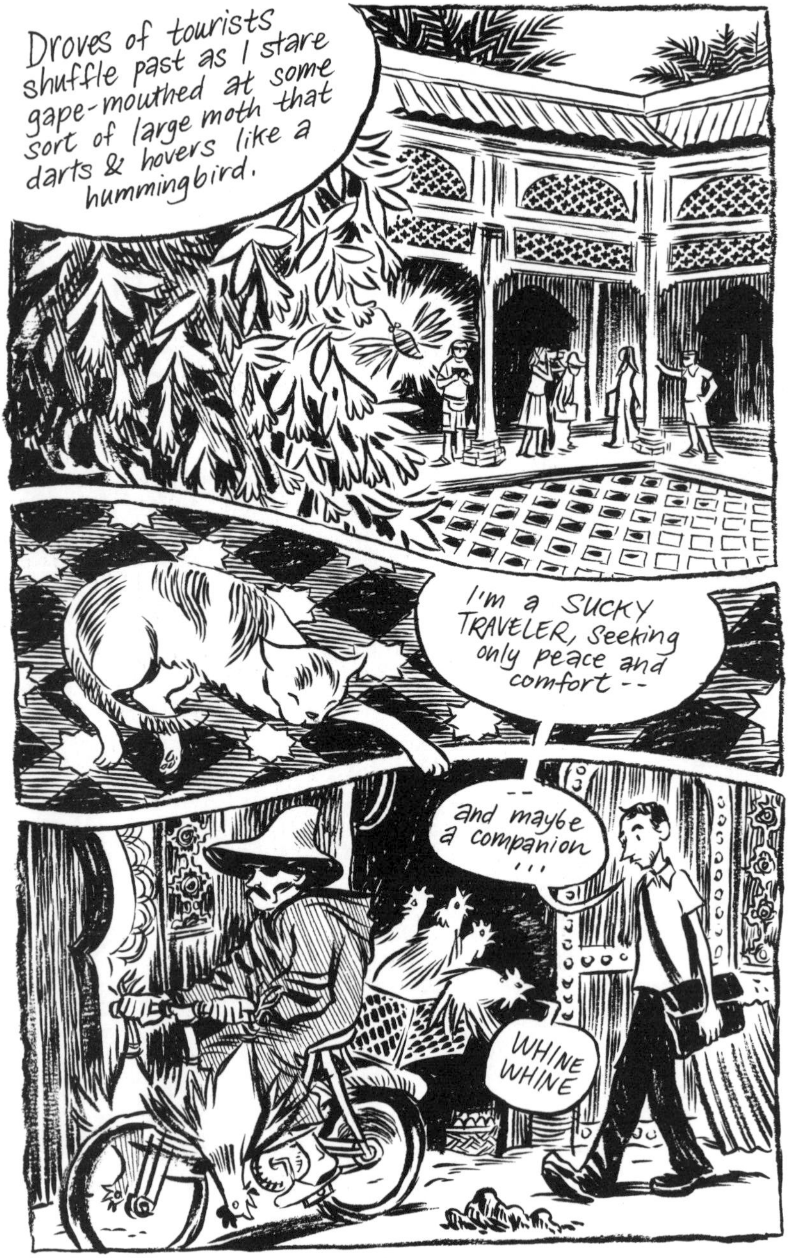
Droves of tourists shuffle past as I stare gape-mouthed at some sort of large moth that darts & hovers like a hummingbird.
I'm a SUCKY TRAVELER, seeking only peace and comfort --
-- and maybe a companion ...
WHINE WHINE

19
mars
04

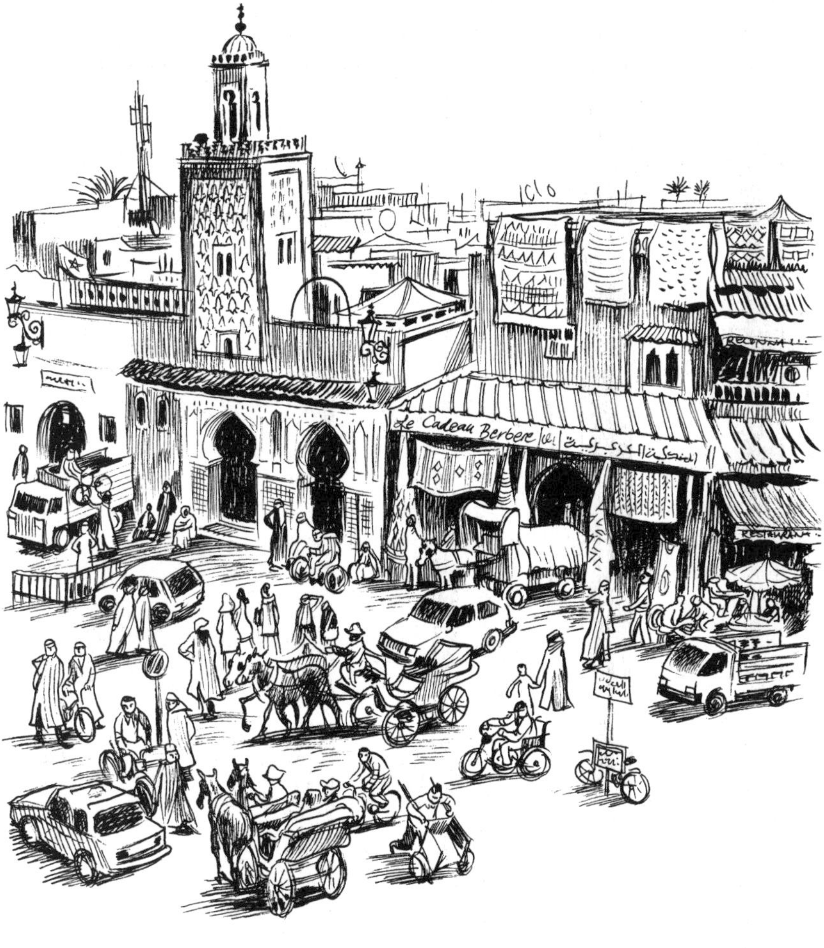
Le Cadeau Berbere

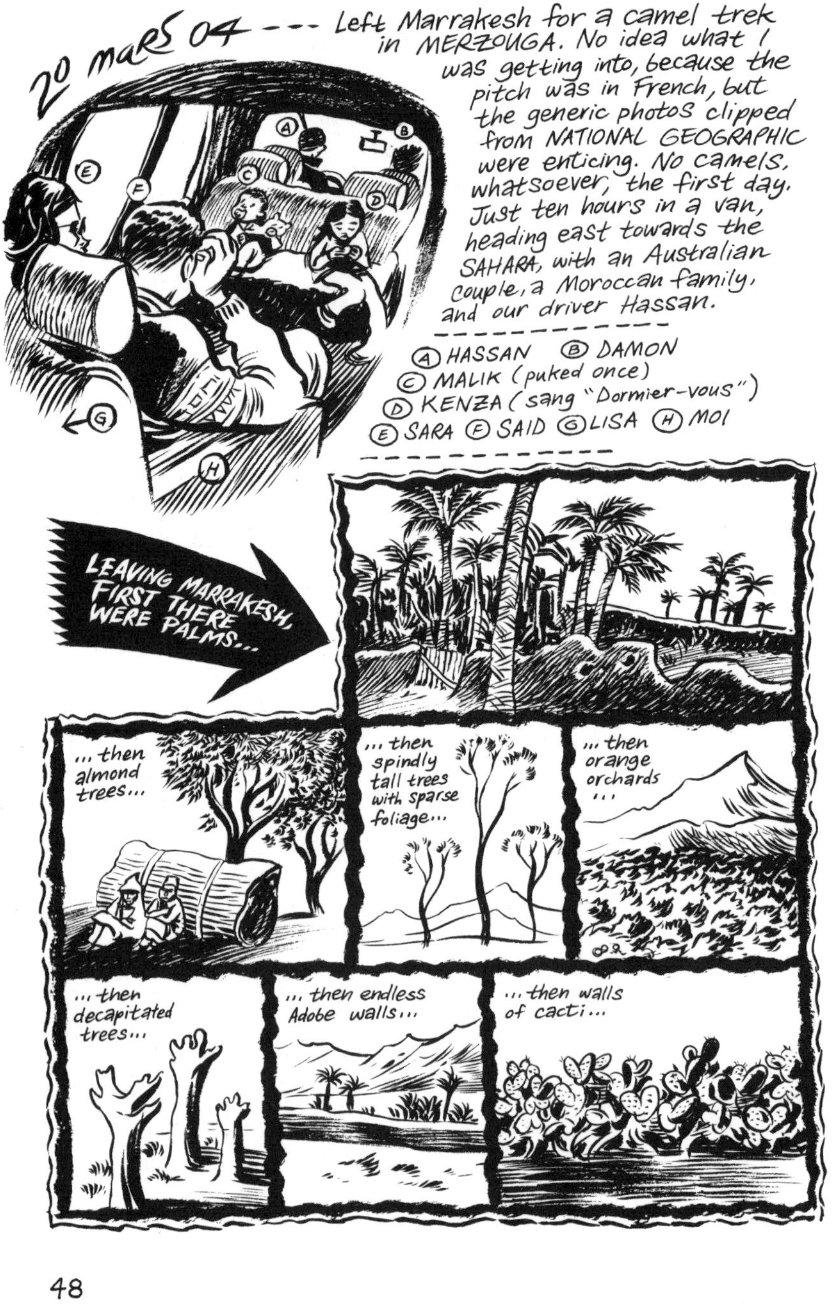
20 MARS 04 --- Left Marrakesh for a camel trek in MERZOUGA. No idea what I was getting into, because the pitch was in French, but the generic photos clipped from NATIONAL GEOGRAPHIC were enticing. No camels, whatsoever, the first day. Just ten hours in a van, heading east towards the SAHARA, with an Australian couple, a Moroccan family, and our driver Hassan.
A HASSAN B DAMON
C MALIK (puked once)
D KENZA (sang "Dormier-vous")
E SARA F SAID G LISA H MOI
A
B
C
D
E
F
G
H
LEAVING MARRAKESH, FIRST THERE WERE PALMS...
... then almond trees...
... then spindly tall trees with sparse foliage...
... then orange orchards ...
... then decapitated trees...
... then endless Adobe walls...
... then walls of cacti...

... then desert (or "designated dump" with plastic bags as tumbleweeds) ... then locusts splattered across the windshield ...

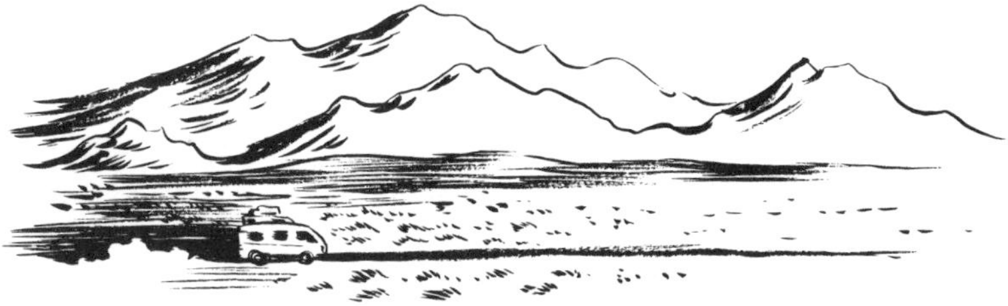

... and then all this:

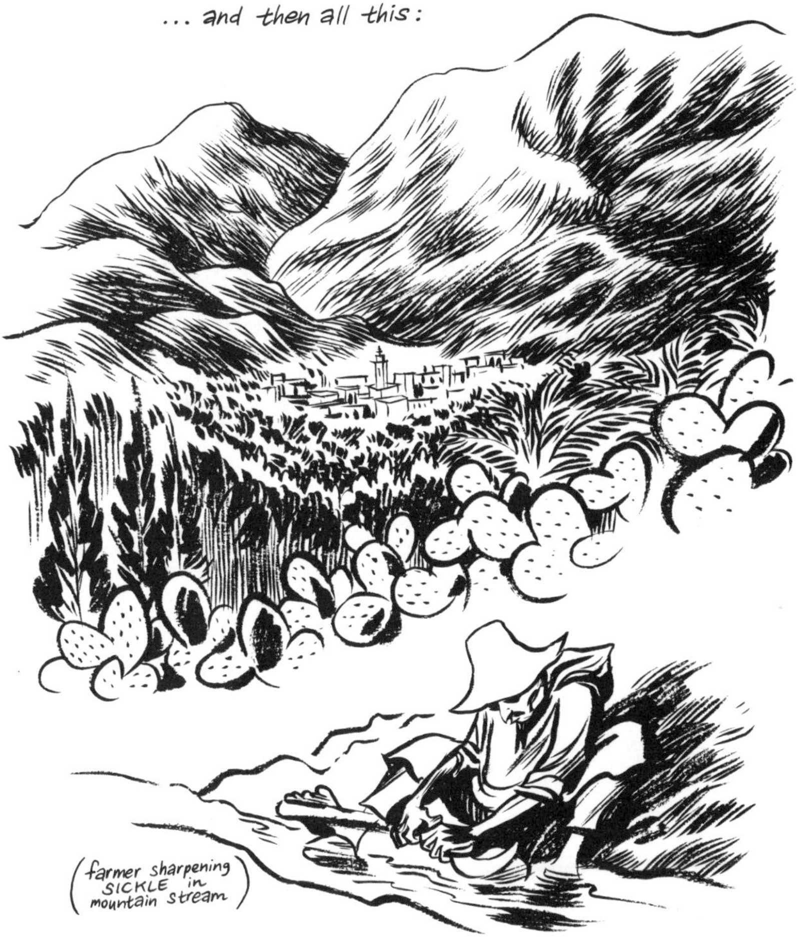
(farmer sharpening SICKLE in mountain stream)

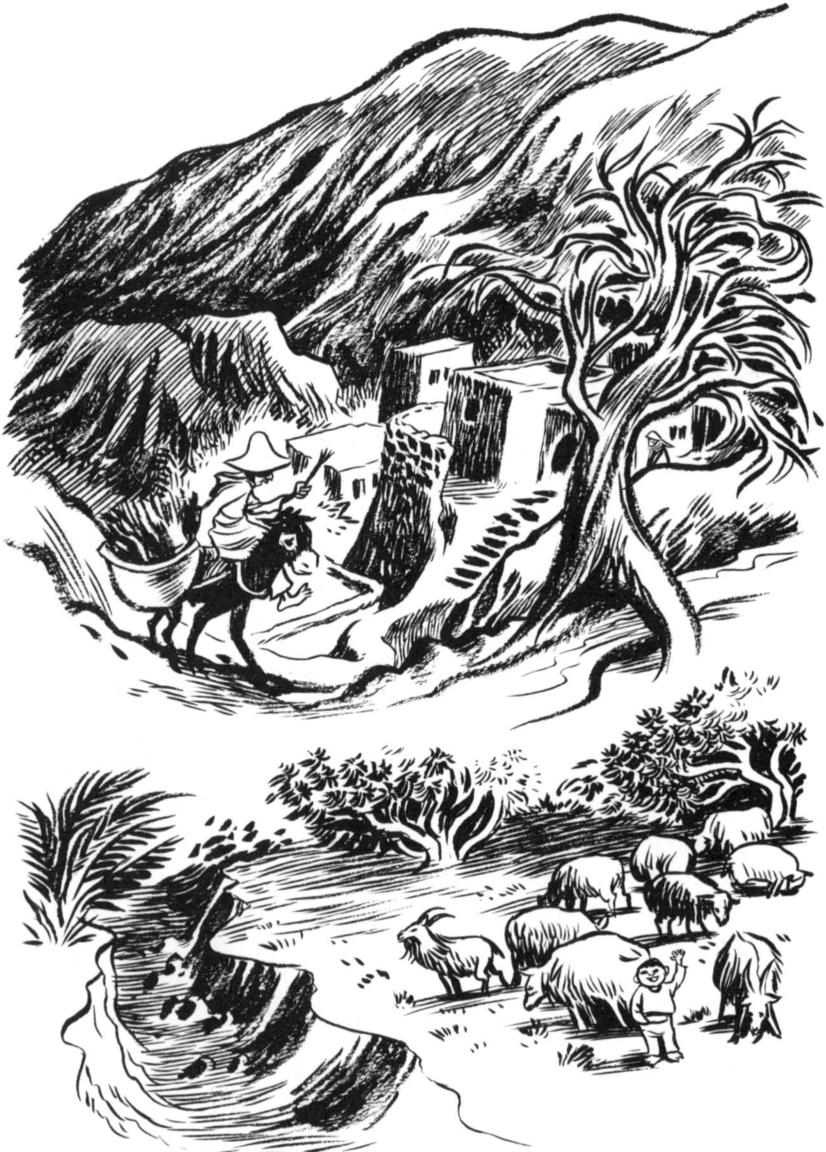

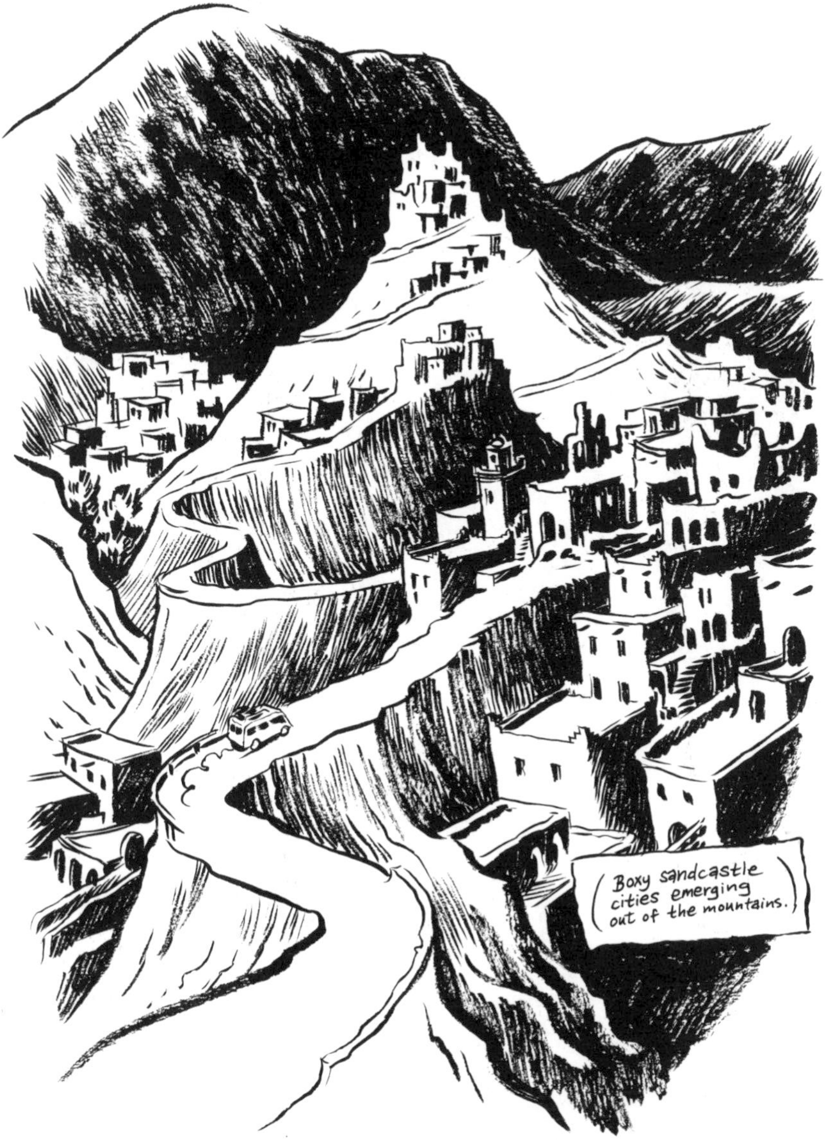
Boxy sandcastle
cities emerging
out of the mountains.

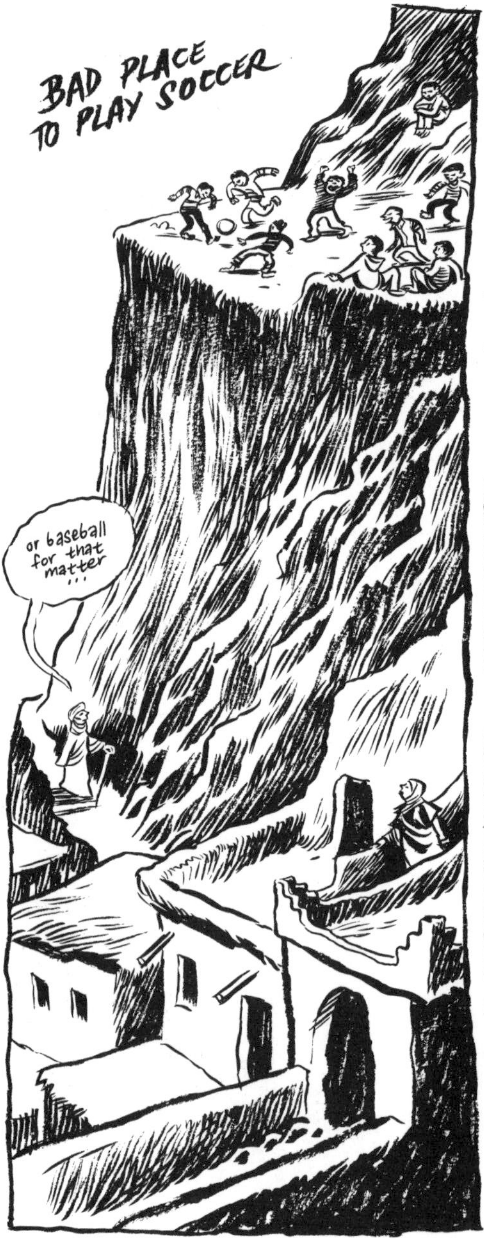
BAD PLACE TO PLAY SOCCER
or baseball for that matter ...

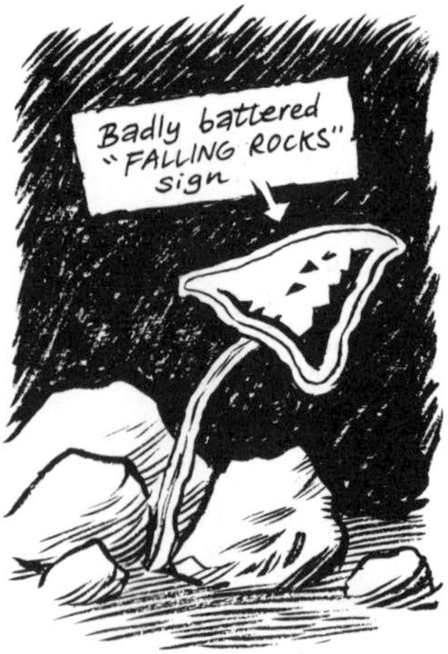
Badly battered "FALLING ROCKS" sign

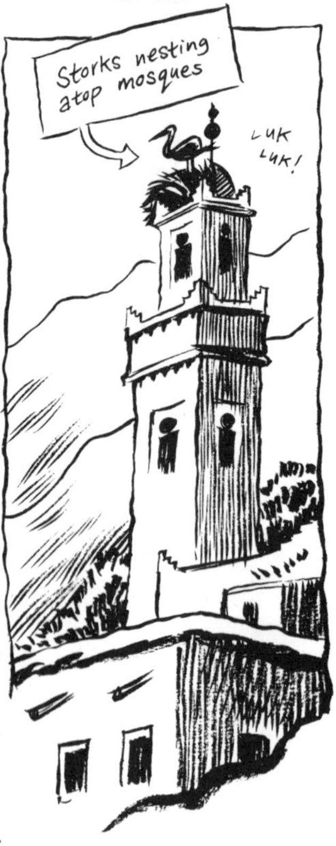
Storks nesting atop mosques
LUK LUK!

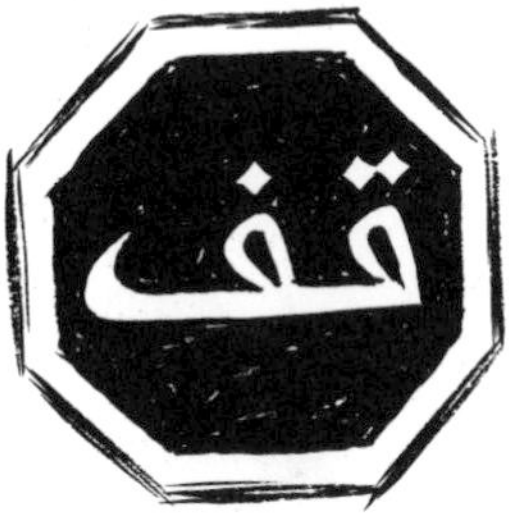
قف

We stopped THRICE – For food, for a kasbah tourist trap, and for a FLAT. We stayed the night in a regal mountain inn, having seen zero camels.

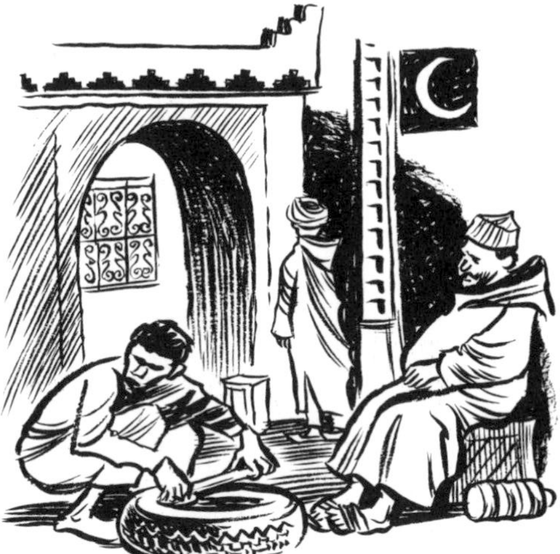

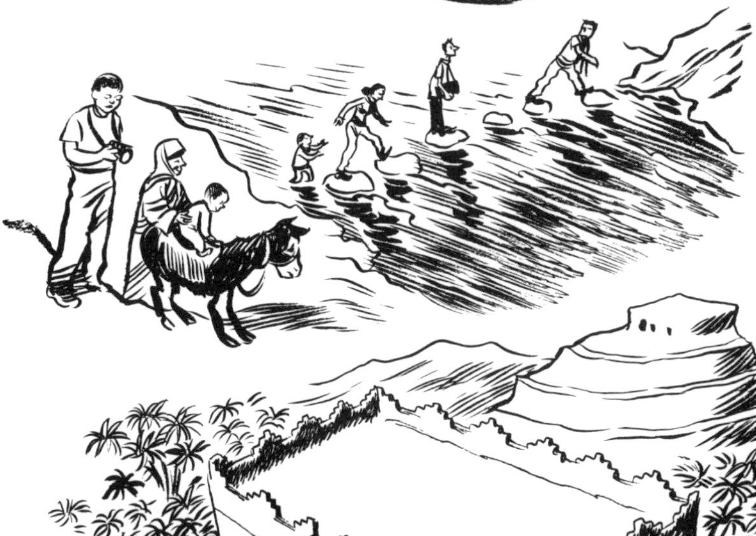

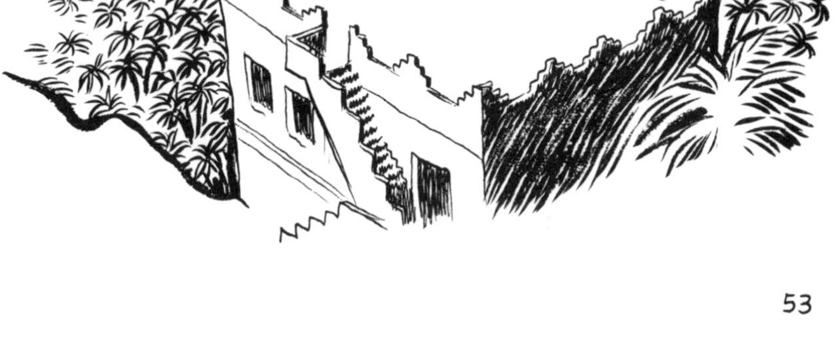

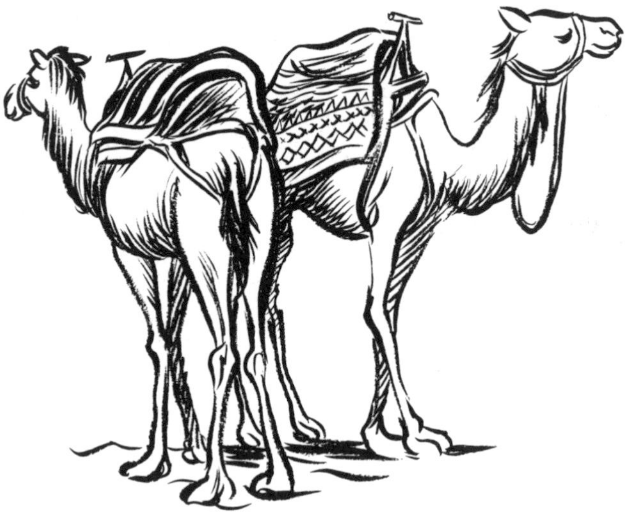

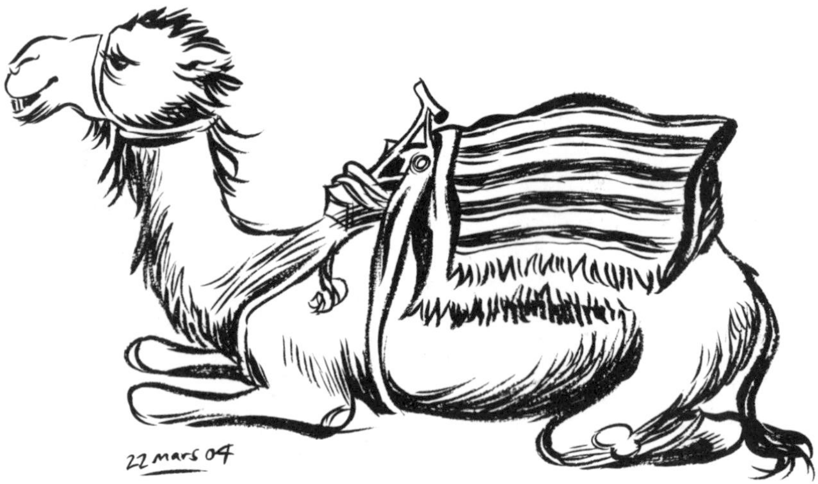
22 mars 04

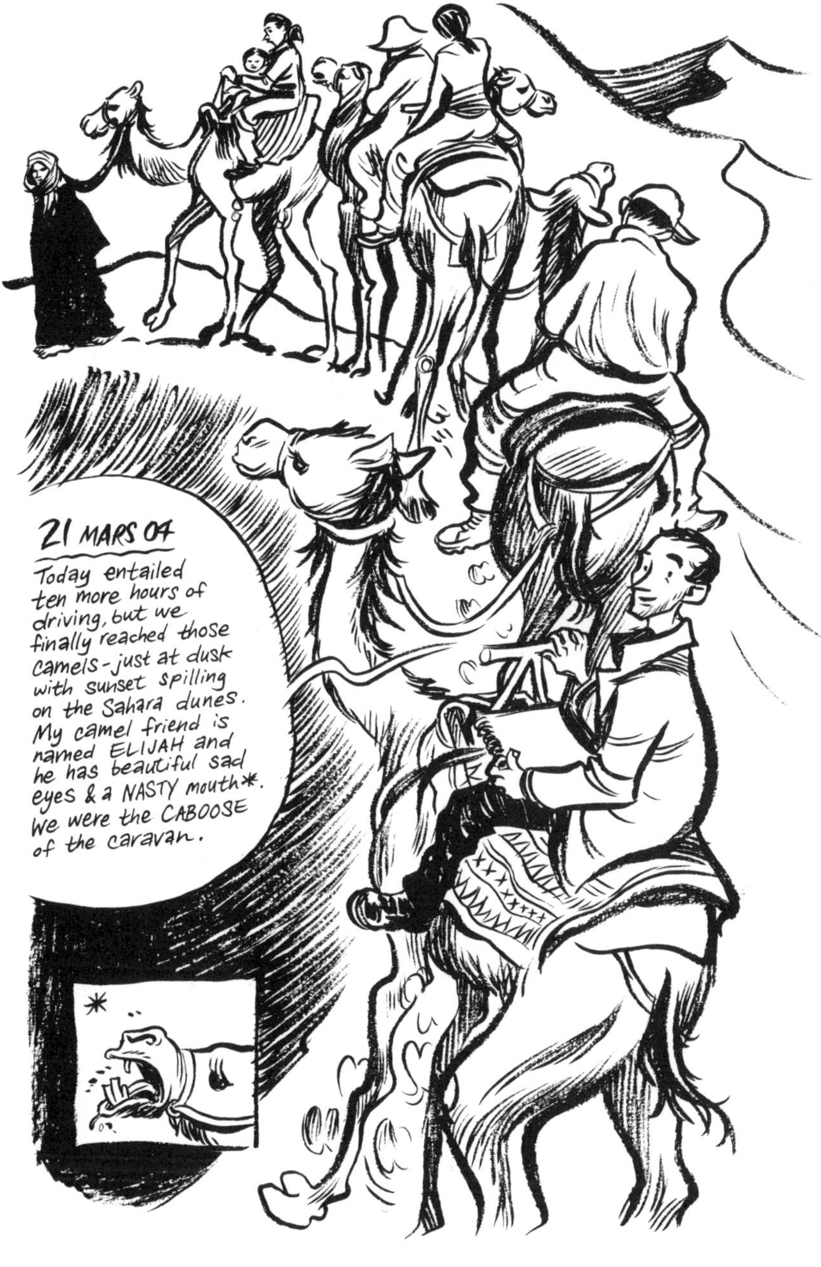
21 MARS 04
Today entailed ten more hours of driving, but we finally reached those camels - just at dusk with sunset spilling on the Sahara dunes. My camel friend is named ELIJAH and he has beautiful sad eyes & a NASTY mouth*. We were the CABOOSE of the caravan.

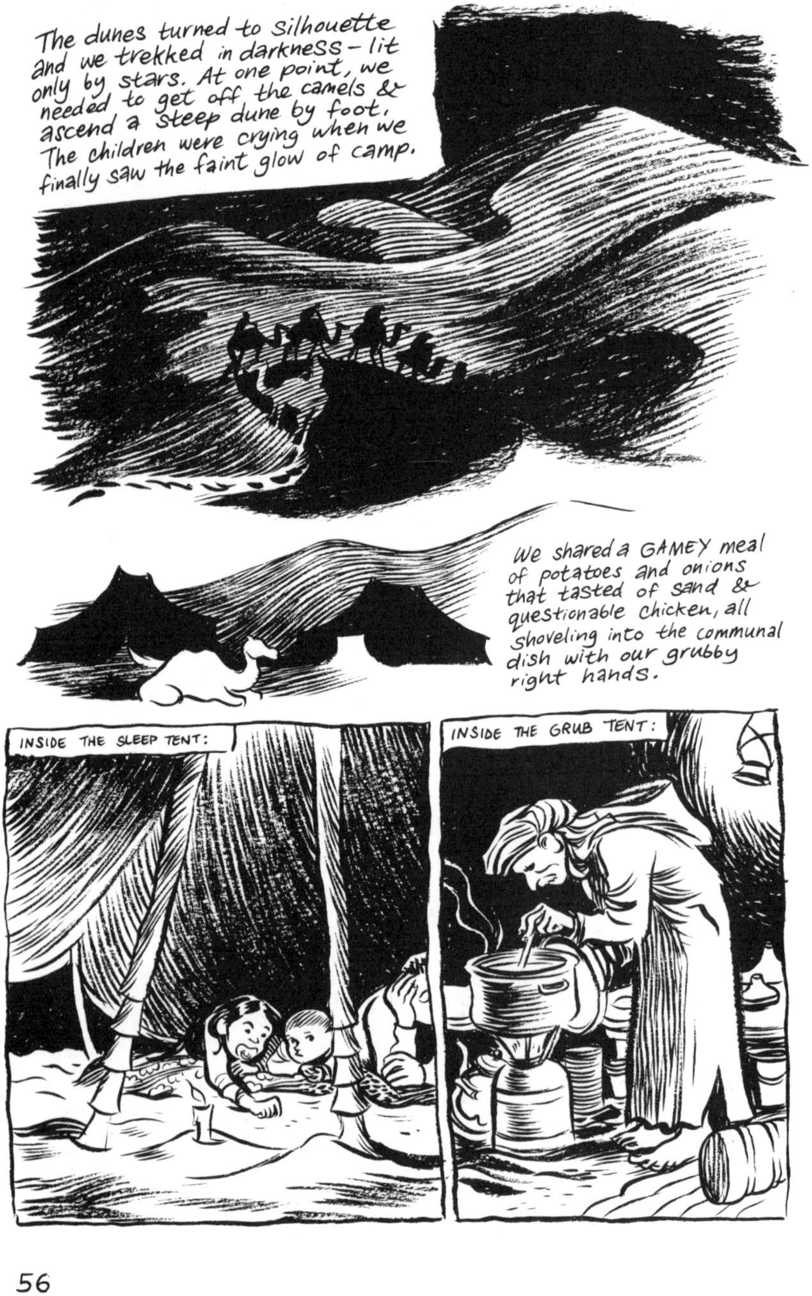
The dunes turned to silhouette and we trekked in darkness - lit only by stars. At one point, we needed to get off the camels & ascend a steep dune by foot. The children were crying when we finally saw the faint glow of camp.
We shared a GAMEY meal of potatoes and onions that tasted of sand & questionable chicken, all shoveling into the communal dish with our grubby right hands.
INSIDE THE SLEEP TENT:
INSIDE THE GRUB TENT:

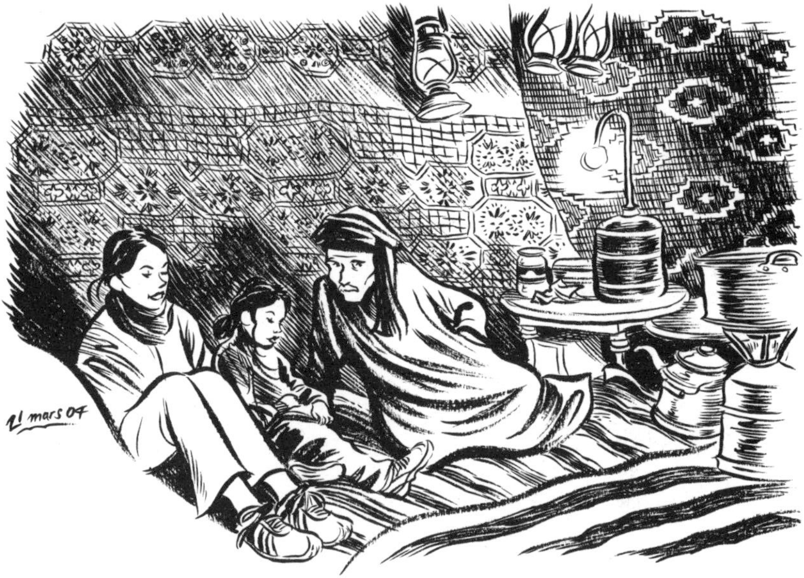
21 mars 04

Exhausted in the utter silence of the Sahara, Damon joked, "If you can't sleep tonight, then there's something wrong with you."

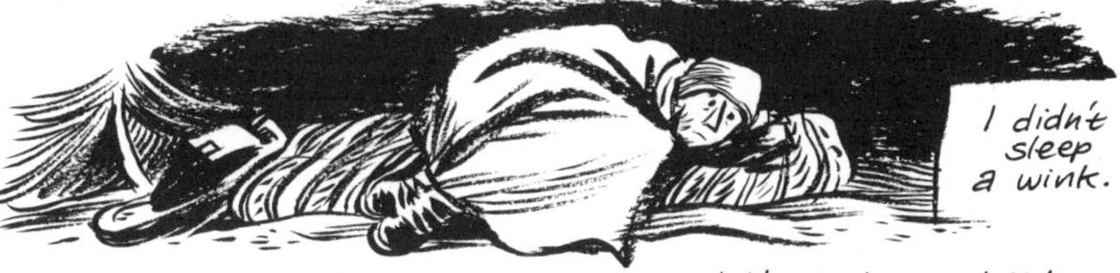
I didn't sleep a wink.

-Freezing cold with hat, wool overcoat and blankets-and I'd a nasty case of the CAMEL BOWELS--tummy messed up from the jolting lilt. Squirming out of the tent to crap in the middle of the night, there was something primitive & mystical--a shooting star above and single kleenex to take care of my bottom.

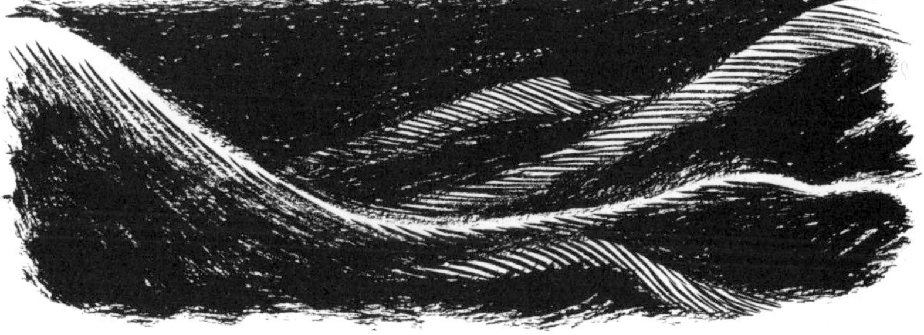

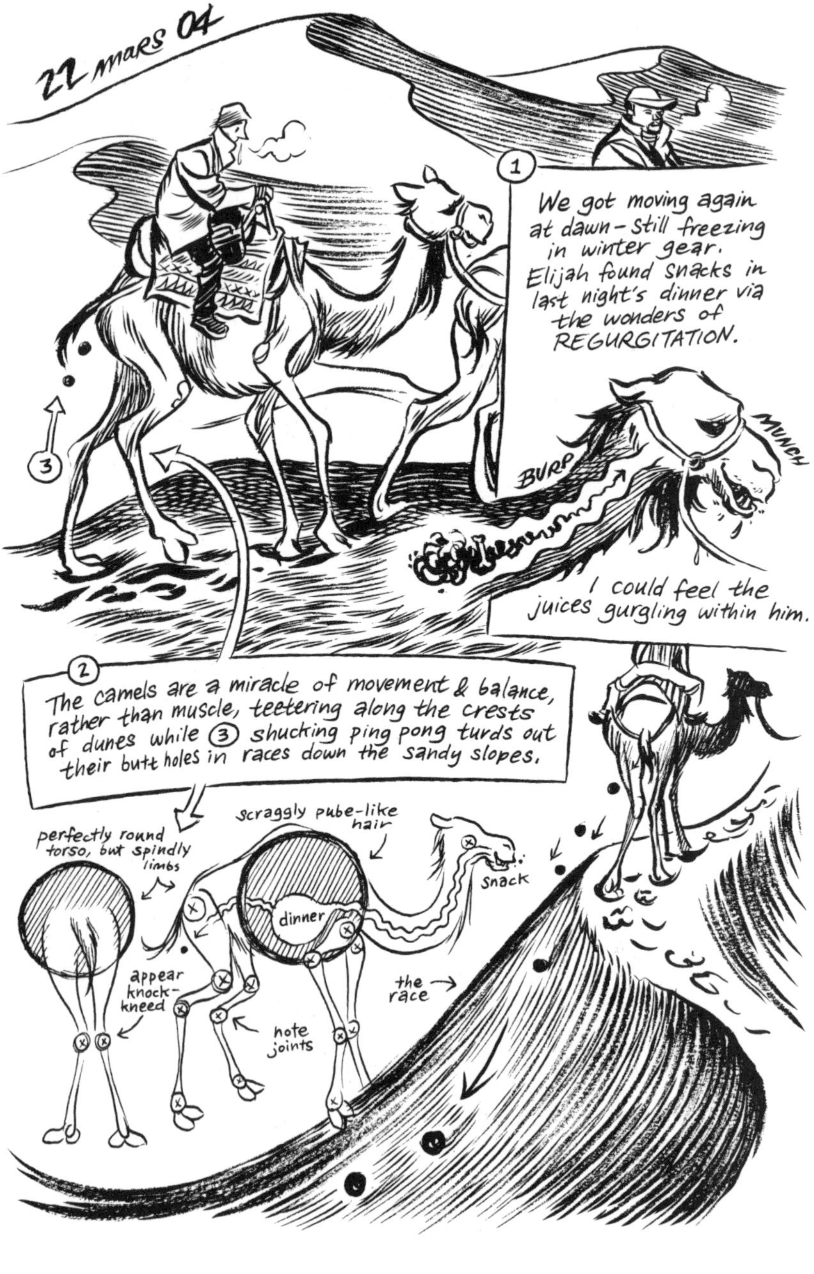

22 MARS 04
① We got moving again at dawn - still freezing in winter gear. Elijah found snacks in last night's dinner via the wonders of REGURGITATION.
BURP
MUNCH
I could feel the juices gurgling within him.
② The camels are a miracle of movement & balance, rather than muscle, teetering along the crests of dunes while ③ shucking ping pong turds out their butt holes in races down the sandy slopes.
③
perfectly round torso, but spindly limbs
scraggly pube-like hair
snack
dinner
appear knock-kneed
note joints
the race

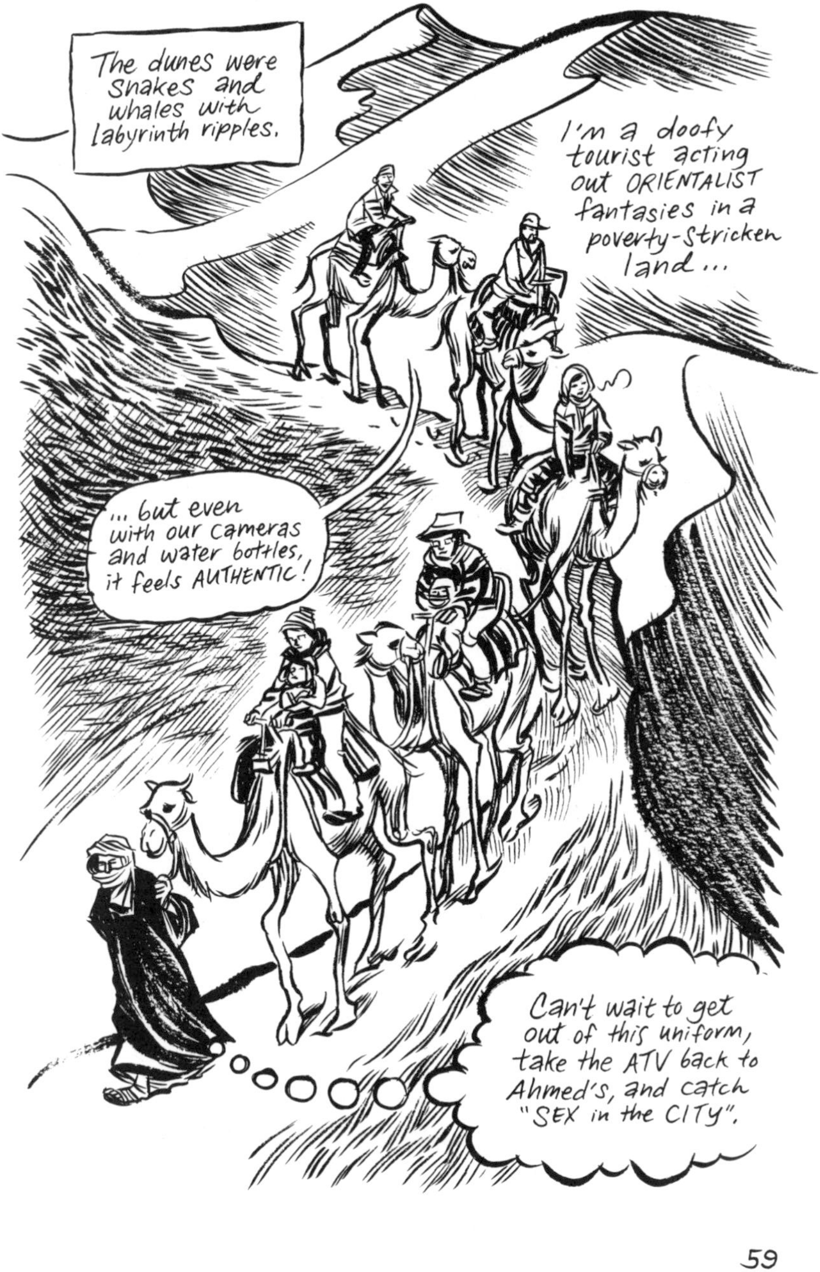

The dunes were snakes and whales with labyrinth ripples.
I'm a doofy tourist acting out ORIENTALIST fantasies in a poverty-stricken land...
... but even with our cameras and water bottles, it feels AUTHENTIC!
Can't wait to get out of this uniform, take the ATV back to Ahmed's, and catch "SEX in the CITY".

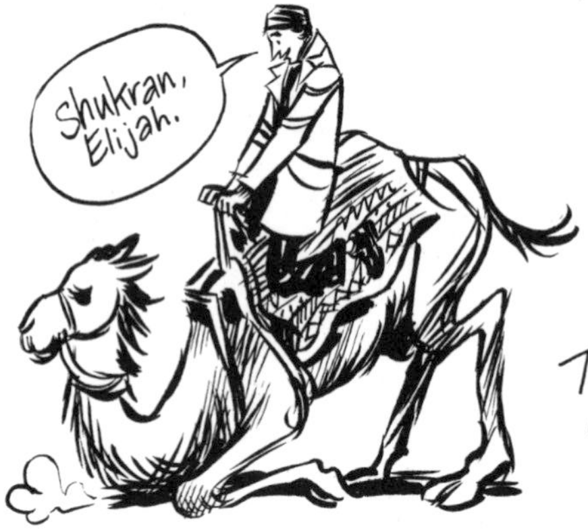
Shukran, Elijah.

Two hours or so west, we emerged from the dunes to palm trees and the van

Driving back to Marrakesh, we were weakened by exhaustion, and the same terrain seemed monotonous.

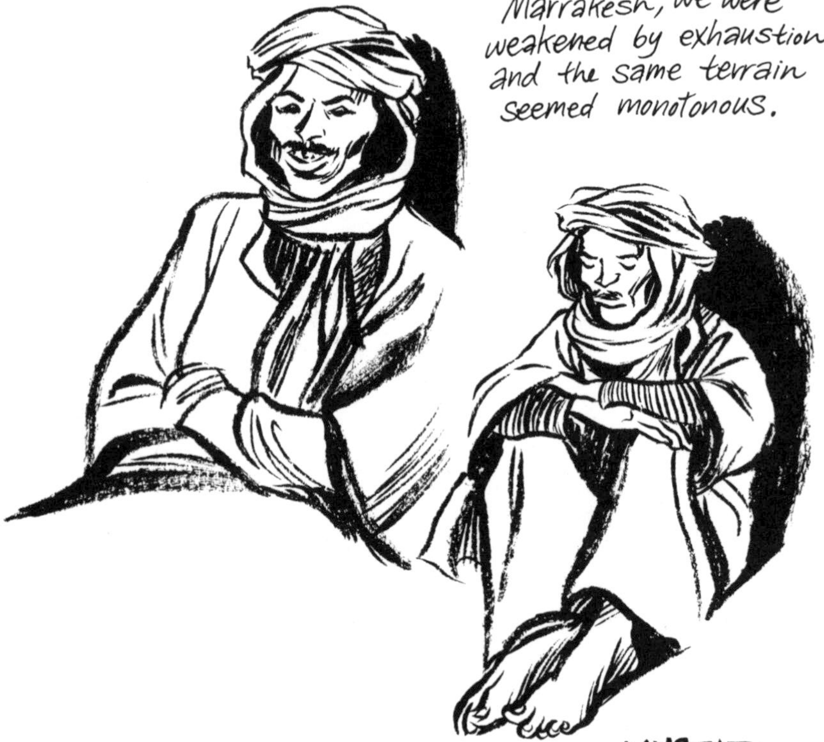

MUSTAFA

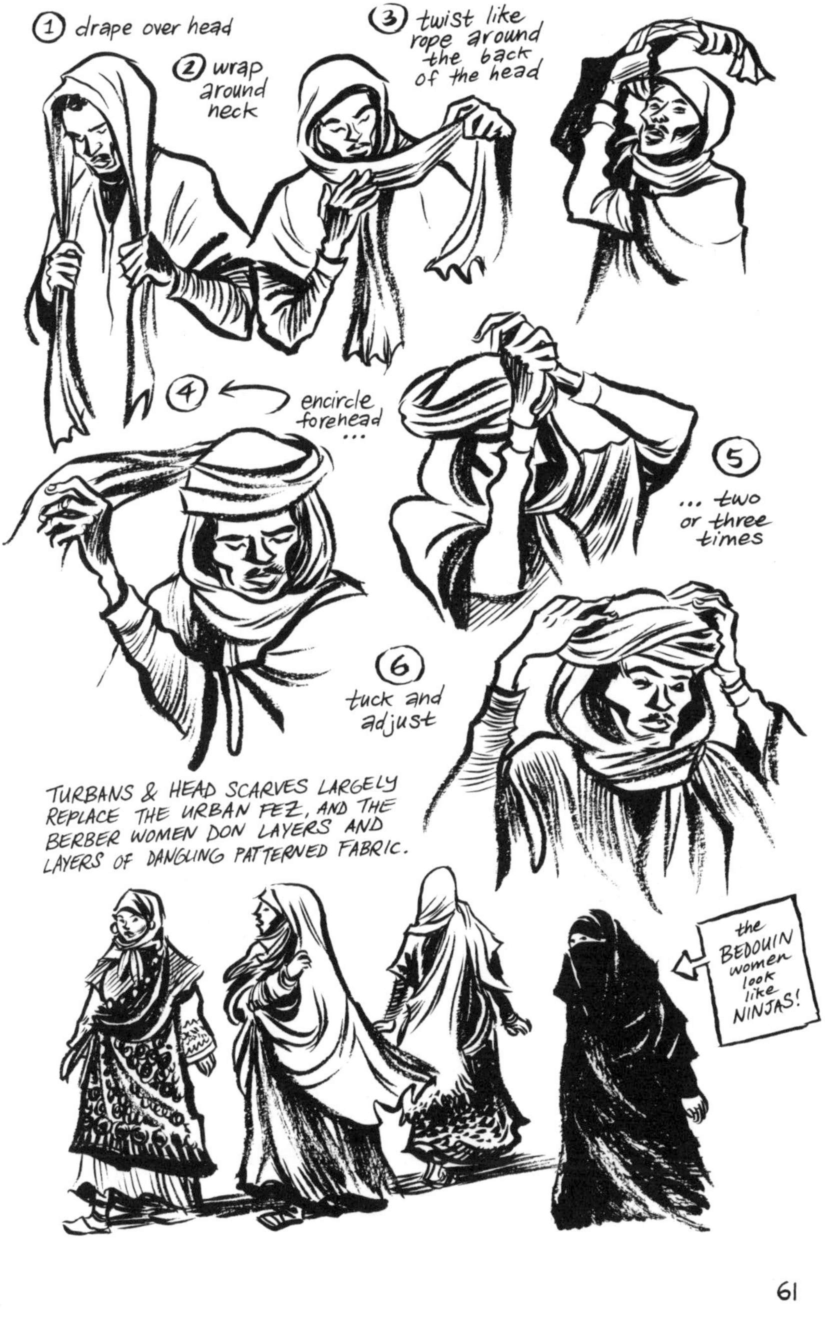

1 drape over head
2 wrap around neck
3 twist like rope around the back of the head
4 encircle forehead ...
5 ... two or three times
6 tuck and adjust
TURBANS & HEAD SCARVES LARGELY REPLACE THE URBAN FEZ, AND THE BERBER WOMEN DON LAYERS AND LAYERS OF DANGLING PATTERNED FABRIC.
the BEDOUIN women look like NINJAS!

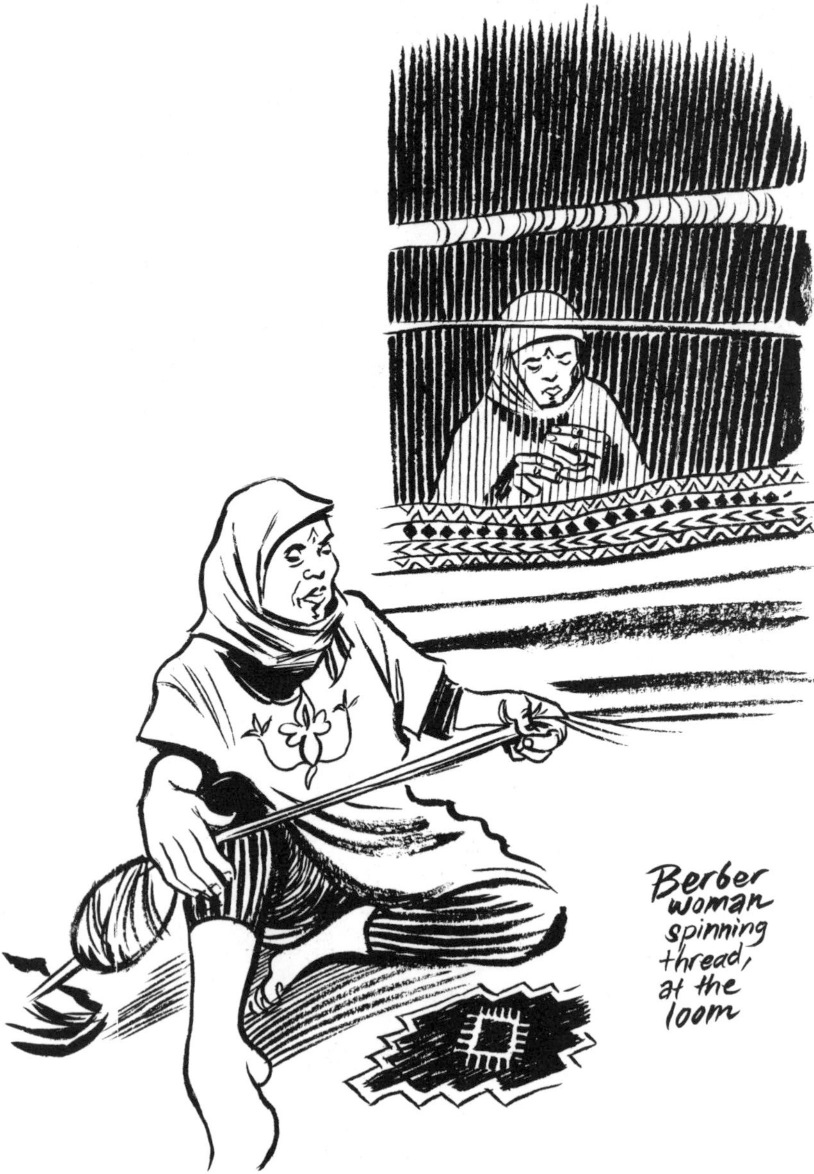
Berber woman spinning thread, at the loom

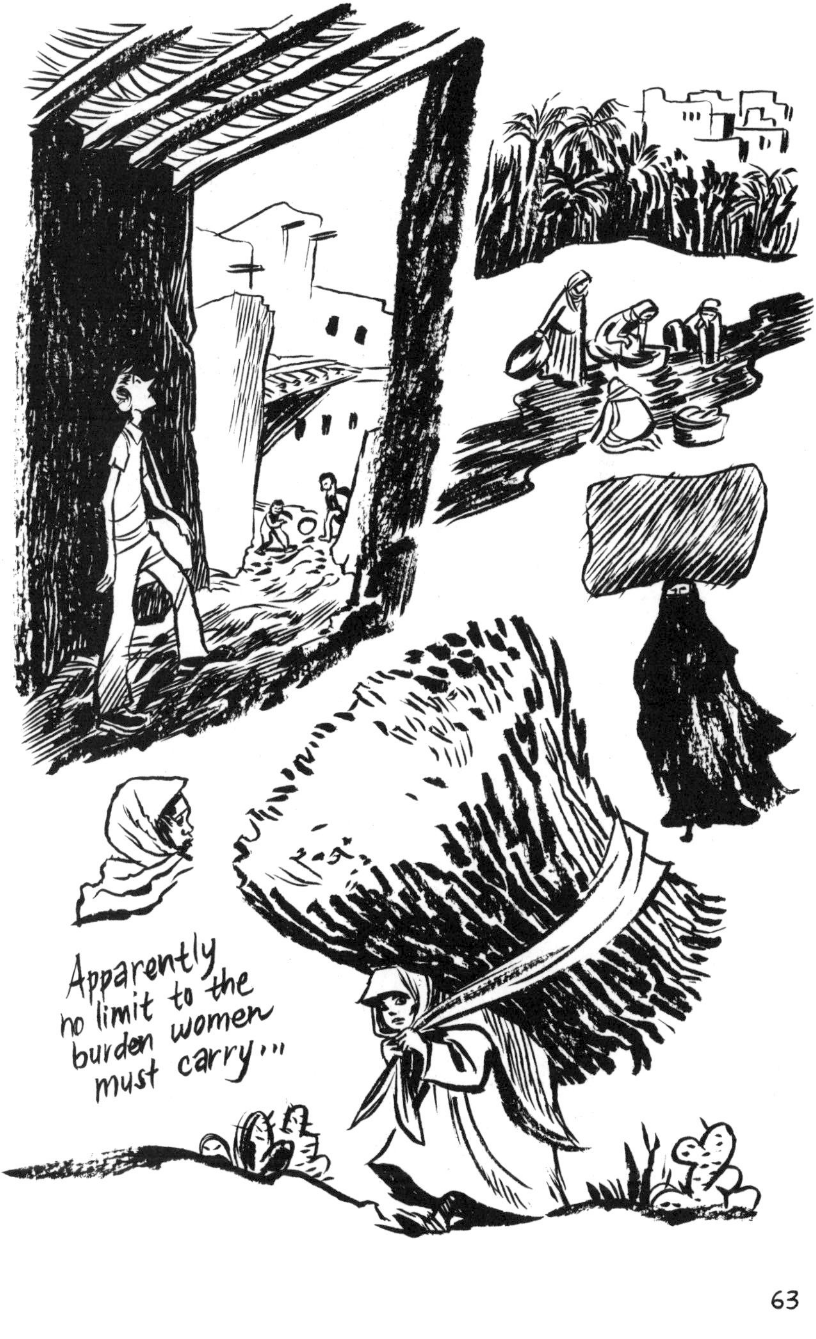
Apparently no limit to the burden women must carry...

23 MARS 04 As soon as I returned to Marrakesh from the rural east, I was desperate to leave again. It felt like a cheezy circus put on for the tourists & full of unctuous CARNIES. I booked a ticket for the bus west to coastal Essaouira and then the "kind fellow" who helped stow my baggage nabbed me for 20 dirham. (This was the third time I was ripped off by unsolicited generosity.) At each stop heading west, beggars would jump aboard and scour the aisles. One particular stop, the man next to me said we'd reached Essaouira and I deported.. but he'd lied. Crawling back on the bus, my seat was gone and a "new friend" approached me about alternative routes to the coast. Once the beggars cleared out, a new "seat" presented itself, next to a fanatical nose-picker. The smell of crap and vomit further fueled my grumpiness.

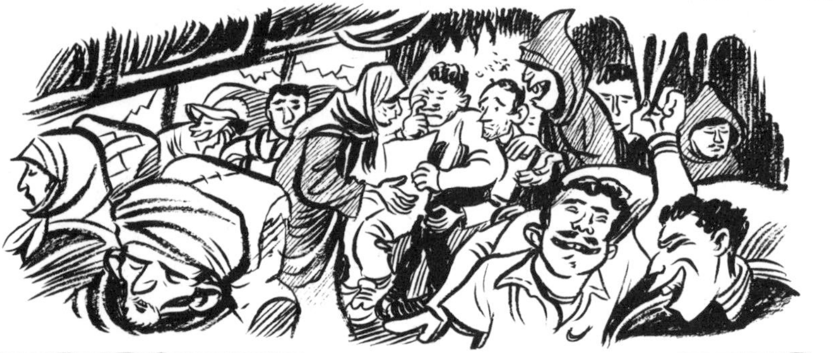

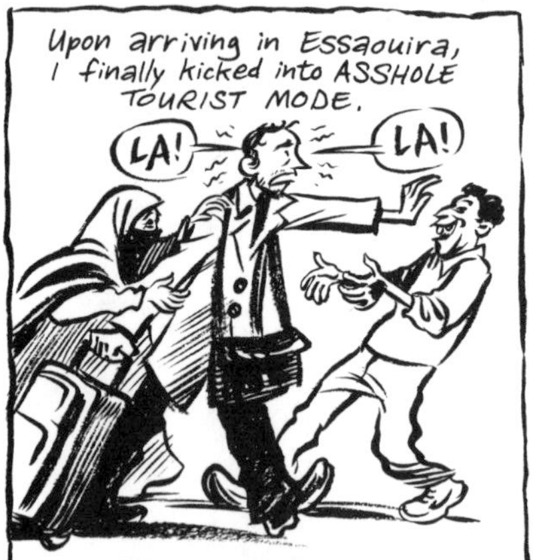
Upon arriving in Essaouira, I finally kicked into ASSHOLE TOURIST MODE.
LA!
LA!

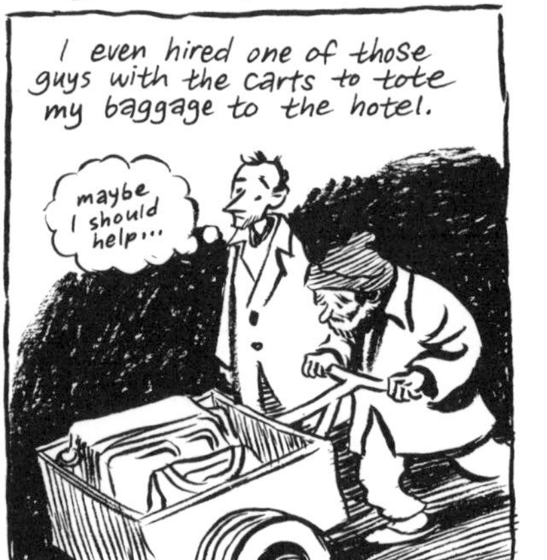
I even hired one of those guys with the carts to tote my baggage to the hotel.
maybe I should help...

I resolved to pamper myself with a room at the HÔTEL RIAD AL-MADINA. The guide book recommended if you "fancy yourself as a bit of a ROCK STAR and want to treat yourself*."

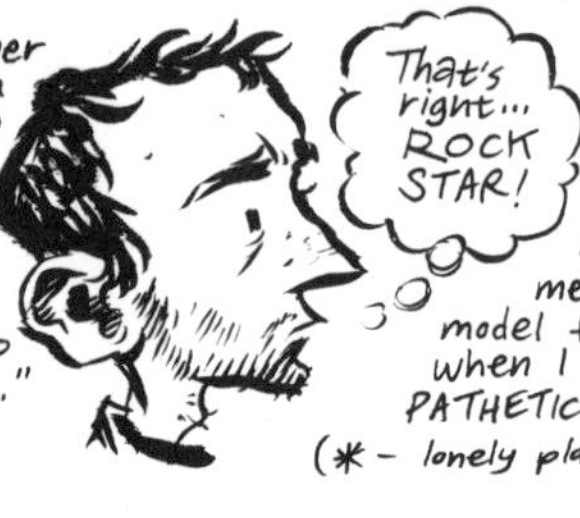
That's right... ROCK STAR!

Actually, the selling point was that LEONARD COHEN stayed there. I love his music, we share the same birthday, and just yesterday I was meditating on him as a role model for the POETIC RAKE when I was feeling like a PATHETIC WORM.

(* - lonely planet)

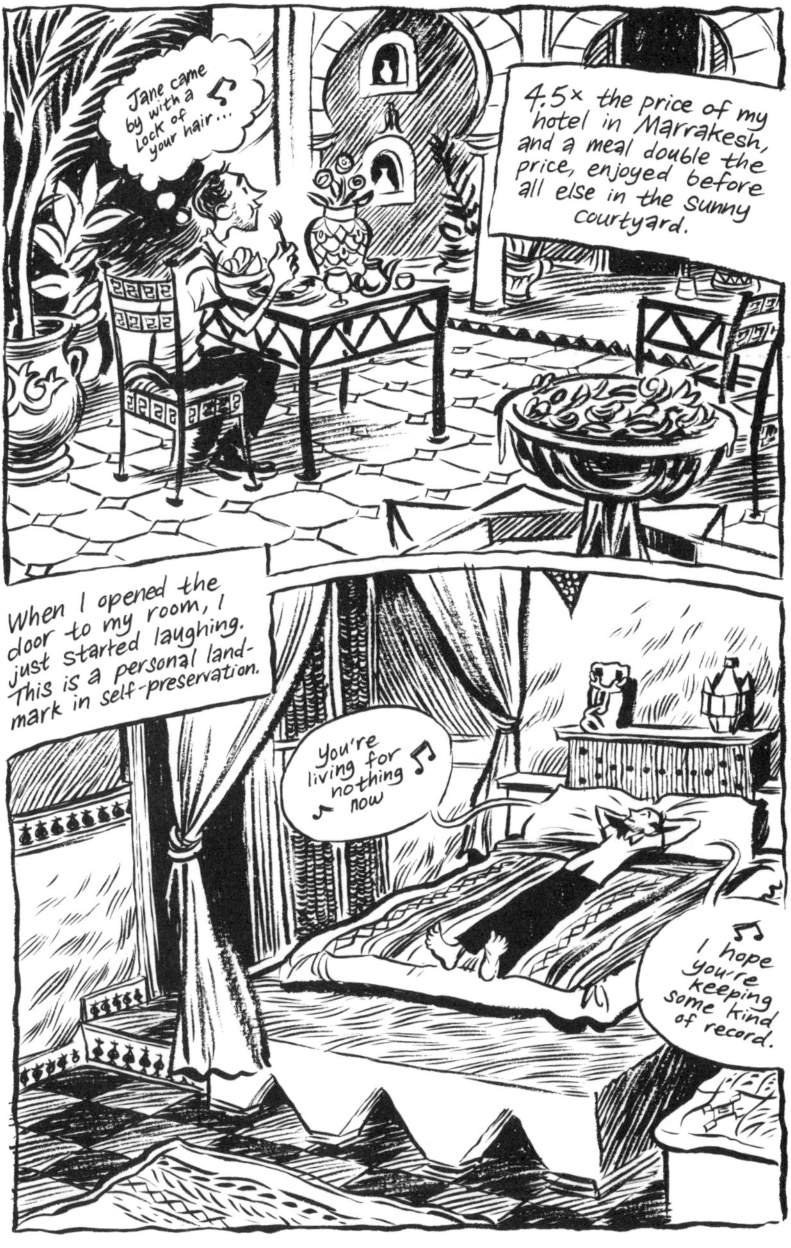
Jane came by with a lock of your hair...
4.5× the price of my hotel in Marrakesh, and a meal double the price, enjoyed before all else in the sunny courtyard.
When I opened the door to my room, I just started laughing. This is a personal landmark in self-preservation.
You're living for nothing now
I hope you're keeping some kind of record.

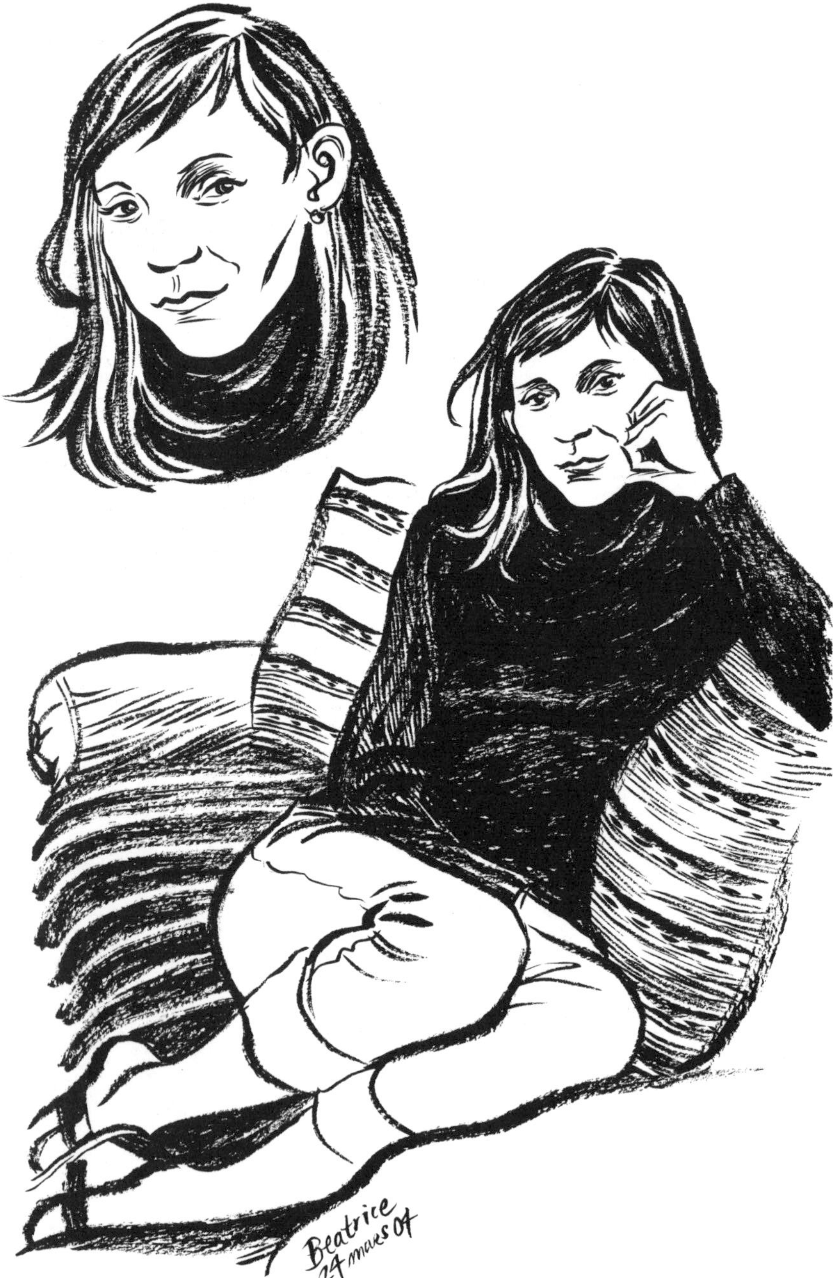
Beatrice
24 mars 04

24 MARS 04

Did very little. First some laundry in the bathroom sink (not very rock star of me)- Then a stroll along the beach, but my foot still hurt too much. I ran into another sweet couple (Parisians), but it's always COUPLES! Returning to the hotel, a slew of retirees/package tourists had arrived and the place was more a nursing home than a rock star hangout. Then I finally met another LONE traveler-- Her name's Beatrice and she's a bit older than me & quite sexy - an assistant director from Luxembourg (worked on 8½ WOMEN and SHADOW OF THE VAMPIRE among others)- she becomes, like ANGE, a source of connection & encouragement in the midst of my self-imposed loneliness.

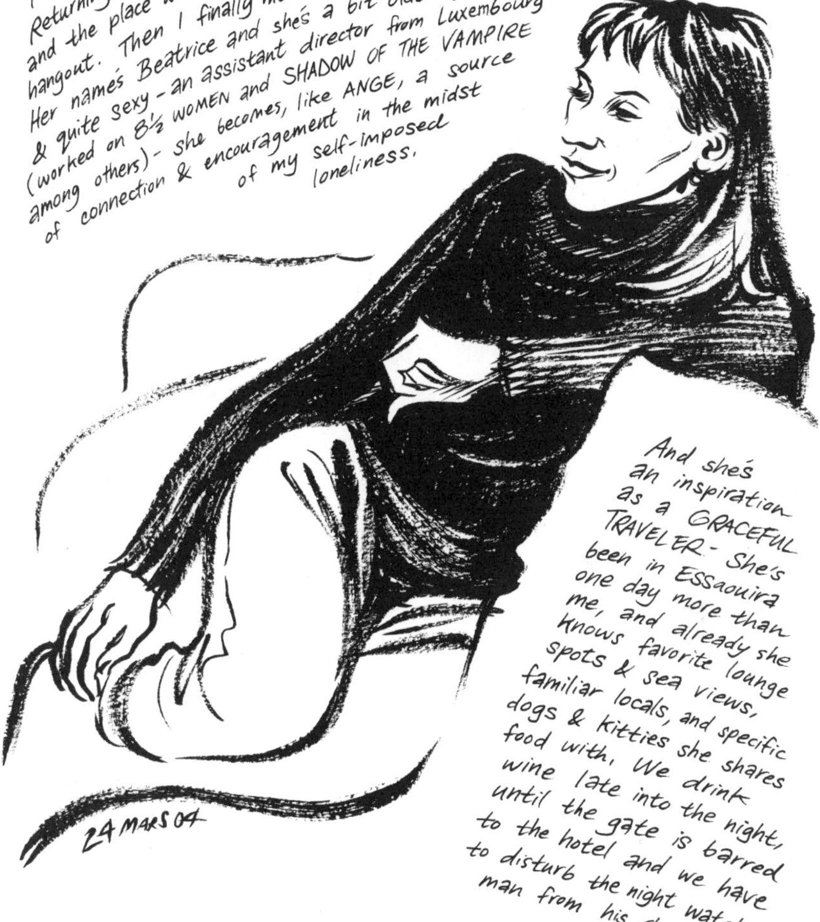
24 MARS 04

And she's an inspiration as a GRACEFUL TRAVELER- She's been in ESSAOUIRA one day more than me, and already she knows favorite lounge spots & sea views, familiar locals, and specific dogs & kitties she shares food with. We drink wine late into the night, until the gate is barred to the hotel and we have to disturb the night watch-man from his slumber.

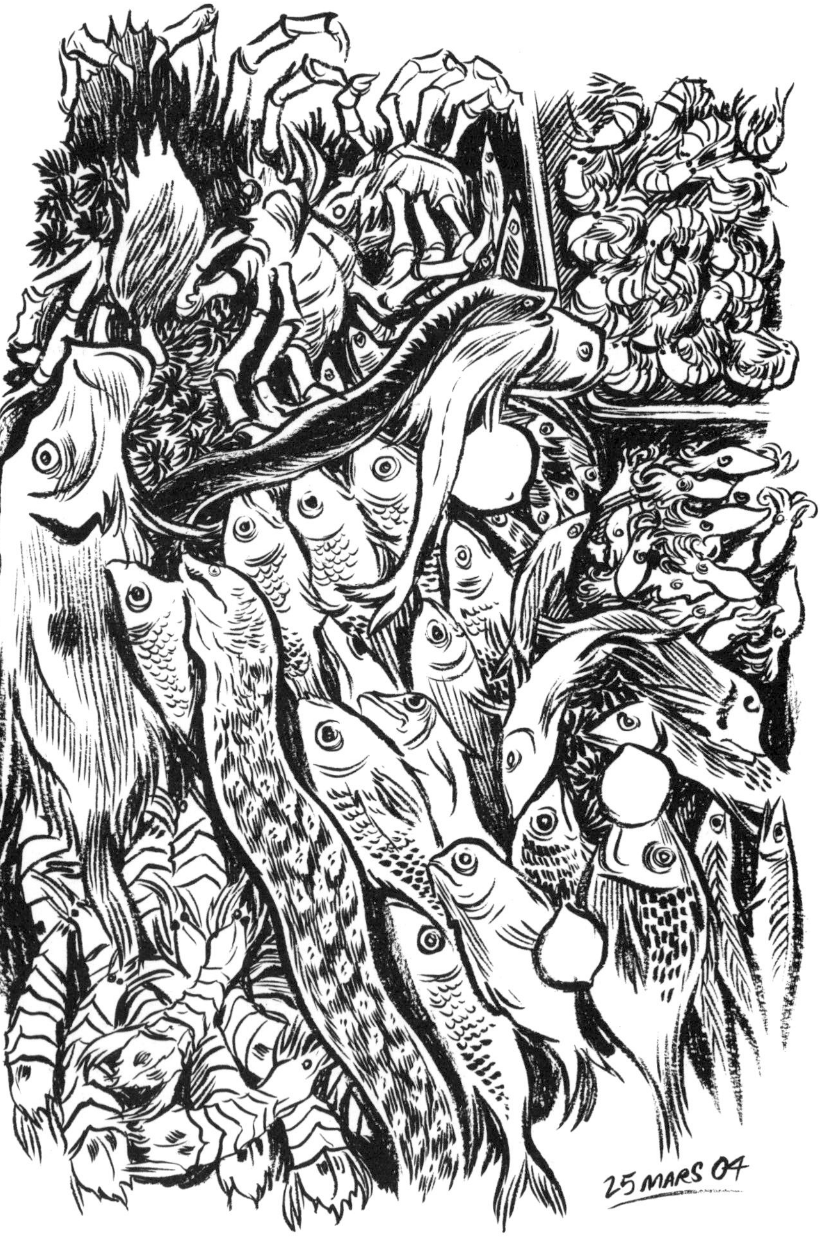
25 MARS 04

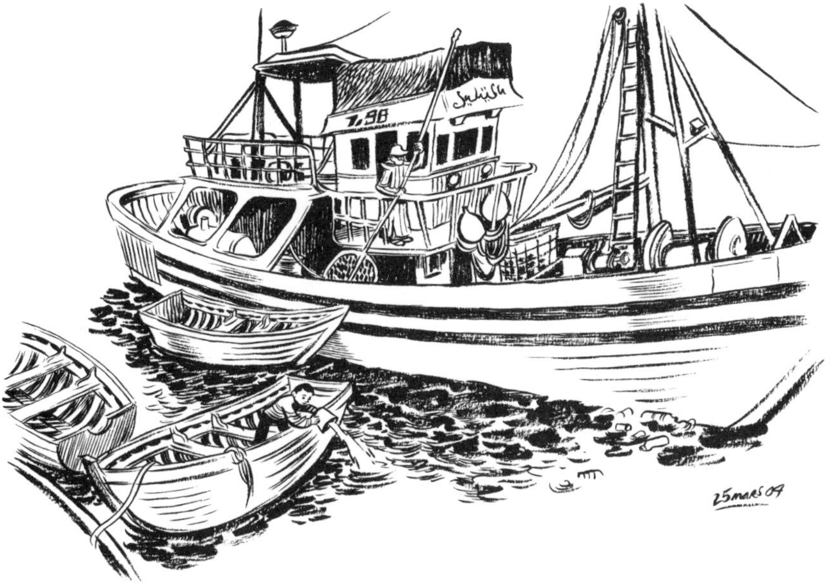
25mars04

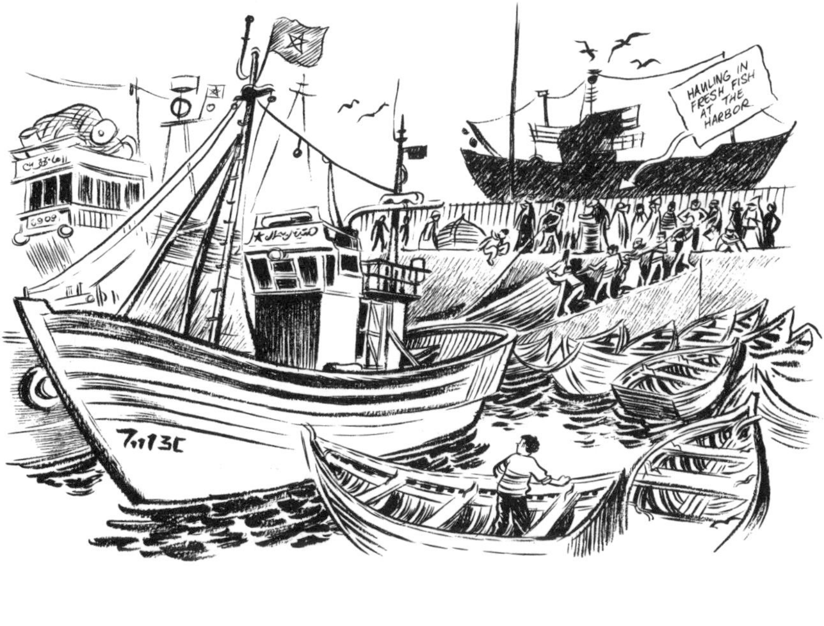
HAULING IN FRESH FISH AT THE HARBOR

25 MARS 04

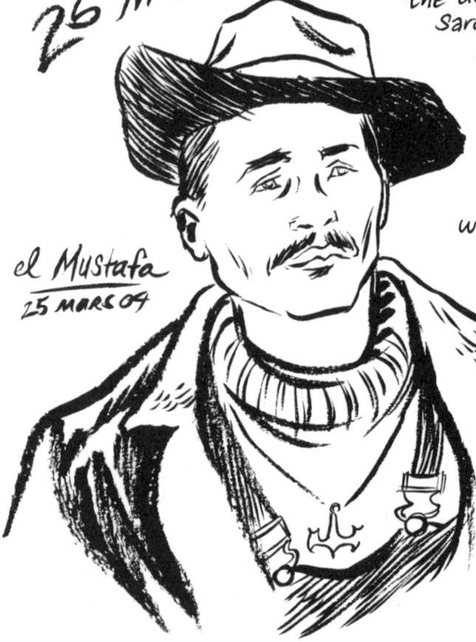
el Mustafa
25 MARS 04

Beatrice and I spent the first half of the day together – eating shrimp and sardines at the outdoor fish grills, and perched on the ramparts overlooking the sea. She spoke fluent English, but often we were simply silent, conditioned to traveling alone. She left for Luxembourg in the early afternoon, and I went to the docks to draw boats and watch the catch come in. Afterwards, I returned to the fish grills and buddied up to a few locals by drawing portraits.

In the evening, I met another kind couple, and they remarked that they hadn't met any other lone travelers.

"I know," I said, already missing my one day travel companion.

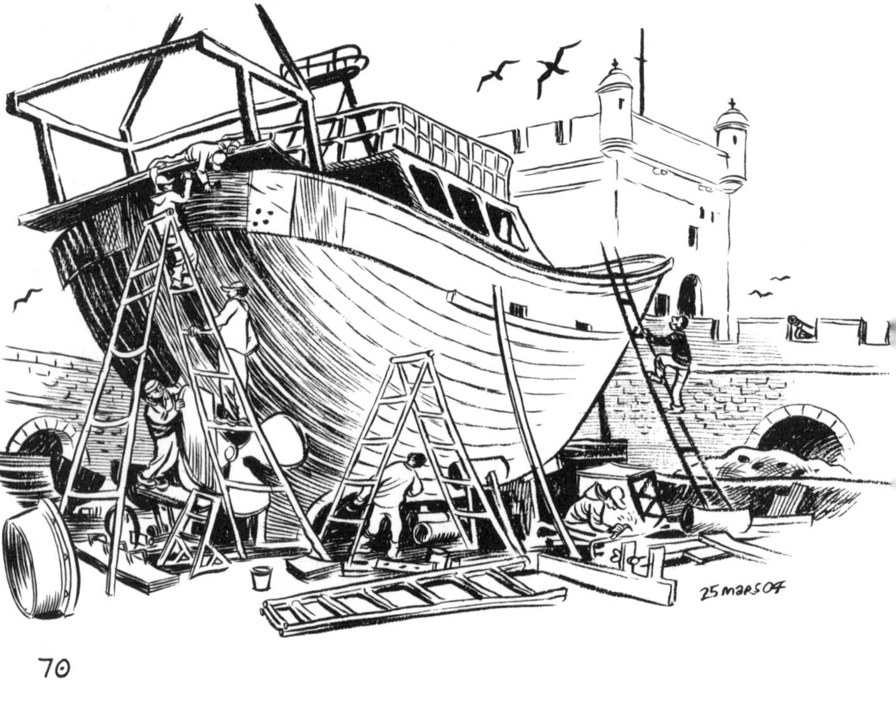
25 MARS 04

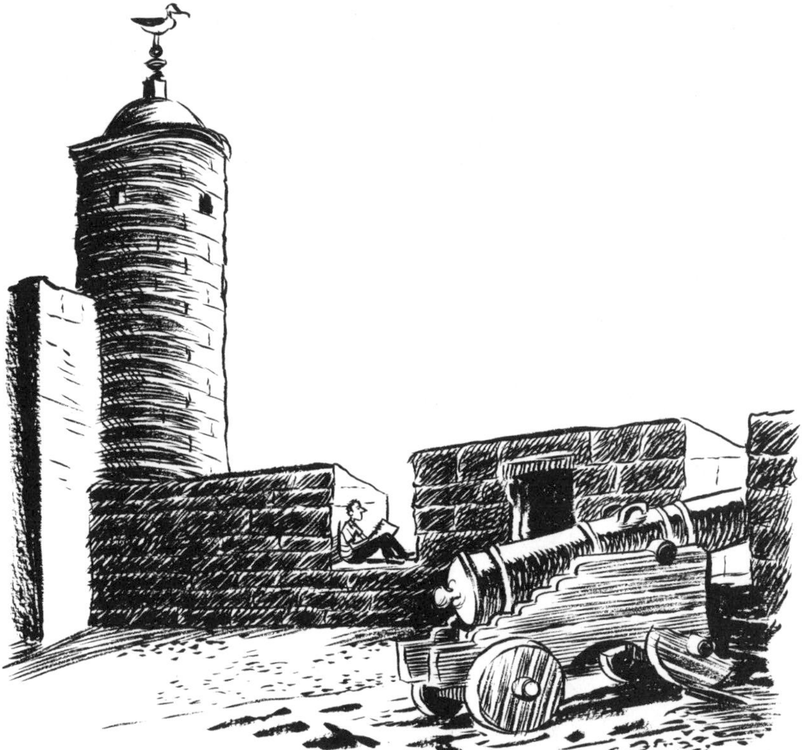

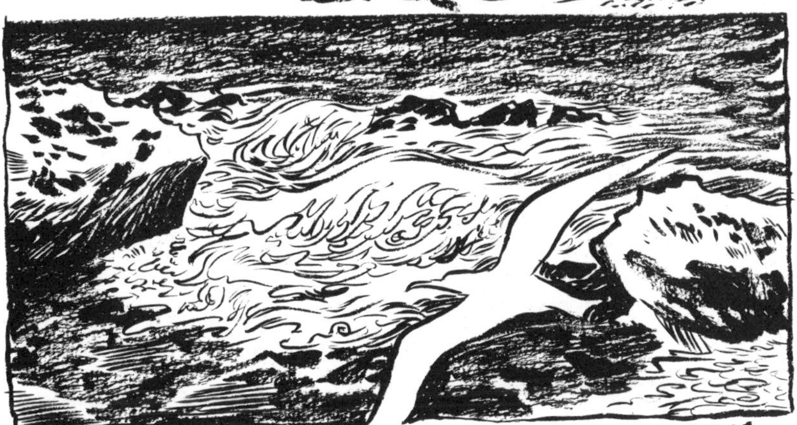

26 MARS 04

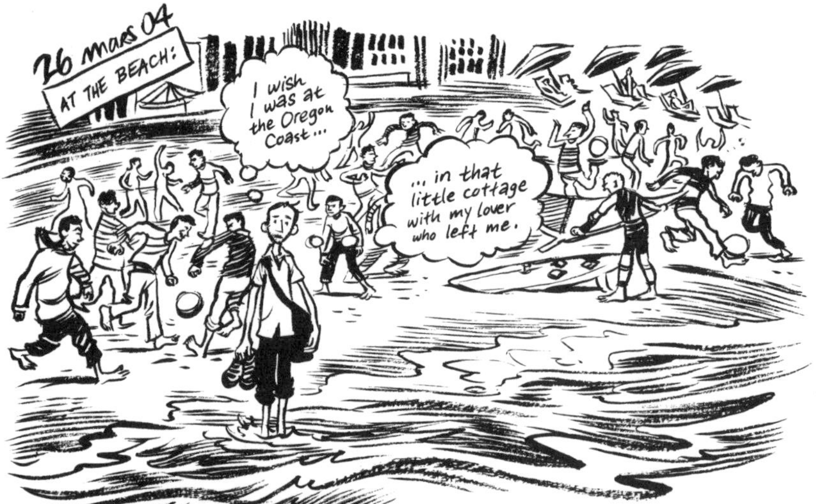
26 mars 04
AT THE BEACH:
I wish I was at the Oregon Coast...
... in that little cottage with my lover who left me.

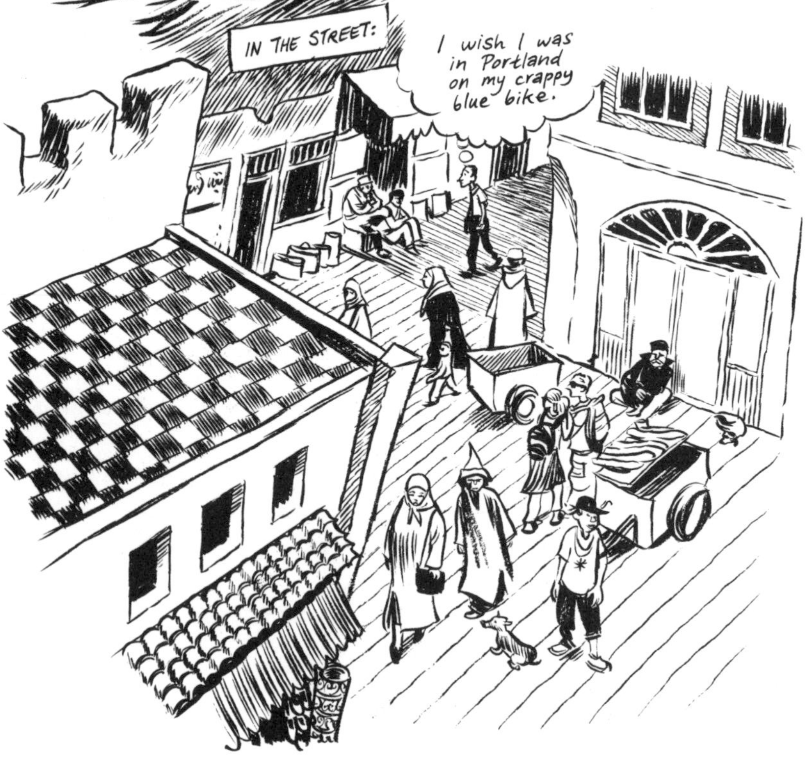
IN THE STREET:
I wish I was in Portland on my crappy blue bike.

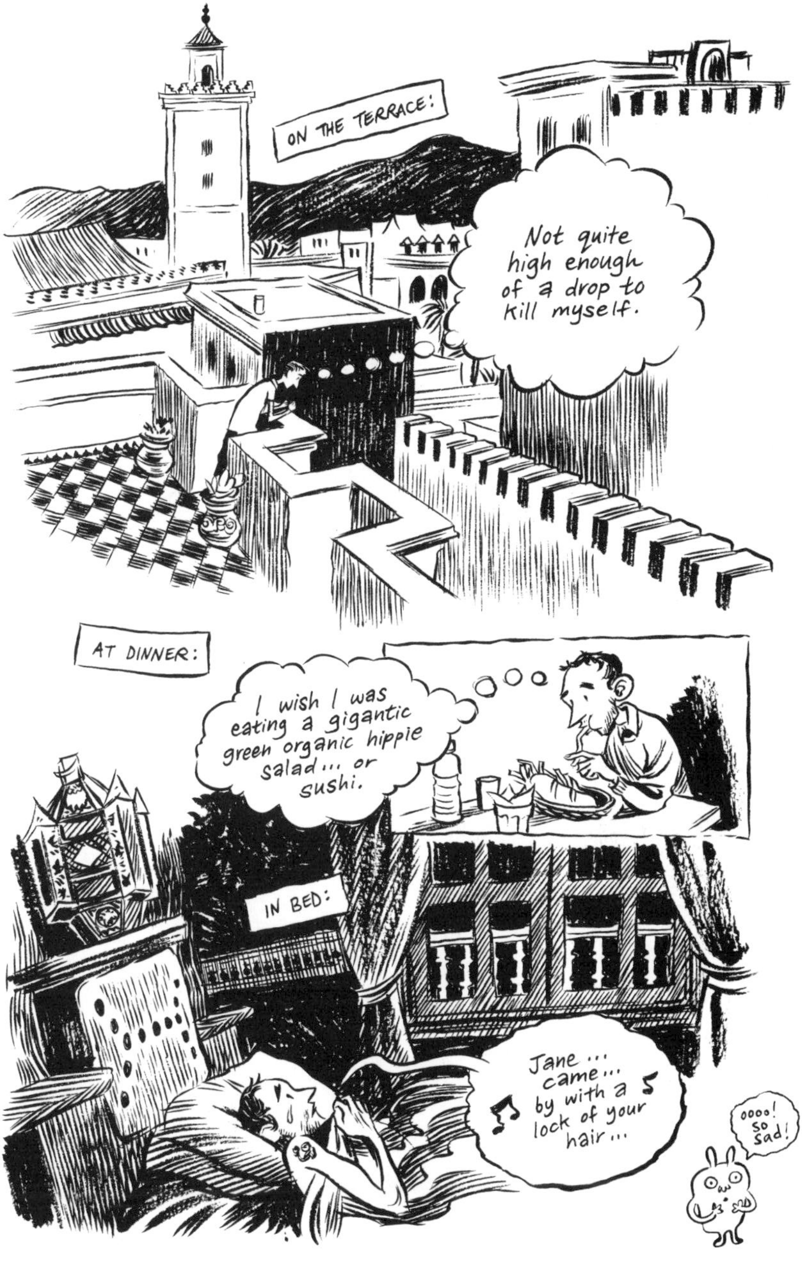
ON THE TERRACE:
Not quite high enough of a drop to kill myself.
AT DINNER:
I wish I was eating a gigantic green organic hippie salad... or sushi.
IN BED:
Jane ... came... by with a lock of your hair...
oooo! so sad!

27 mars 04

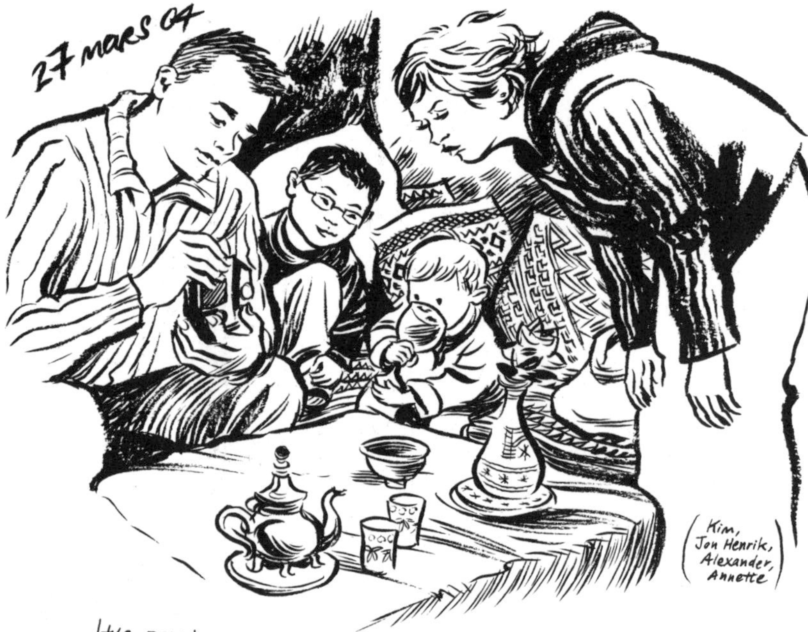
(Kim, Jon Henrik, Alexander, Annette)

It's pouring rain in Essaouria & I'm becoming a professional portrait artist. Yesterday at the fish grills, I was cajoled by the locals to do another portrait for free lunch -- that's about three dollars for an hour's work, but I was hoping to mingle with the Moroccans. Instead, I felt like a novelty & they want me to return today.

This morning, a friendly Norwegian family took me to lunch for a portrait of their children - Jon Henrik & Alexander.

While I drew them in the hotel lounge, other tourists stopped me to ask my rate.

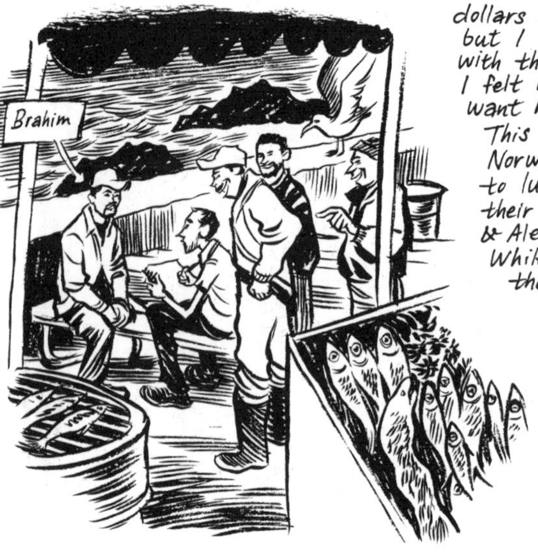
Brahim

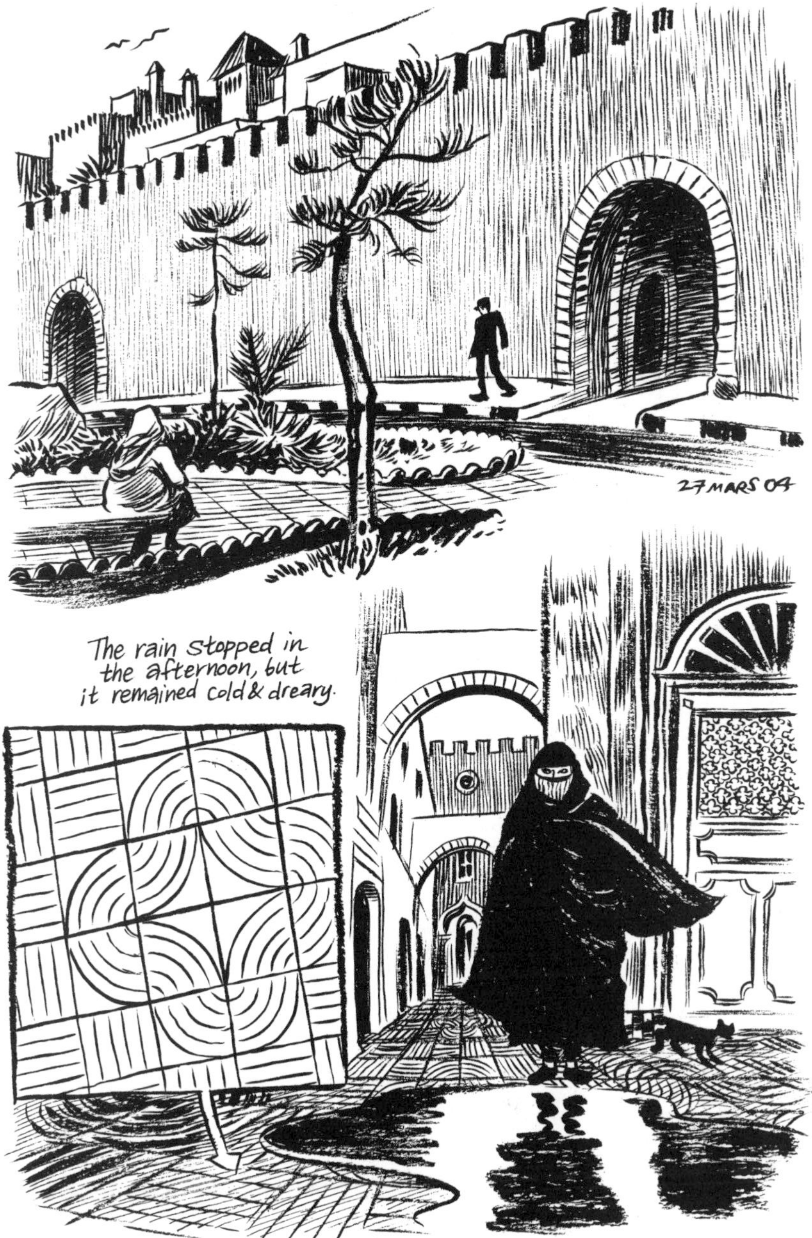
27 MARS 04
The rain stopped in the afternoon, but it remained cold & dreary.

I reluctantly returned to the fish grills, but the guys were genuinely happy to see me & insisted I join them for dinner -- digging into fish chunks and tomatoes with our right hands, and tossing the heads to the kitties & gulls.

SKRAWK

SKREEK

drip

Later, another meal at a familiar sandwich shop where I ran into a familiar German fellow - Christophe - for the second night in a row. He's in Essaouria studying Arabic, and he introduced me to his local friend SAID - an apprentice in a wood-shop. Said and I agreed to visit the SOUQ HAD DRA - the big Sunday market on the outskirts of the city - together the next morning.

26 MARS 04

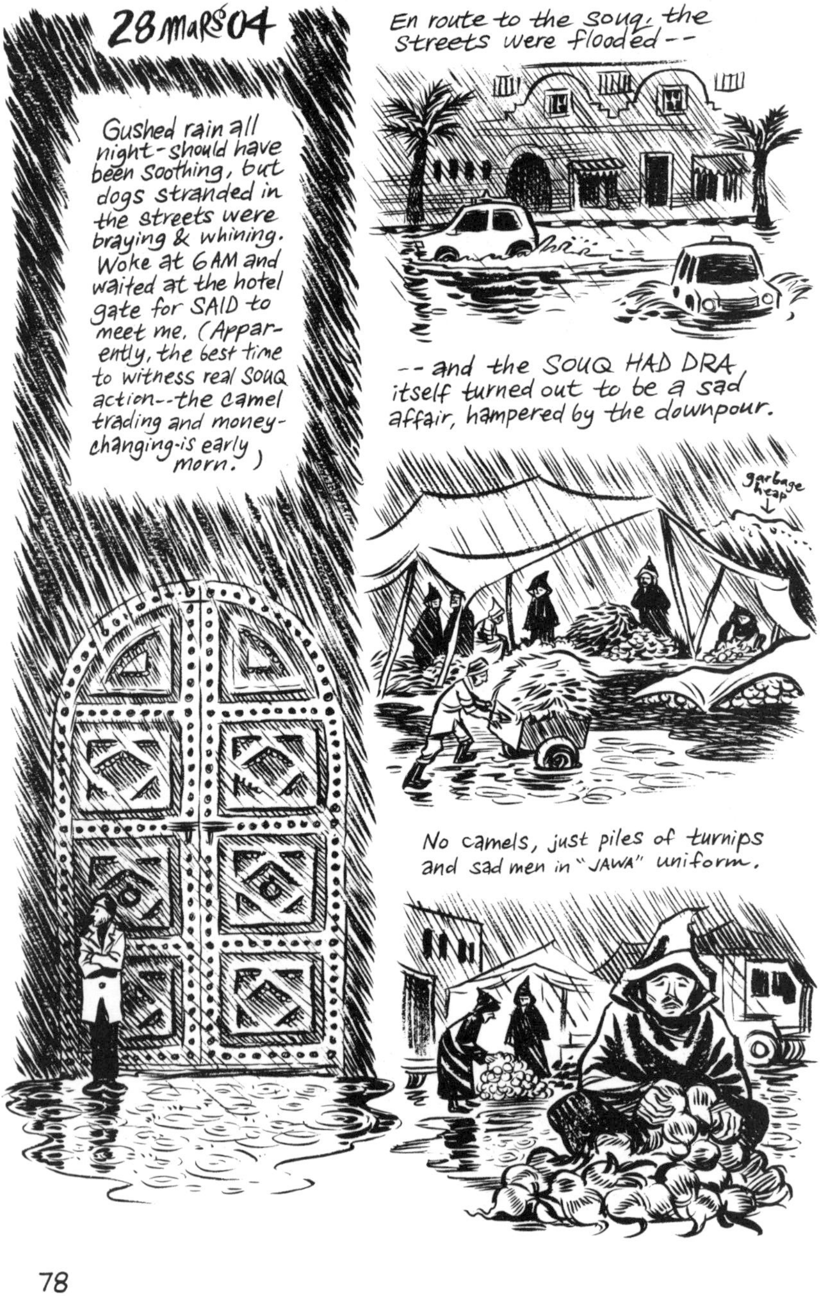
28 MARS 04
Gushed rain all night-should have been soothing, but dogs stranded in the streets were braying & whining. Woke at 6AM and waited at the hotel gate for SAID to meet me. (Apparently, the best time to witness real SOUQ action--the camel trading and money-changing-is early morn.)
En route to the souq, the streets were flooded--
--and the SOUQ HAD DRA itself turned out to be a sad affair, hampered by the downpour.
garbage heap
No camels, just piles of turnips and sad men in "JAWA" uniform.

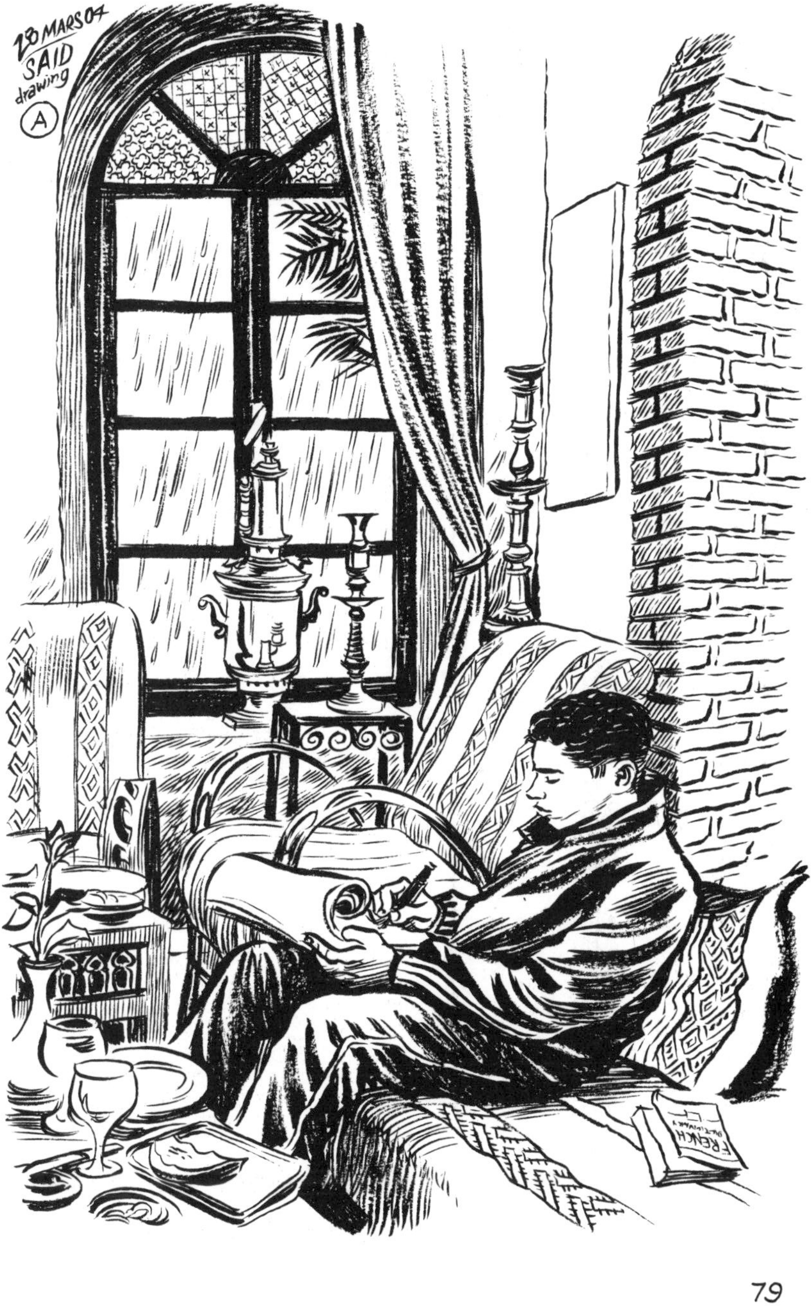
28 MARS 04
SAID
drawing
A
FRENCH

(A) Said and I returned to the hotel lounge to draw while the rain continued.
It withdrew, once again, in the afternoon.

(B) I walked (my foot is beginning to WORK!) to a Jewish cemetery outside the medina. I keep gravitating towards quiet spaces, though this was no first-world leisure garden. The graves were crammed together in a chaotic heap, somehow creating a habitat for...

(C) small turtles...
and dogs. I met an attractive Parisian couple --

(D) Here's Cecile...
Julien is behind me playing with the turtles (©).

(C)

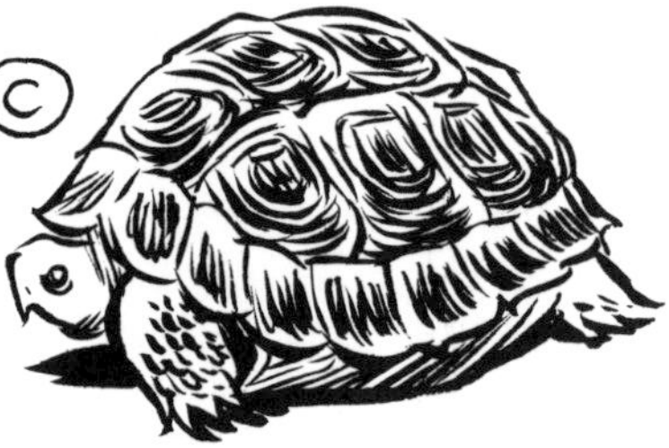

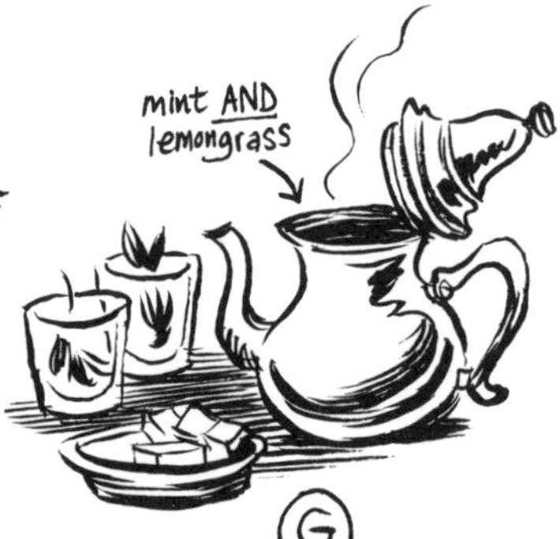
mint AND lemongrass

(G)

(E) In the afternoon, I wandered the medina souqs.
-- vegetables, meat, and kitties -- Gave away another portrait, but kept this one of

(F) KARIM — a modern day spice dealer with a RASTA edge. He's one of the first to show me the famous Arabic hospitality -- inviting me in for

(G) tea
and talk with no sneaky sales pitch.

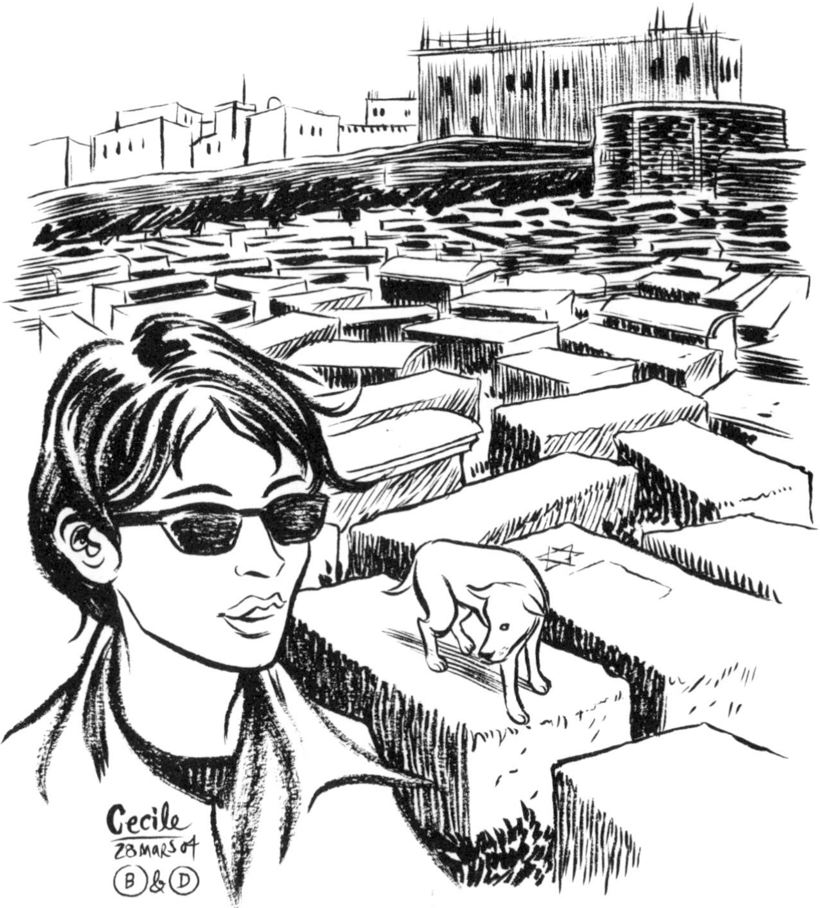
Cecile
28 MARS 04
B & D

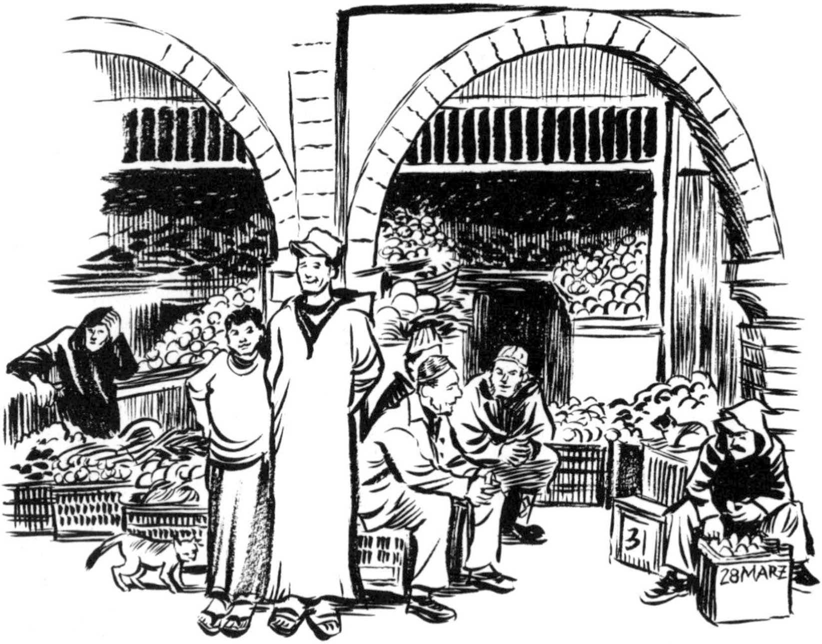
31
28MARZ

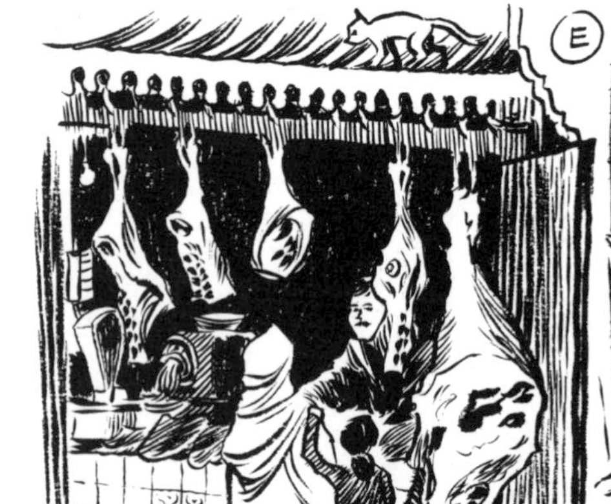
E
28
MARS
04

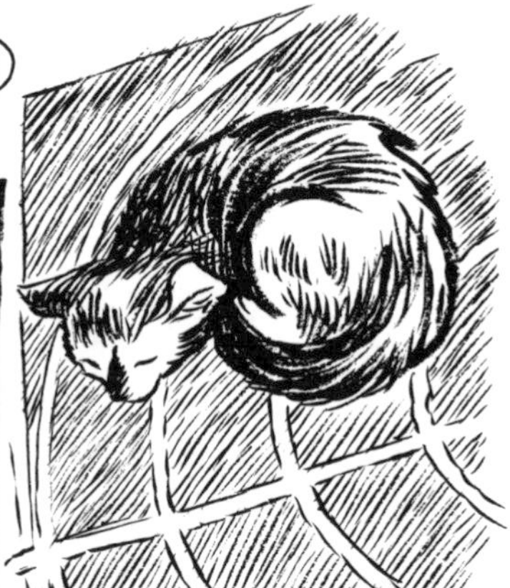

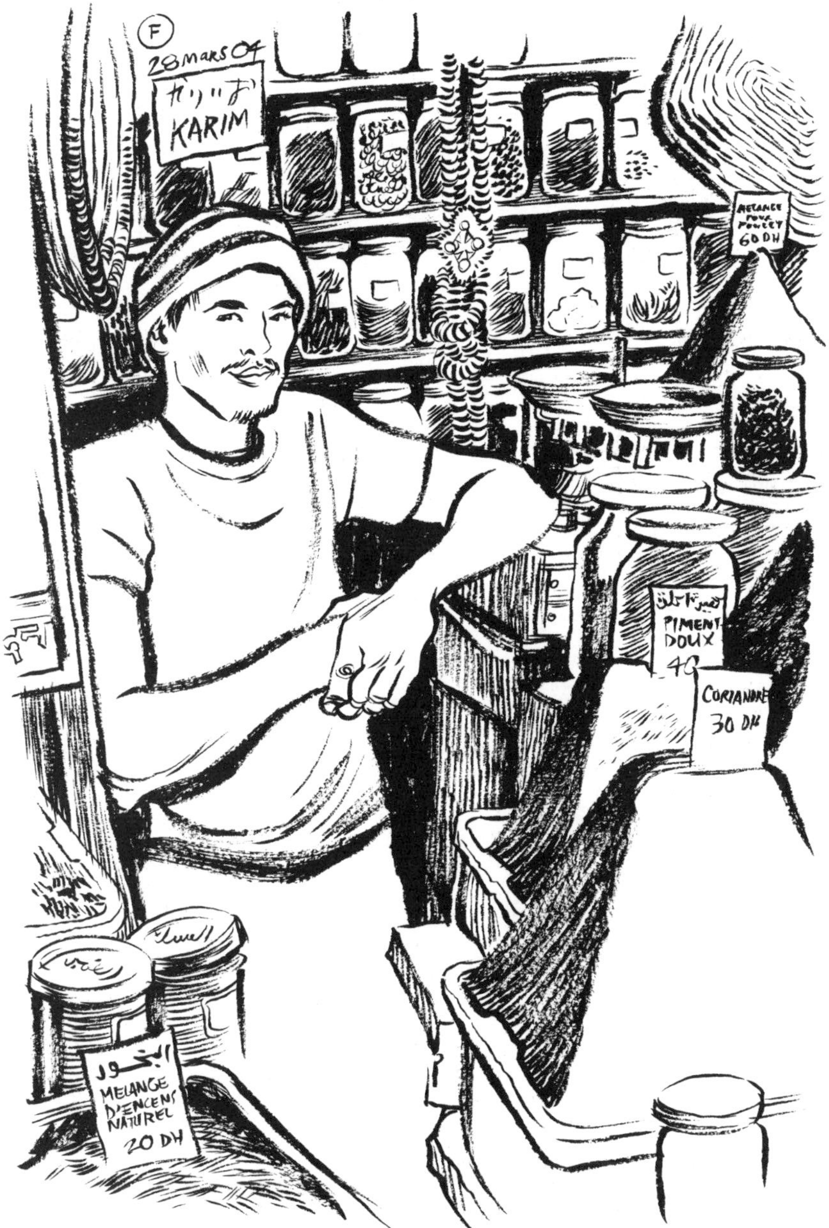
F
28 MARS 04
KARIM
PIMENT DOUX
40
CORIANDRE
30 DH
MELANGE D'ENCENS NATUREL
20 DH

29 MARS 04

Yesterday, drawing that delicate curled-up kitten was my most content moment in Morocco,

So I inquired about bus schedules, made a photocopy for Karim, and said good-bye to the guys at "my—

But then today, eating lunch alone again at a sidewalk cafe, I was restless to leave.

— regular sandwich shop and the hotel.

Once I was waiting at the bus stop, I was sad to leave-- feeling like it was all too sudden. Never touched base with Christophe or Said, or the fish grill fellas- Brahim, Mustafa & Fattaf...

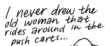

I never drew the old woman that rides around in the push carts...

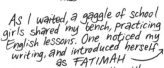

...or bought a painting from the man with cerebral palsey who paints with his mouth.

As I waited, a gaggle of school girls shared my bench, practicing English lessons. One noticed my writing, and introduced herself as FATIMAH

It's refreshing to talk with someone other than "the guys." --The separation of the sexes being a frustrating element of Moroccan culture

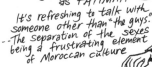

So easy to love a place on the day you're leaving.

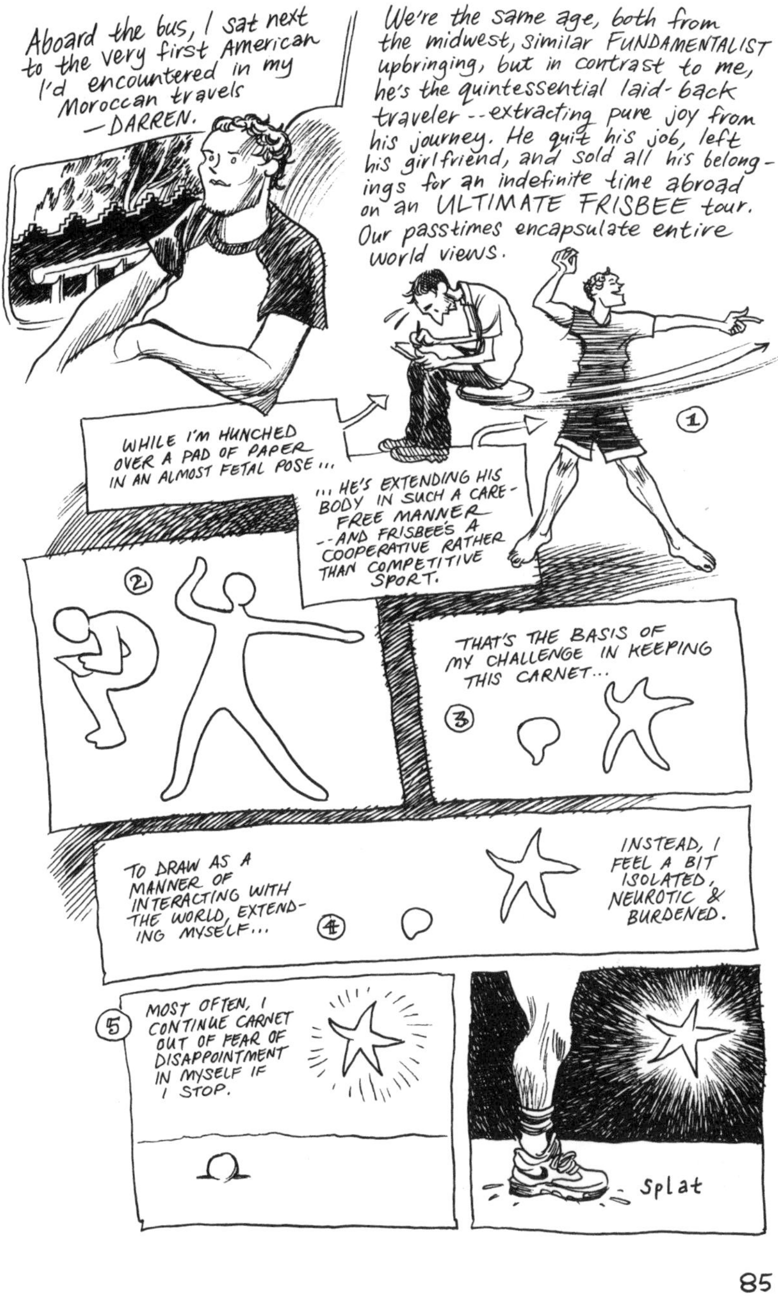

Aboard the bus, I sat next to the very first American I'd encountered in my Moroccan travels —DARREN.
We're the same age, both from the midwest, similar FUNDAMENTALIST upbringing, but in contrast to me, he's the quintessential laid-back traveler --extracting pure joy from his journey. He quit his job, left his girlfriend, and sold all his belongings for an indefinite time abroad on an ULTIMATE FRISBEE tour. Our passtimes encapsulate entire world views.
WHILE I'M HUNCHED OVER A PAD OF PAPER IN AN ALMOST FETAL POSE...
...HE'S EXTENDING HIS BODY IN SUCH A CAREFREE MANNER --AND FRISBEE'S A COOPERATIVE RATHER THAN COMPETITIVE SPORT.
1
2
THAT'S THE BASIS OF MY CHALLENGE IN KEEPING THIS CARNET...
3
TO DRAW AS A MANNER OF INTERACTING WITH THE WORLD, EXTENDING MYSELF...
4
INSTEAD, I FEEL A BIT ISOLATED, NEUROTIC & BURDENED.
5
MOST OFTEN, I CONTINUE CARNET OUT OF FEAR OF DISAPPOINTMENT IN MYSELF IF I STOP.
Splat

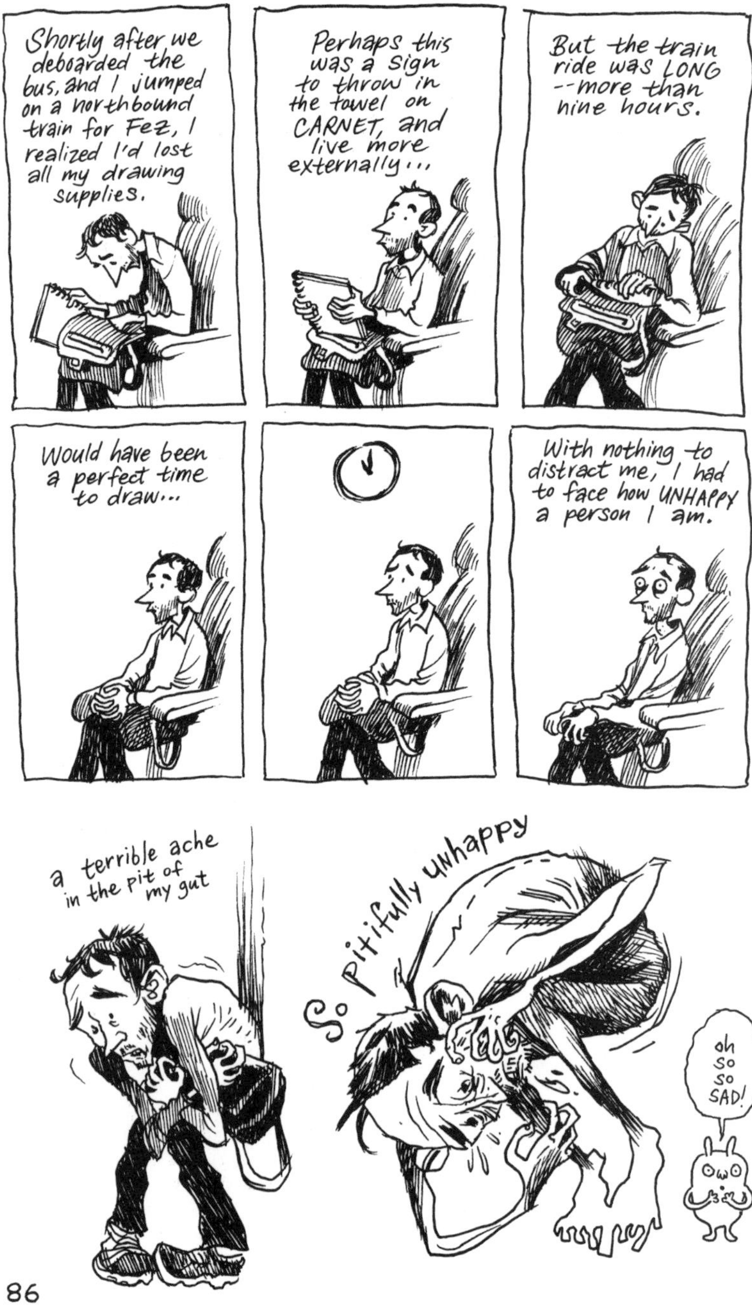

Shortly after we deboarded the bus, and I jumped on a northbound train for Fez, I realized I'd lost all my drawing supplies.
Perhaps this was a sign to throw in the towel on CARNET, and live more externally...
But the train ride was LONG --more than nine hours.
Would have been a perfect time to draw...
With nothing to distract me, I had to face how UNHAPPY a person I am.
a terrible ache in the pit of my gut
So pitifully unhappy
oh so so SAD!

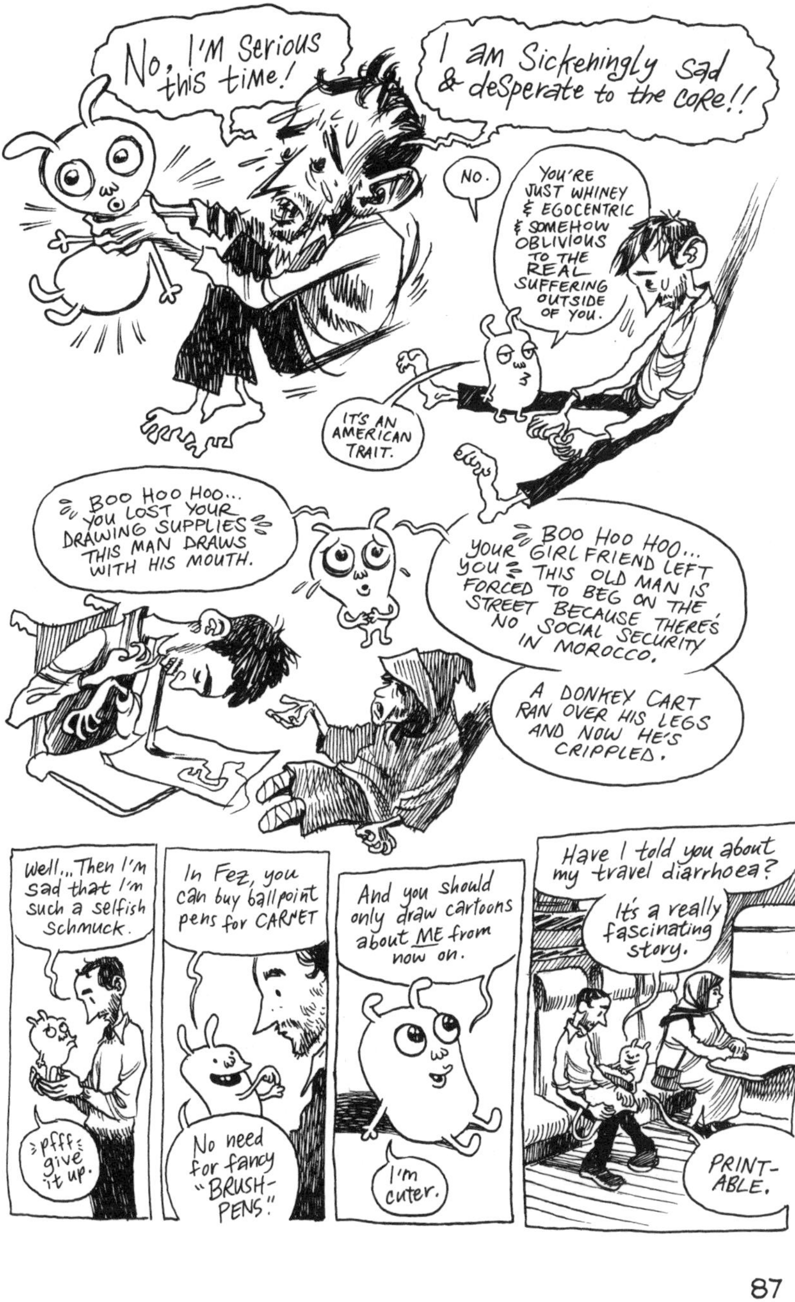
No, I'M Serious this time!
I am Sickeningly sad & desperate to the core!!
NO.
YOU'RE JUST WHINEY & EGOCENTRIC & SOMEHOW OBLIVIOUS TO THE REAL SUFFERING OUTSIDE OF YOU.
IT'S AN AMERICAN TRAIT.
BOO HOO HOO... YOU LOST YOUR DRAWING SUPPLIES THIS MAN DRAWS WITH HIS MOUTH.
BOO HOO HOO... YOUR GIRLFRIEND LEFT YOU THIS OLD MAN IS FORCED TO BEG ON THE STREET BECAUSE THERE'S NO SOCIAL SECURITY IN MOROCCO.
A DONKEY CART RAN OVER HIS LEGS AND NOW HE'S CRIPPLED.
Well... Then I'm sad that I'm such a selfish schmuck.
pfff give it up.
In Fez, you can buy ballpoint pens for CARNET
No need for fancy "BRUSH-PENS."
And you should only draw cartoons about ME from now on.
I'm cuter.
Have I told you about my travel diarrhoea?
It's a really fascinating story.
PRINT-ABLE.

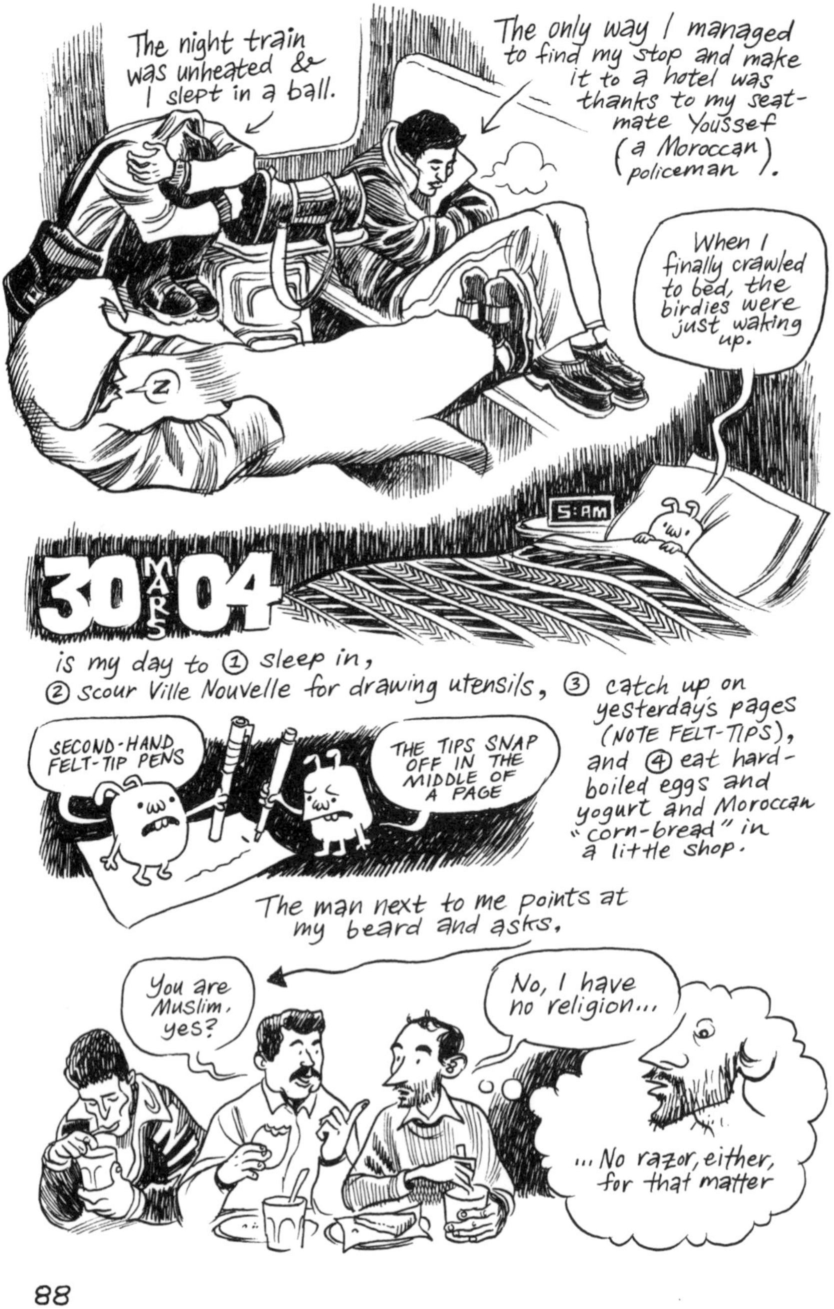
The night train was unheated & I slept in a ball.
The only way I managed to find my stop and make it to a hotel was thanks to my seat-mate Youssef (a Moroccan policeman).
Z
When I finally crawled to bed, the birdies were just waking up.
5:AM
30 MARS 04
is my day to ① sleep in, ② scour Ville Nouvelle for drawing utensils, ③ catch up on yesterday's pages (NOTE FELT-TIPS), and ④ eat hard-boiled eggs and yogurt and Moroccan "corn-bread" in a little shop.
SECOND-HAND FELT-TIP PENS
THE TIPS SNAP OFF IN THE MIDDLE OF A PAGE
The man next to me points at my beard and asks,
You are Muslim, yes?
No, I have no religion...
...No razor, either, for that matter

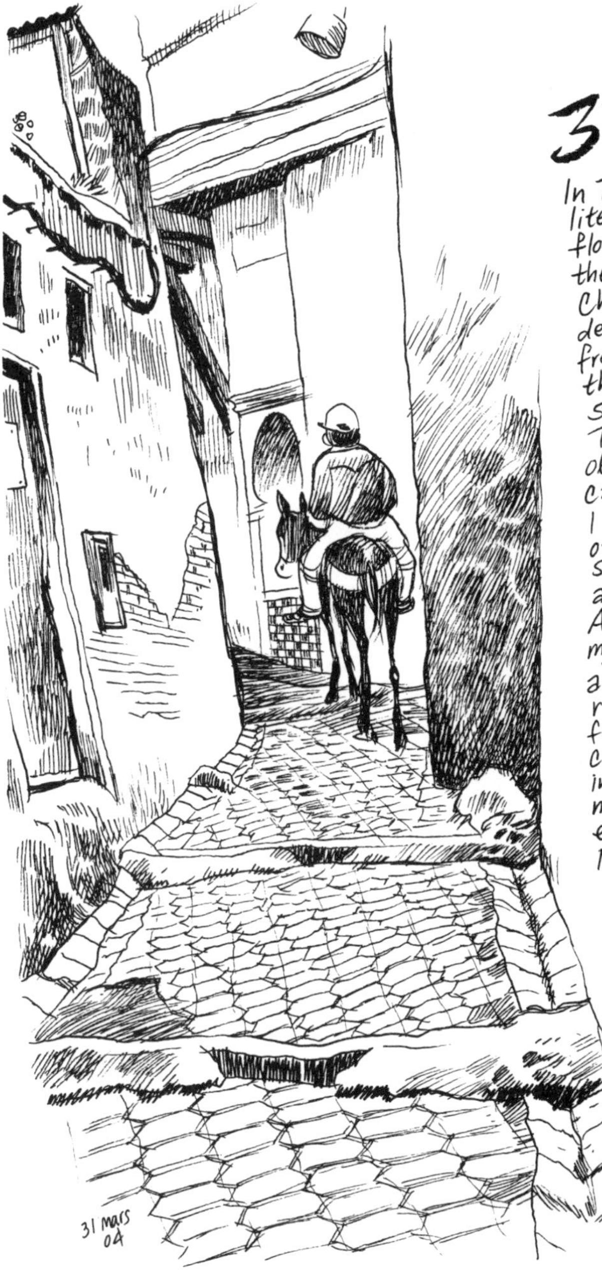
31 mars
04

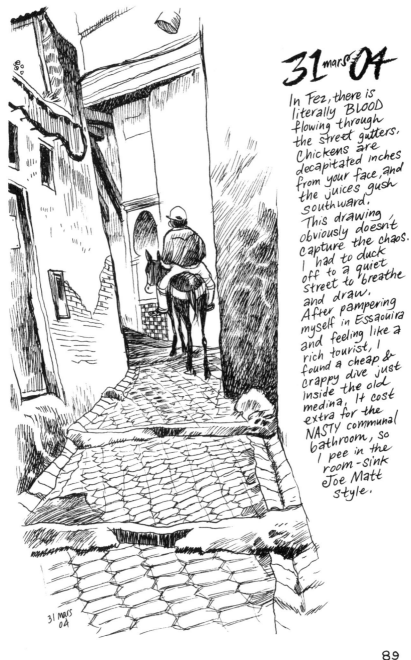

31 mars 04

In Fez, there is literally BLOOD flowing through the street gutters. Chickens are decapitated inches from your face, and the juices gush southward. This drawing obviously doesn't capture the chaos. I had to duck off to a quiet street to breathe and draw. After pampering myself in Essaouira and feeling like a rich tourist, I found a cheap & crappy dive just inside the old medina. It cost extra for the NASTY communal bathroom, so I pee in the room-sink eJoe Matt style.

The streets are crawling with Faux-guides and hustlers, and I end up in a lamp shop with two questionably friendly fellows —HUSSEIN and DRISS. I speak bad French with Hussein, but Driss is fluent in English. We talk religion. He says he is Muslim, but in casual/personal way. He says he doesn't often attend mosque or get caught up in the dogma, but believes in God and prays. I tell him that I believe Muslims, Christians, & Jews all worship the same God, and he agrees. And we agree that nobody knows anything.

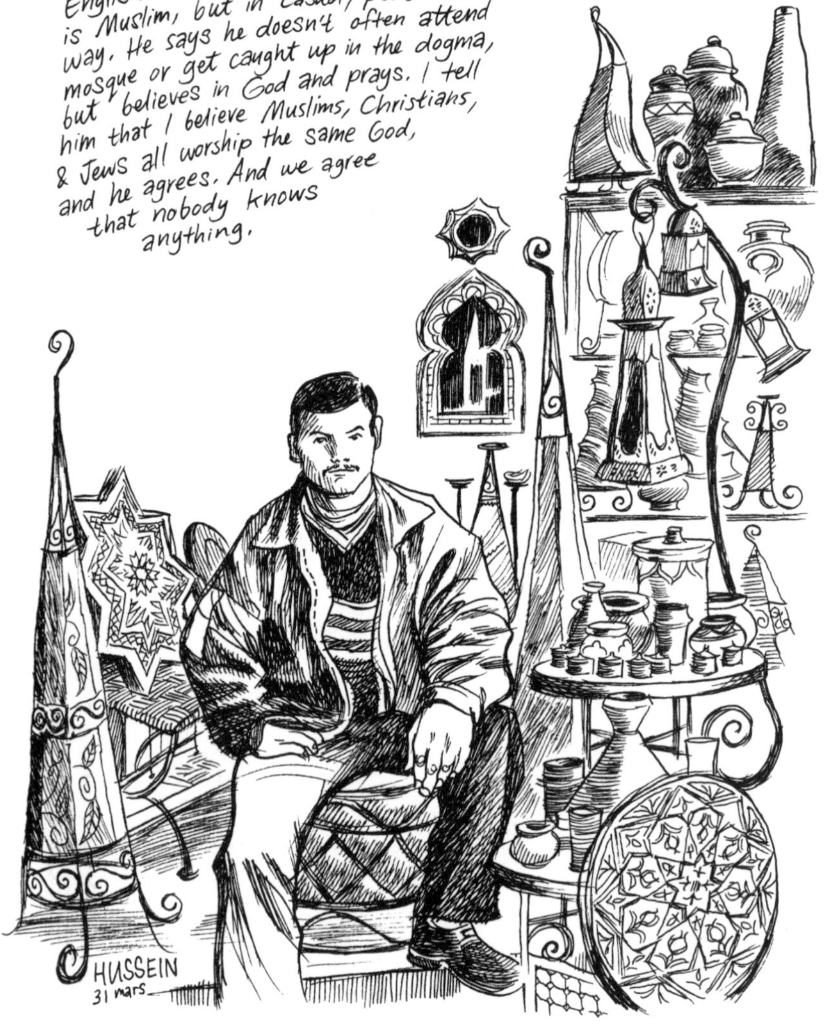
HUSSEIN
31 mars

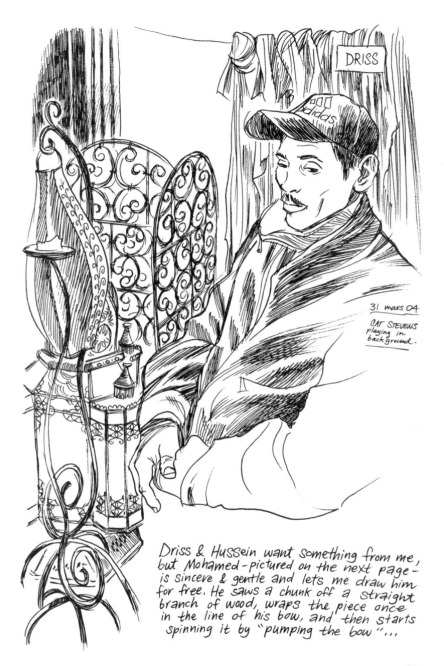

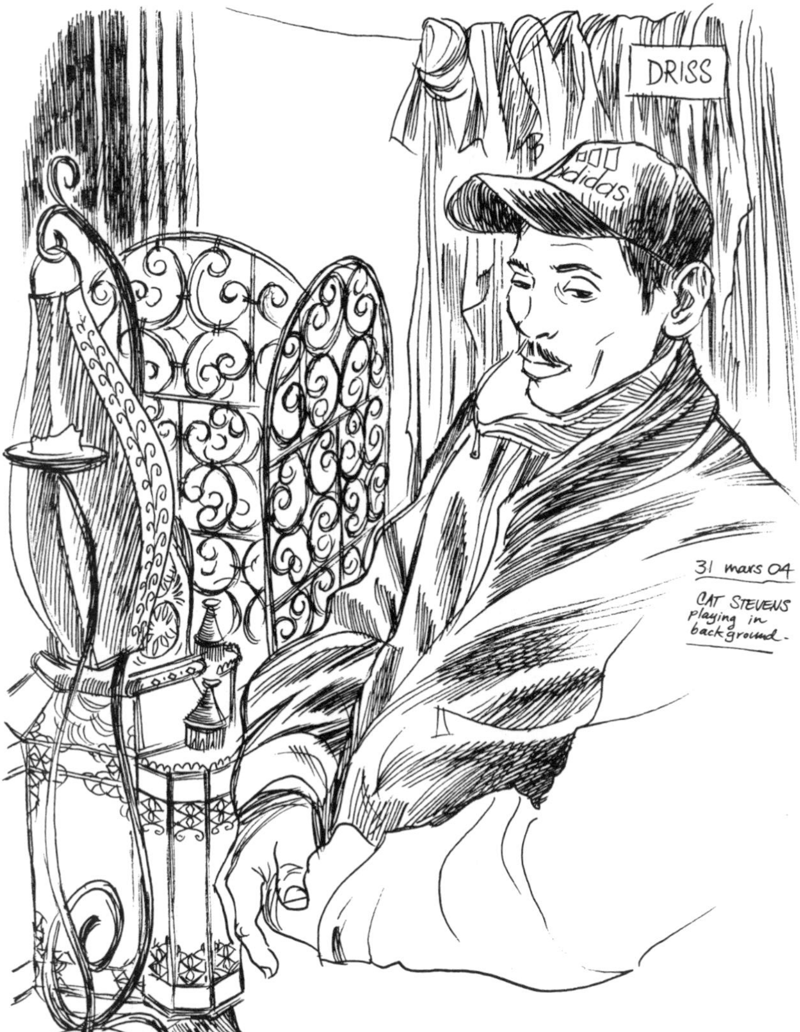
DRISS
adidas
31 mars 04
CAT STEVENS playing in background -

Driss & Hussein want something from me, but Mohamed - pictured on the next page - is sincere & gentle and lets me draw him for free. He saws a chunk off a straight branch of wood, wraps the piece once in the line of his bow, and then starts spinning it by "pumping the bow"...

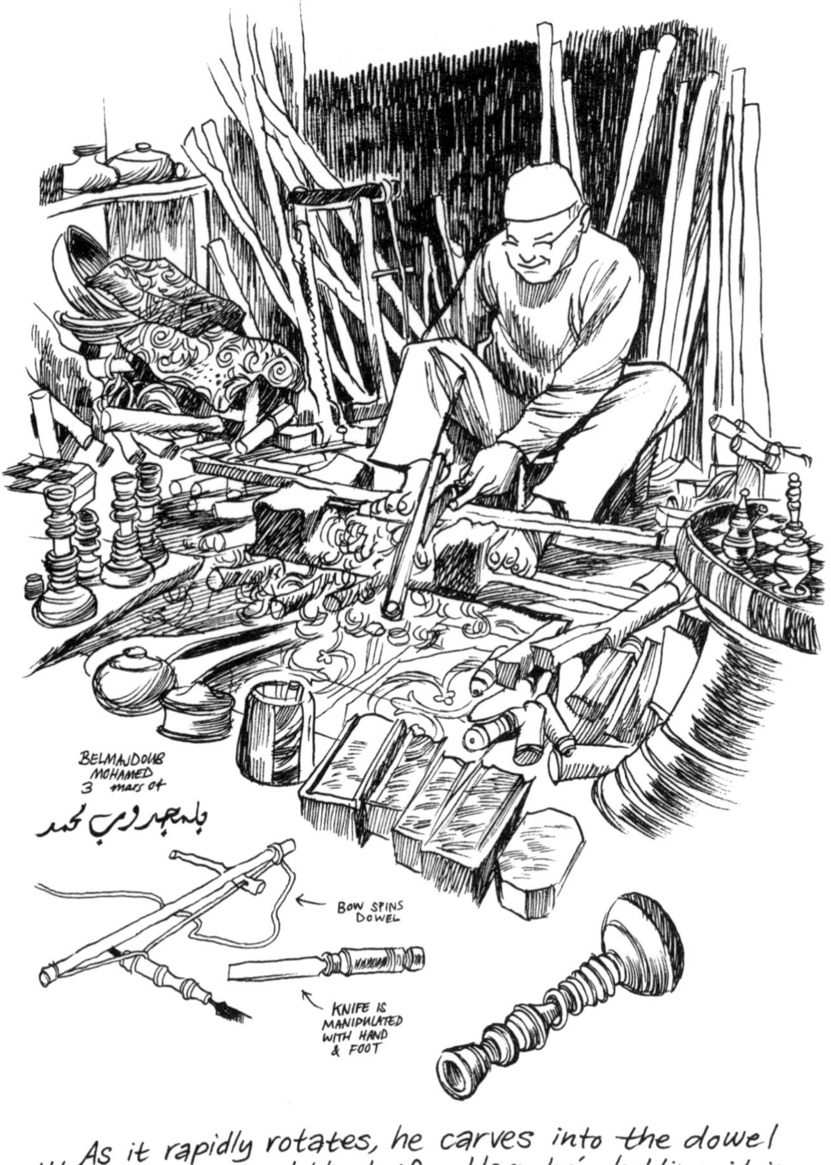
BELMAJDOUB
MOHAMED
3 mars 04
بلمجدوب محمد
BOW SPINS
DOWEL
KNIFE IS
MANIPULATED
WITH HAND
& FOOT

... As it rapidly rotates, he carves into the dowel with a flat, chisel-like knife. Here he's holding it in his hand, though he primarily manipulated the knife with his left foot.

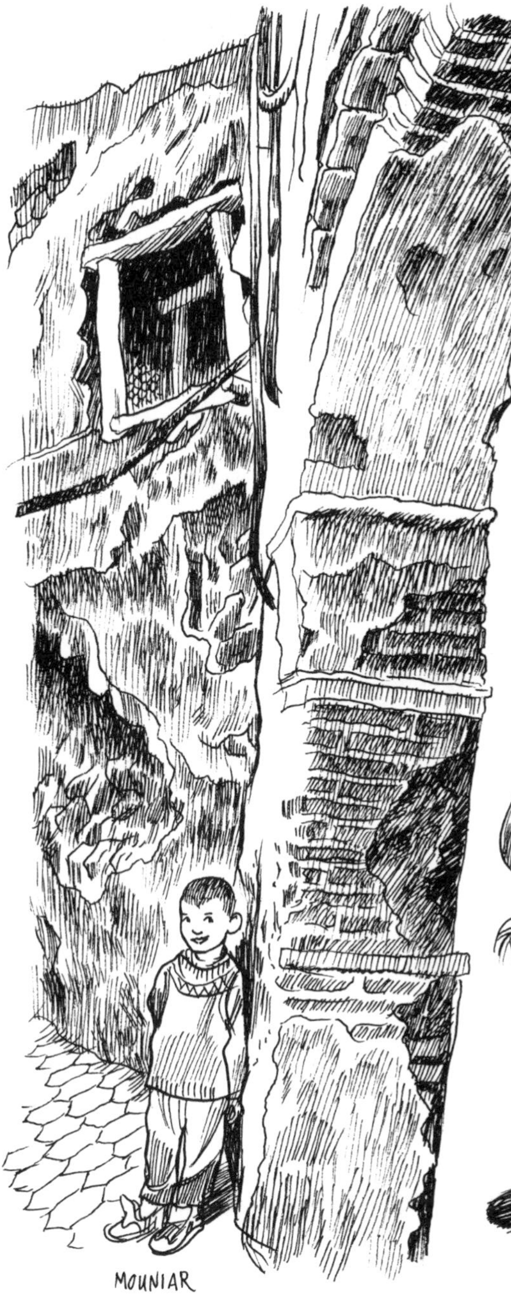

MOUNIAR

I pay this cute little kid a few dirham for a sketch, and for a second, I'm comfortable in Fez. But then once again, my CHAOS TOLERANCE is overloaded. I have trouble breathing; winding back through the turmoil, I linger at a snail cart.

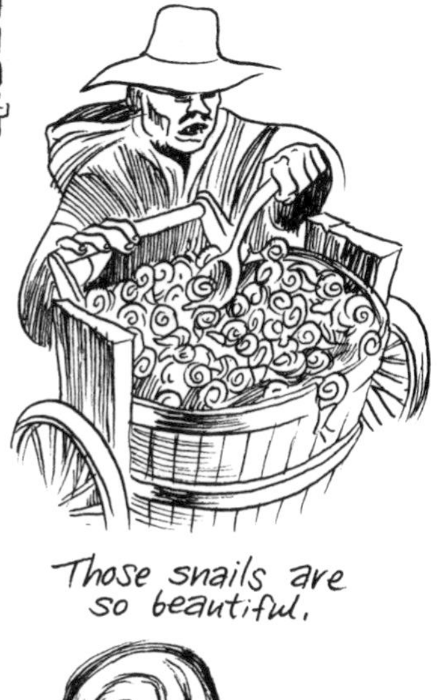

Those snails are so beautiful.

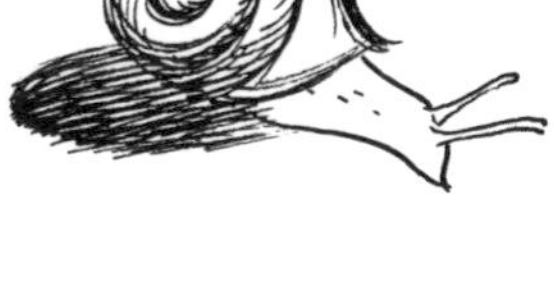

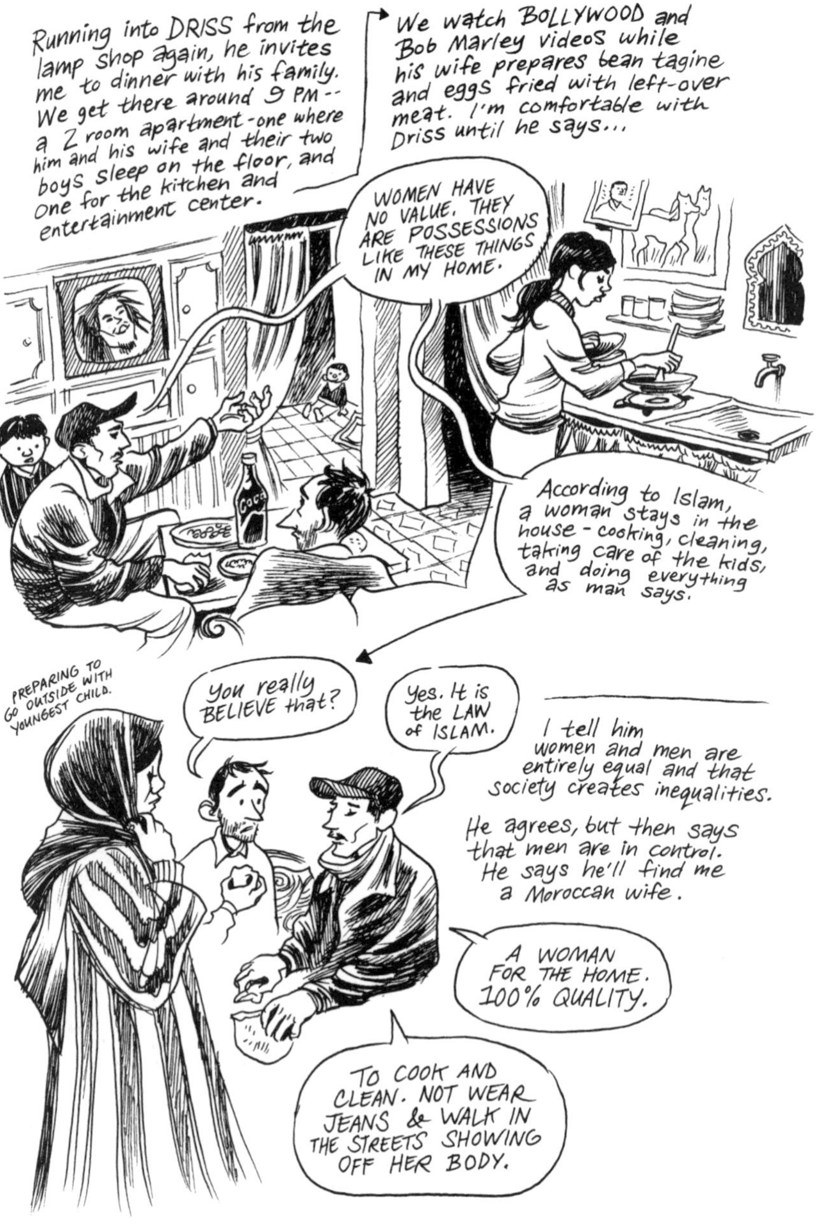
Running into DRISS from the lamp shop again, he invites me to dinner with his family. We get there around 9 PM -- We get there around 9 PM -- a 2 room apartment - one where him and his wife and their two boys sleep on the floor, and one for the kitchen and entertainment center.
We watch BOLLYWOOD and Bob Marley videos while his wife prepares bean tagine and eggs fried with left-over meat. I'm comfortable with Driss until he says...
WOMEN HAVE NO VALUE. THEY ARE POSSESSIONS LIKE THESE THINGS IN MY HOME.
According to Islam, a woman stays in the house - cooking, cleaning, taking care of the kids, and doing everything as man says.
PREPARING TO GO OUTSIDE WITH YOUNGEST CHILD.
You really BELIEVE that?
Yes. It is the LAW of ISLAM.
I tell him women and men are entirely equal and that society creates inequalities.
He agrees, but then says that men are in control. He says he'll find me a Moroccan wife.
A WOMAN FOR THE HOME. 100% QUALITY.
TO COOK AND CLEAN. NOT WEAR JEANS & WALK IN THE STREETS SHOWING OFF HER BODY.

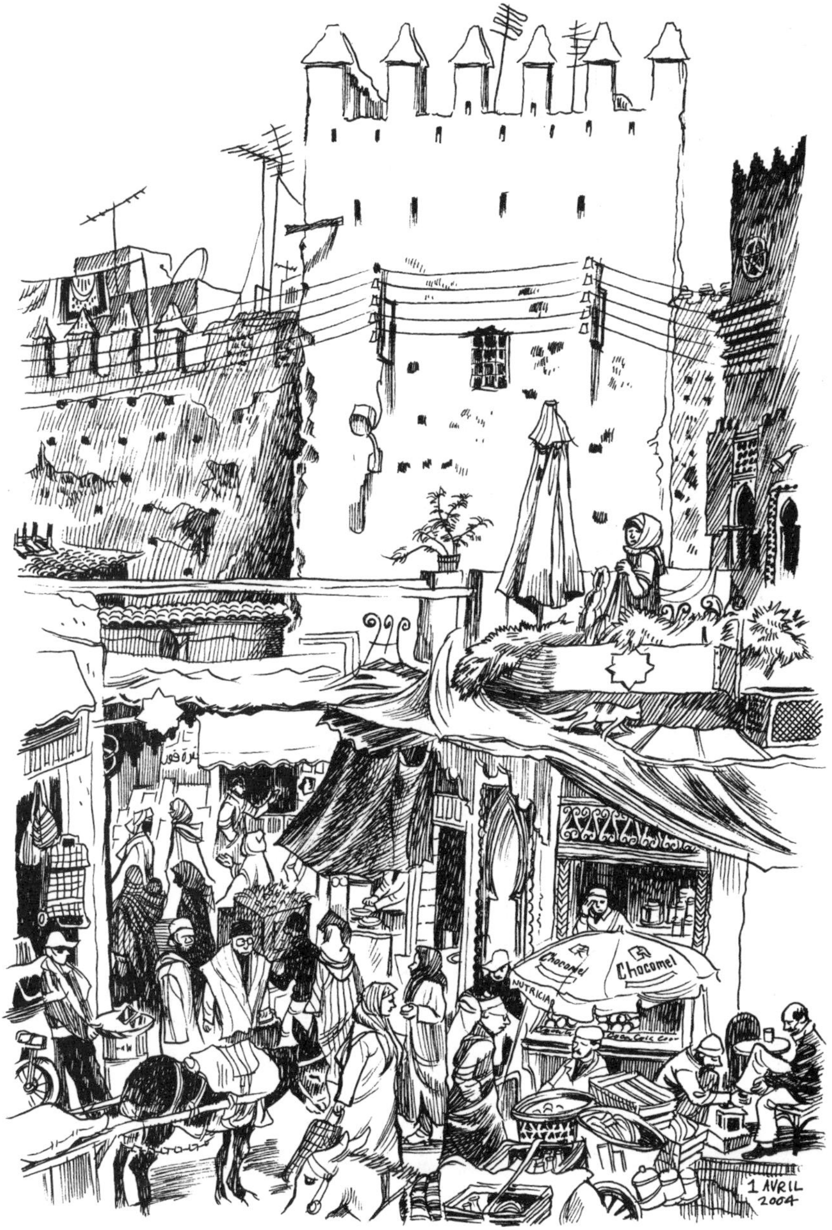
Chocomel
Chocomel
NUTRICIA
1 AVRIL
2004

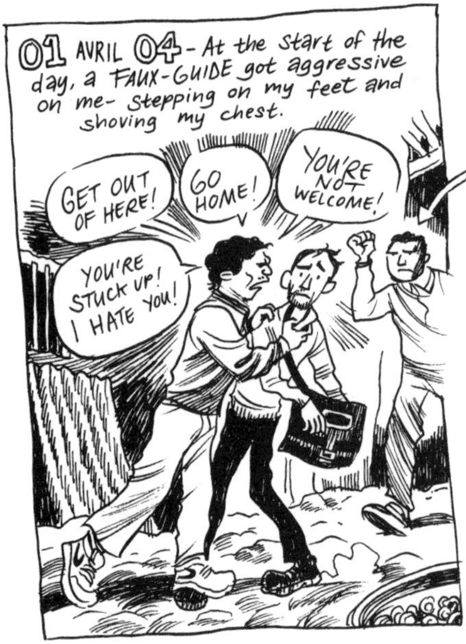
01 AVRIL 04 - At the start of the day, a FAUX-GUIDE got aggressive on me- stepping on my feet and shoving my chest.
GET OUT OF HERE!
GO HOME!
YOU'RE NOT WELCOME!
YOU'RE STUCK UP! I HATE YOU!

But then another faux-guide came to my defence.

I managed 2.5 sketches for CARNET (which, once again, fail to reflect the filth and commotion of the medina), but gave away four portraits (including two women!?) as I was swarmed by "spectators." I churned out portraits until my hand was numb and I was fearing a relapse of crippling tendonitis, trying in some small way to compensate for the reputation Bush has given America.

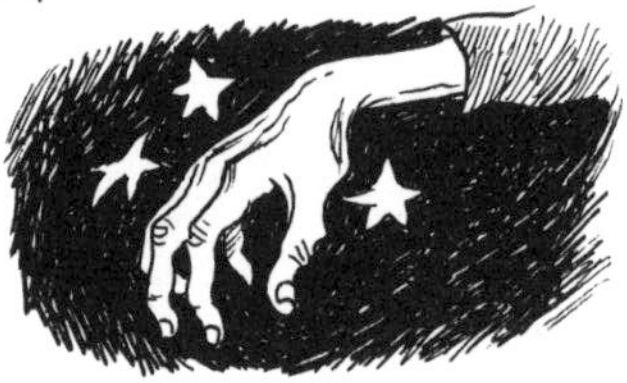

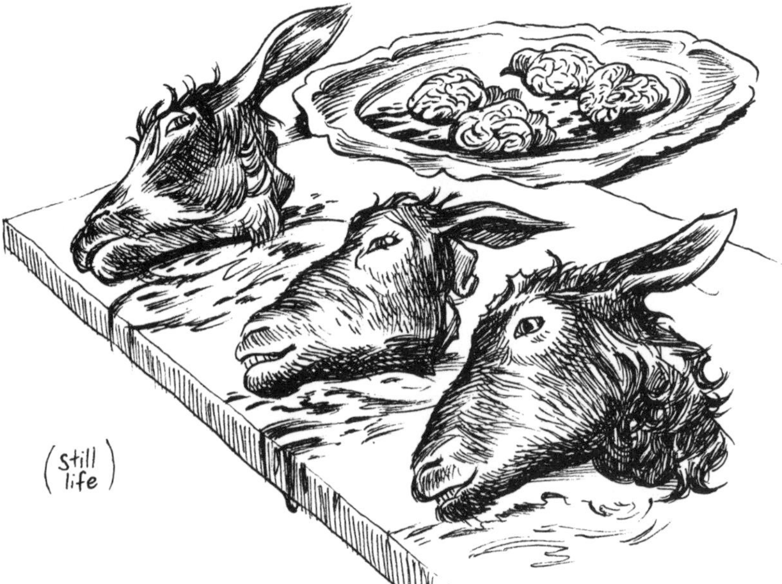

(still life)

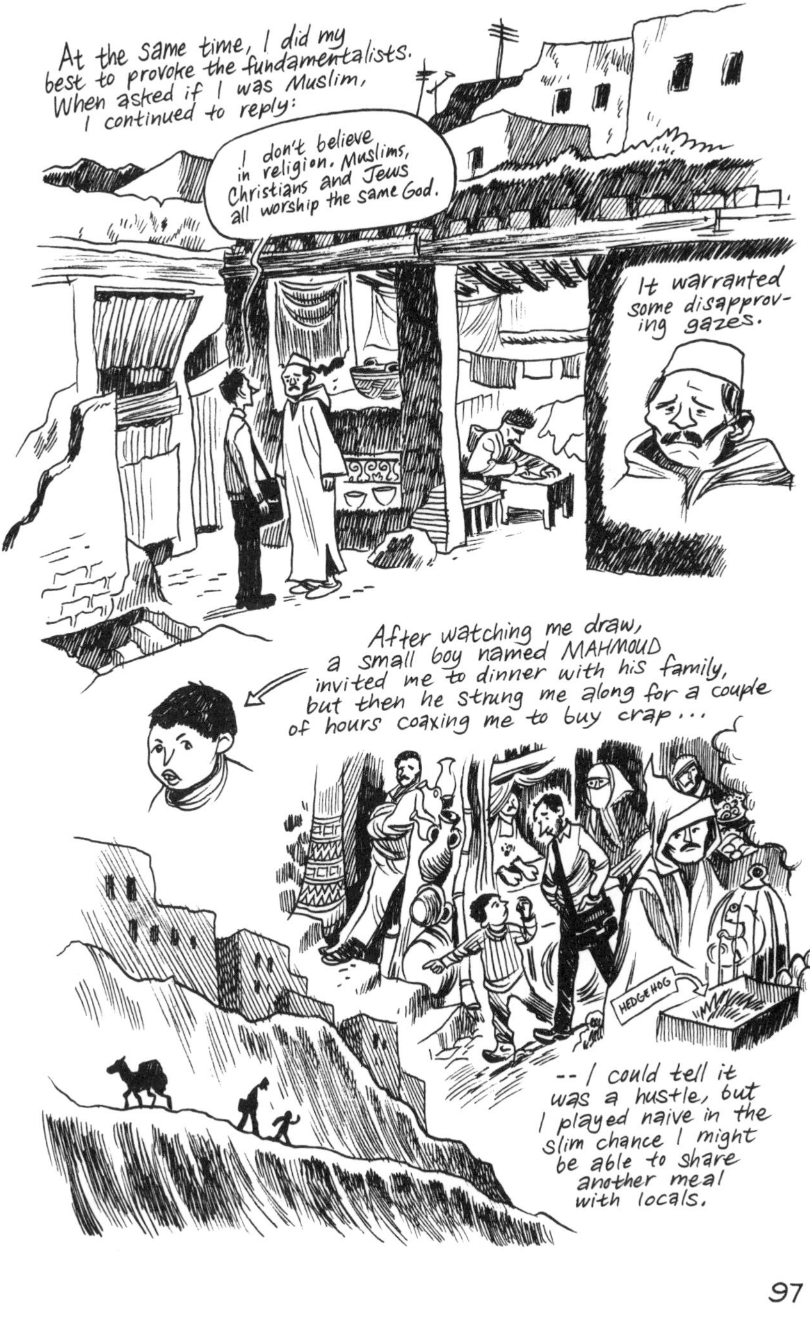
At the same time, I did my best to provoke the fundamentalists. When asked if I was Muslim, I continued to reply:
I don't believe in religion. Muslims, Christians and Jews all worship the same God.
It warranted some disapproving gazes.
After watching me draw, a small boy named MAHMOUD invited me to dinner with his family, but then he strung me along for a couple of hours coaxing me to buy crap...
HEDGEHOG
-- I could tell it was a hustle, but I played naive in the slim chance I might be able to share another meal with locals.

When we arrived, mother-with 2 one-month-old twins-seemed wary, but the two older sisters and their friend were enthusiastic to meet me. Of course I drew more portraits, despite the hand pain. When father got home, evidently peeved, I picked up on my cue to leave. As I got up to go, I handed him a few bucks.

That's all it took. He urged that I join them, and we sat down to bread and olives and lentils. As the night wore on, the welcome felt sincere. The girls showed me photo albums, and older brother and his buddies arrived later and chatted in English.

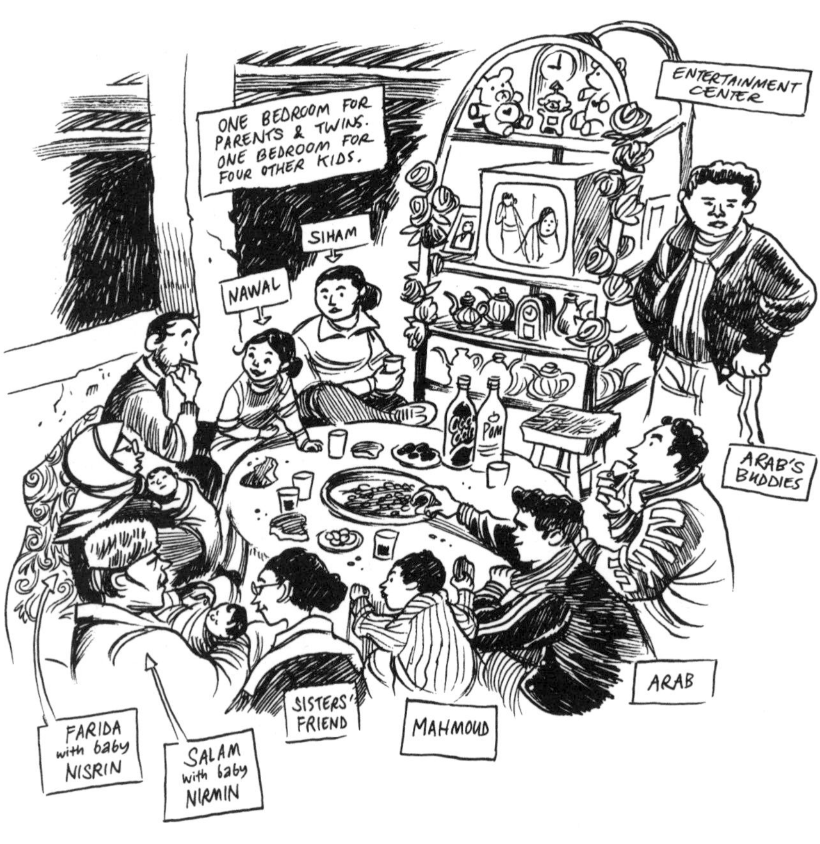

ONE BEDROOM FOR PARENTS & TWINS. ONE BEDROOM FOR FOUR OTHER KIDS.
ENTERTAINMENT CENTER
SIHAM
NAWAL
ARAB'S BUDDIES
ARAB
MAHMOUD
SISTERS' FRIEND
FARIDA with baby NISRIN
SALAM with baby NIRMIN

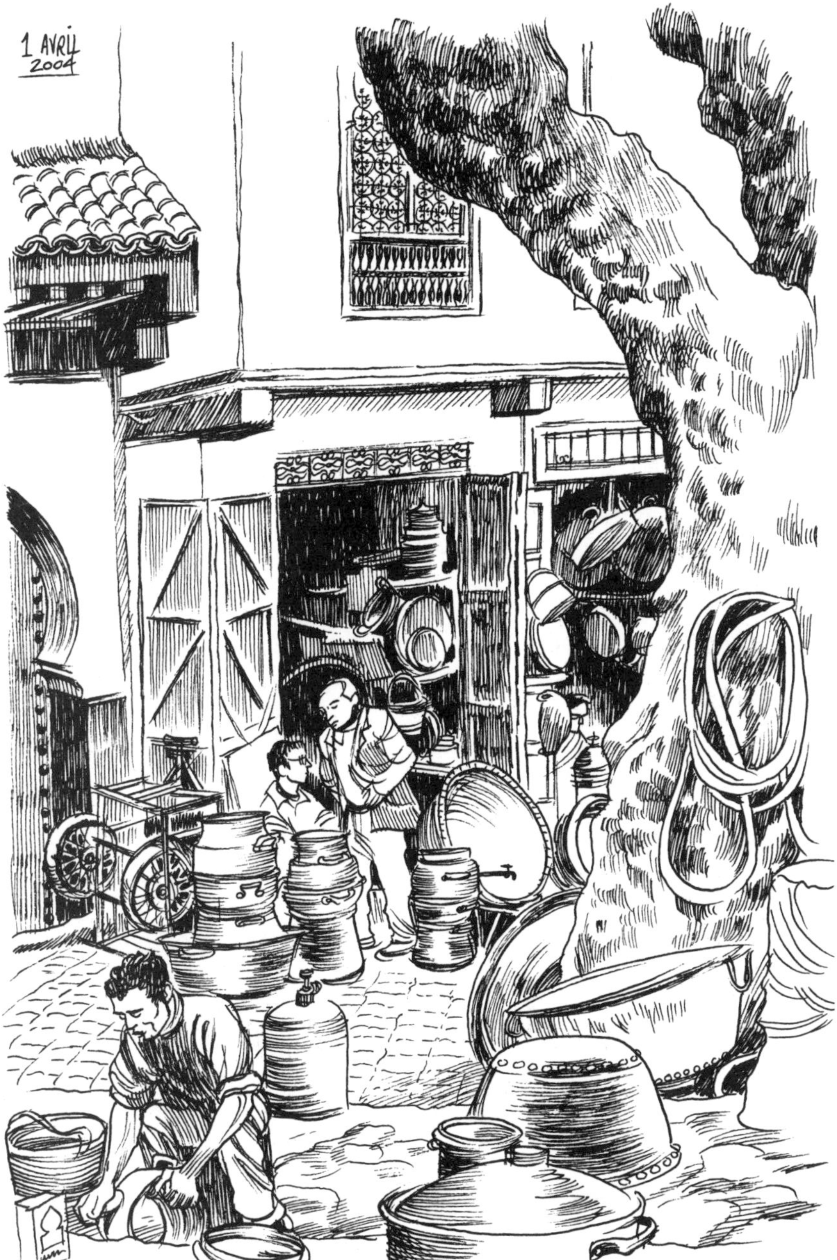
1 AVRIL
2004

02 avril 04 Last night, Mahmoud's eldest brother - Arab - invited me to be a guest at his university English class. His friend Tourik & Mahmoud arrived at my hotel early in the morning to accompany me. When we got there, the campus was much like those in America, only unheated, sparcely lit with fluorescents, birds nesting in the rafters, the occasional beggar, and giant murals like this:

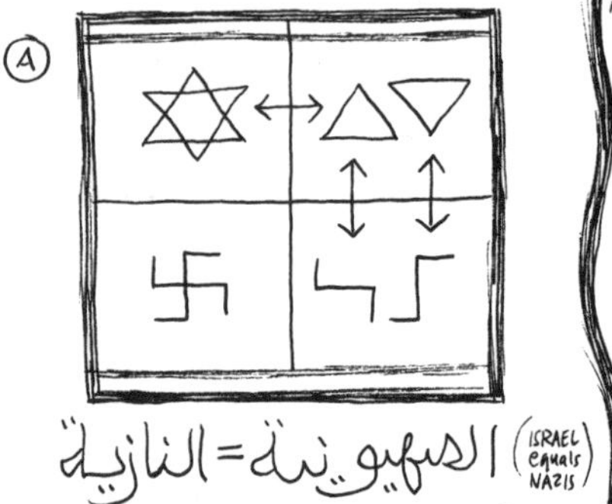

A
الصهيونية=النازية
(ISRAEL equals NAZIS)

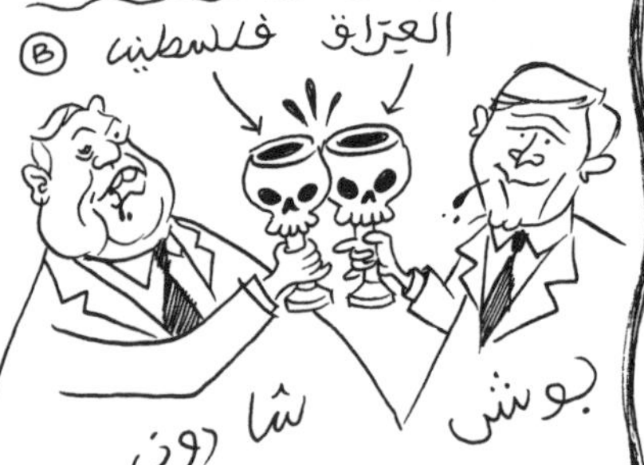

B
العراق فلسطين
شارون
بوش

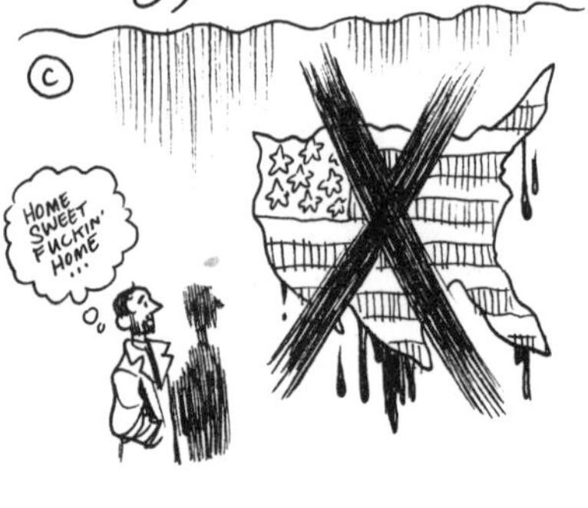

C
HOME SWEET FUCKIN' HOME ...

It turned out there was no English class & I was just being dragged around campus. Little Mahmoud was acting all shifty-eyed & I was suspicious this might be another unsolicited tour to extract more money from me.

Tourik was curious about girls and dating in America.

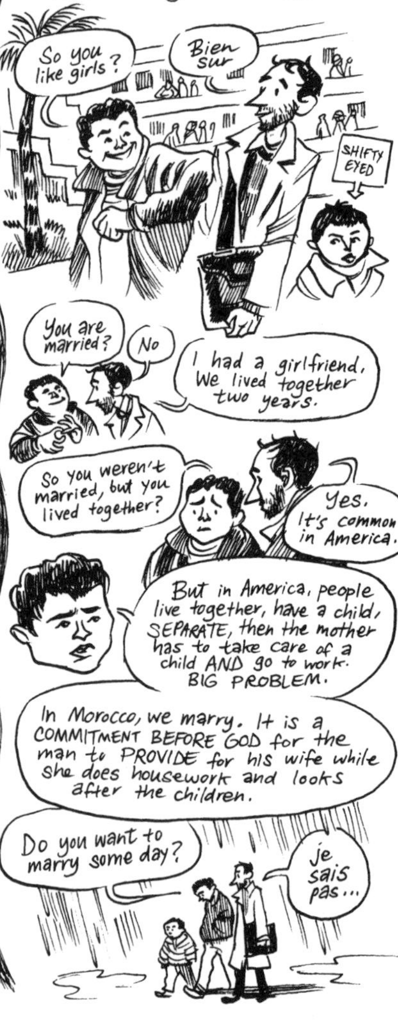

So you like girls?
Bien sur
SHIFTY EYED
You are married?
No
I had a girlfriend. We lived together two years.
So you weren't married, but you lived together?
Yes. It's common in America.
But in America, people live together, have a child, SEPARATE, then the mother has to take care of a child AND go to work. BIG PROBLEM.
In Morocco, we marry. It is a COMMITMENT BEFORE GOD for the man to PROVIDE for his wife while she does housework and looks after the children.
Do you want to marry some day?
je sais pas...

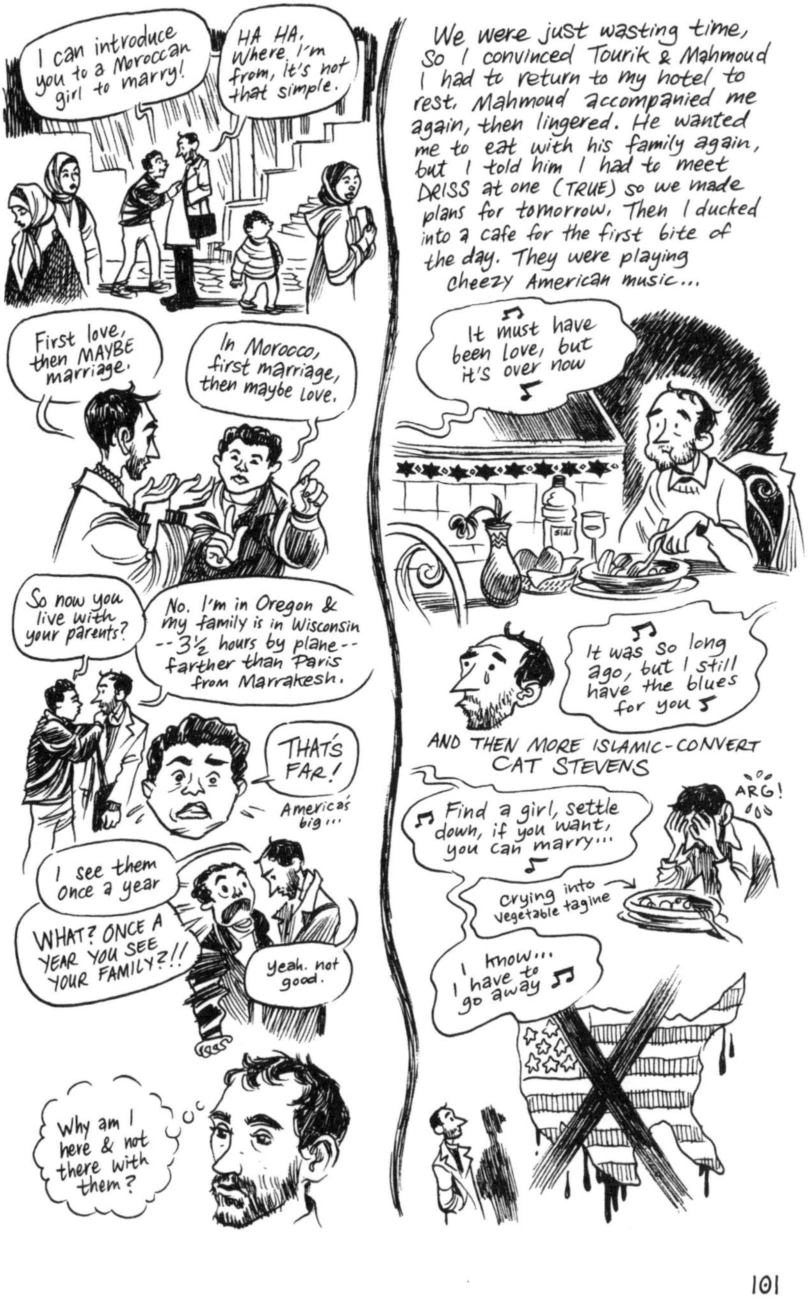
I can introduce you to a Moroccan girl to marry!
HA HA, where I'm from, it's not that simple.
First love, then MAYBE marriage.
In Morocco, first marriage, then maybe love.
So now you live with your parents?
No. I'm in Oregon & my family is in Wisconsin --3½ hours by plane-- farther than Paris from Marrakesh.
THAT'S FAR!
America's big...
I see them once a year
WHAT? ONCE A YEAR YOU SEE YOUR FAMILY?!!
Yeah. not good.
Why am I here & not there with them?
We were just wasting time, so I convinced Tourik & Mahmoud I had to return to my hotel to rest. Mahmoud accompanied me again, then lingered. He wanted me to eat with his family again, but I told him I had to meet DRISS at one (TRUE) so we made plans for tomorrow. Then I ducked into a cafe for the first bite of the day. They were playing cheezy American music...
It must have been love, but it's over now
It was so long ago, but I still have the blues for you
AND THEN MORE ISLAMIC-CONVERT CAT STEVENS
Find a girl, settle down, if you want, you can marry...
ARG!
crying into vegetable tagine
I know... I have to go away

While eating, I was being shadowed by Mahmoud, who kept peering in the door. Then, when I slipped back to the hotel, the usual hustlers were waving and calling to me through the window. On the way to meet Driss, someone stopped me and said Driss was dangerous. I pretty much believed them, but I was having an impossible time finding someone to trust.

At DRISS', we ate couscous and drank a little wine while more BOLLYWOOD movies played. Then I collapsed with illness -- It'd rained all day, I'd barely slept the night before, and I was just generally worn raw with home sickness.

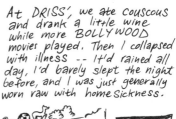

mon ami

my friend

I'm not here to watch TV...

After a couple of hours passed out on Driss' couch, I excused myself & returned to my hotel. The same hustlers were loitering. I packed my bags, checked out, and found a new crappy dive in Ville Nouvelle — away from the medina. Paranoia was setting in.

PETIT TAXI

03 AVRIL 04 I made the right decision in getting out of the old medina. The new hotel is another crapper, but quiet enough for me to get six hours of rest. Woke with a raw throat and a headache. Eating breakfast at the yogurt stand, met a friendly man named Ahmed - a professor at the Arabic Language Institute - who urged that I not let the hustle of the medina mar my opinion of Arabic people. My experience, in fact, is that most everyone is welcoming & generous outside of the concentrated tourist pockets.

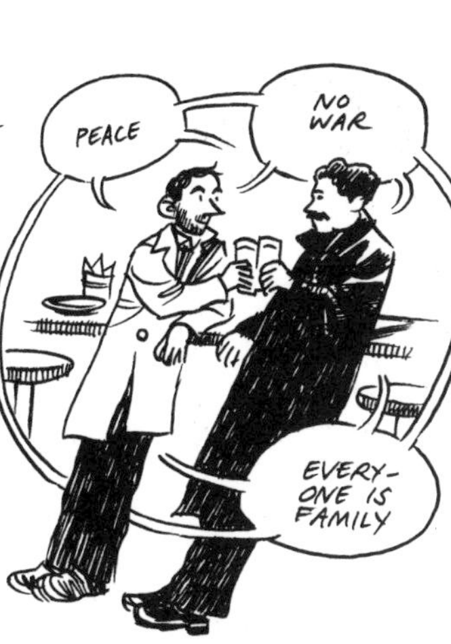
PEACE
NO WAR
EVERY-ONE IS FAMILY

I met with little Mahmoud at twelve as promised, but again he was shifty-eyed. Instead of taking me to his home for lunch, he led me to and fro about the medina, talking constantly of money. Under the weather and exhausted, I finally lost my patience, telling him I'd rather spend the rest of the day alone. He got pissed off and indignant.

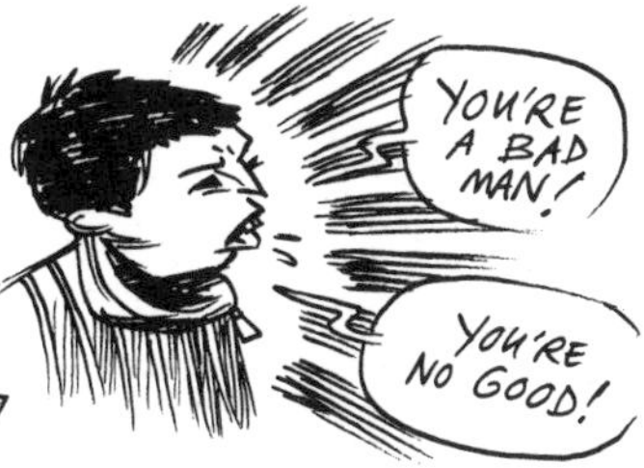
YOU'RE A BAD MAN!
YOU'RE NO GOOD!

I want to like the kid. His family's quite poor, and he's just looking to scratch up a few dirham to help out, but I was just too tired to handle it today.

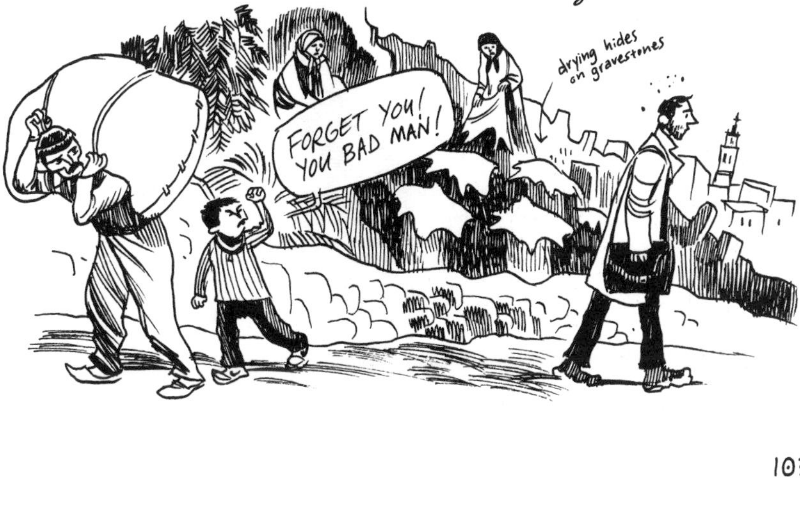
drying hides on gravestones
FORGET YOU! YOU BAD MAN!

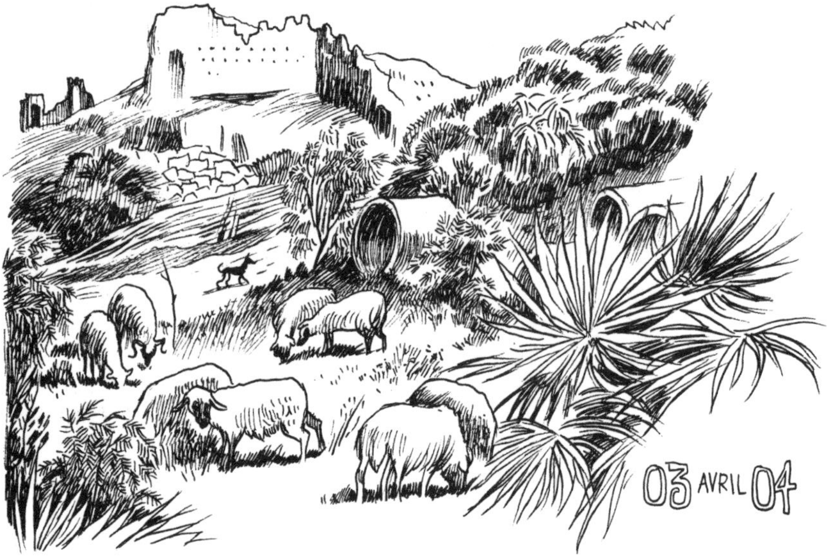
03 AVRIL 04

Instead, I drew sheep.

At a cyber cafe back in ville nouvelle...

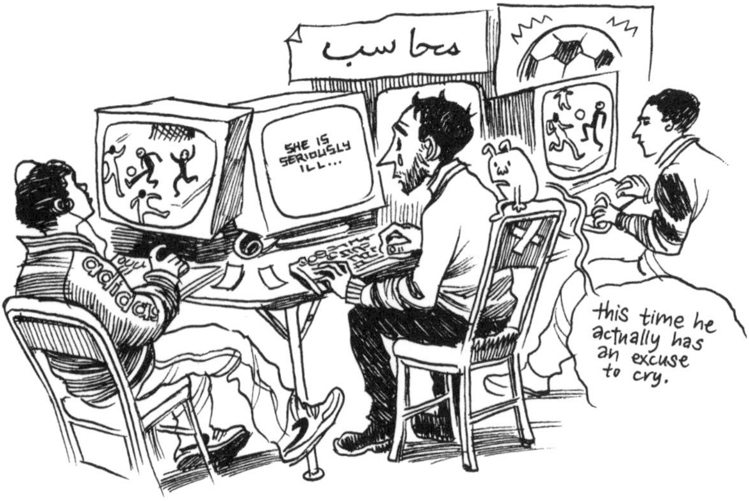
محاسب
SHE IS SERIOUSLY ILL...
adidas
this time he actually has an excuse to cry.

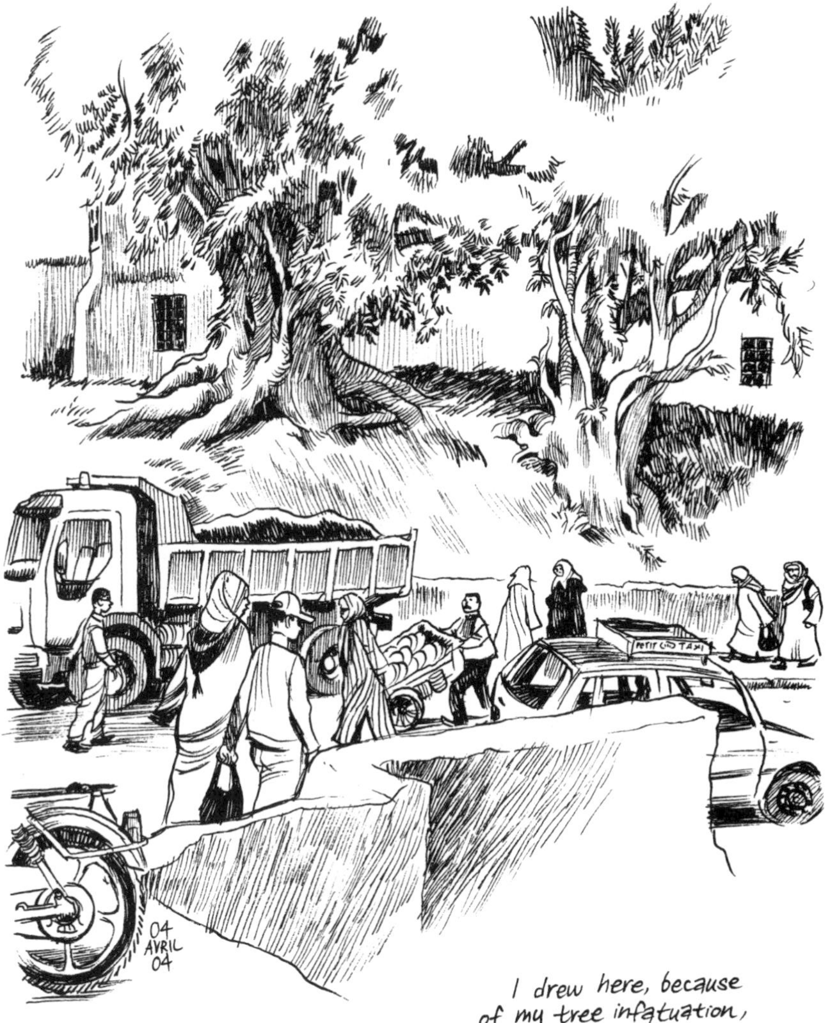
PETIT TAXI
04 AVRIL 04

I drew here, because of my tree infatuation, and because it was a quiet, modern street where I thought I wouldn't attract too much attention. On the contrary, no less than twenty people stopped me and asked that I draw their portraits. I refused - quite sick of giving away my drawings - though I did hand out coins to beggars.

This is the blue gate at Bab Bou Jeloud as viewed from the balcony of my original Fez hotel. Upon returning there, I met a friendly band of Spaniards who invited me to dinner.

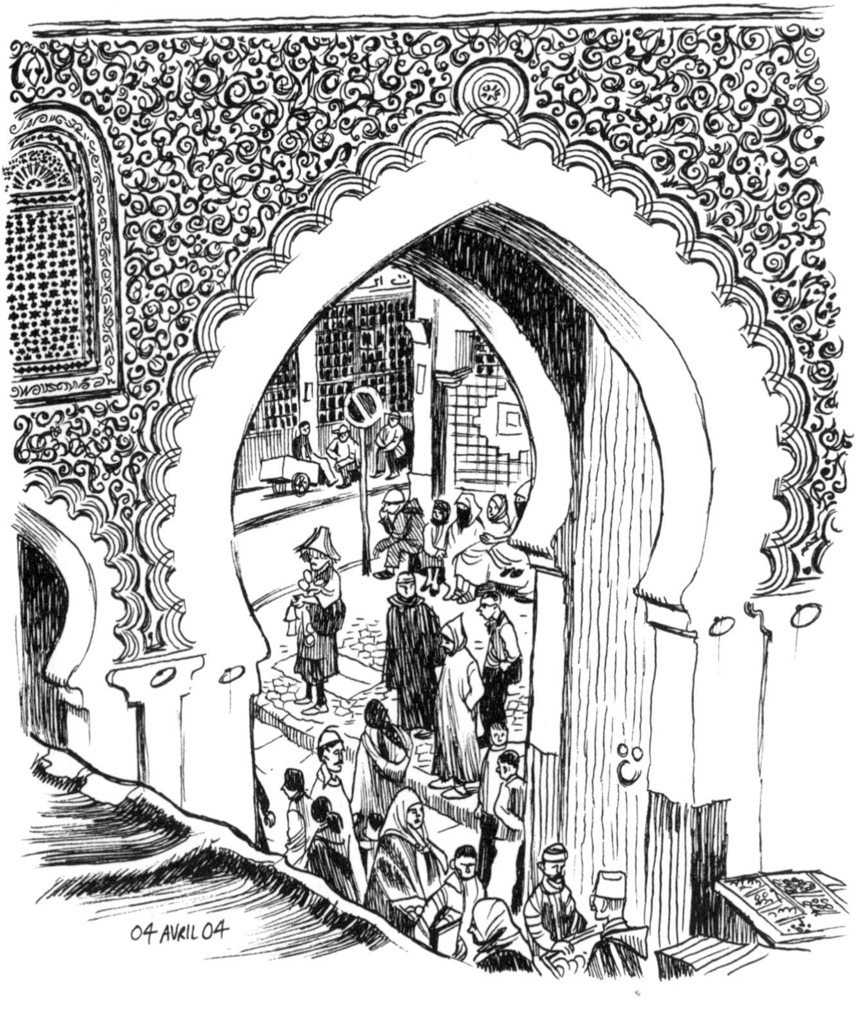
04 AVRIL 04

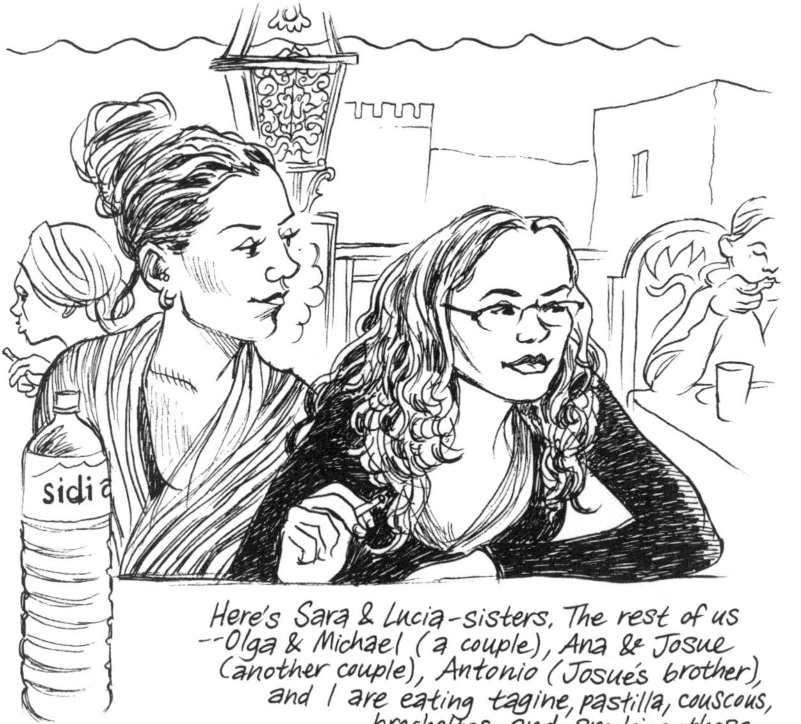
sidi a

Here's Sara & Lucia-sisters. The rest of us --Olga & Michael (a couple), Ana & Josue (another couple), Antonio (Josué's brother), and I are eating tagine, pastilla, couscous, brochettes, and smoking those hashish cigarettes. (I hate to say it, but it's mellow & cozy to share time with Europeans again.)

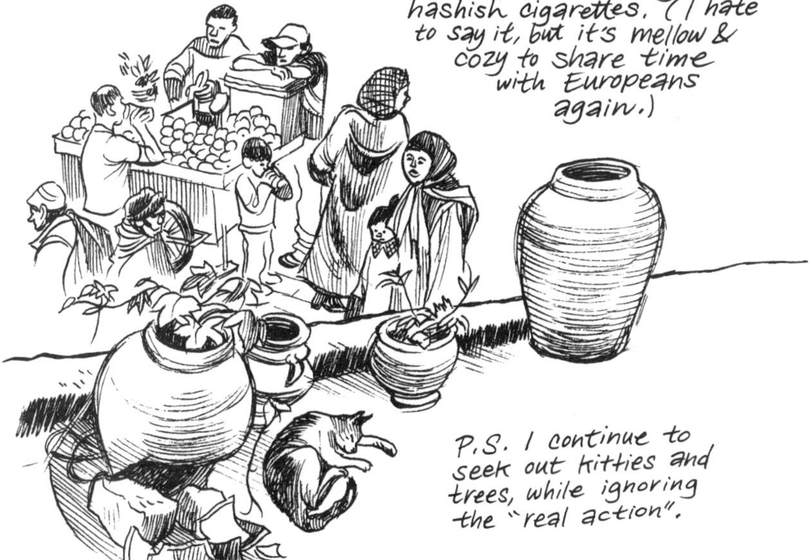

P.S. I continue to seek out kitties and trees, while ignoring the "real action".

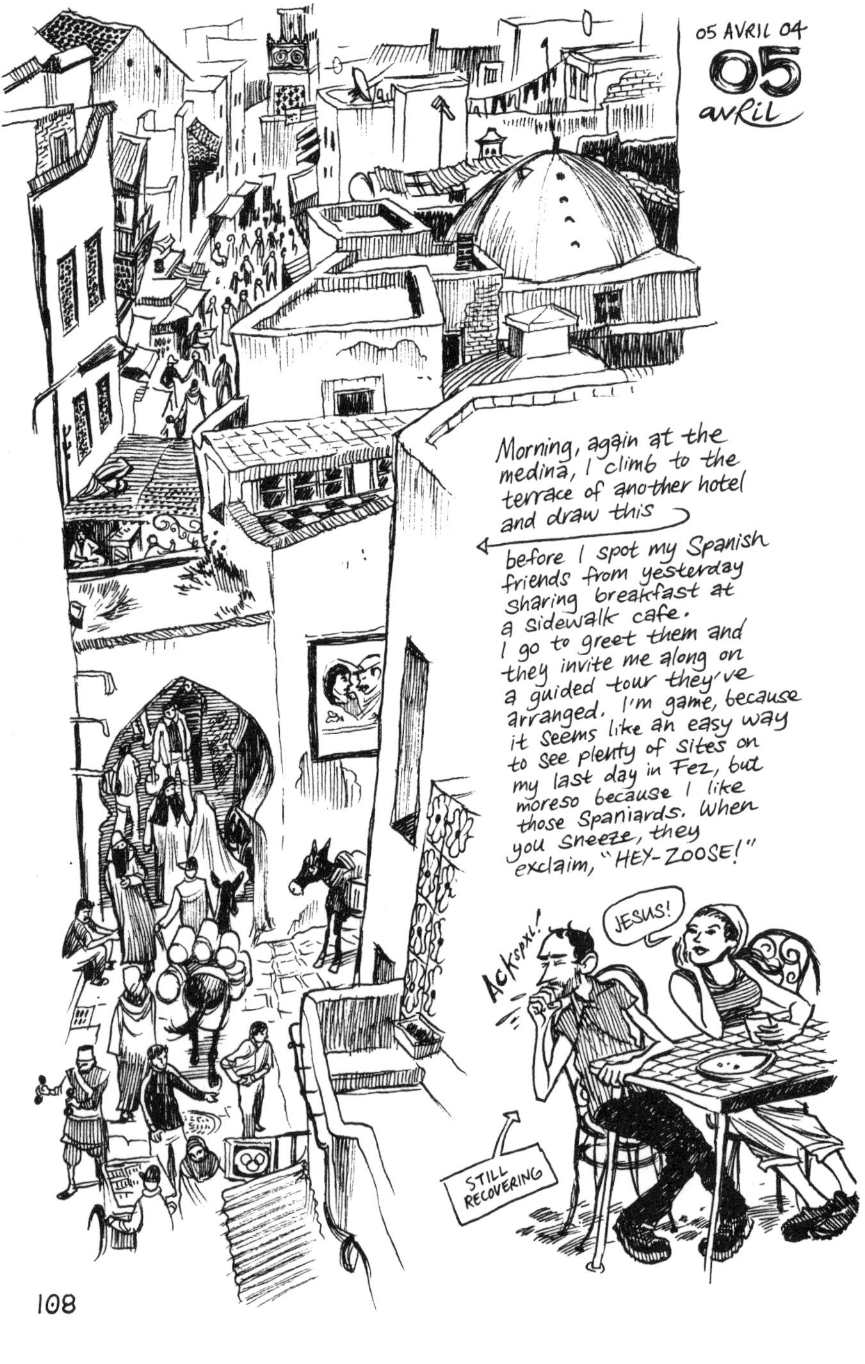
05 AVRIL 04
05
avril
Morning, again at the medina, I climb to the terrace of another hotel and draw this
before I spot my Spanish friends from yesterday sharing breakfast at a sidewalk cafe. I go to greet them and they invite me along on a guided tour they've arranged. I'm game, because it seems like an easy way to see plenty of sites on my last day in Fez, but moreso because I like those Spaniards. When you sneeze, they exclaim, "HEY-ZOOSE!"
JESUS!
ACKspxl!
STILL RECOVERING

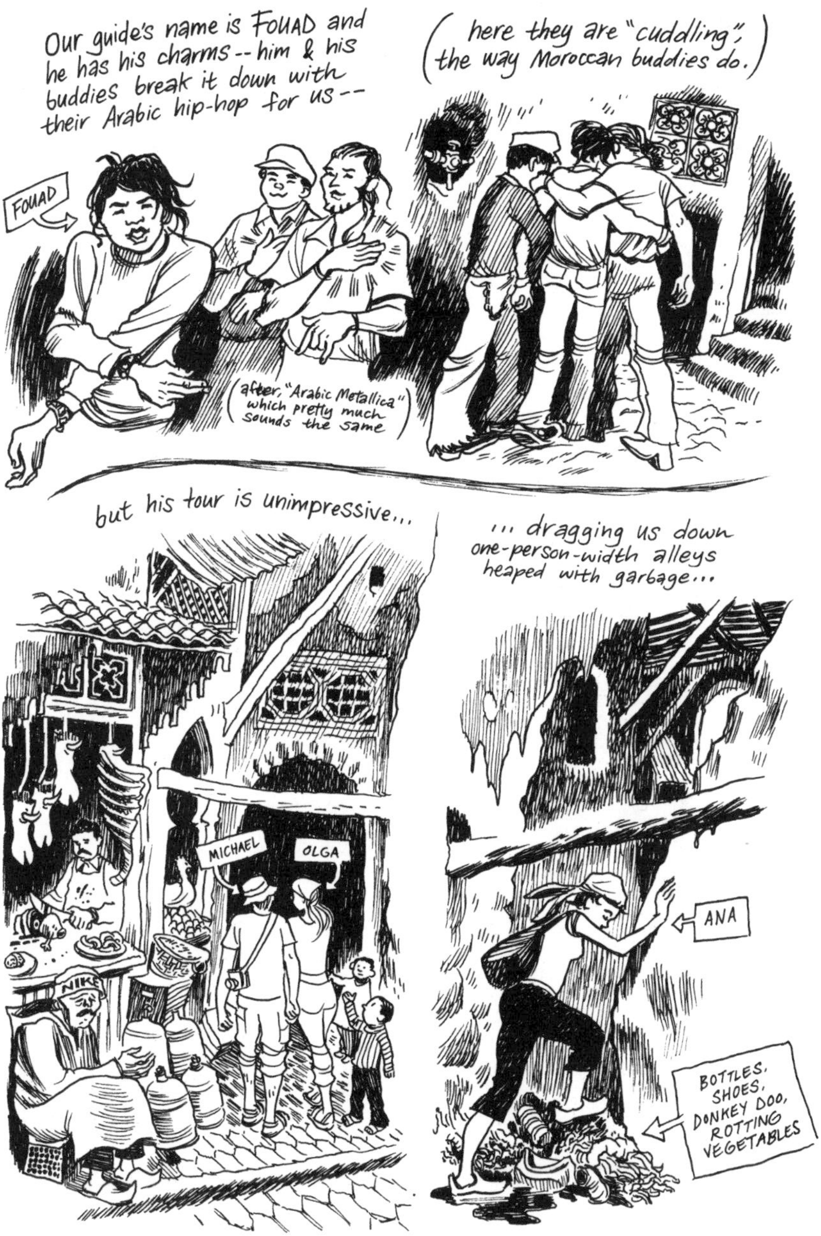
Our guide's name is FOUAD and he has his charms -- him & his buddies break it down with their Arabic hip-hop for us --
FOUAD
(after, "Arabic Metallica" which pretty much sounds the same
(here they are "cuddling", the way Moroccan buddies do.)
but his tour is unimpressive...
MICHAEL
OLGA
NIKE
... dragging us down one-person-width alleys heaped with garbage...
ANA
BOTTLES, SHOES, DONKEY DOO, ROTTING VEGETABLES

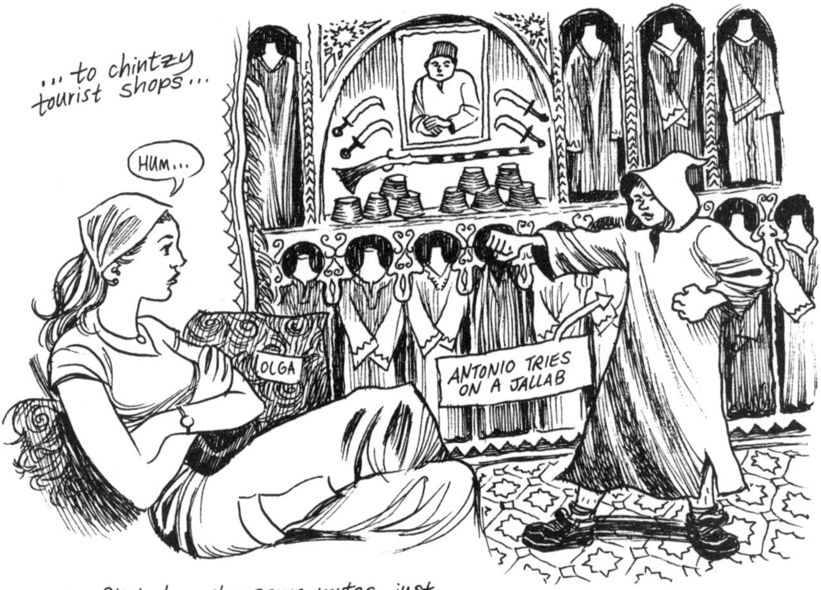
... to chintzy tourist shops...
HUM...
OLGA
ANTONIO TRIES ON A JALLAB

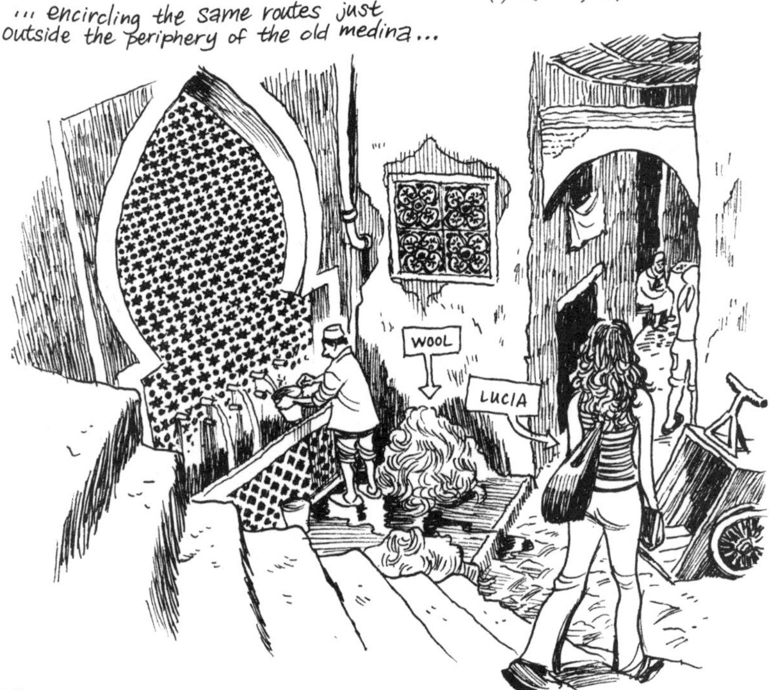
... encircling the same routes just outside the periphery of the old medina...
WOOL
LUCIA

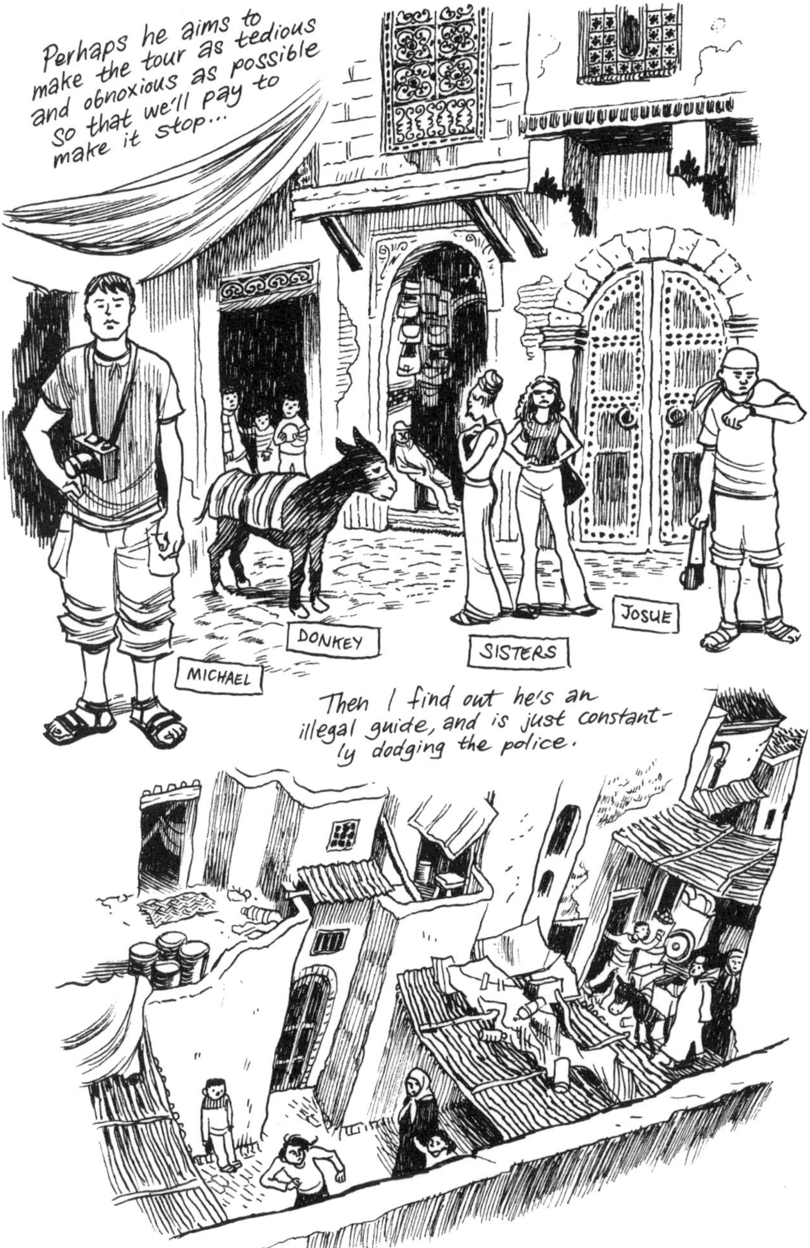
Perhaps he aims to make the tour as tedious and obnoxious as possible so that we'll pay to make it stop...
DONKEY
SISTERS
JOSUE
MICHAEL
Then I find out he's an illegal guide, and is just constantly dodging the police.

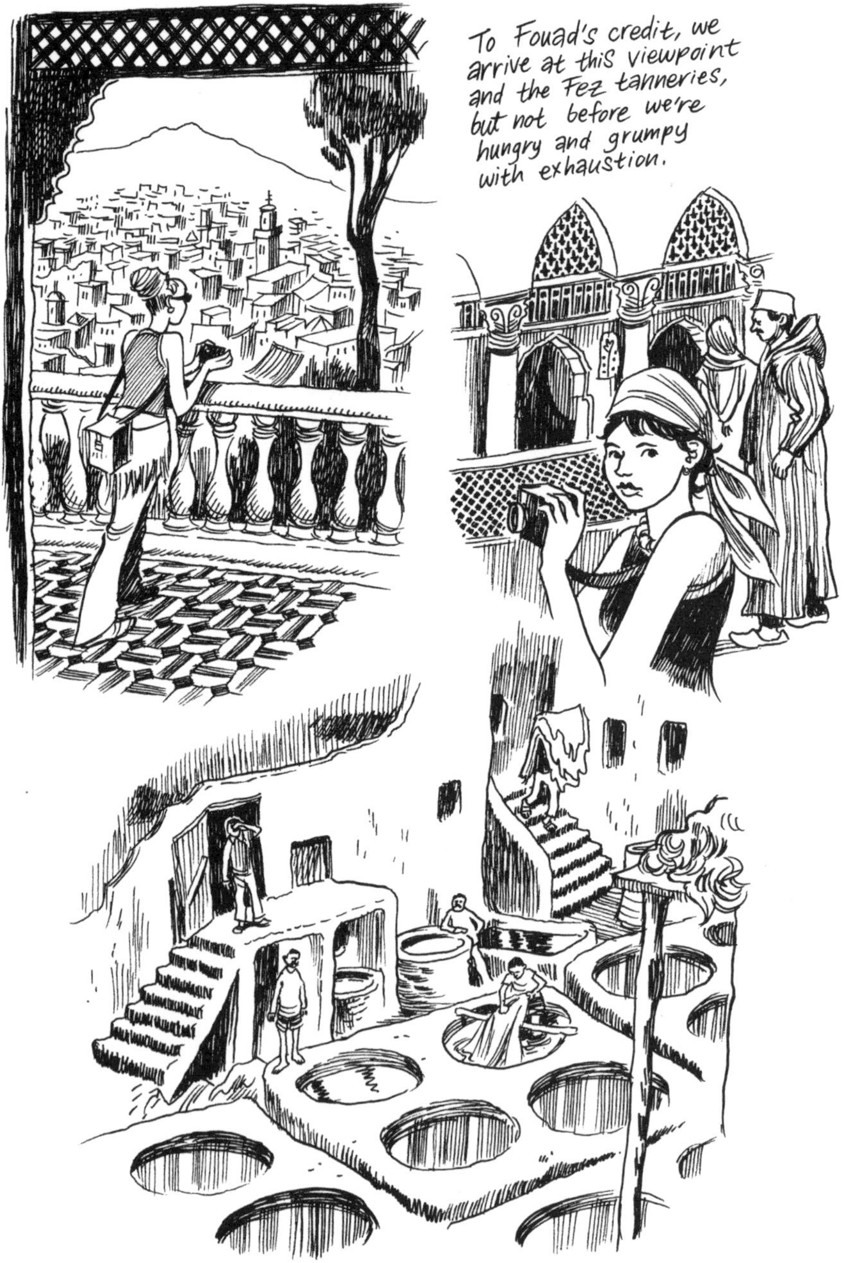
To Fouad's credit, we arrive at this viewpoint and the Fez tanneries, but not before we're hungry and grumpy with exhaustion.

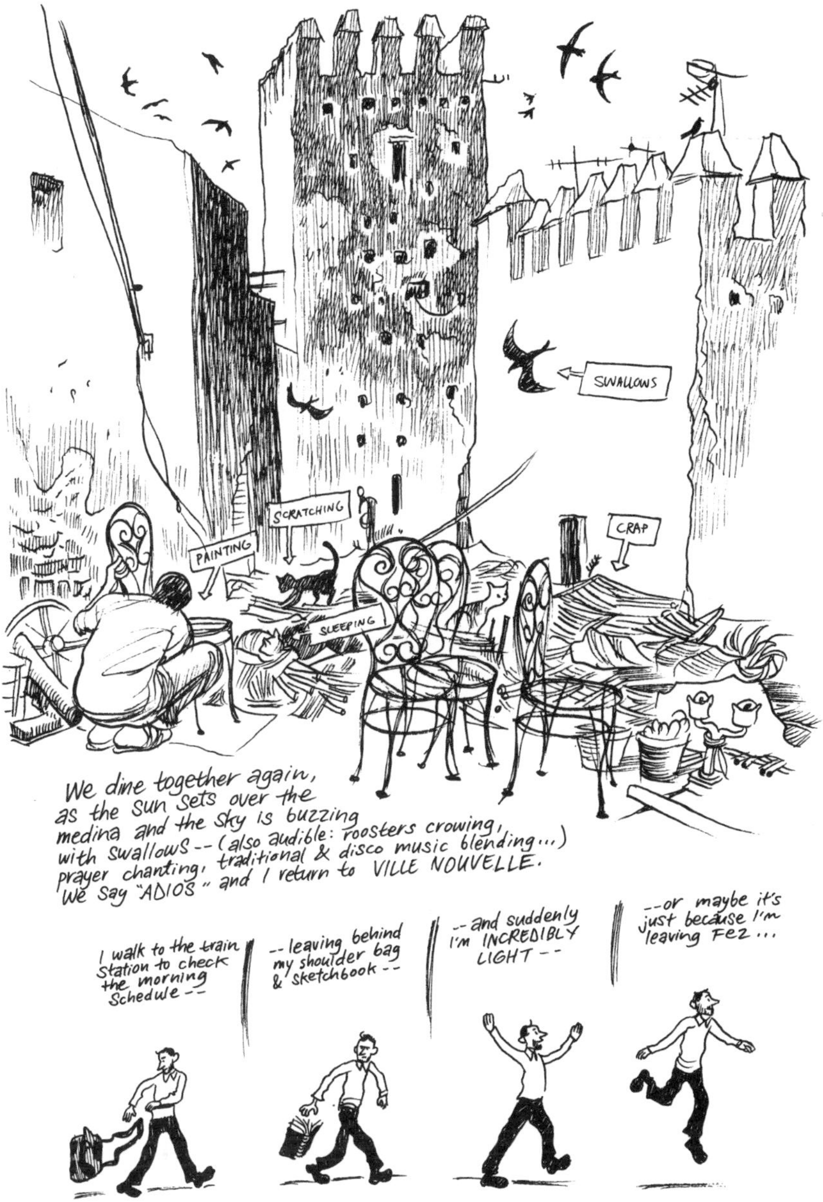
SWALLOWS
SCRATCHING
PAINTING
CRAP
SLEEPING
We dine together again, as the sun sets over the medina and the sky is buzzing with swallows -- (also audible: roosters crowing, prayer chanting, traditional & disco music blending...) We say "ADIOS" and I return to VILLE NOUVELLE.
I walk to the train station to check the morning schedule --
-- leaving behind my shoulder bag & sketchbook --
-- and suddenly I'm INCREDIBLY LIGHT --
-- or maybe it's just because I'm leaving Fez...

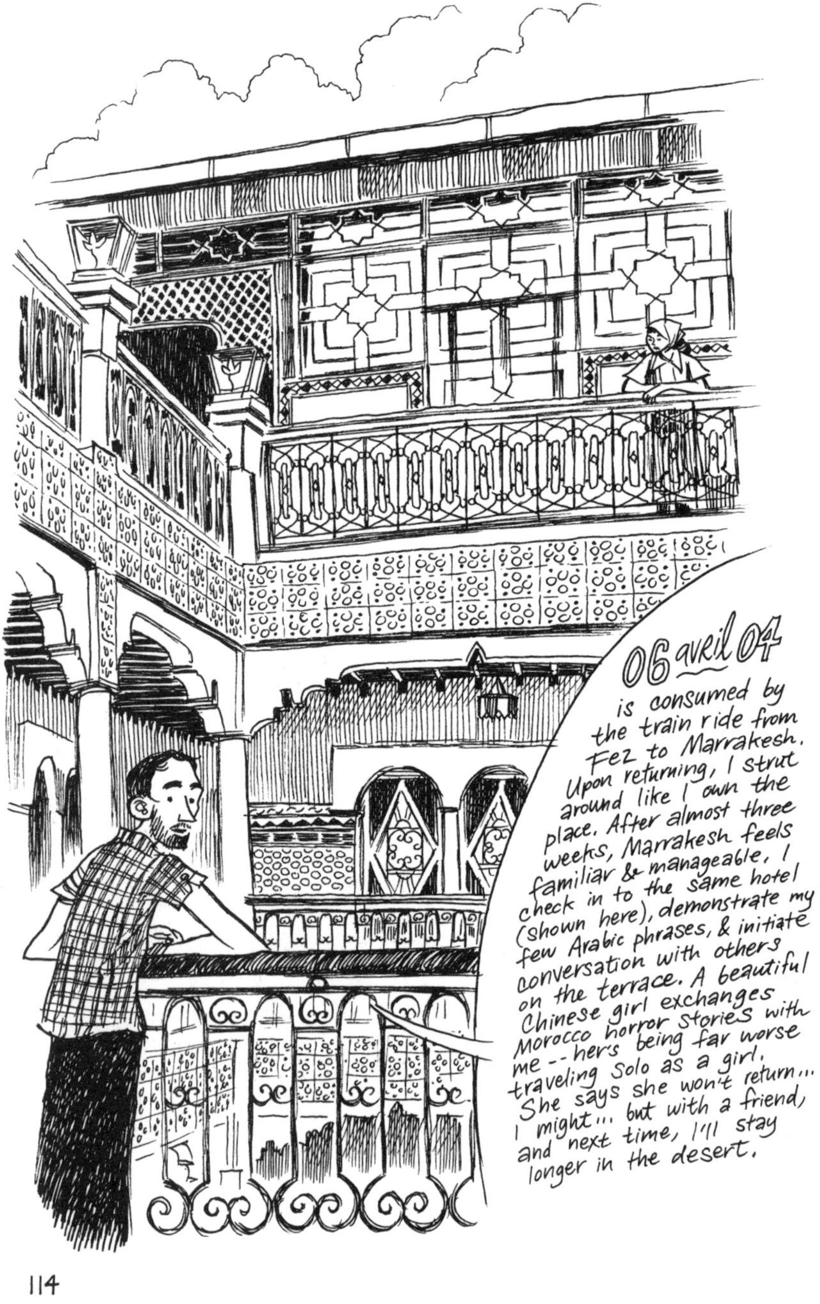
06 avril 04
is consumed by the train ride from Fez to Marrakesh. Upon returning, I strut around like I own the place. After almost three weeks, Marrakesh feels familiar & manageable. I check in to the same hotel (shown here), demonstrate my few Arabic phrases, & initiate conversation with others on the terrace. A beautiful Chinese girl exchanges Morocco horror stories with me -- hers being far worse traveling solo as a girl. She says she won't return... I might... but with a friend, and next time, I'll stay longer in the desert.

07 AVRIL 04 - What to do on one's last day in a country... I opt for the minimal. Taking the morning slow, sipping those yogurt drinks at the hotel lounge, I meet a sweet British couple, Gillian & Ged. They've great expressions like "BLOODY CHEEK" and "I'M JUST A JIGALO WHEREVER I GO." As they begin looking at my sketchbook, they say, "I LIKE YOU A LOT. YOU'RE A NICE PERSON TO KNOW." It almost makes me cry.

Gillian &
Ged
07 AVRIL 04

The weather is sweltering. When I draw, the ink from the crappy pens is smeared by my sweat. I visit HUSSEIN at JUICE STAND number six and draw my very last free portrait for Morocco. He trades me for an orange juice & I hang around a bit watching Marrakesh, transformed by the tourist season, mill past.

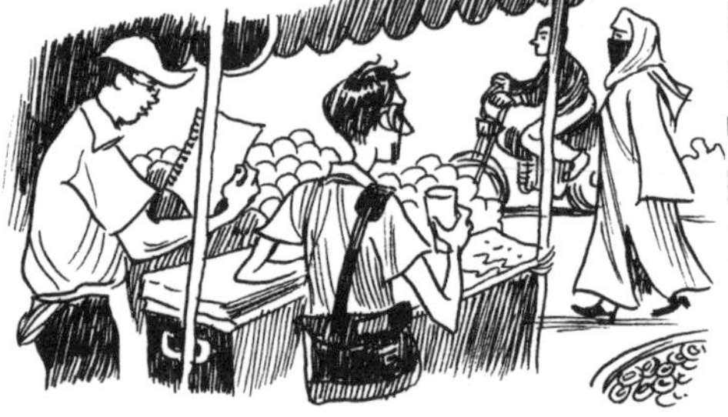

Then rain erupts, and I dash to a cyber cafe for shelter.

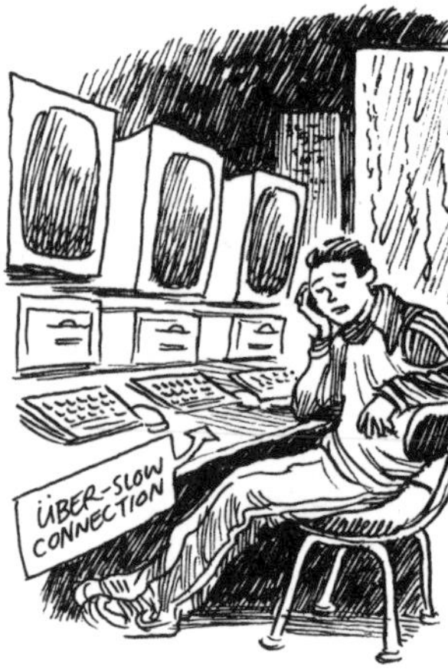

ÜBER-SLOW CONNECTION

Back to the hotel to lounge with more Spaniards. (Smoking the KIFFI is abrasive on my delicate lungs.)

(Elena, Raffa & Laticia)

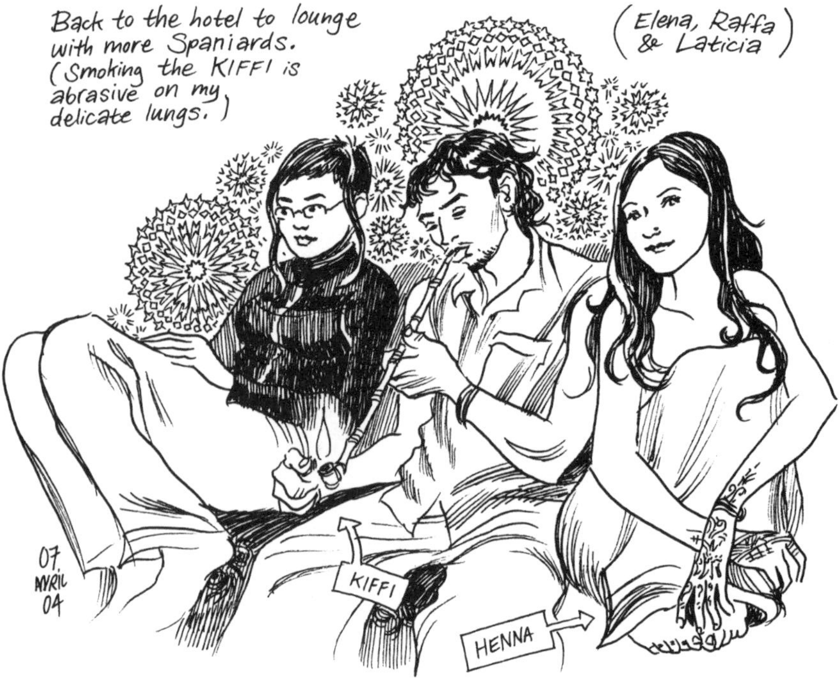

KIFFI
HENNA
07 AVRIL 04

Then, I rendezvous again with Gillian & Ged. It's Gillian's 63rd birthday, and they invite me to dinner to celebrate. Like Ange and Beatrice and my friends from Madrid, they are my support line for the night -- wise, engaging, and funny, too.

Then, by chance, I spot sisters Sara & Lucia in the manic zoo of Djemaa el-Fna. They've just arrived in Marrakesh. I tell them where I'm staying as they hunt for a hotel.

Later, moments after I've crawled to bed, they drop by to wish adios one last time.

KNOCK KNOCK

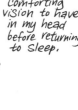

They're a comforting vision to have in my head before returning to sleep.

117

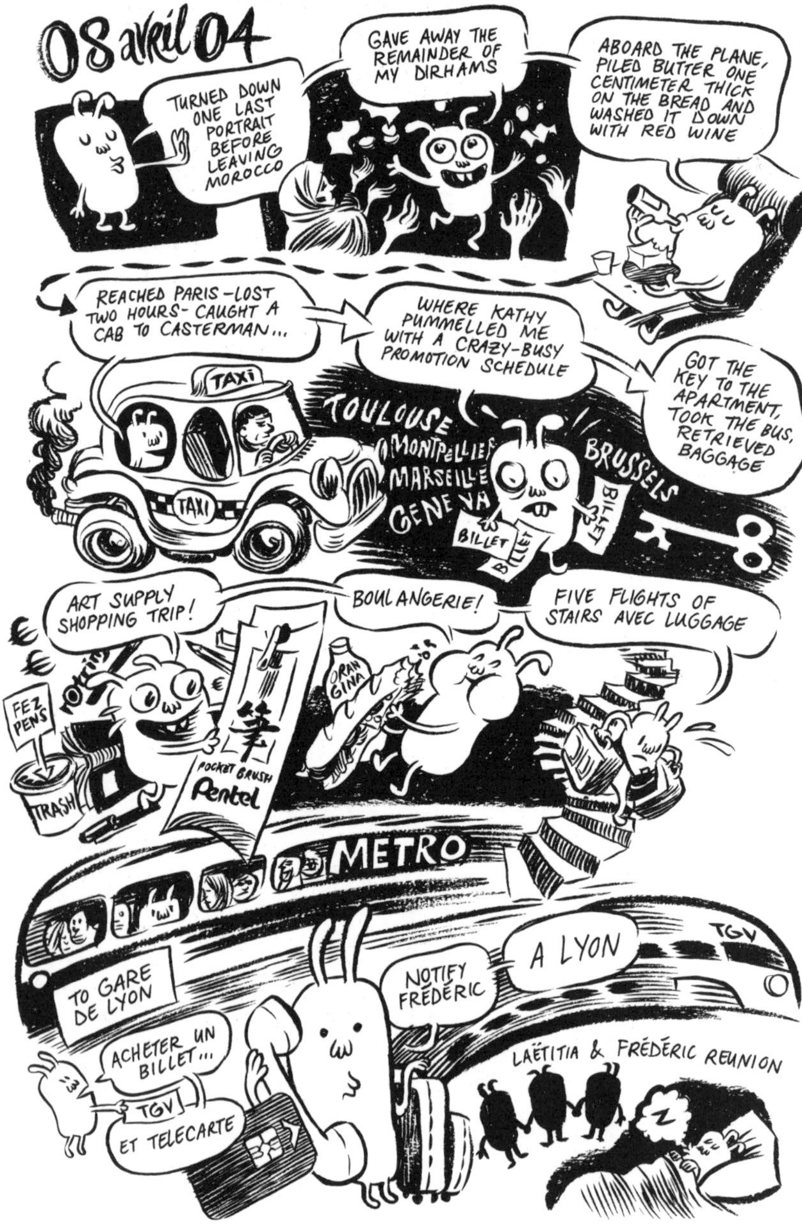
08 avril 04
TURNED DOWN ONE LAST PORTRAIT BEFORE LEAVING MOROCCO
GAVE AWAY THE REMAINDER OF MY DIRHAMS
ABOARD THE PLANE, PILED BUTTER ONE CENTIMETER THICK ON THE BREAD AND WASHED IT DOWN WITH RED WINE
REACHED PARIS - LOST TWO HOURS - CAUGHT A CAB TO CASTERMAN...
TAXI
TAXI
WHERE KATHY PUMMELLED ME WITH A CRAZY-BUSY PROMOTION SCHEDULE
TOULOUSE
MONTPELLIER
MARSEILLE
GENEVA
BRUSSELS
BILLET
BILLET
BILLET
BILLET
GOT THE KEY TO THE APARTMENT, TOOK THE BUS, RETRIEVED BAGGAGE
ART SUPPLY SHOPPING TRIP!
BOULANGERIE!
FIVE FLIGHTS OF STAIRS AVEC LUGGAGE
FEZ PENS
TRASH
POCKET BRUSH
Pentel
ORANGINA
METRO
TGV
TO GARE DE LYON
NOTIFY FRÉDÉRIC
A LYON
ACHETER UN BILLET...
TGV
ET TELECARTE
LAËTITIA & FRÉDÉRIC REUNION

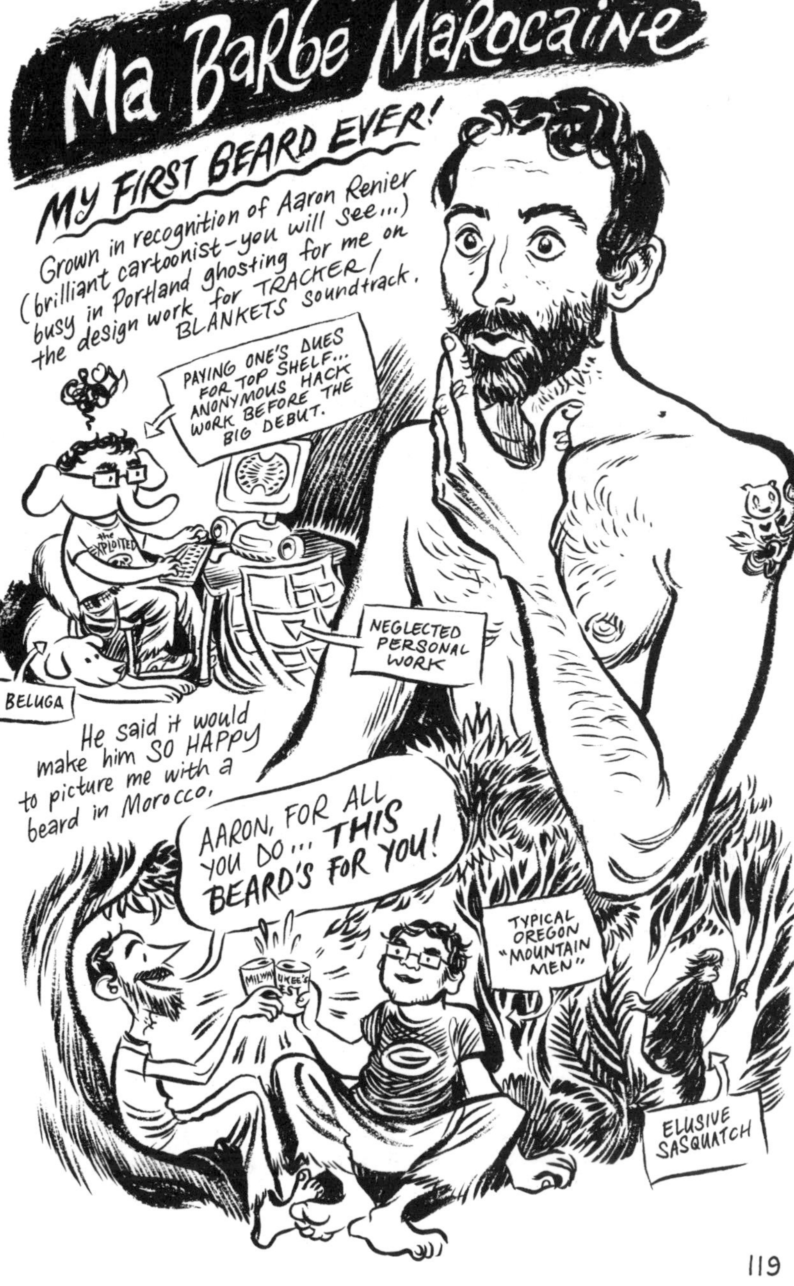
Ma Barbe Marocaine
MY FIRST BEARD EVER!
Grown in recognition of Aaron Renier (brilliant cartoonist—you will see...) busy in Portland ghosting for me on the design work for TRACKER/ BLANKETS soundtrack.
PAYING ONE'S DUES FOR TOP SHELF... ANONYMOUS HACK WORK BEFORE THE BIG DEBUT.
NEGLECTED PERSONAL WORK
BELUGA
He said it would make him SO HAPPY to picture me with a beard in Morocco.
AARON, FOR ALL YOU DO... THIS BEARD'S FOR YOU!
TYPICAL OREGON "MOUNTAIN MEN"
ELUSIVE SASQUATCH

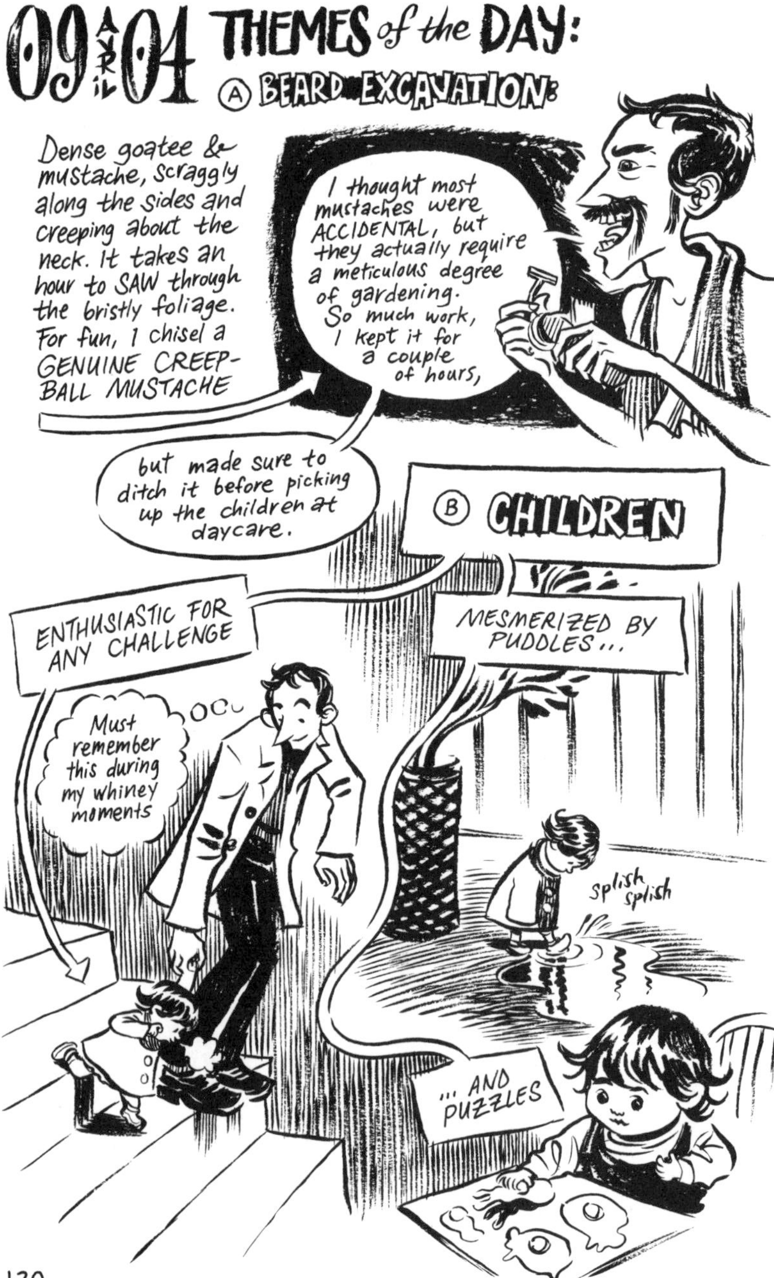
09 APRIL 04 THEMES of the DAY:
A BEARD EXCAVATION:
Dense goatee & mustache, scraggly along the sides and creeping about the neck. It takes an hour to SAW through the bristly foliage. For fun, I chisel a GENUINE CREEP-BALL MUSTACHE
I thought most mustaches were ACCIDENTAL, but they actually require a meticulous degree of gardening. So much work, I kept it for a couple of hours,
but made sure to ditch it before picking up the children at daycare.
B CHILDREN
ENTHUSIASTIC FOR ANY CHALLENGE
Must remember this during my whiney moments
MESMERIZED BY PUDDLES...
splish splish
... AND PUZZLES

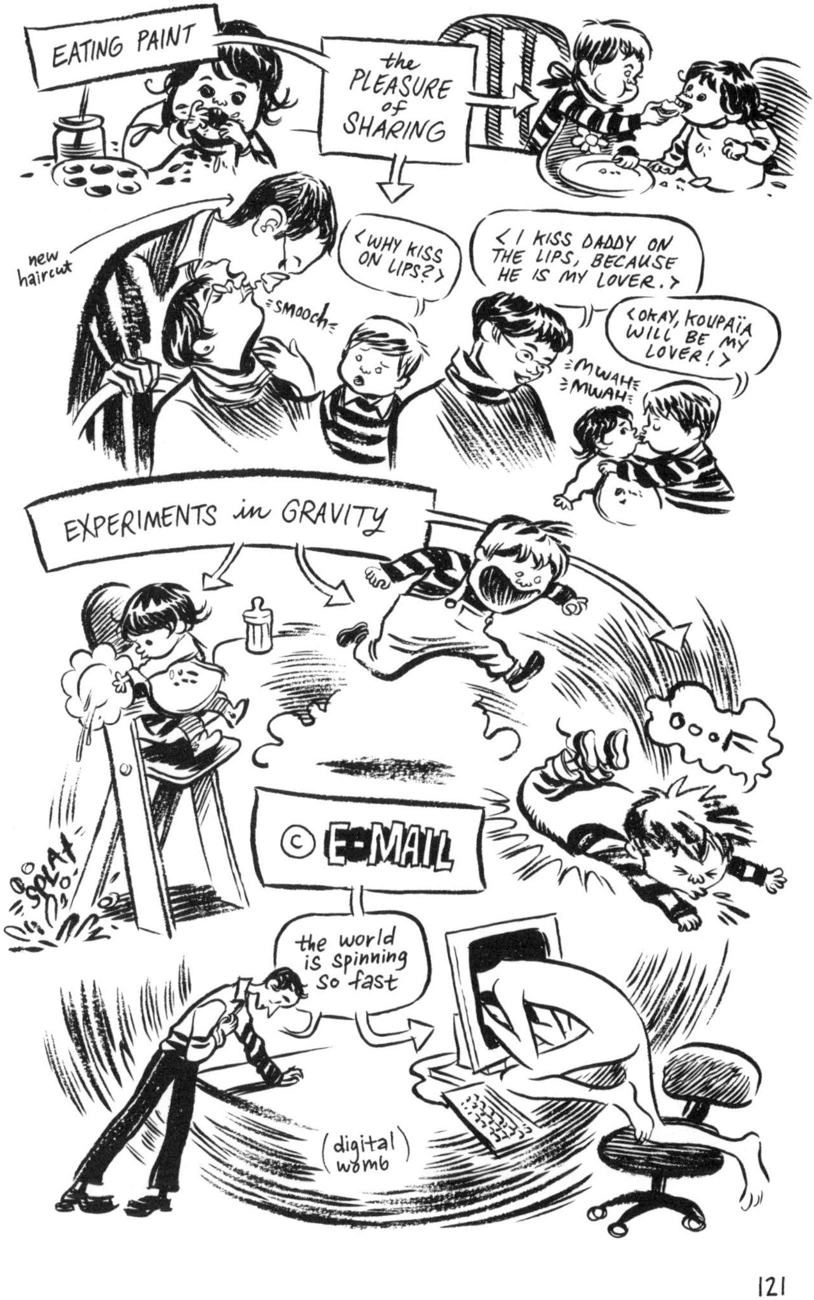
EATING PAINT
the PLEASURE of SHARING
new haircut
SMOOCH
<WHY KISS ON LIPS?>
<I KISS DADDY ON THE LIPS, BECAUSE HE IS MY LOVER.>
<OKAY, KOUPAÏA WILL BE MY LOVER!>
MWAH MWAH
EXPERIMENTS in GRAVITY
OOOF
SPLAT
© E-MAIL
the world is spinning so fast
(digital womb)

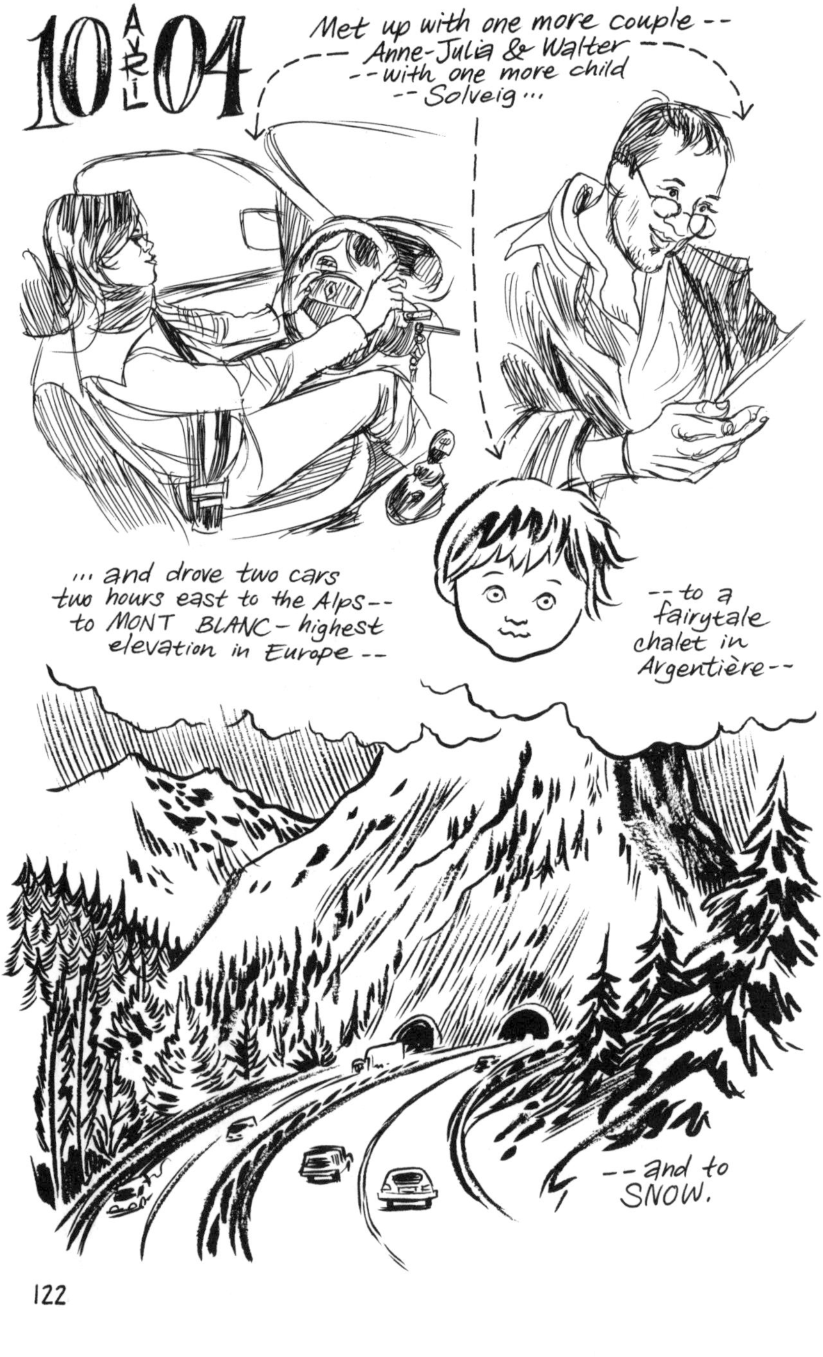
10 AVRIL 04
Met up with one more couple -- Anne-Julia & Walter -- with one more child -- Solveig ...
... and drove two cars two hours east to the Alps -- to MONT BLANC - highest elevation in Europe --
-- to a fairytale chalet in Argentière --
-- and to SNOW.

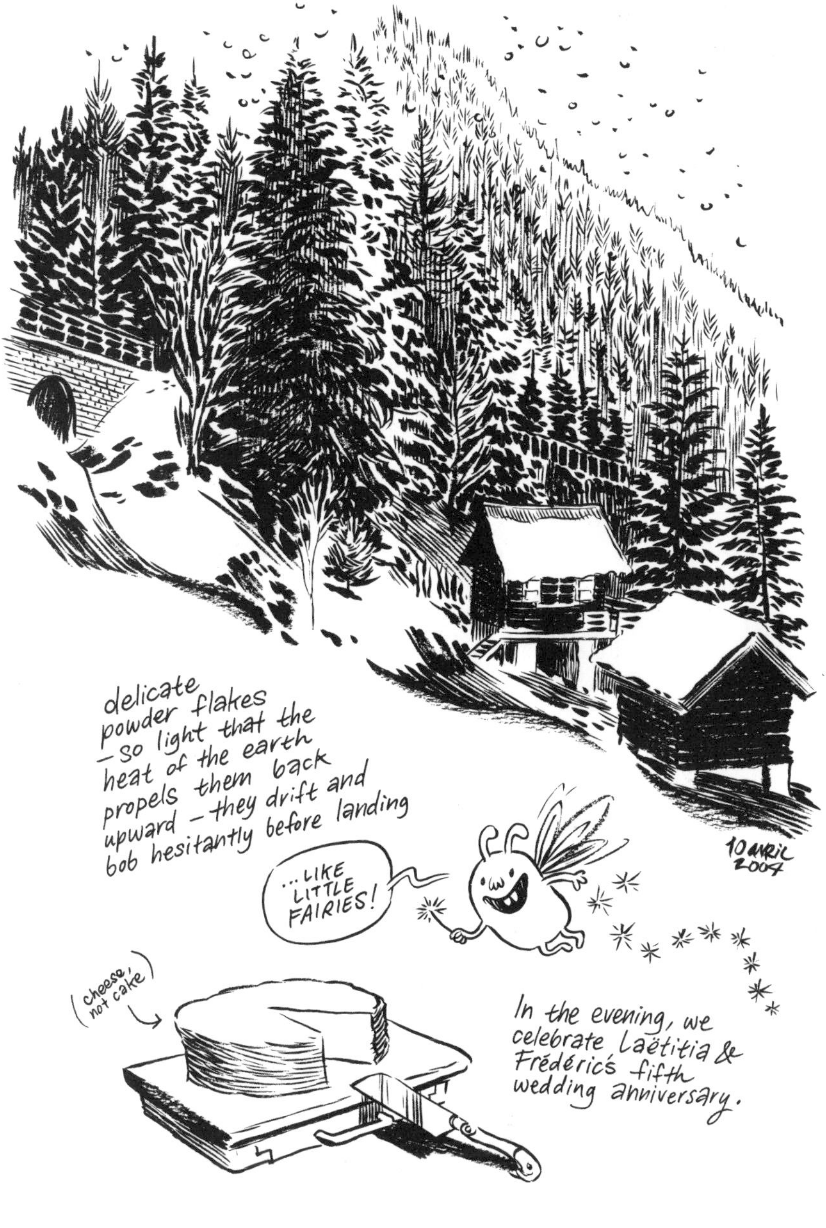
delicate powder flakes — so light that the heat of the earth propels them back upward — they drift and bob hesitantly before landing
10 AVRIL 2007
...LIKE LITTLE FAIRIES!
(cheese, not cake)
In the evening, we celebrate Laëtitia & Frédéric's fifth wedding anniversary.

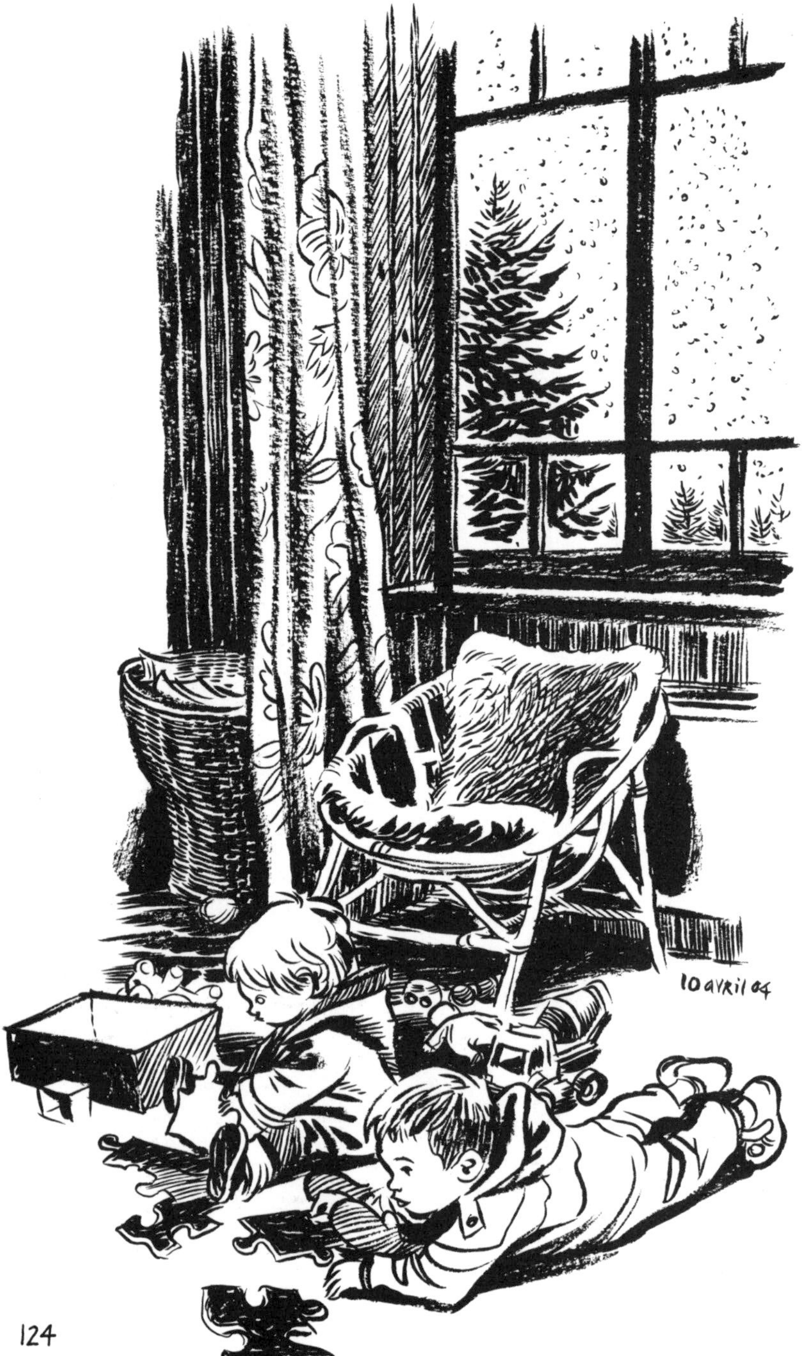
10 avril 04

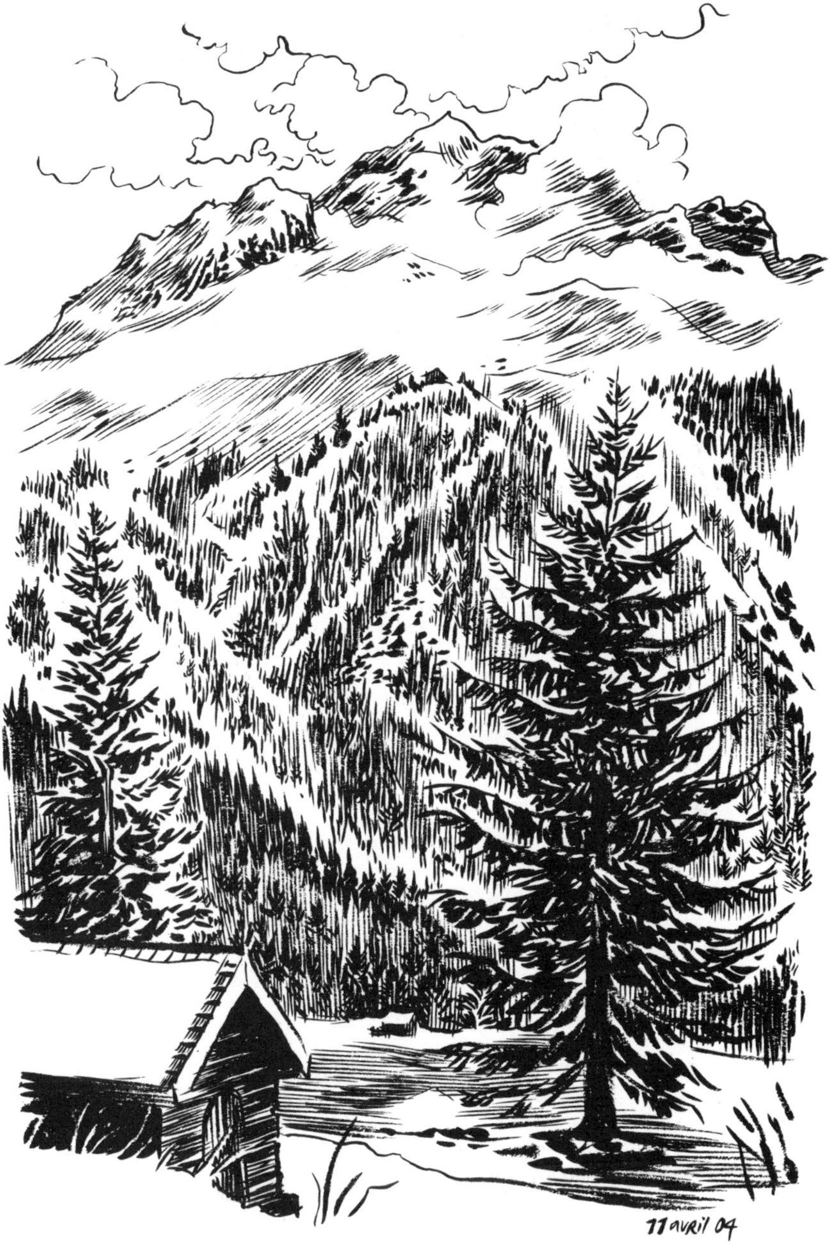
11 avril 04

11 avril 04

The fairytale chalet has a fairytale story -- built in 1936 by Laëtitia's great grandfather

AIMÉ COUTAGNE

- a pioneer in hydrology, one of the first to ski in France, a poet for 55 years, and most of all, a DEVOTEE of the MOUNTAINS.

He endured much hardship in his lifetime. His first wife Marie died giving birth to their fourth child. The child died, too. Their second had already died, and the third would die at age 19 of tuberculosis. Only his first child, Elizabeth, survived.

He remarried - to Marie's sister Jeanne (so the children would have the same grandparents). They had 8 children _ three never reached adulthood -- of the five surviving boys, four became priests/monks, except for Jean - Laëtitia's grandfather.

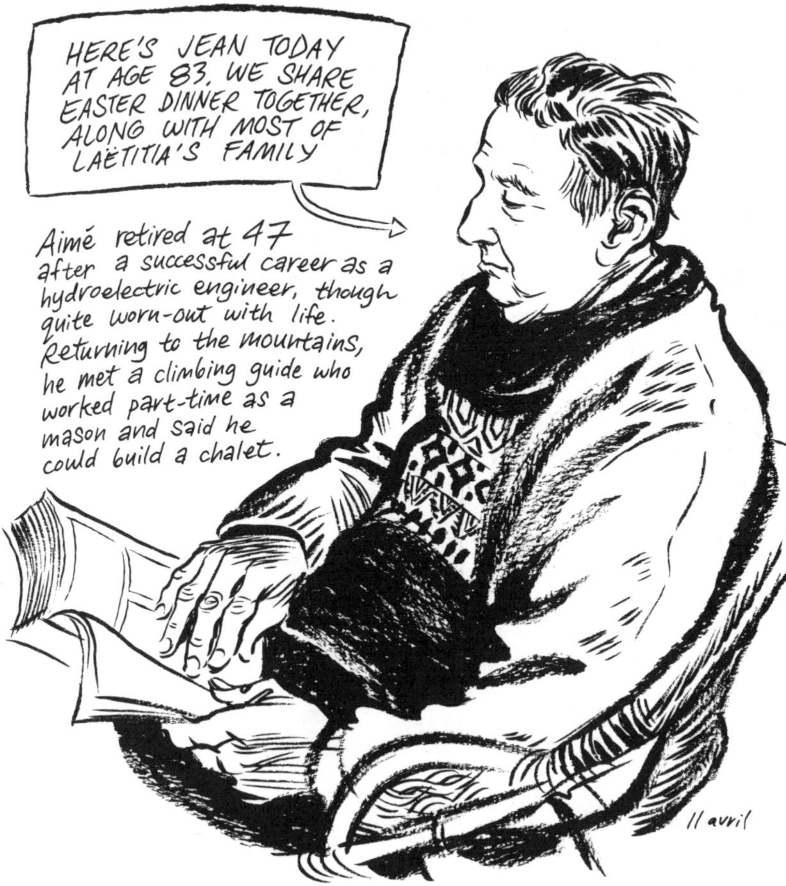
HERE'S JEAN TODAY AT AGE 83. WE SHARE EASTER DINNER TOGETHER, ALONG WITH MOST OF LAËTITIA'S FAMILY
Aimé retired at 47 after a successful career as a hydroelectric engineer, though quite worn-out with life. Returning to the mountains, he met a climbing guide who worked part-time as a mason and said he could build a chalet.
11 avril

Six months later, it materialized -- a life-long dream for Aimé and a REBIRTH.

The place is brimming with old photos, handmade books, tattered maps, cuckoo clocks, old gadgets, copper teapots, well-stoked fireplace, the smell of chocolate & cognac & aged wood, and a huge bed with soft wool blankets all to myself. After bouts of insomnia preceding this trip and miserable bedtimes in Morocco, I curl into the dense slumber of high-elevation nights ... and my dreams are hopeful.

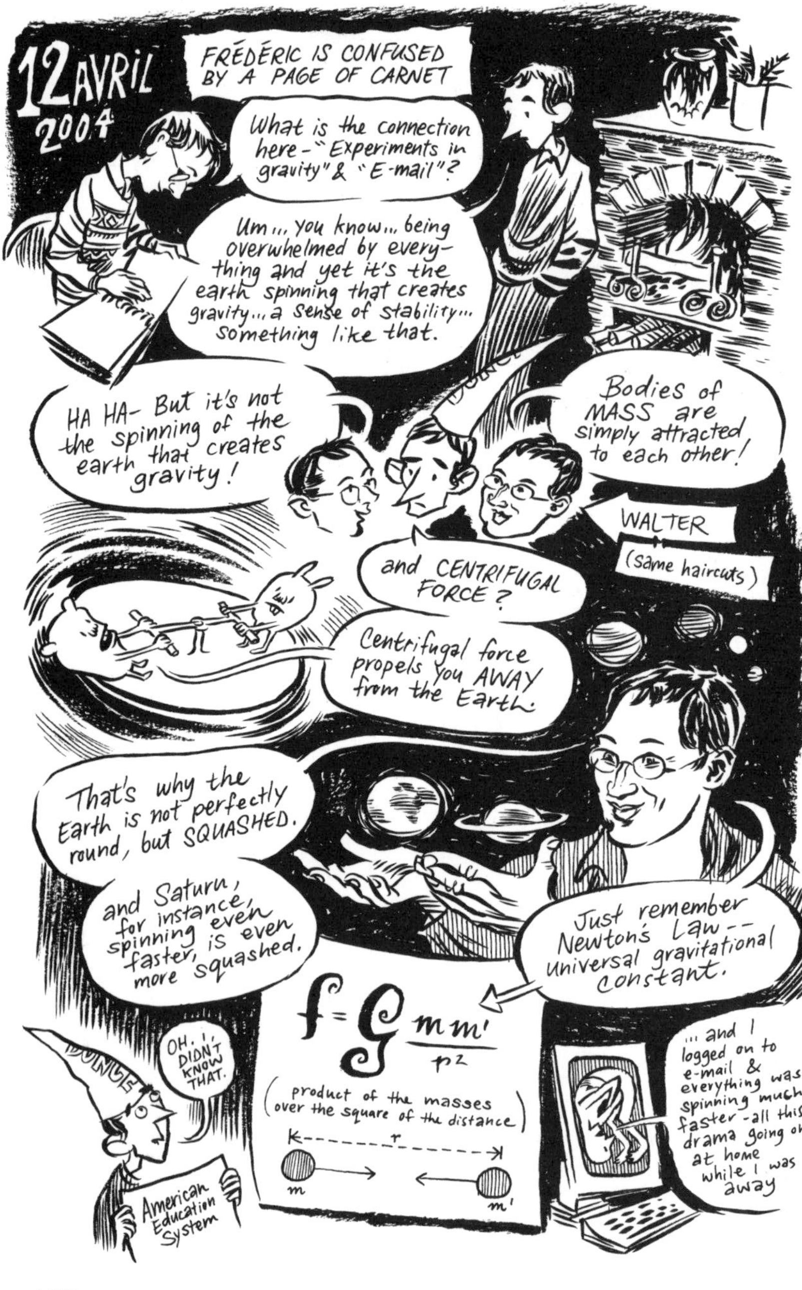

12 AVRIL 2004
FRÉDÉRIC IS CONFUSED BY A PAGE OF CARNET
What is the connection here - "Experiments in gravity" & "E-mail"?
Um... you know... being overwhelmed by everything and yet it's the earth spinning that creates gravity... a sense of stability... something like that.
HA HA- But it's not the spinning of the earth that creates gravity!
Bodies of MASS are simply attracted to each other!
WALTER
(same haircuts)
and CENTRIFUGAL FORCE?
Centrifugal force propels you AWAY from the Earth.
That's why the Earth is not perfectly round, but SQUASHED.
and Saturn, for instance, spinning even faster, is even more squashed.
Just remember Newton's Law-- universal gravitational constant.
f = G mm'/r²
(product of the masses over the square of the distance)
r
m
m'
OH. I, DIDN'T KNOW THAT.
American Education System
... and I logged on to e-mail & everything was spinning much faster - all this drama going on at home while I was away

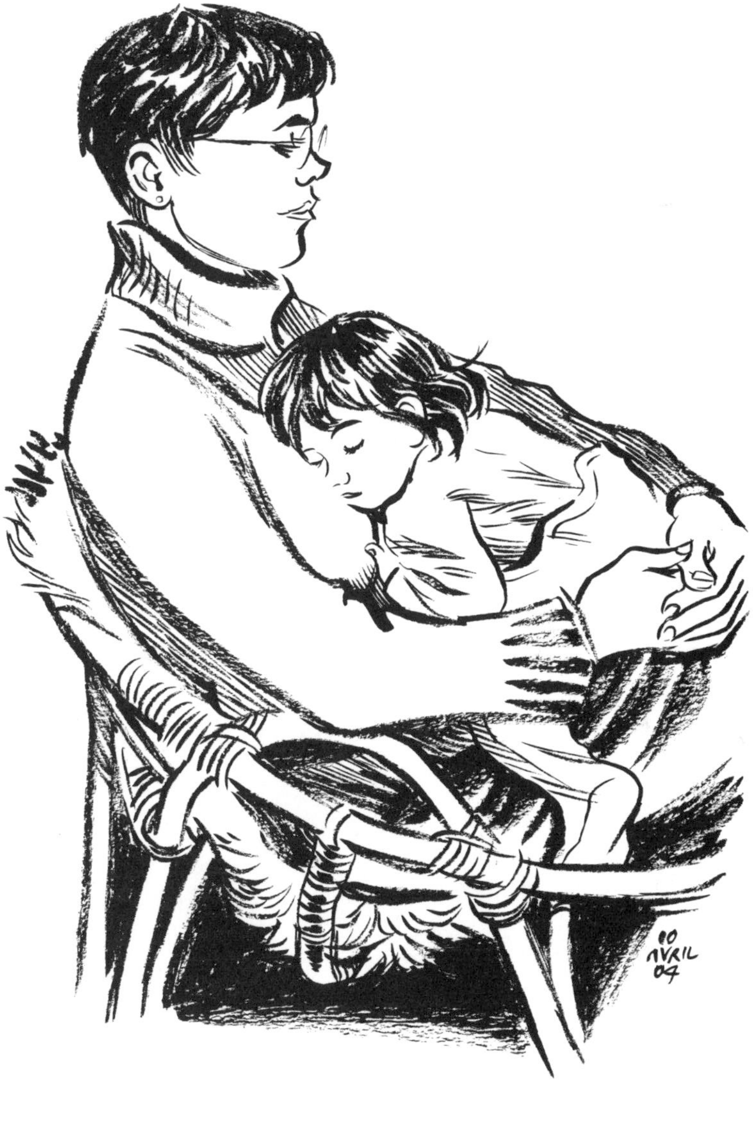
AVRIL
04

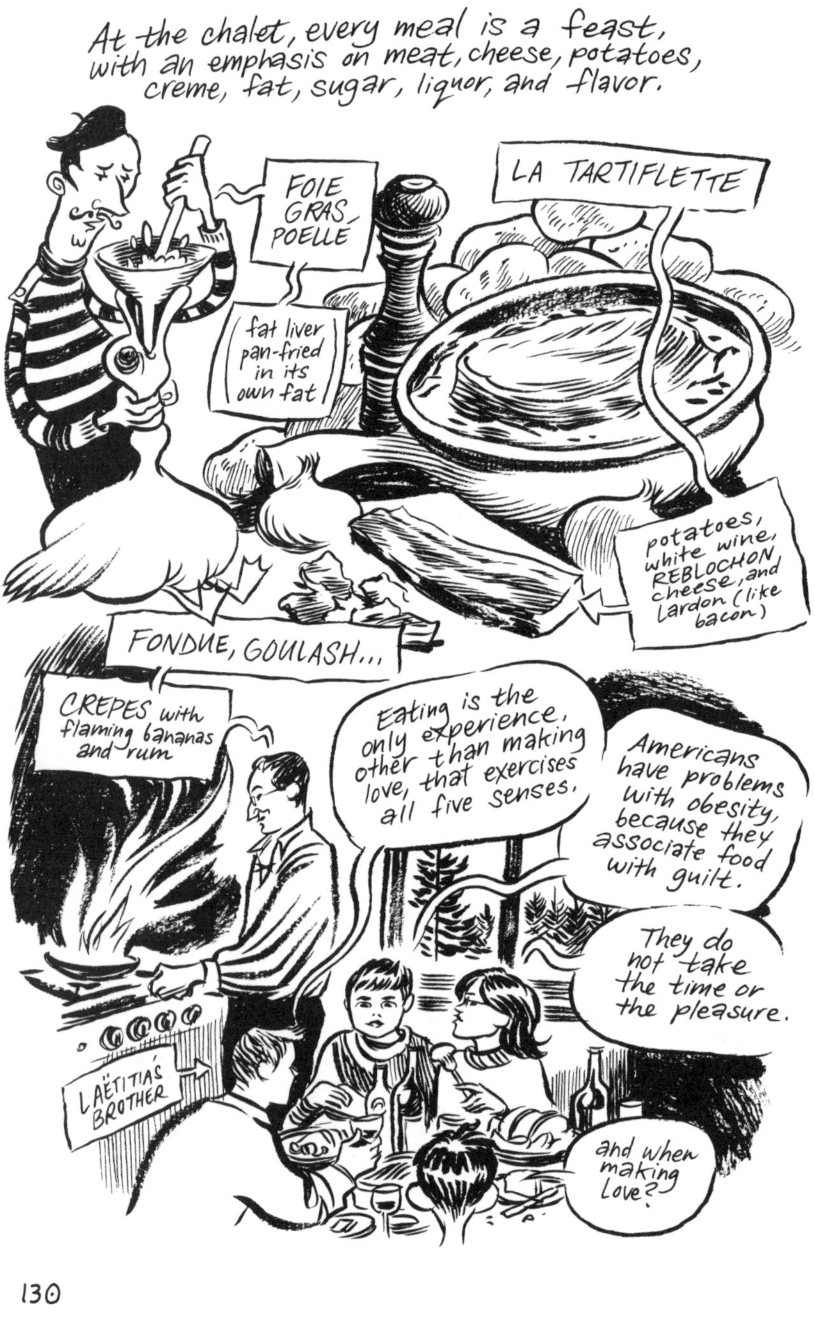
At the chalet, every meal is a feast, with an emphasis on meat, cheese, potatoes, creme, fat, sugar, liquor, and flavor.
FOIE GRAS POELLÉ
fat liver pan-fried in its own fat
LA TARTIFLETTE
potatoes, white wine, REBLOCHON cheese, and Lardon (like bacon)
FONDUE, GOULASH...
CREPES with flaming bananas and rum
LAËTITIA'S BROTHER
Eating is the only experience, other than making love, that exercises all five senses.
Americans have problems with obesity, because they associate food with guilt.
They do not take the time or the pleasure.
and when making love?

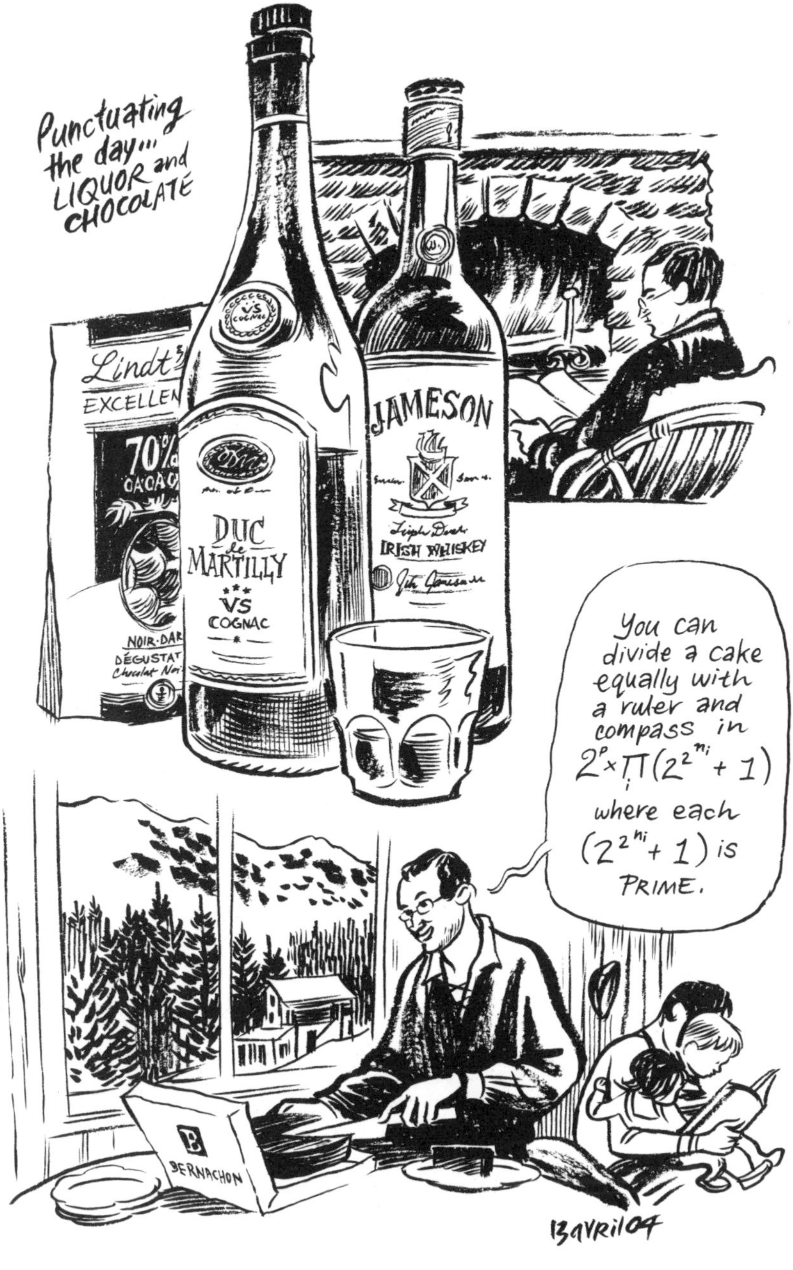
Punctuating the day... LIQUOR and CHOCOLATE
Lindt
EXCELLEN
70%
CACAO
NOIR·DAR
DÉGUSTAT
DUC de MARTILLY
VS
COGNAC
JAMESON
IRISH WHISKEY
You can divide a cake equally with a ruler and compass in $2^p \times \prod_i (2^{2^{n_i}} + 1)$ where each $(2^{2^{n_i}} + 1)$ is PRIME.
BERNACHON
13avril04

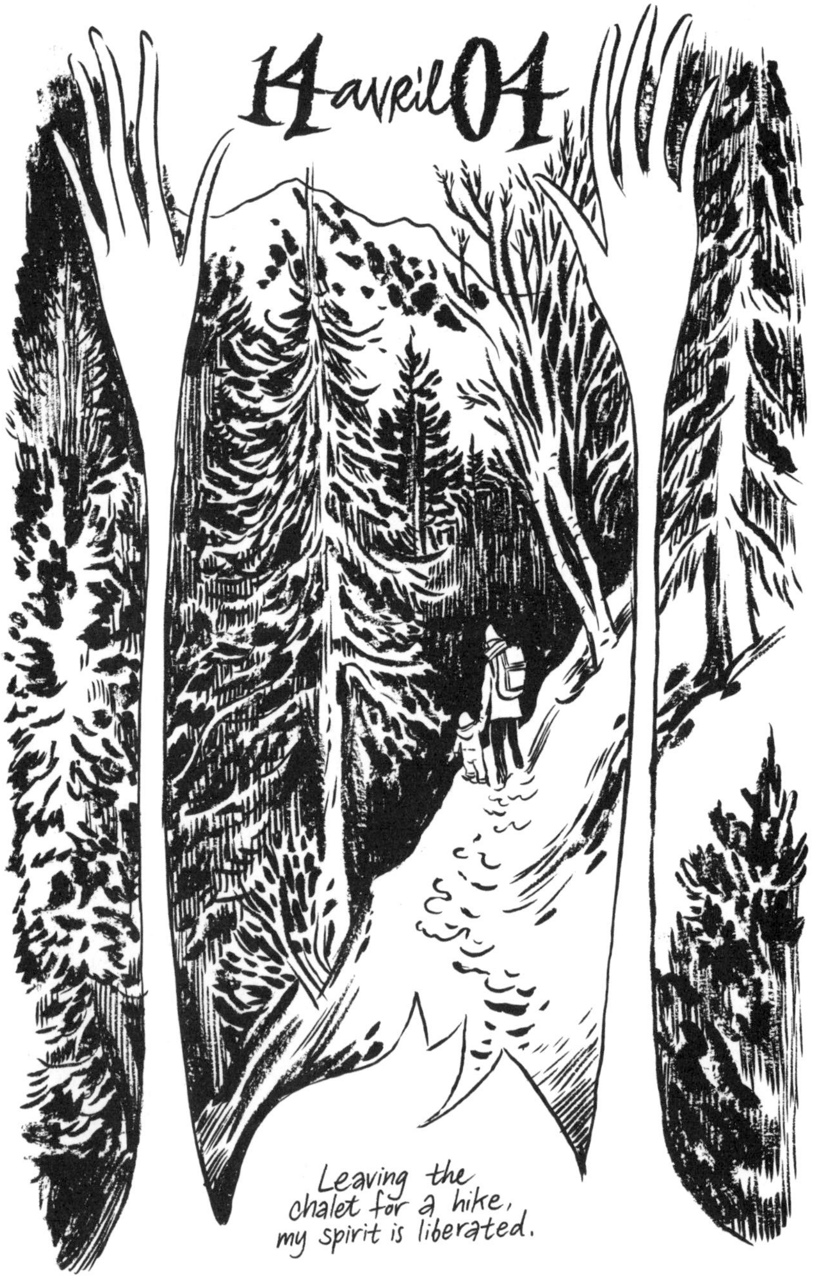
14 avril 04
Leaving the chalet for a hike, my spirit is liberated.

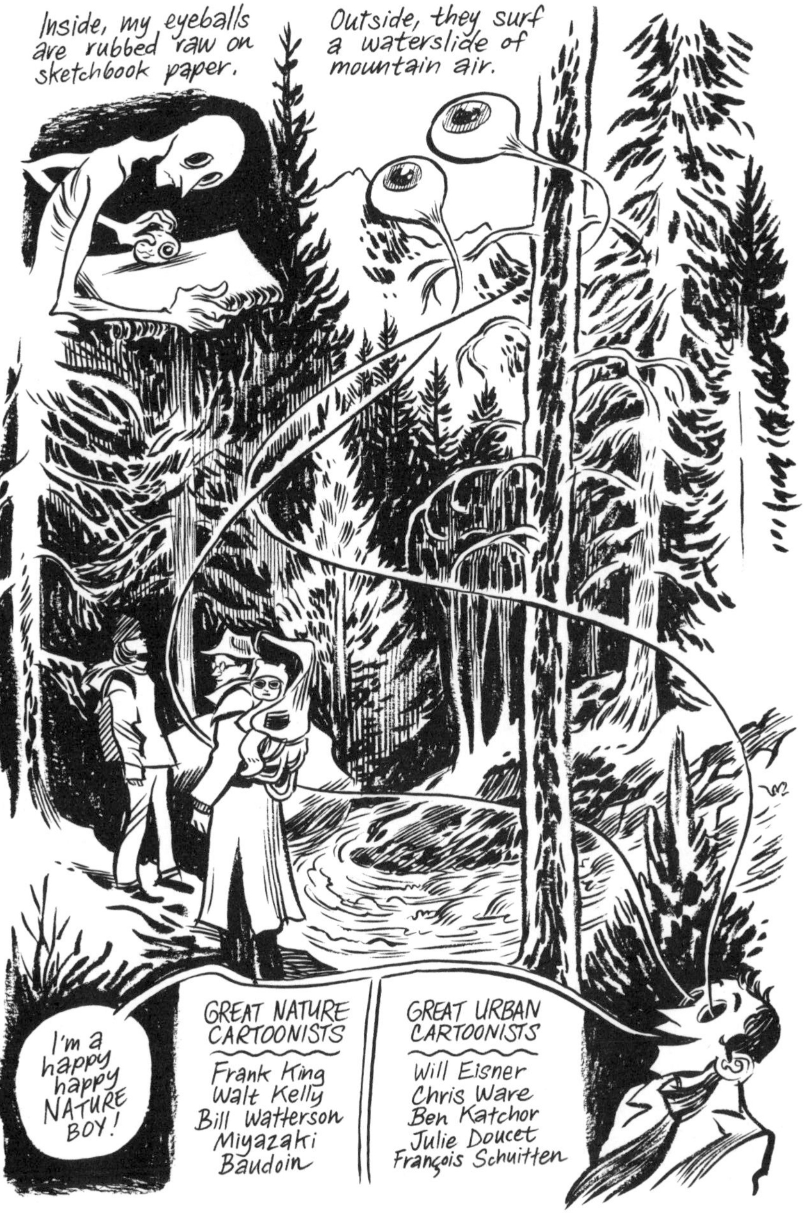

Inside, my eyeballs are rubbed raw on sketchbook paper.
Outside, they surf a waterslide of mountain air.
I'm a happy happy NATURE BOY!
GREAT NATURE CARTOONISTS
Frank King
Walt Kelly
Bill Watterson
Miyazaki
Baudoin
GREAT URBAN CARTOONISTS
Will Eisner
Chris Ware
Ben Katchor
Julie Doucet
François Schuitten

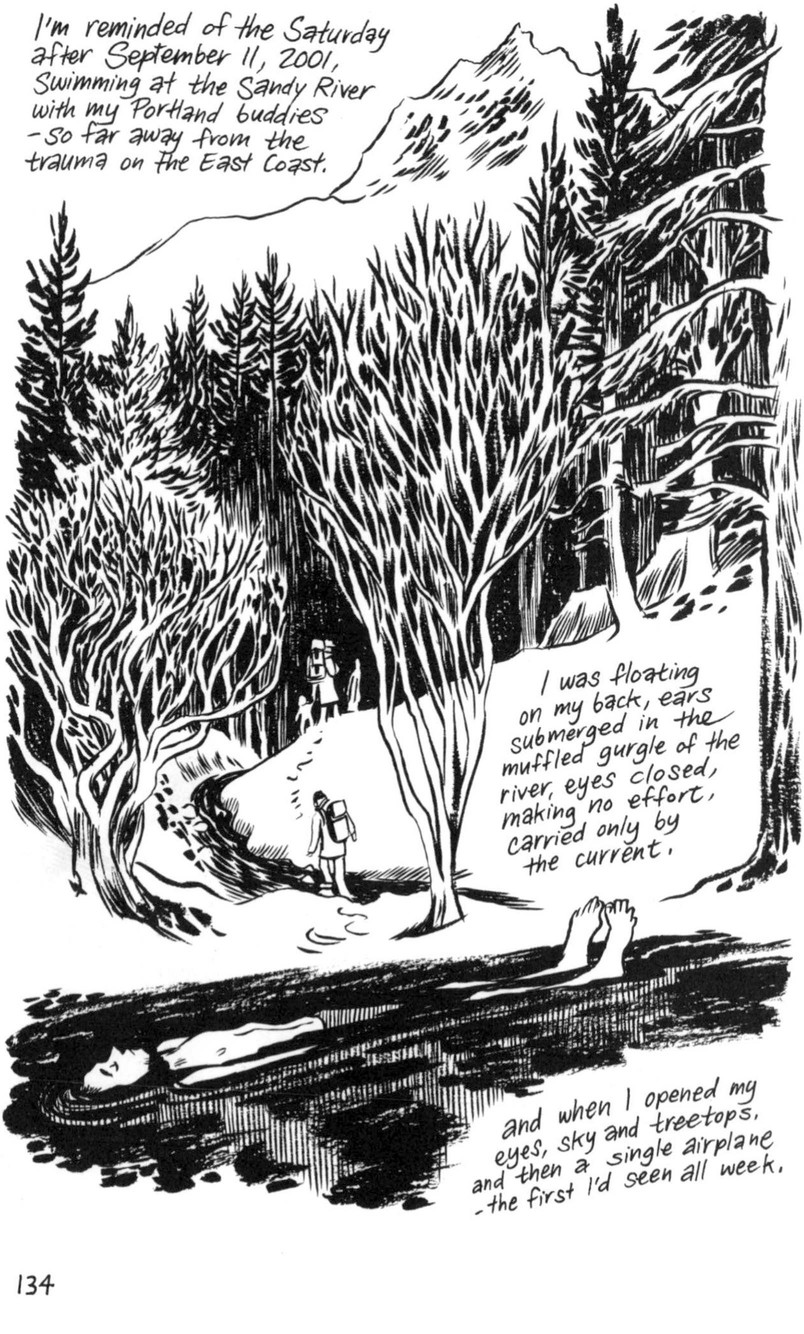
I'm reminded of the Saturday after September 11, 2001, Swimming at the Sandy River with my Portland buddies -so far away from the trauma on the East Coast.
I was floating on my back, ears submerged in the muffled gurgle of the river, eyes closed, making no effort, carried only by the current.
and when I opened my eyes, sky and treetops, and then a single airplane -the first I'd seen all week.

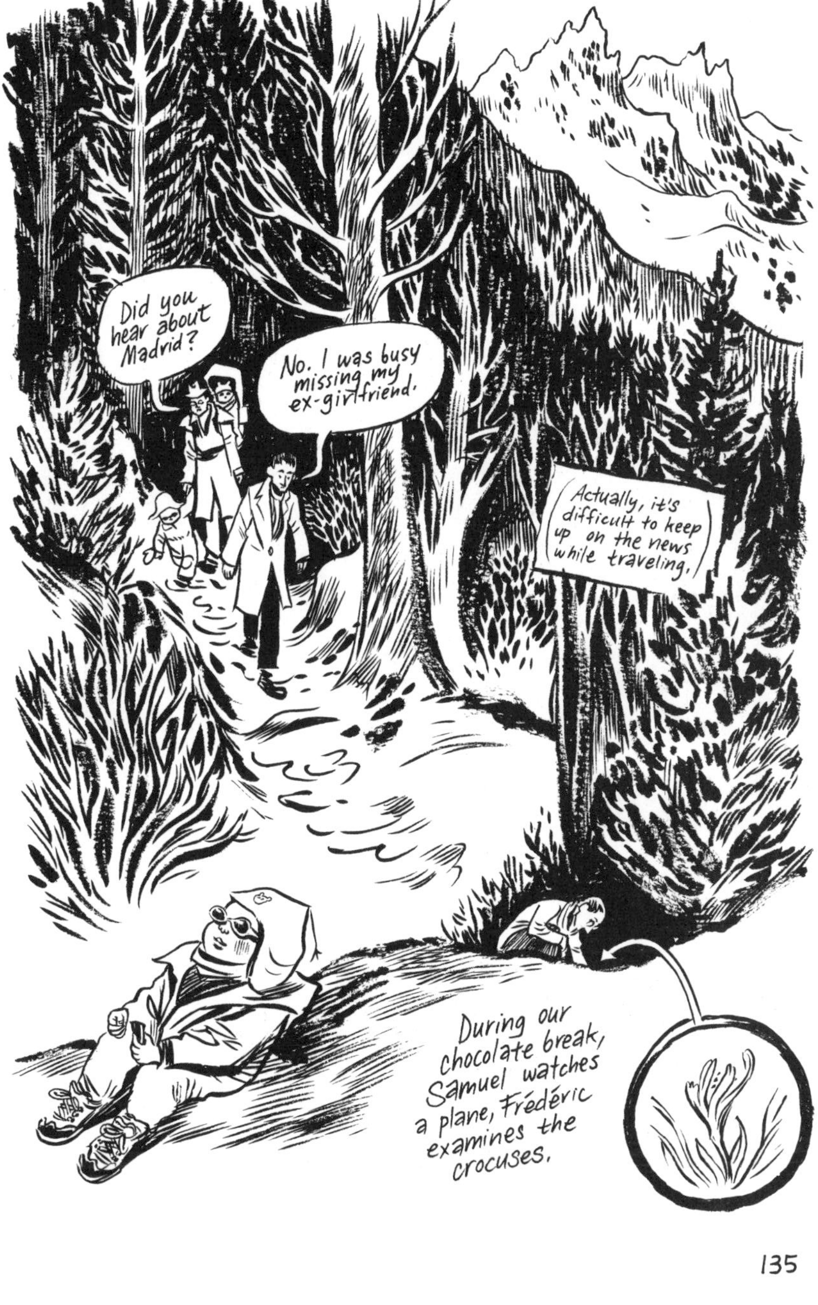

Did you hear about Madrid?
No. I was busy missing my ex-girlfriend.
(Actually, it's difficult to keep up on the news while traveling.)
During our chocolate break, Samuel watches a plane, Frédéric examines the crocuses.

15 AVRIL 04 There's been talk of skiing, but the mountains are shrouded in clouds. It rains all day, so we're trapped inside again, where there are but two distractions: (1) **CHILDREN...**

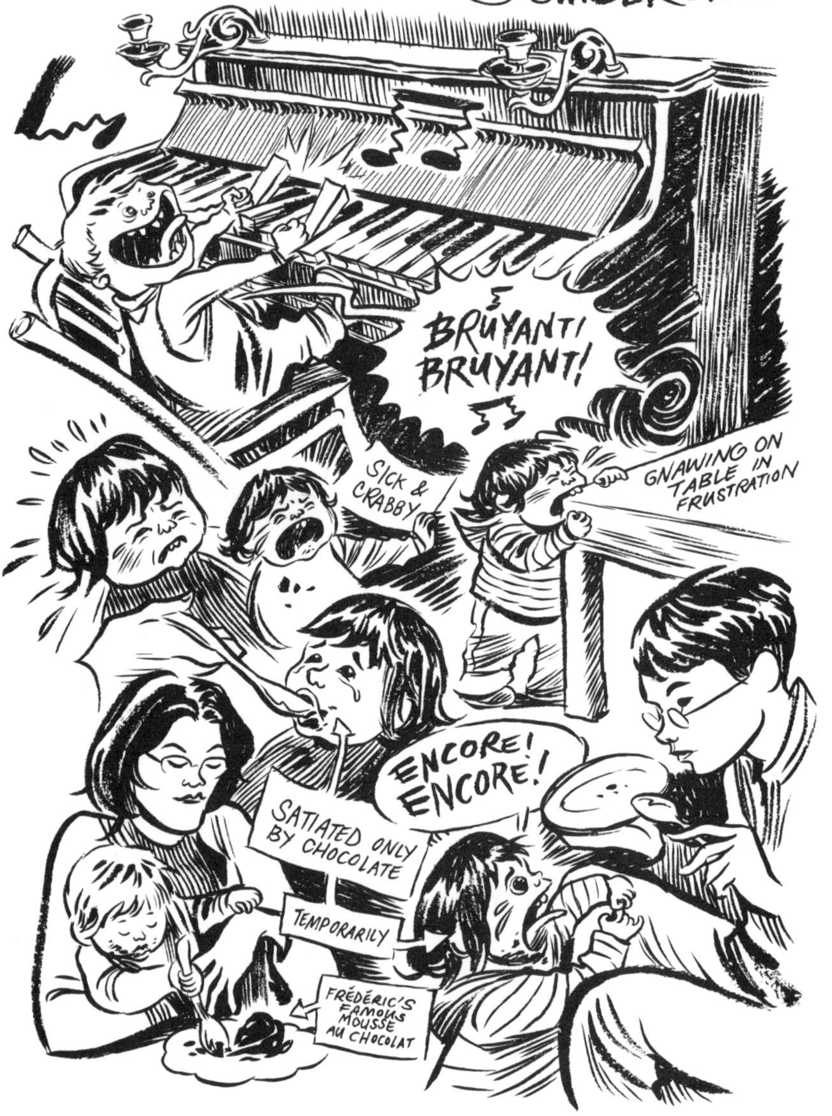
BRUYANT! BRUYANT!
SICK & CRABBY
GNAWING ON TABLE IN FRUSTRATION
ENCORE! ENCORE!
SATIATED ONLY BY CHOCOLATE
TEMPORARILY
FRÉDÉRIC'S FAMOUS MOUSSE AU CHOCOLAT

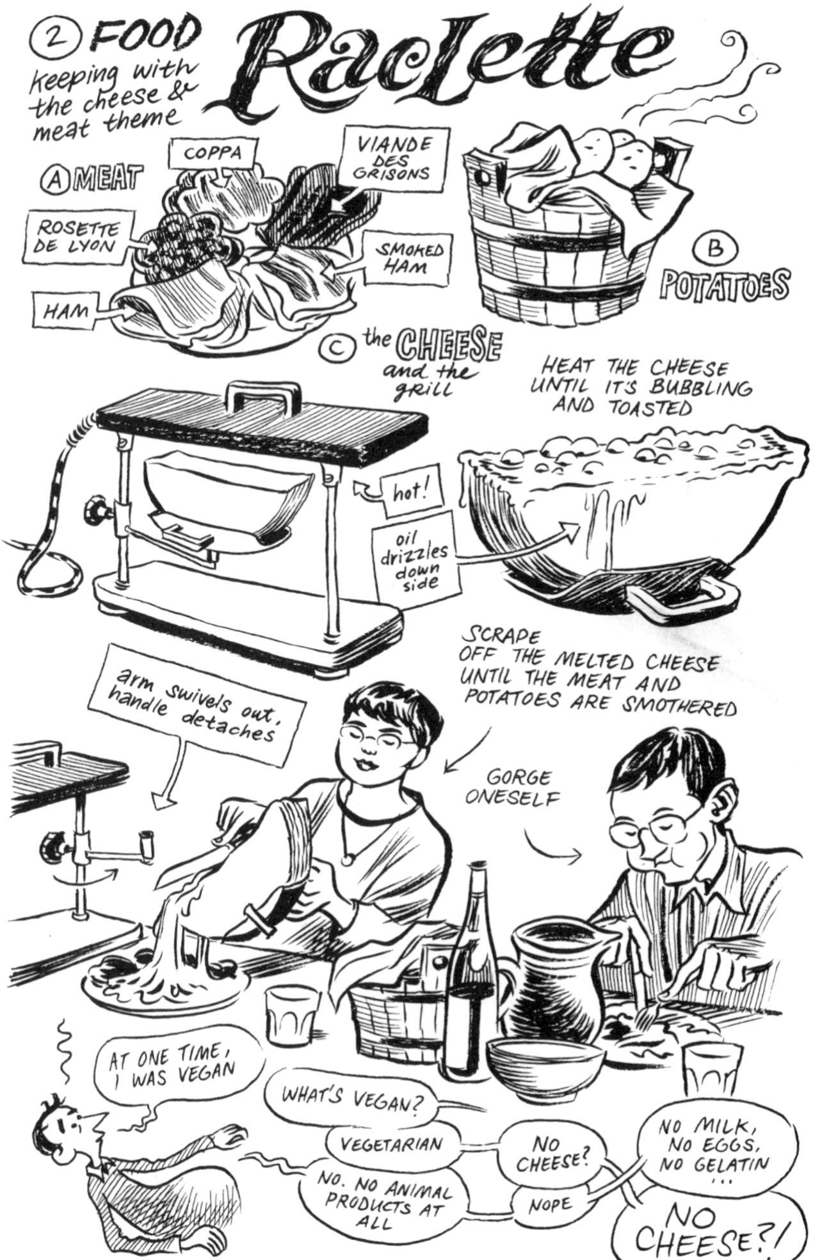

2 FOOD
Raclette
keeping with the cheese & meat theme
A MEAT
COPPA
VIANDE DES GRISONS
ROSETTE DE LYON
SMOKED HAM
HAM
B POTATOES
C the CHEESE and the grill
HEAT THE CHEESE UNTIL IT'S BUBBLING AND TOASTED
hot!
oil drizzles down side
SCRAPE OFF THE MELTED CHEESE UNTIL THE MEAT AND POTATOES ARE SMOTHERED
arm swivels out, handle detaches
GORGE ONESELF
AT ONE TIME, I WAS VEGAN
WHAT'S VEGAN?
VEGETARIAN
NO. NO ANIMAL PRODUCTS AT ALL
NO CHEESE?
NOPE
NO MILK, NO EGGS, NO GELATIN ...
NO CHEESE?!

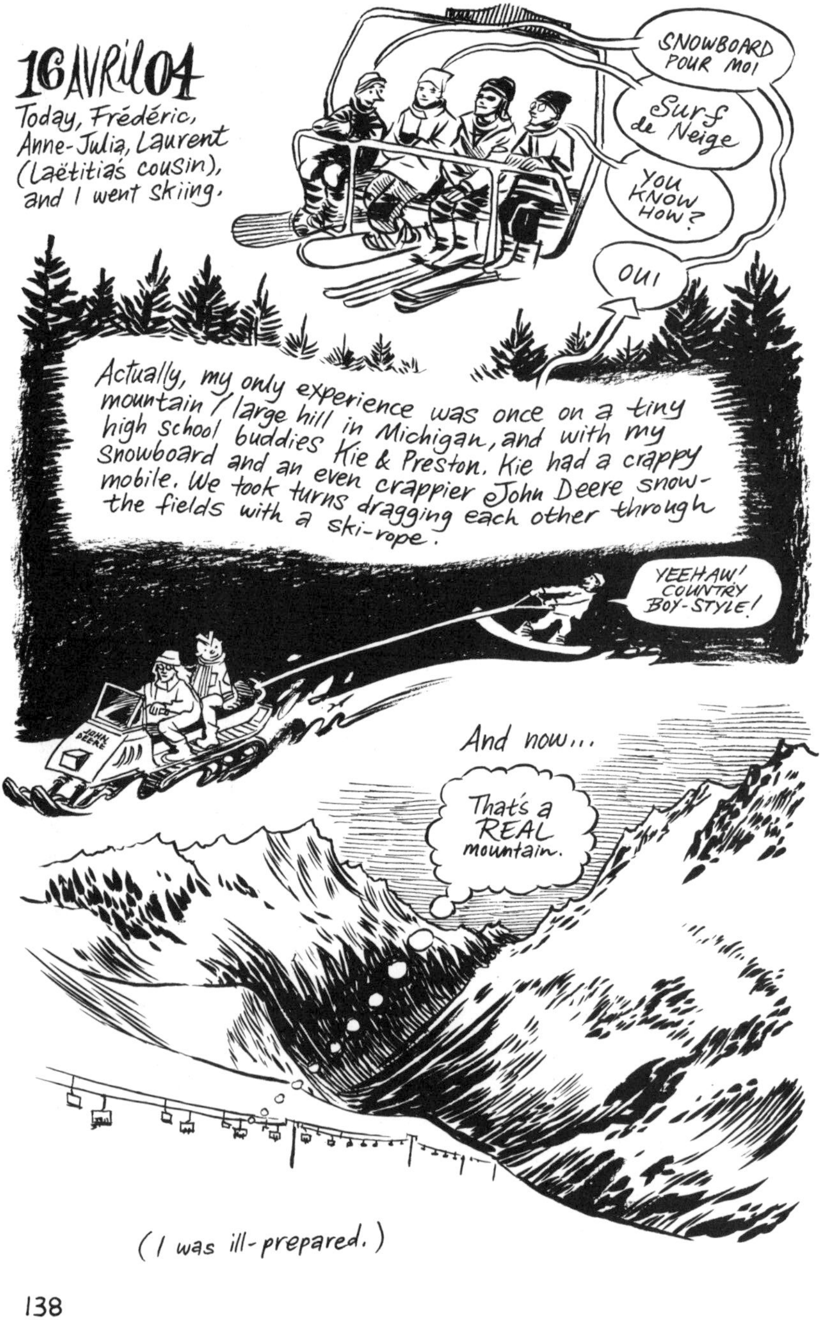
16 AVRIL 04
Today, Frédéric, Anne-Julia, Laurent (Laëtitia's cousin), and I went skiing.
SNOWBOARD POUR MOI
Surf de Neige
YOU KNOW HOW?
OUI
Actually, my only experience was once on a tiny
mountain / large hill in Michigan, and with my
high school buddies Kie & Preston. Kie had a crappy
snowboard and an even crappier John Deere snow-
mobile. We took turns dragging each other through
the fields with a ski-rope.
YEEHAW! COUNTRY BOY-STYLE!
JOHN DEERE
And now...
That's a REAL mountain.
(I was ill-prepared.)

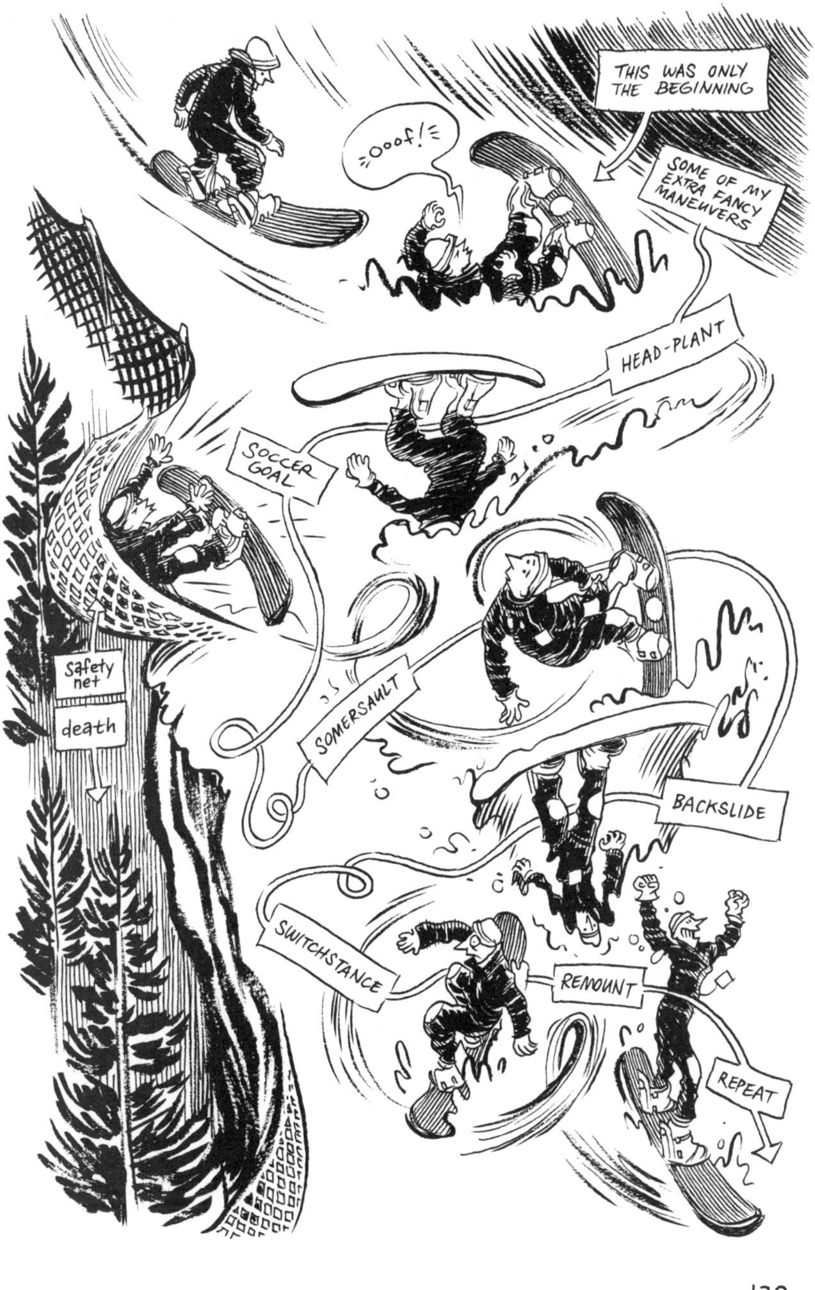

THIS WAS ONLY THE BEGINNING
OOOF!
SOME OF MY EXTRA FANCY MANEUVERS
HEAD-PLANT
SOCCER GOAL
SOMERSAULT
BACKSLIDE
SWITCHSTANCE
REMOUNT
REPEAT
Safety net
death

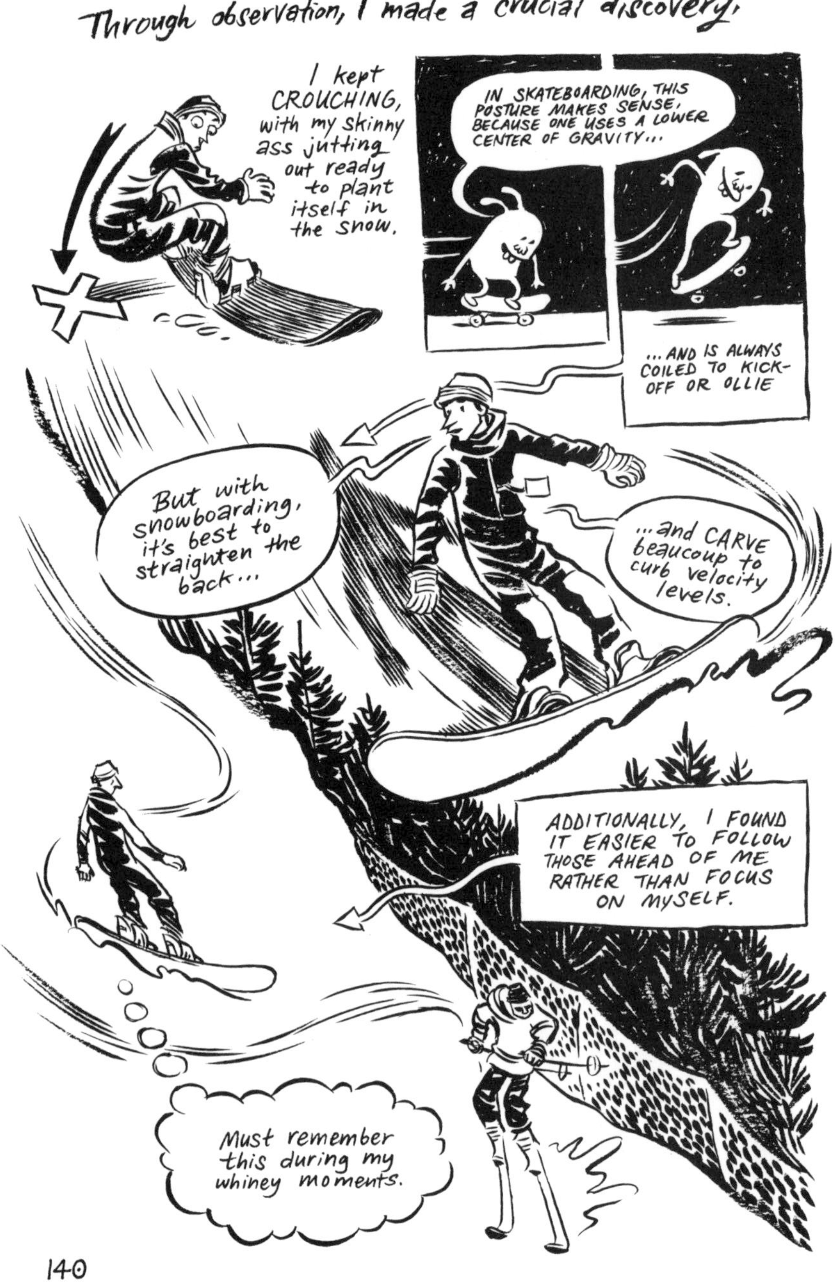

Through observation, I made a crucial discovery.
I kept CROUCHING, with my skinny ass jutting out ready to plant itself in the snow.
IN SKATEBOARDING, THIS POSTURE MAKES SENSE, BECAUSE ONE USES A LOWER CENTER OF GRAVITY...
...AND IS ALWAYS COILED TO KICK-OFF OR OLLIE
But with snowboarding, it's best to straighten the back...
...and CARVE beaucoup to curb velocity levels.
ADDITIONALLY, I FOUND IT EASIER TO FOLLOW THOSE AHEAD OF ME RATHER THAN FOCUS ON MYSELF.
Must remember this during my whiney moments.

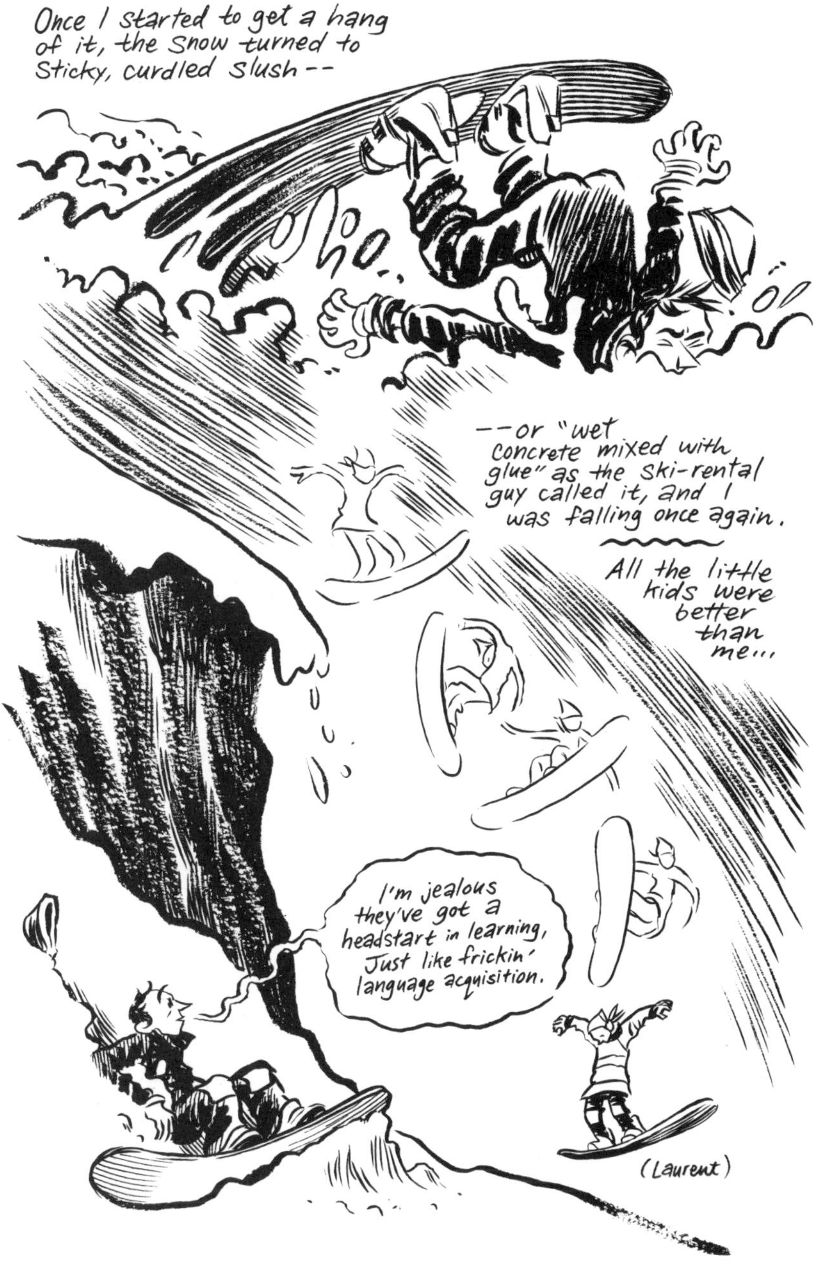
Once I started to get a hang of it, the snow turned to sticky, curdled slush--
--or "wet concrete mixed with glue" as the ski-rental guy called it, and I was falling once again.
All the little kids were better than me...
I'm jealous they've got a headstart in learning, just like frickin' language acquisition.
(Laurent)

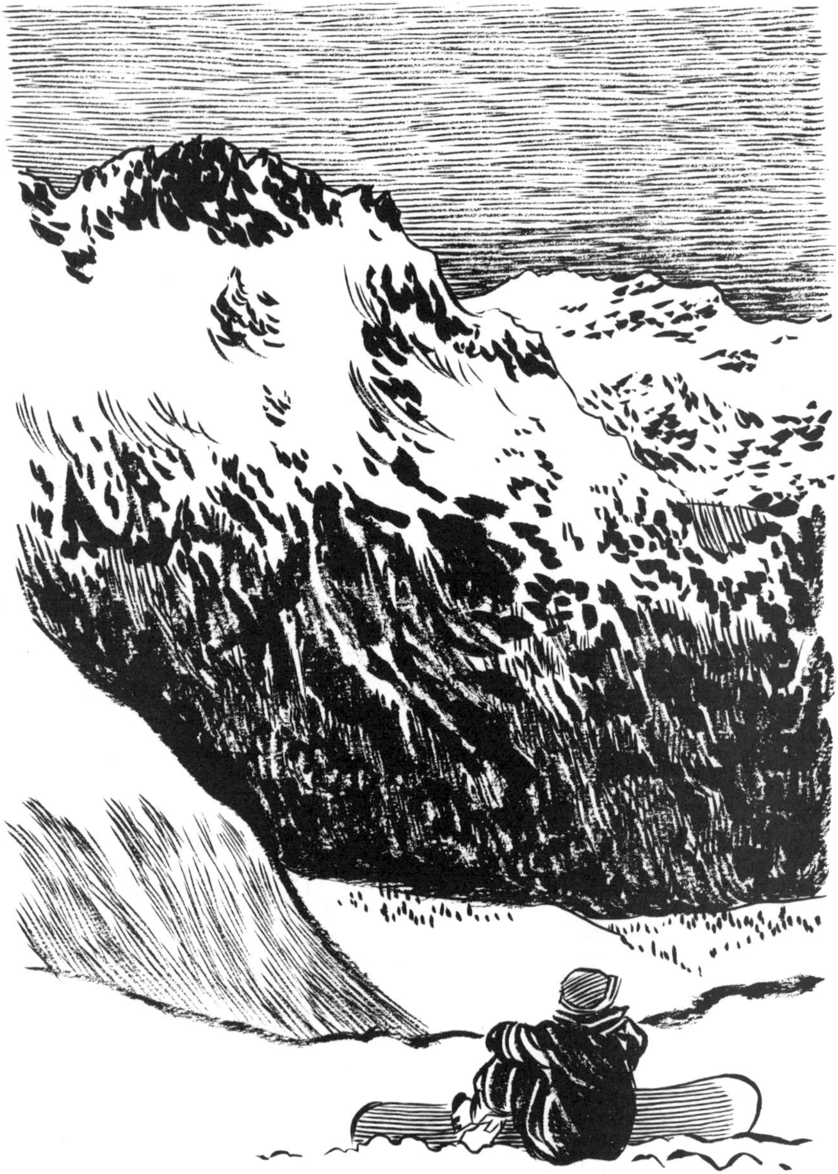

At least I didn't miss the view.

17 avril 04 Spent half of the day cleaning the chalet before packing up, wishing good-bye to Walter, Anne-Julia & Solveig, and driving to Laëtitia's parents' (Christian & Florence) for dinner and a night's rest.

18 avril 04 While Christian & Florence looked after the children, Laëtitia, Frédéric & I went walking in Annecy -- through the Sunday market...

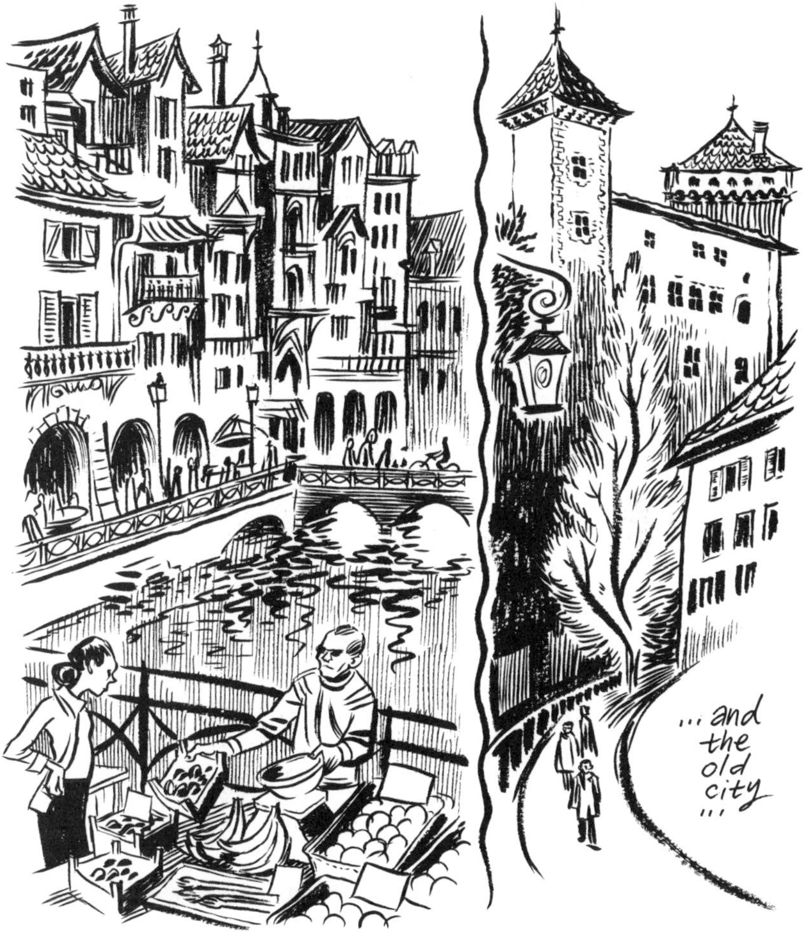

...and the old city...

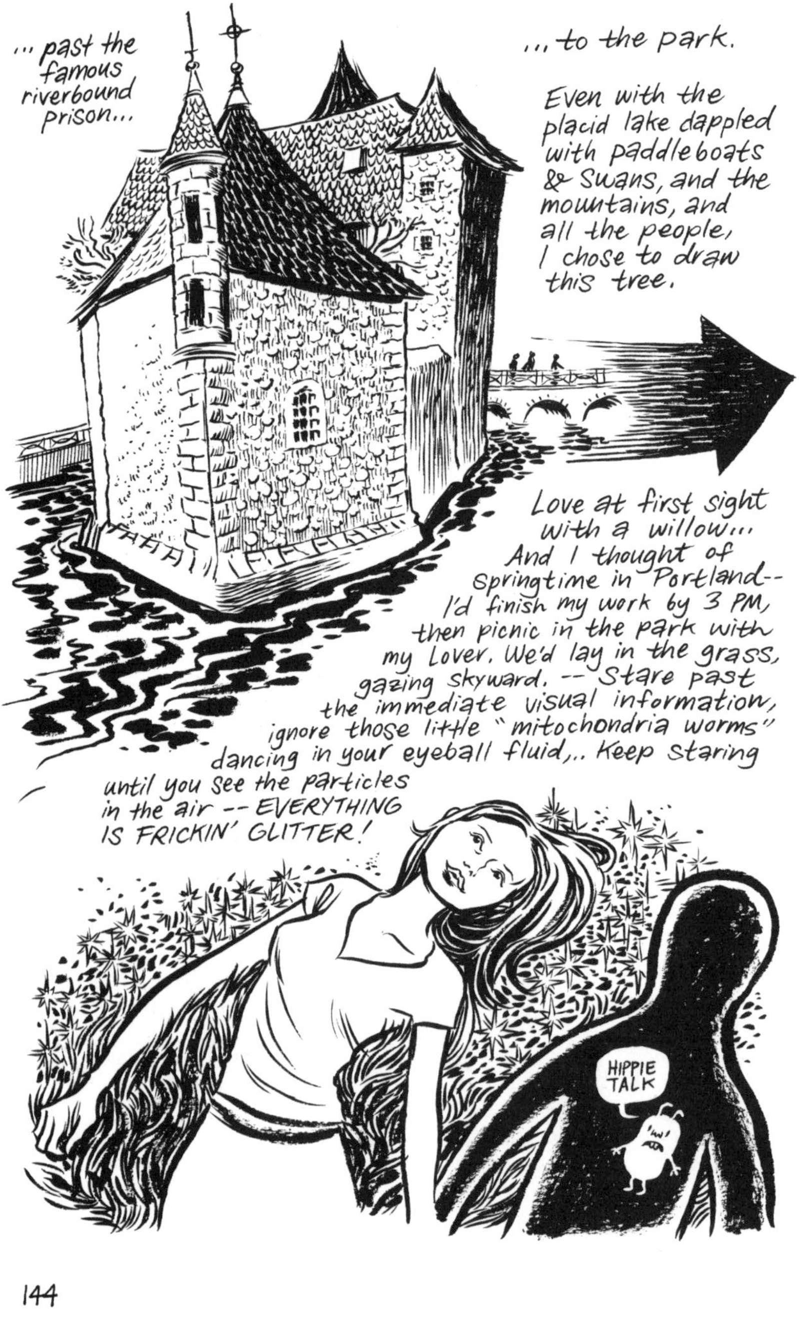
... past the famous riverbound prison...
... to the park.
Even with the placid lake dappled with paddleboats & swans, and the mountains, and all the people, I chose to draw this tree.
Love at first sight with a willow... And I thought of springtime in Portland-- I'd finish my work by 3 PM, then picnic in the park with my lover. We'd lay in the grass, gazing skyward. -- Stare past the immediate visual information, ignore those little "mitochondria worms" dancing in your eyeball fluid,.. Keep staring until you see the particles in the air -- EVERYTHING IS FRICKIN' GLITTER!
HIPPIE TALK

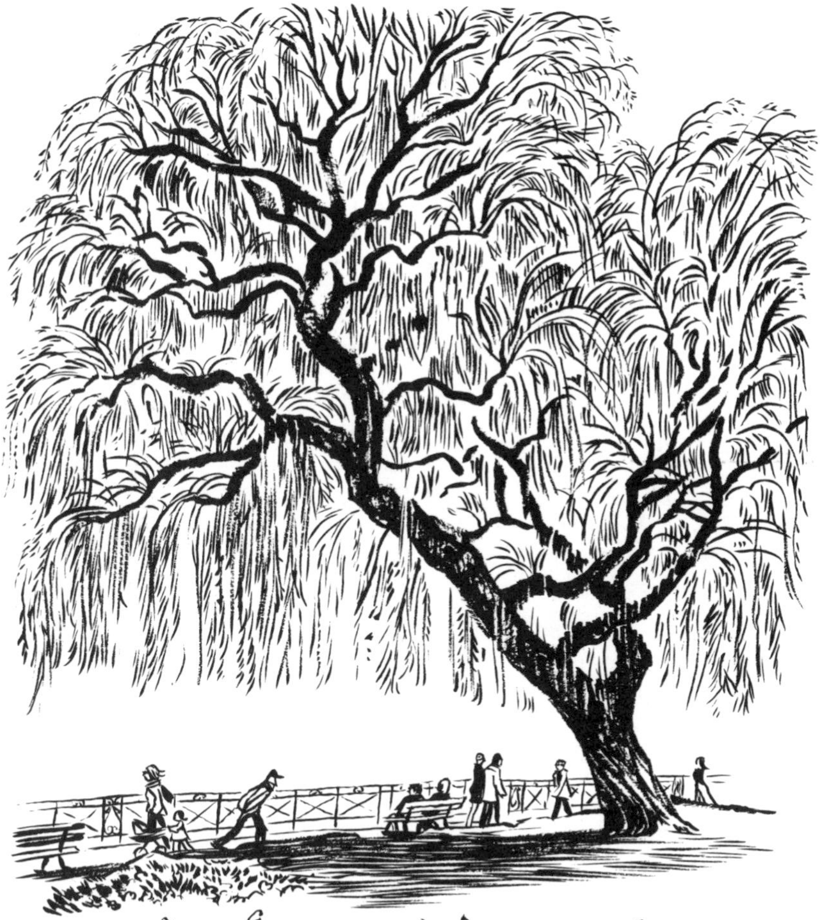

↖ I'm not sure if my willow is a "WEEPING WILLOW," because her melancholy is peaceful and inviting. The trees that really make me sad are the manicured platanes (the French bonzai) in the parking lot. They remind me of my gnarled hands.

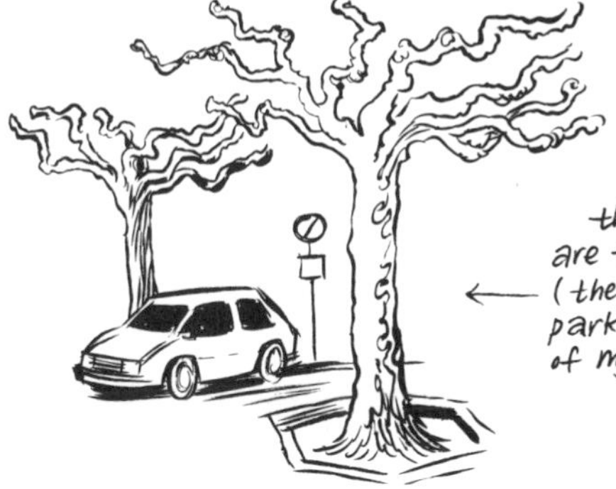

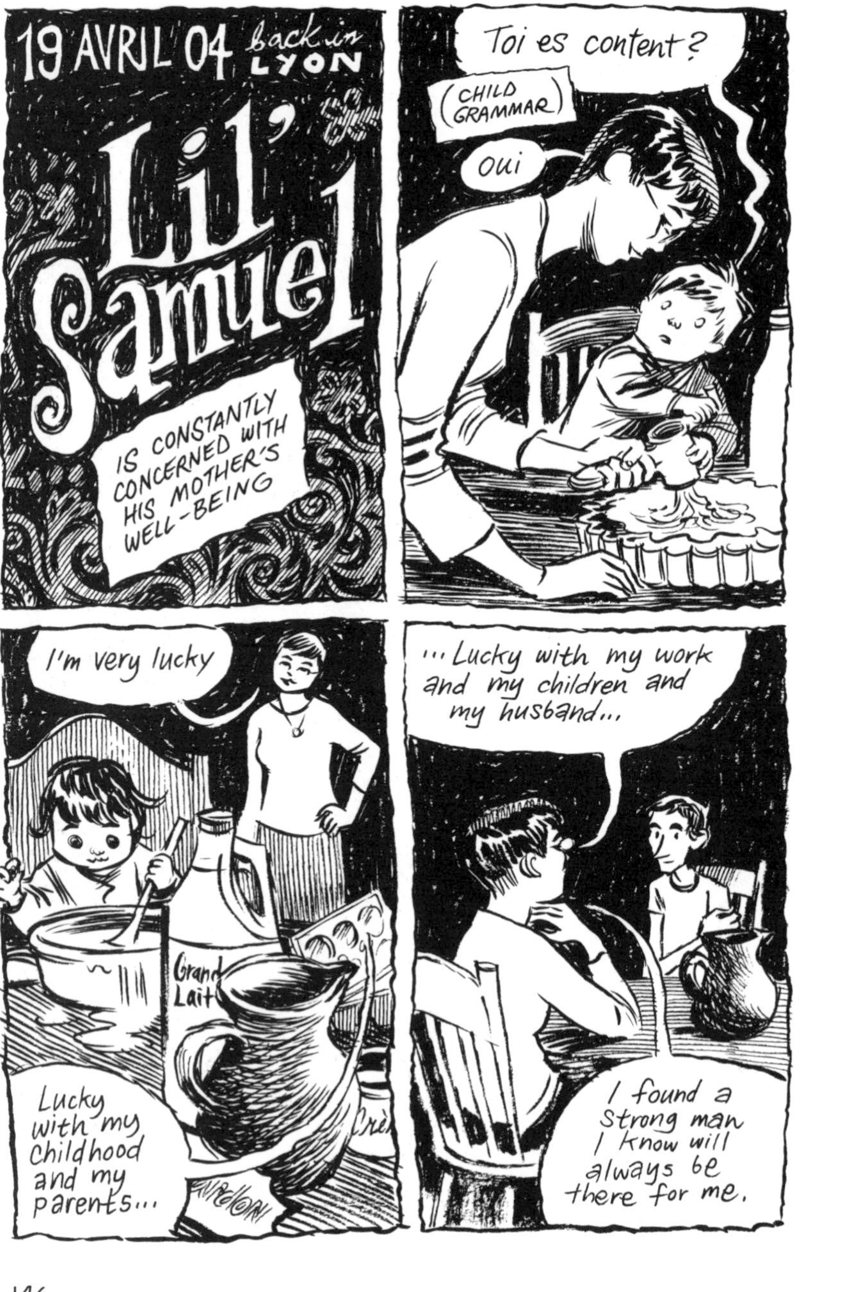
19 AVRIL 04 back in LYON
Lil' Samuel
IS CONSTANTLY CONCERNED WITH HIS MOTHER'S WELL-BEING
Toi es content?
(CHILD GRAMMAR)
Oui
I'm very lucky
Grand Lait
Lucky with my childhood and my parents...
...Lucky with my work and my children and my husband...
I found a strong man I know will always be there for me.

LAËTITIA SAYS SHE WANTED TO MARRY TO SHARE HER PLEASURE WITH FRIENDS - TO HAVE A CELEBRATION. SHE WANTED TO HAVE CHILDREN TO SHARE THE PLEASURE OF LIFE WITH THEM.

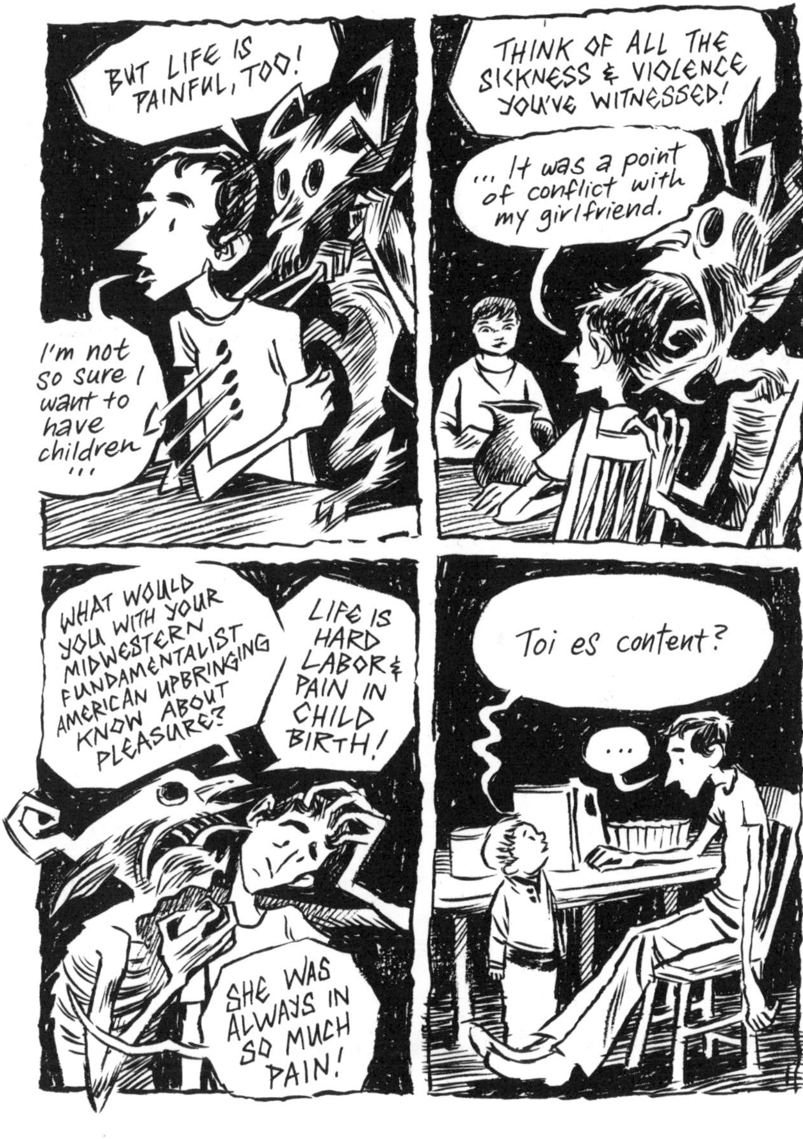
BUT LIFE IS PAINFUL, TOO!
I'm not so sure I want to have children ...
THINK OF ALL THE SICKNESS & VIOLENCE YOU'VE WITNESSED!
... It was a point of conflict with my girlfriend.
WHAT WOULD YOU WITH YOUR MIDWESTERN FUNDAMENTALIST AMERICAN UPBRINGING KNOW ABOUT PLEASURE?
LIFE IS HARD LABOR & PAIN IN CHILD BIRTH!
SHE WAS ALWAYS IN SO MUCH PAIN!
Toi es content?
...

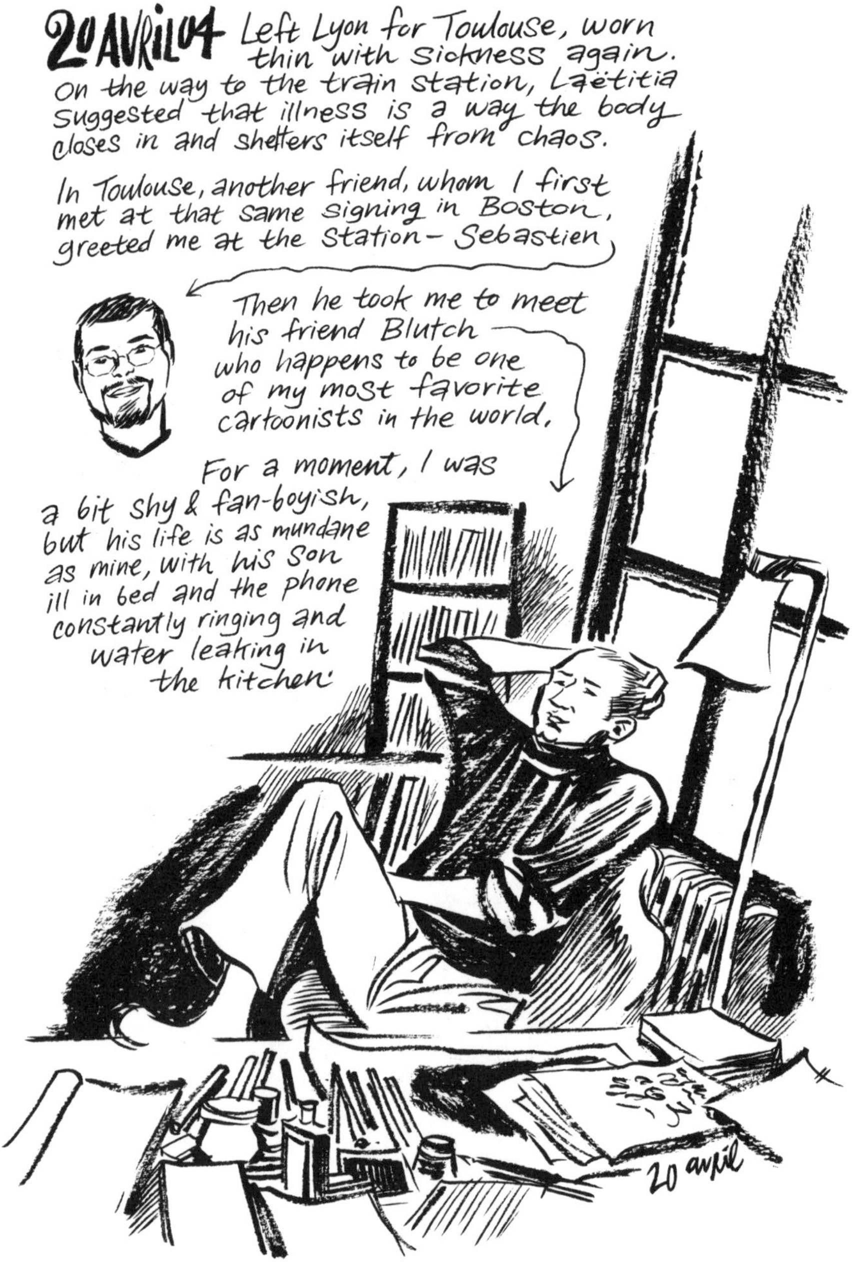
20 AVRIL 04 Left Lyon for Toulouse, worn thin with sickness again. On the way to the train station, Laëtitia suggested that illness is a way the body closes in and shelters itself from chaos.
In Toulouse, another friend, whom I first met at that same signing in Boston, greeted me at the station – Sebastien
Then he took me to meet his friend Blutch who happens to be one of my most favorite cartoonists in the world.
For a moment, I was a bit shy & fan-boyish, but his life is as mundane as mine, with his son ill in bed and the phone constantly ringing and water leaking in the kitchen.
20 avril

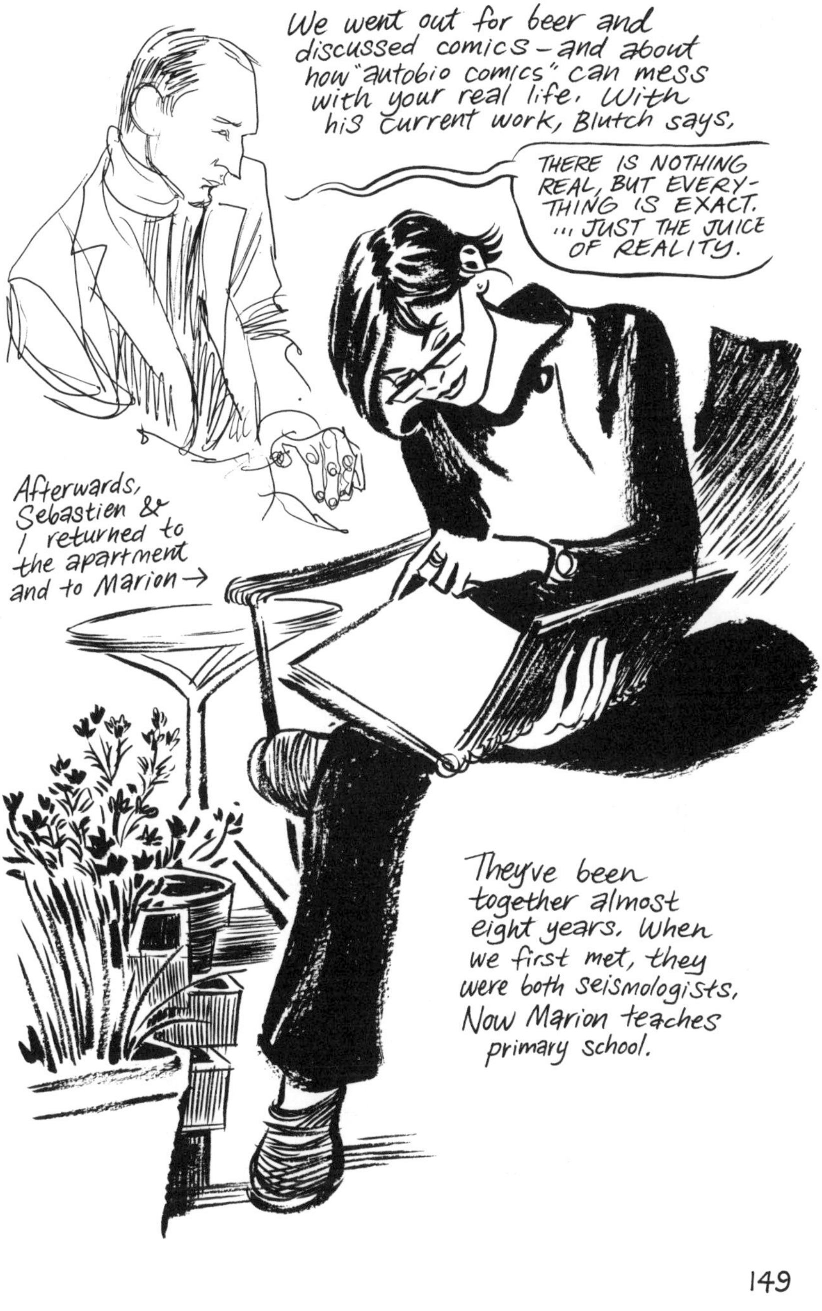

We went out for beer and discussed comics - and about how "autobio comics" can mess with your real life. With his current work, Blutch says,
THERE IS NOTHING REAL, BUT EVERYTHING IS EXACT. ... JUST THE JUICE OF REALITY.
Afterwards, Sebastien & I returned to the apartment and to Marion →
They've been together almost eight years. When we first met, they were both seismologists. Now Marion teaches primary school.

21 avril 04 It's sunny in the south of France, and I've abandoned my neurosis for the day. — Shared breakfast with Sebastien & Marion, then they went to work, and I wandered the city — with no fear of getting lost, no fear of communication, little ambition to be productive drawing, little concern for girls, an infatuation with all the people filing past, and a gigantic love for my ex-lover with no delusions about being back together.

21 avril 04

21 avril 04

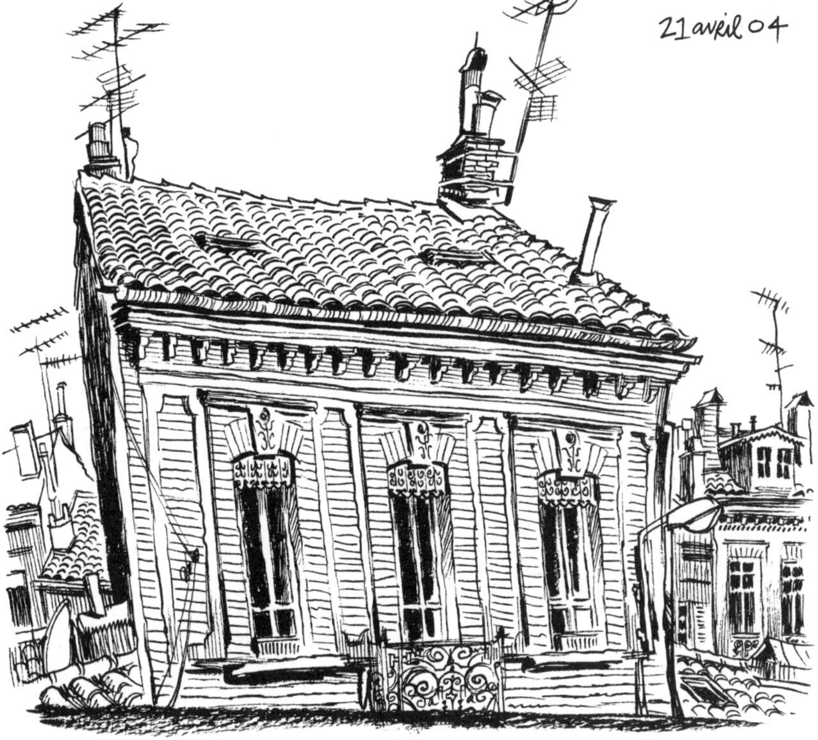

My hair was getting floofy, so I dropped into the first COIFFURE SHOP I spotted -- and since my language skills were lacking, I described my cut with a drawing.

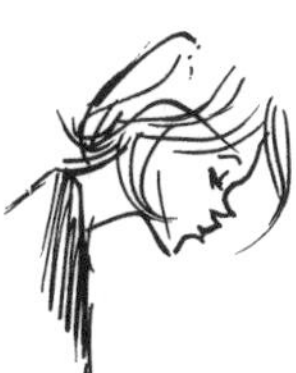

It was a very girly place, quite a contrast to my last three cuts:

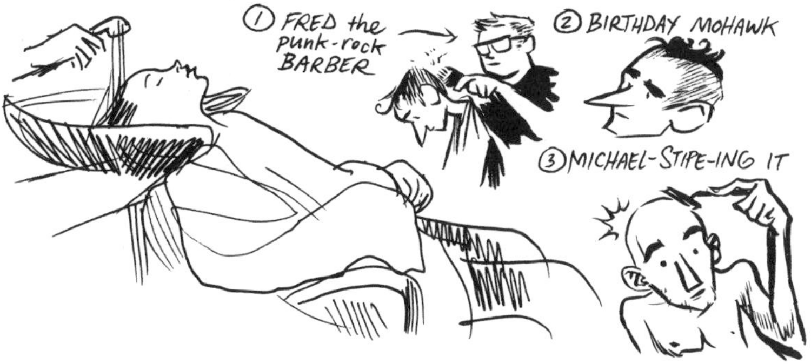

① FRED the punk-rock BARBER
② BIRTHDAY MOHAWK
③ MICHAEL-STIPE-ING IT

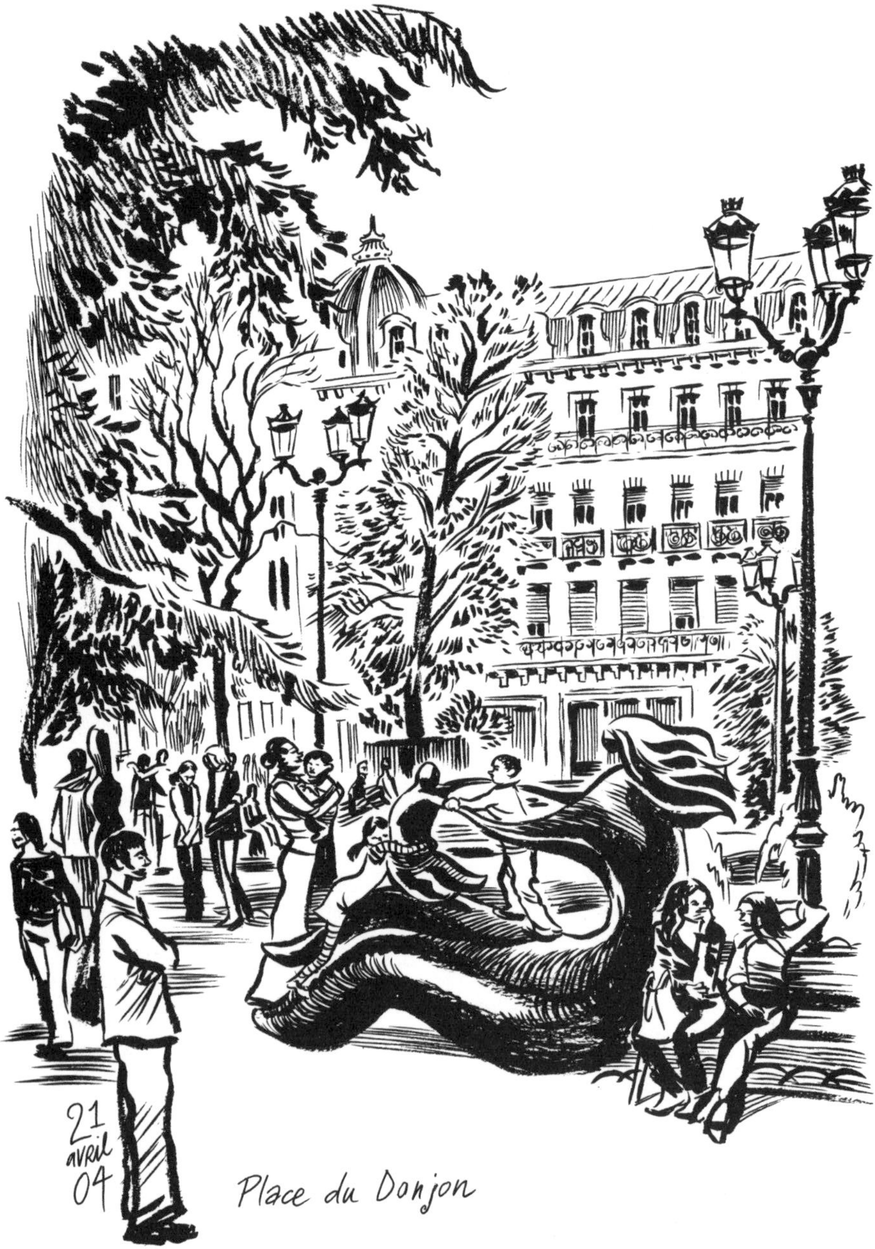

21 avril 04

Place du Donjon

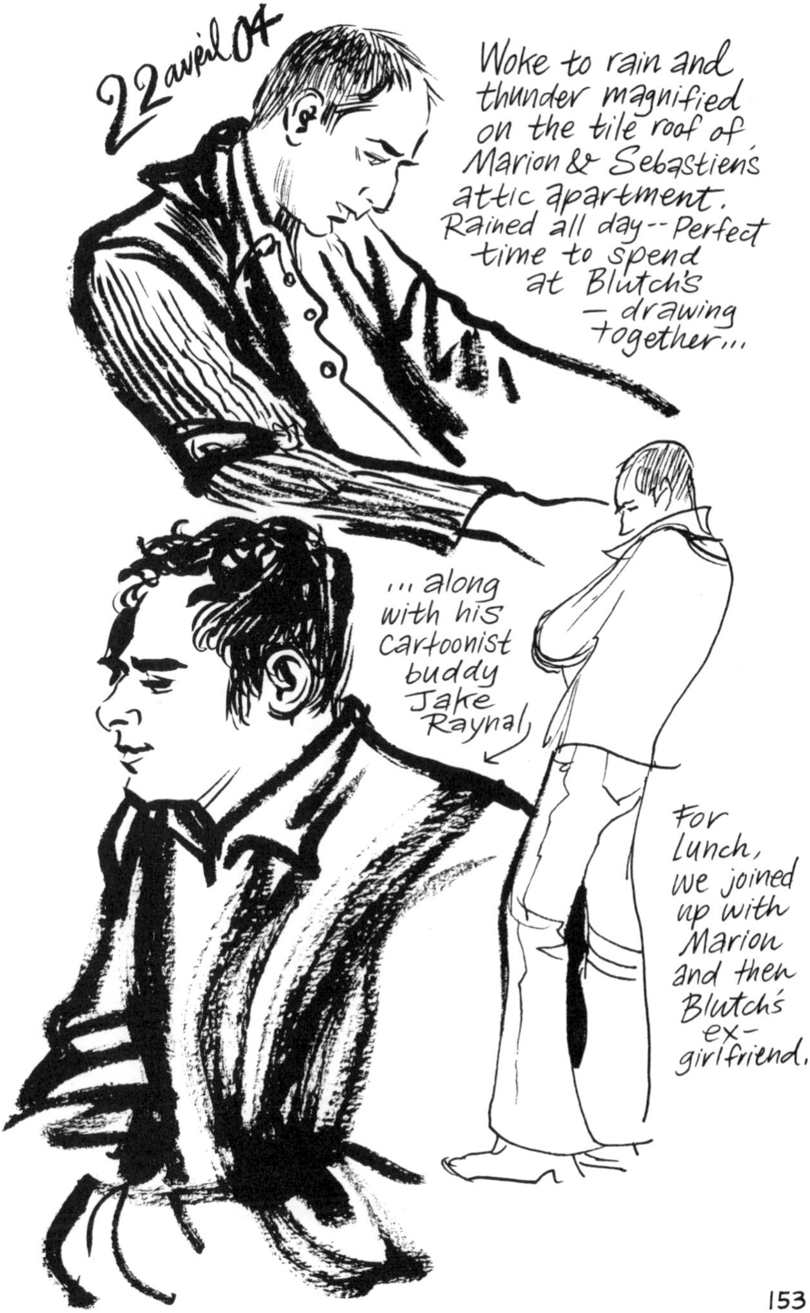
22 avril 04
Woke to rain and thunder magnified on the tile roof of Marion & Sebastien's attic apartment. Rained all day--Perfect time to spend at Blutch's — drawing together...
...along with his cartoonist buddy Jake Raynal
For lunch, we joined up with Marion and then Blutch's ex-girlfriend.

She was instantly recognizable from his drawings, and I said as much, before realizing it might be inappropriate. But it was overwhelming how familiar every nuance of her movement was through my knowledge of Blutch's work.

After she left, I asked him if she was his muse. Of course. She still is. We debated if one can ever abandon their muse, even after the end of a relationship.

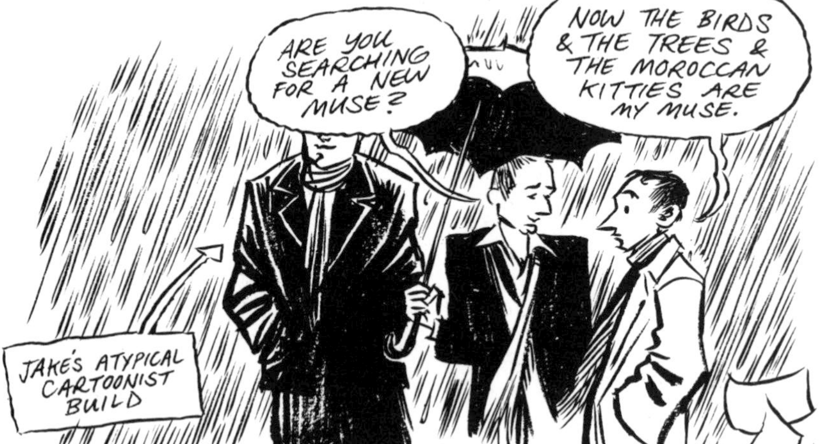
ARE YOU SEARCHING FOR A NEW MUSE?
NOW THE BIRDS & THE TREES & THE MOROCCAN KITTIES ARE MY MUSE.
JAKE'S ATYPICAL CARTOONIST BUILD

Back at his place, I perused hundreds of Blutch's drawings of his ex -- All beautiful, all unpublished --

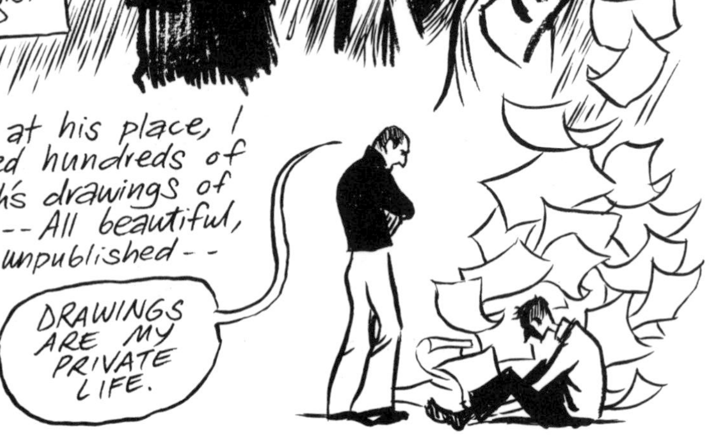
DRAWINGS ARE MY PRIVATE LIFE.

At one point, he drew 126 drawings consecutively while she was reading, most in exactly the same pose.

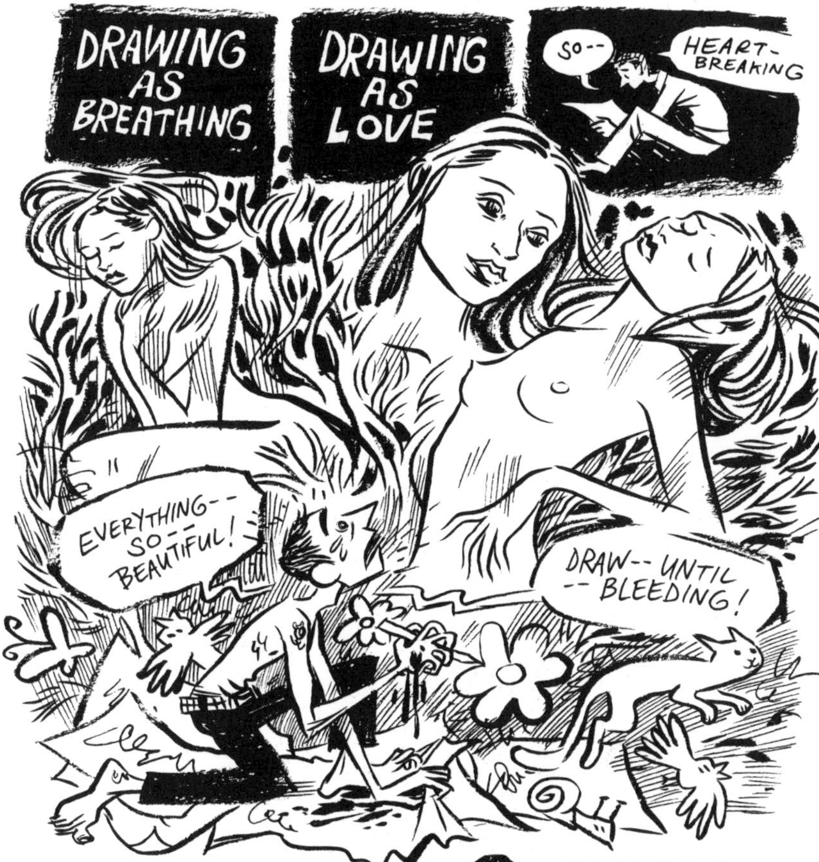
DRAWING AS BREATHING
DRAWING AS LOVE
SO--
HEART-BREAKING
EVERYTHING-- SO-- BEAUTIFUL!
DRAW-- UNTIL -- BLEEDING!

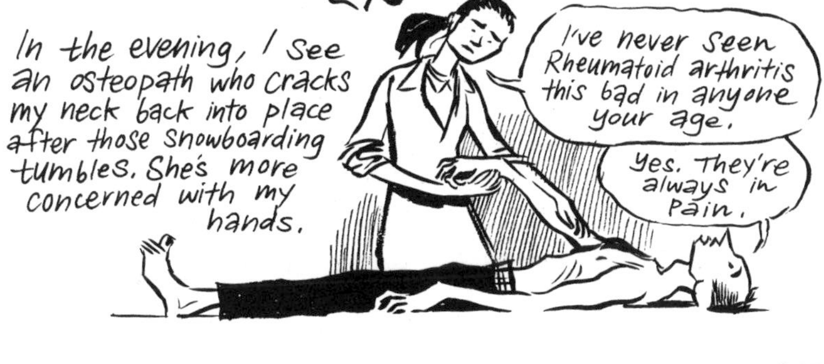
In the evening, I see an osteopath who cracks my neck back into place after those snowboarding tumbles. She's more concerned with my hands.
I've never seen Rheumatoid arthritis this bad in anyone your age.
Yes. They're always in pain.

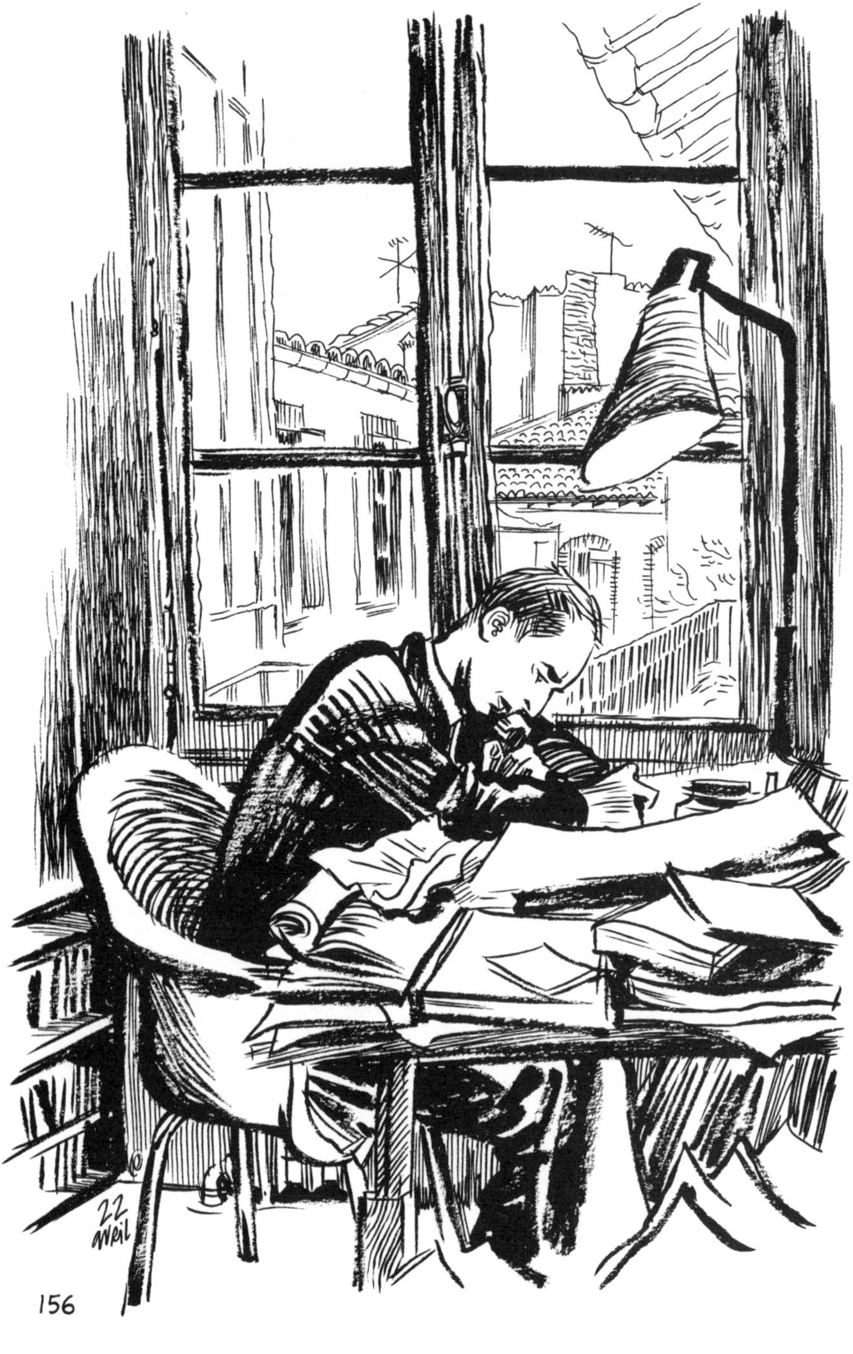
22
avril

23 AVRIL 94 The day begins with an interview for local Toulouse television.

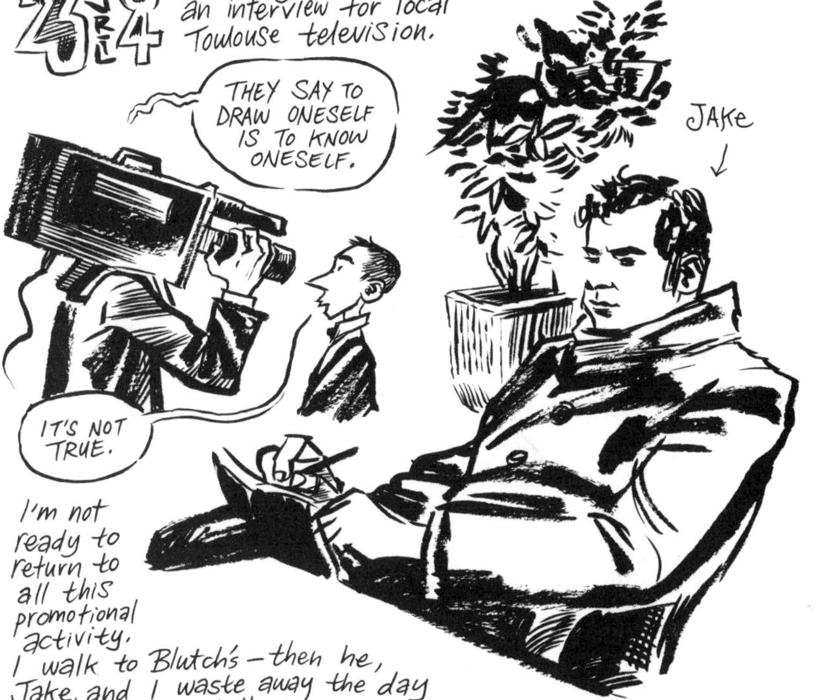
THEY SAY TO DRAW ONESELF IS TO KNOW ONESELF.
IT'S NOT TRUE.
JAKE

I'm not ready to return to all this promotional activity.

I walk to Blutch's – then he, Jake, and I waste away the day looking at books, talking movies, eating, drinking...

Blutch shows me documentary footage of Renoir late in life when his hands were entirely deformed by arthritis and bound in bandages. His son would place the brush in his hand.

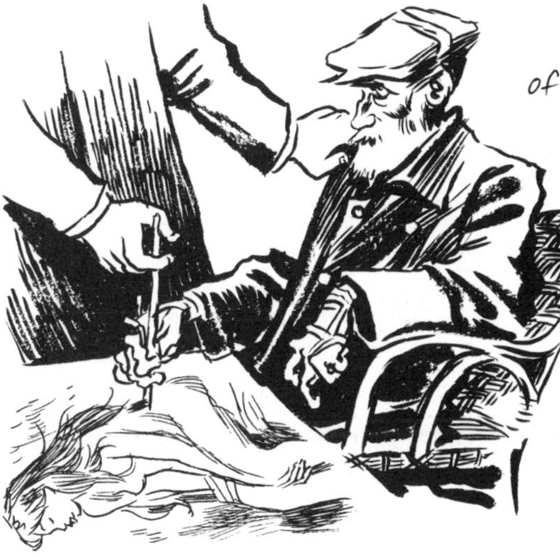

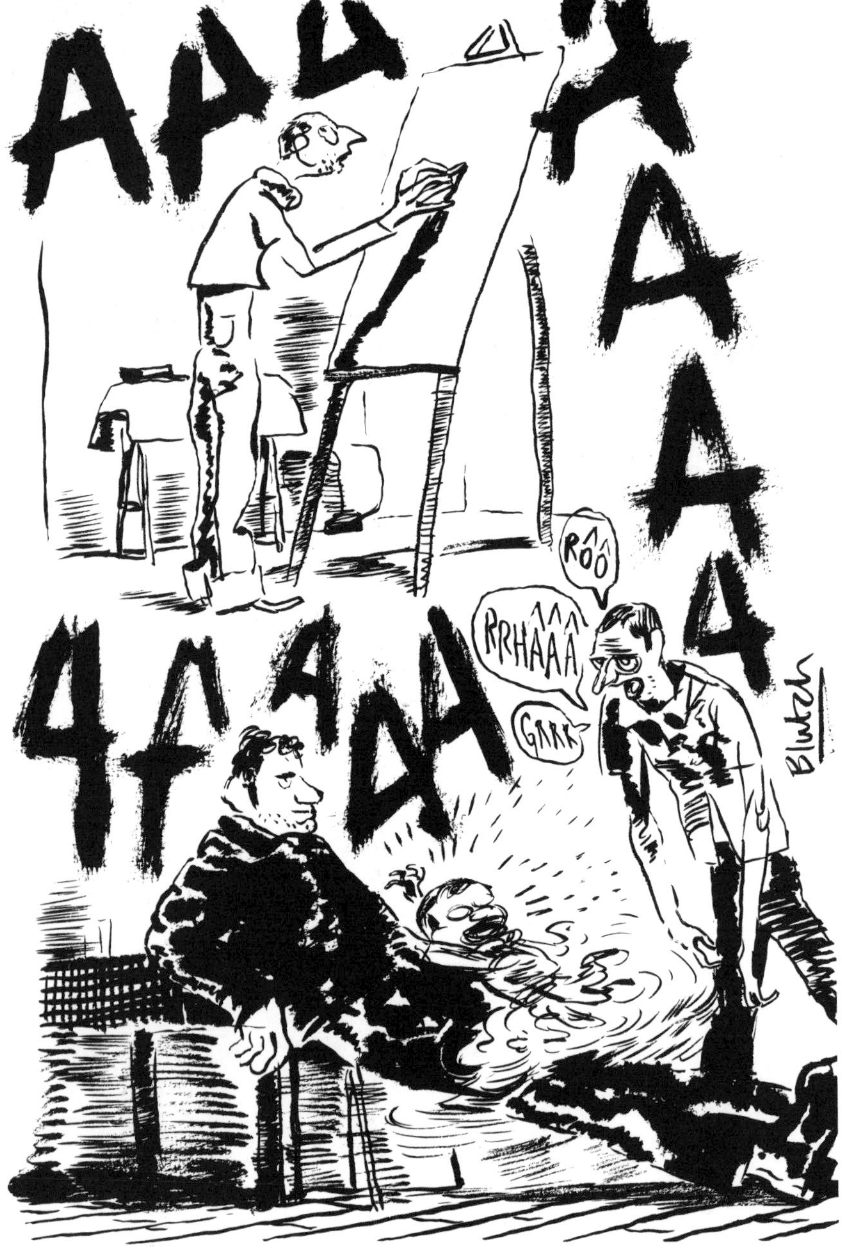

RÔÔ
RRHAÂÂÂ
GARR
Blutch

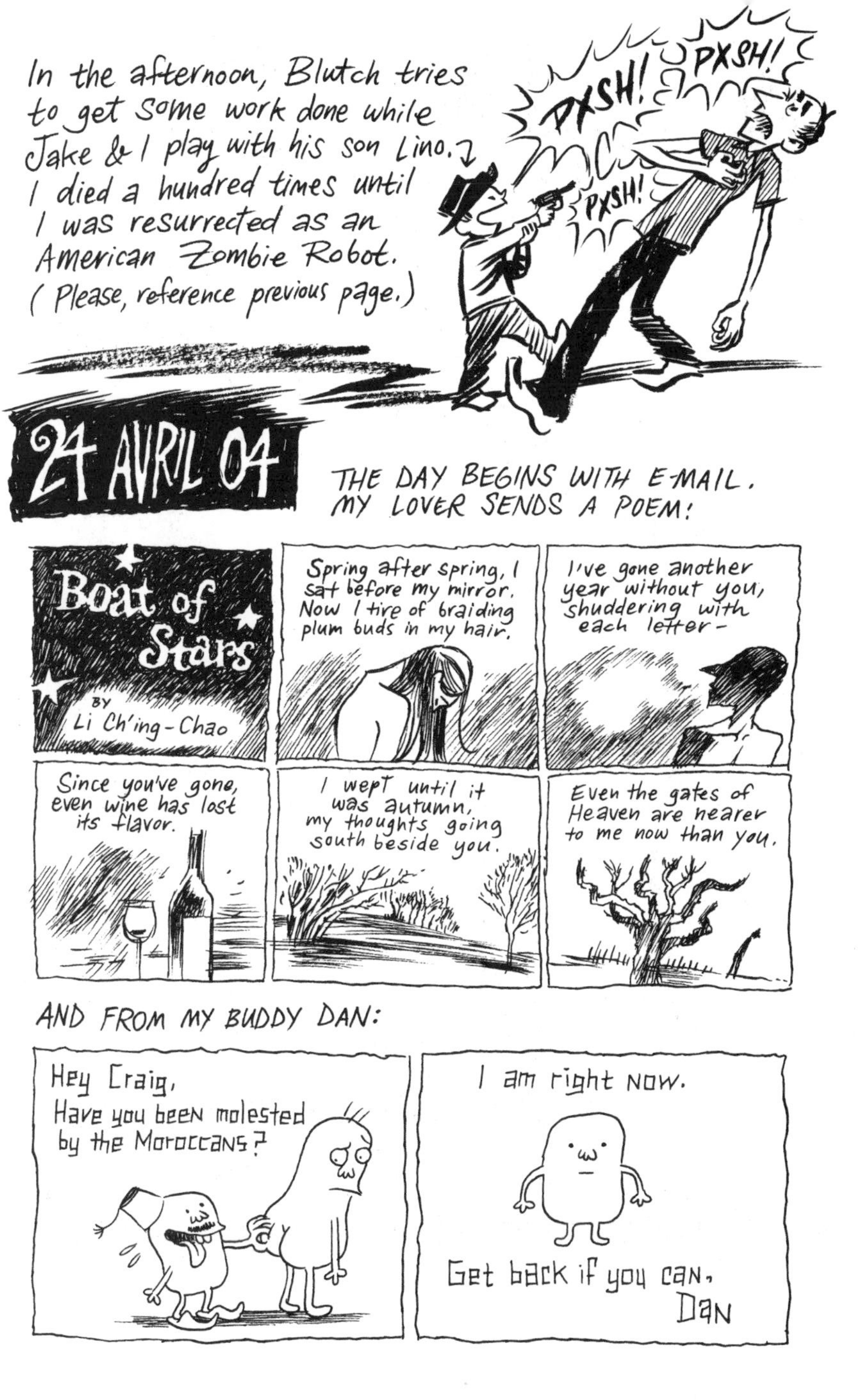
In the afternoon, Blutch tries to get some work done while Jake & I play with his son Lino. I died a hundred times until I was resurrected as an American Zombie Robot. (Please, reference previous page.)
PXSH!
PXSH!
PXSH!
24 AVRIL 04
THE DAY BEGINS WITH E-MAIL. MY LOVER SENDS A POEM:
Boat of Stars
BY Li Ch'ing-Chao
Spring after spring, I sat before my mirror. Now I tire of braiding plum buds in my hair.
I've gone another year without you, shuddering with each letter -
Since you've gone, even wine has lost its flavor.
I wept until it was autumn, my thoughts going south beside you.
Even the gates of Heaven are nearer to me now than you.
AND FROM MY BUDDY DAN:
Hey Craig,
Have you been molested by the Moroccans?
I am right now.
Get back if you can,
Dan

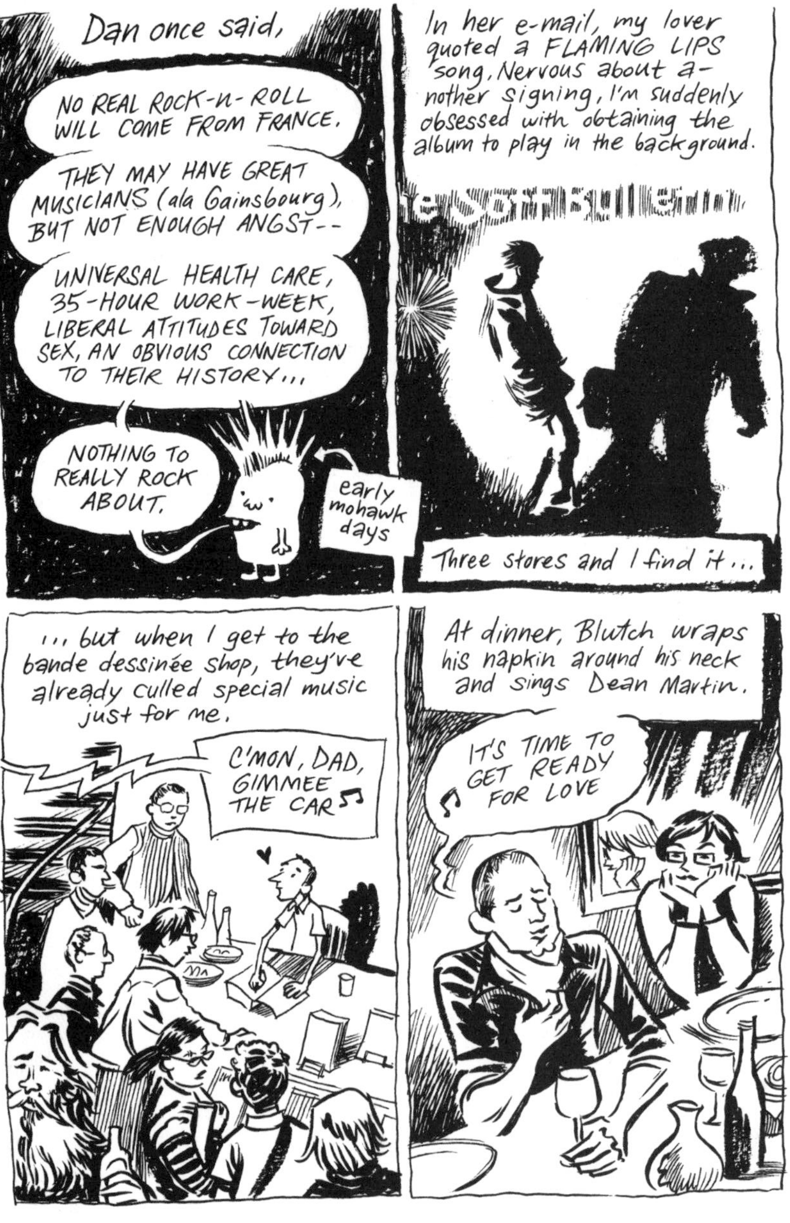
Dan once said,
NO REAL ROCK-N-ROLL WILL COME FROM FRANCE.
THEY MAY HAVE GREAT MUSICIANS (ala Gainsbourg), BUT NOT ENOUGH ANGST--
UNIVERSAL HEALTH CARE, 35-HOUR WORK-WEEK, LIBERAL ATTITUDES TOWARD SEX, AN OBVIOUS CONNECTION TO THEIR HISTORY...
NOTHING TO REALLY ROCK ABOUT.
early mohawk days
In her e-mail, my lover quoted a FLAMING LIPS song. Nervous about another signing, I'm suddenly obsessed with obtaining the album to play in the background.
Three stores and I find it...
...but when I get to the bande dessinée shop, they've already culled special music just for me.
C'MON, DAD, GIMMEE THE CAR
At dinner, Blutch wraps his napkin around his neck and sings Dean Martin.
IT'S TIME TO GET READY FOR LOVE

(Since you've gone, even wine has lost its flavor. | I am right now.)

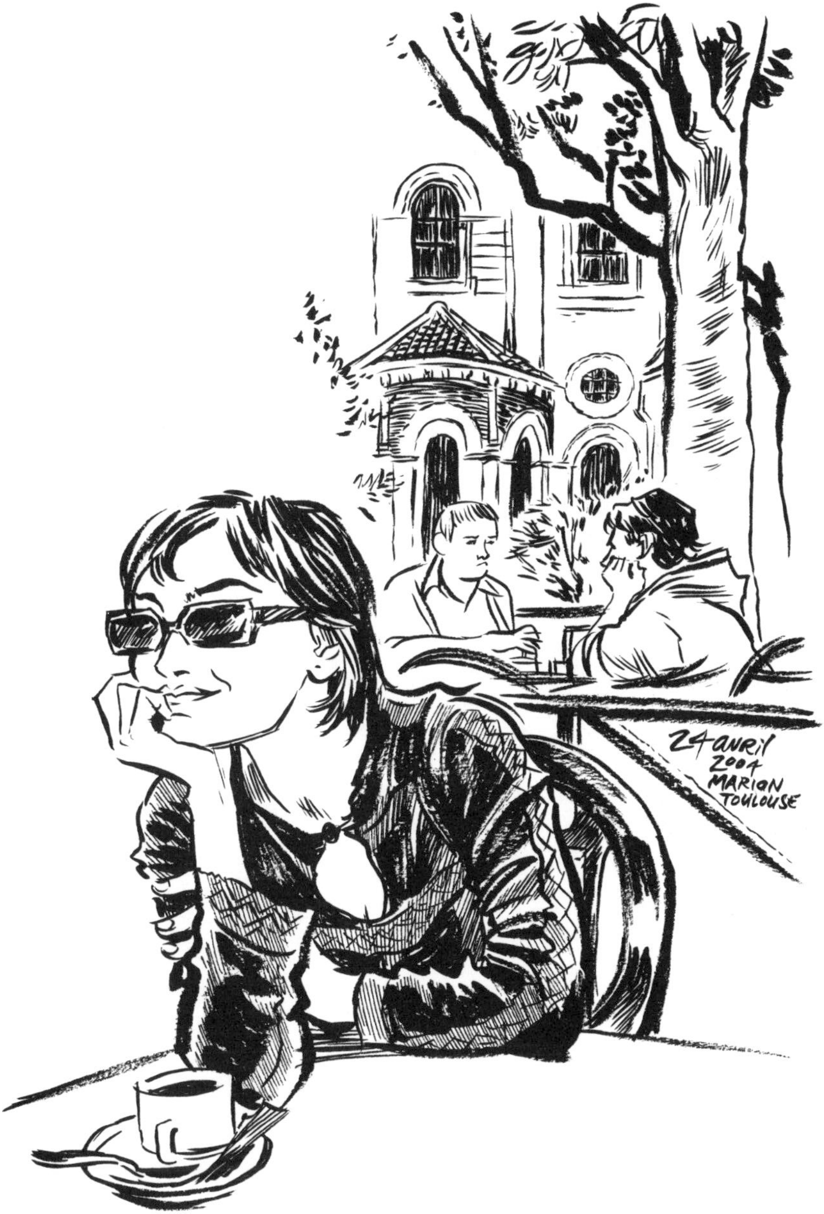
24 avril
2004
MARION
TOULOUSE

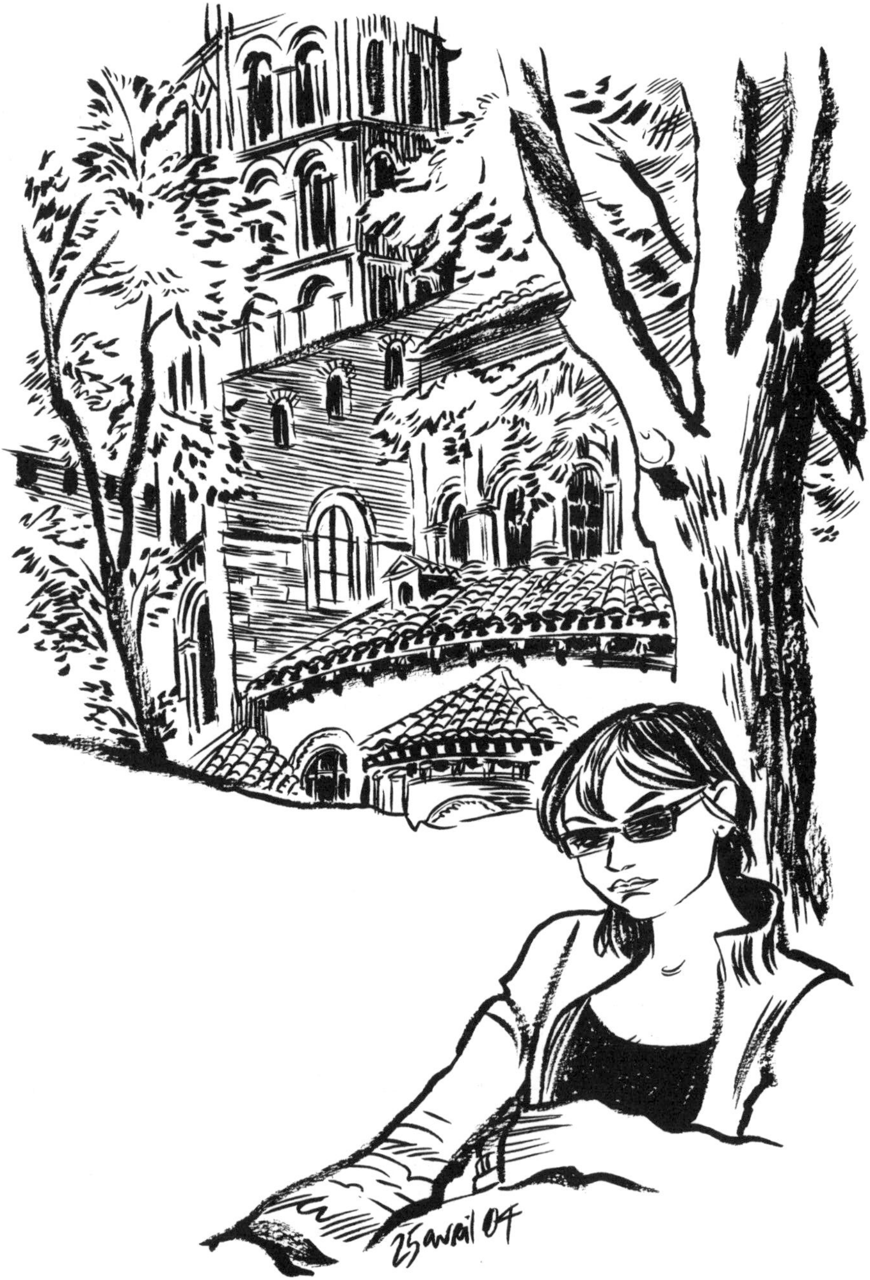
25 avril 04

25 AVRIL 04 The easy life in the South of France: Breakfast in the sun on the roof-top terrace, leisurely strolls, picnic along the river...

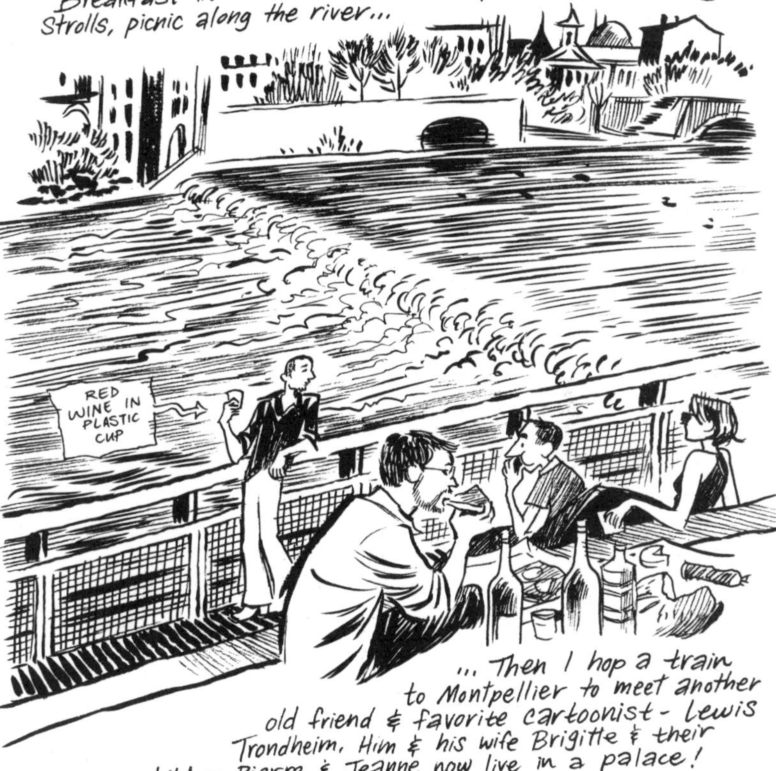
RED WINE IN PLASTIC CUP

... Then I hop a train to Montpellier to meet another old friend & favorite cartoonist - Lewis Trondheim. Him & his wife Brigitte & their children Pierre & Jeanne now live in a palace!

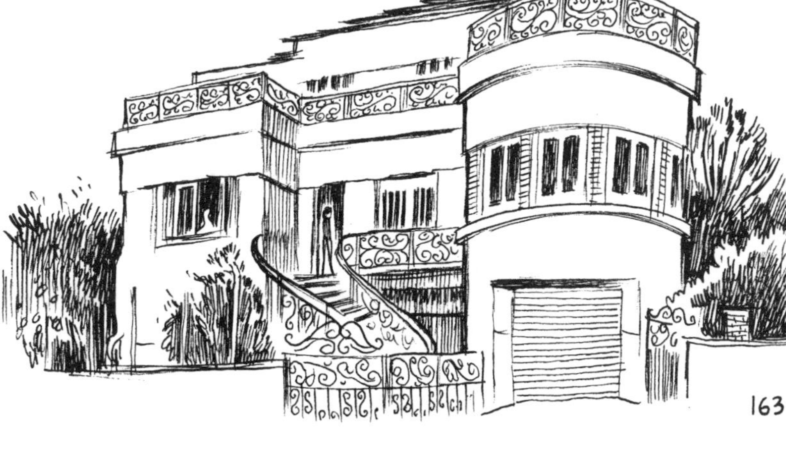

Chère Lewis

lettre écrite à Toulouse le dimanche 25 avril 04 par Blutch.
Nous t'envoyons donc cet américain épris de culture du vieux
[redacted] continent. Il arrive par le train et il en vient.

il vide les frigos

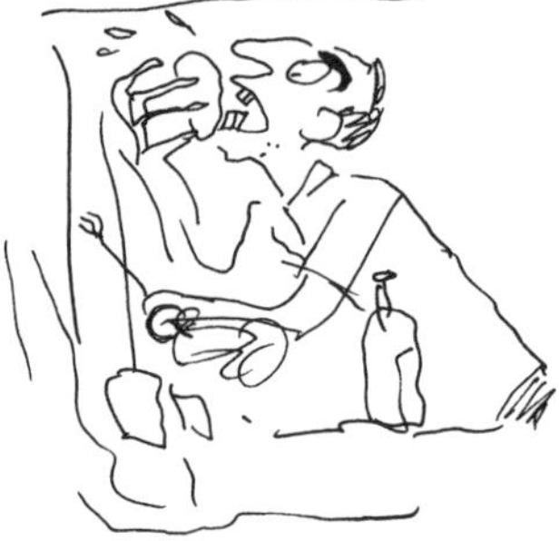

il excite nos enfants

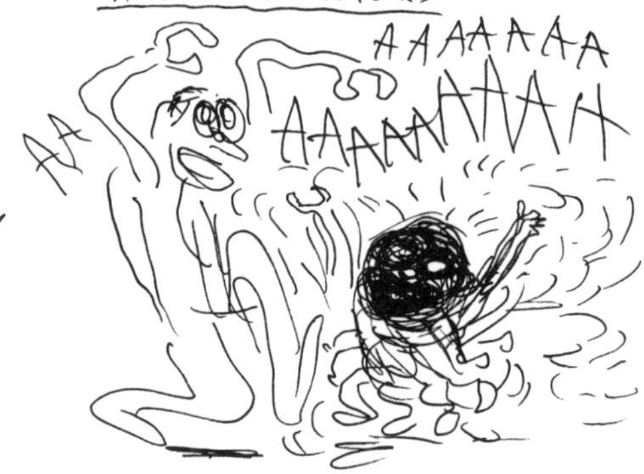
AAAAAA
AAAAAAAAA
AA

il courtise nos femmes

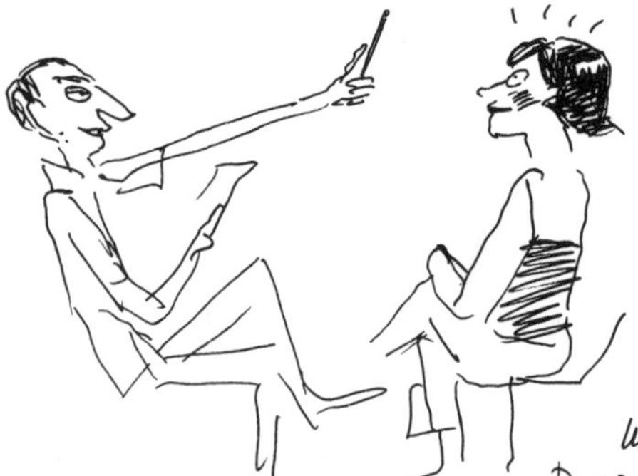

Je sais sûr
néanmoins que tu
lui feras bon accueil

Reçois ma bénédiction
Blutch —

26 avril 04 My first day with Lewis gave the impression that the European life is a charmed one. When I woke, he was plucking away at a ukulele in his studio, birdees accompanying, sun gushing in the window--The kids came home from school to share lunch with us (in this frickin' PALACE)--Then Lewis & I & his cartoonist friend Nicolas lounged at the beach--more sun, topless girls, gentle waves that preserve the pretty shells-- Followed by strolls through the beautiful streets of Montpellier, sipping drinks at a sidewalk cafe... Layer on more sun & leisure & wine & chocolate... oysters for dinner, and a whirlpool bath in my guest-room!

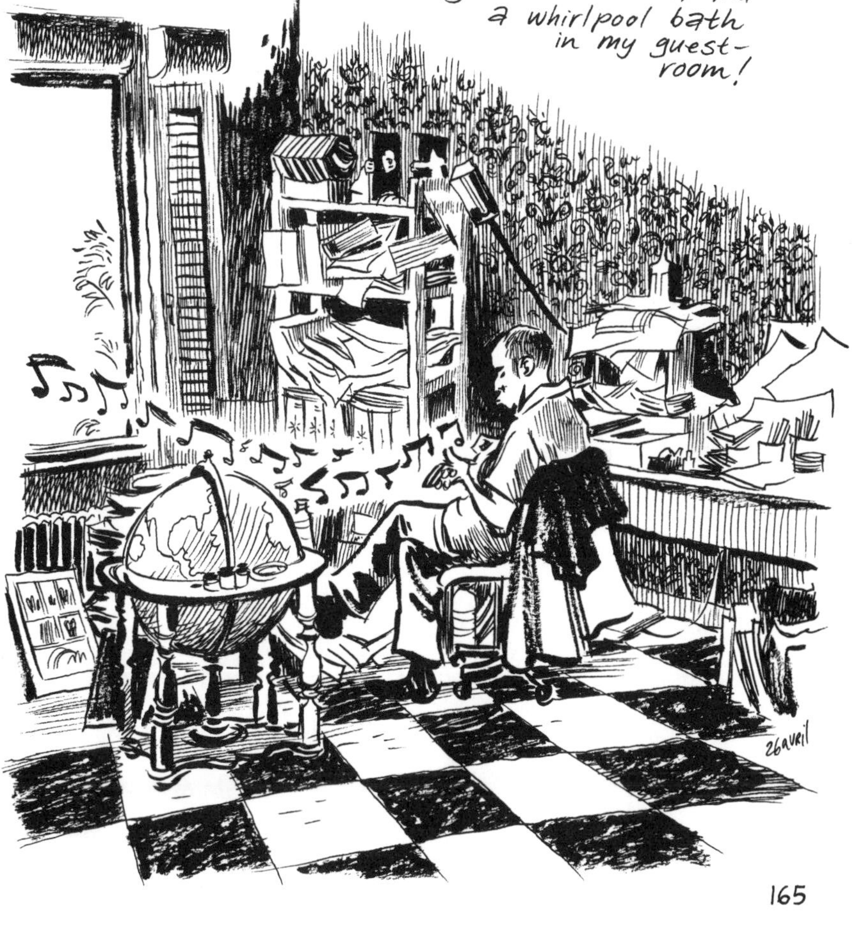
26 avril

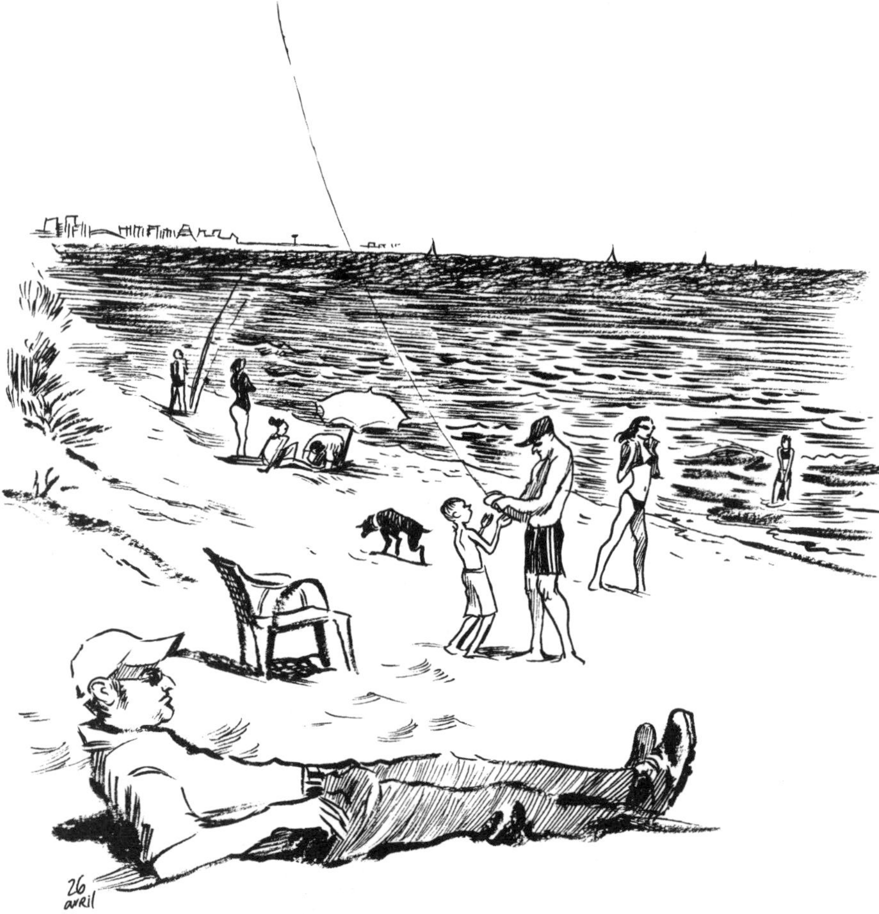
26
avril

But to balance out my idyllic view, the South of France can be cheezy, too-- the youth are obsessed with American athletic wear, much of the old city is grafitti-ed- with no discretion between ugly modern buildings (that deserve decoration) and beautiful historic architecture -- dog crap everywhere, and annoying street performers like the clown who planted his "boom-box" and horns right in front of us at the cafe. Lewis said, "YOU CAN LAUGH AT ANYTHING MAN DOES... BECAUSE MAN IS PATHETIC." I laughed for a very long time.

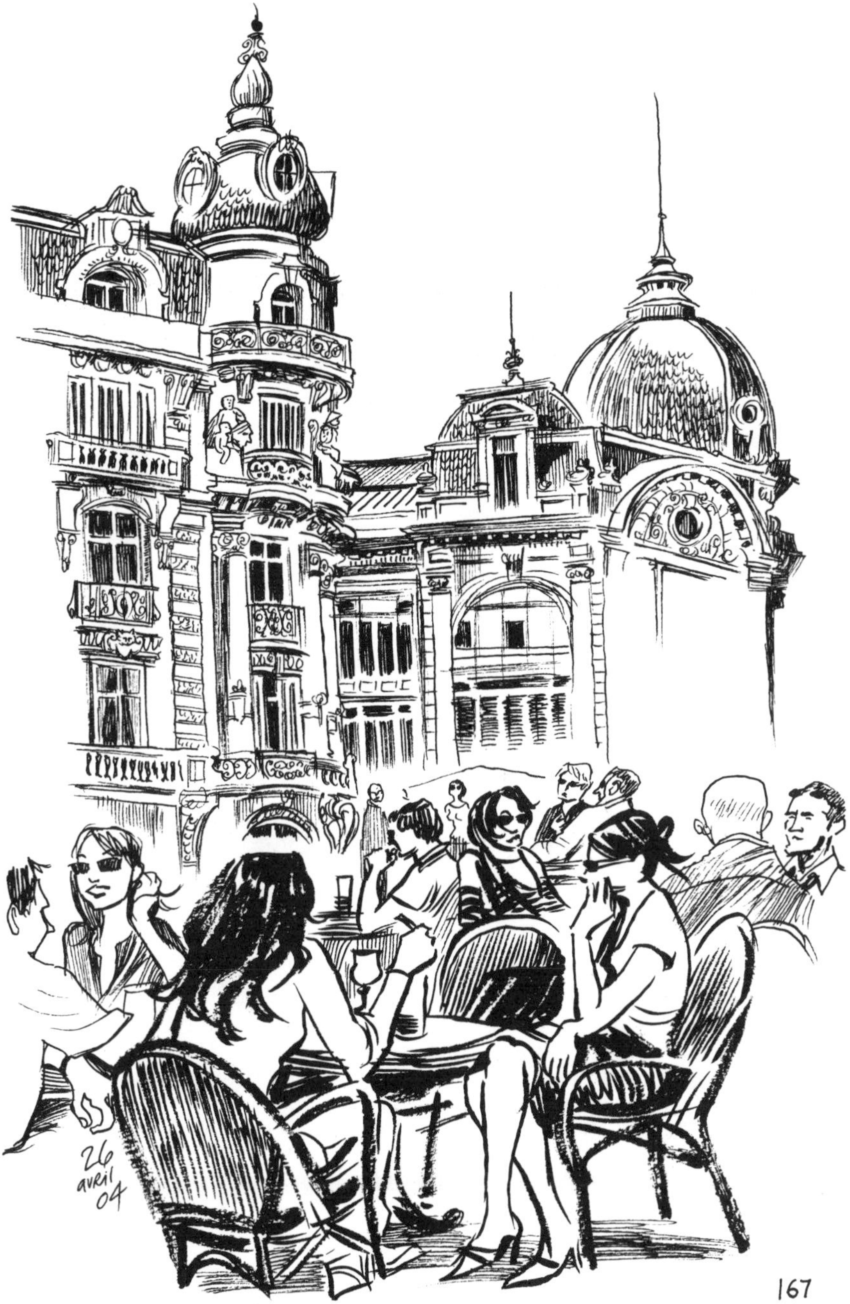
26
avril
04

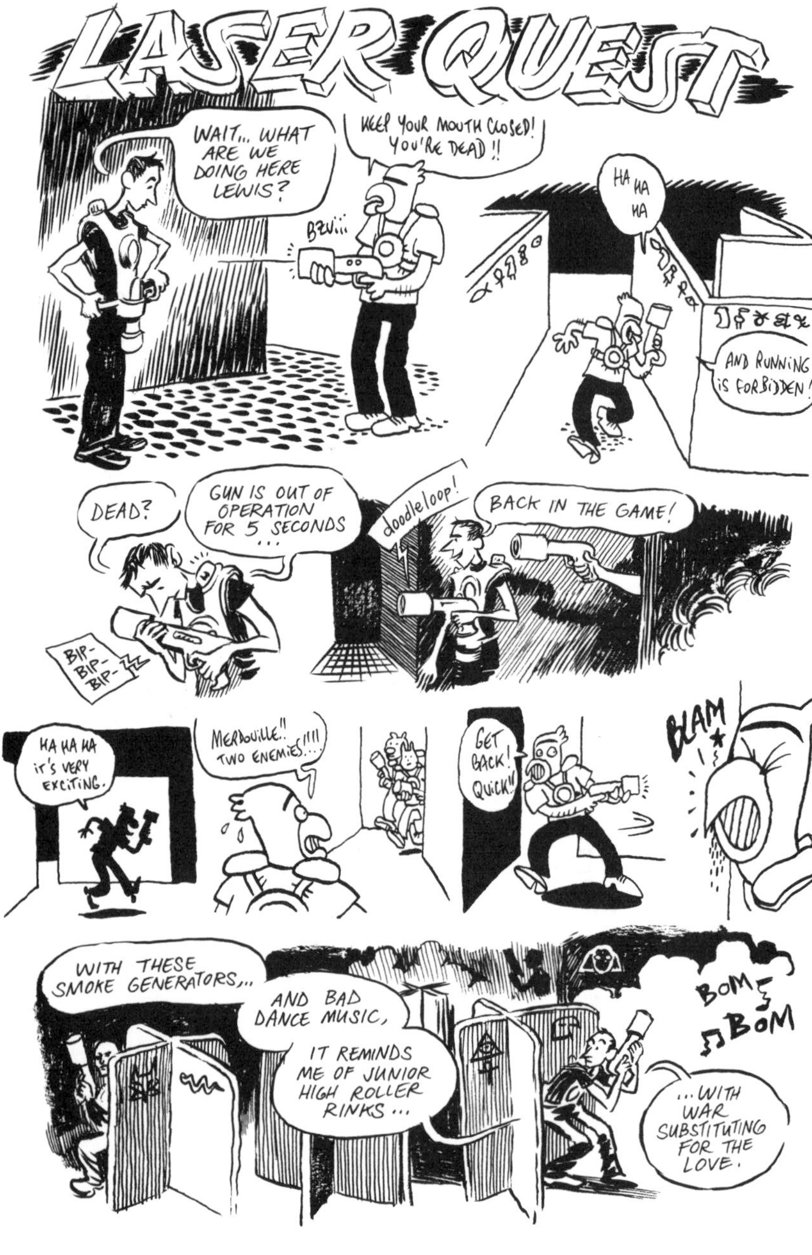
LASER QUEST
WAIT... WHAT ARE WE DOING HERE LEWIS?
KEEP YOUR MOUTH CLOSED! YOU'RE DEAD !!
BZUiii
HA HA HA
AND RUNNING IS FORBIDDEN!
DEAD?
GUN IS OUT OF OPERATION FOR 5 SECONDS ...
BIP-BIP-BIP-
doodleloop!
BACK IN THE GAME!
HA HA HA it's VERY EXCITING.
MERDOUILLE!! TWO ENEMIES!!!!
GET BACK! QUICK!!
BLAM
WITH THESE SMOKE GENERATORS,..
AND BAD DANCE MUSIC,
IT REMINDS ME OF JUNIOR HIGH ROLLER RINKS...
BOM BOM
...WITH WAR SUBSTITUTING FOR THE LOVE.

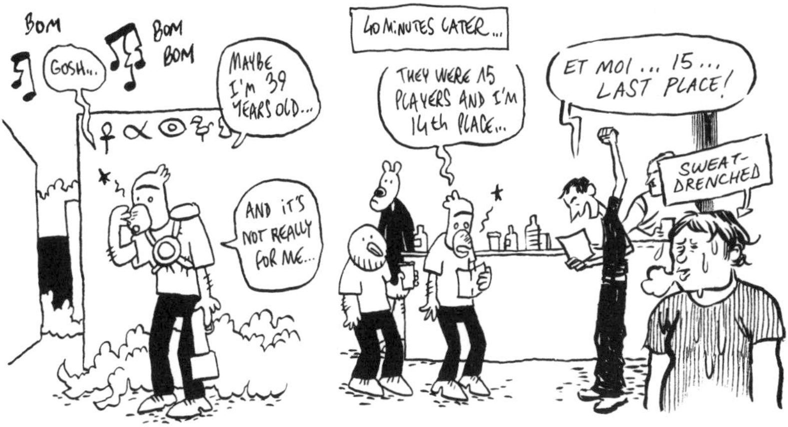
BOM
GOSH...
BOM BOM
MAYBE I'M 39 YEARS OLD...
AND IT'S NOT REALLY FOR ME...
40 MINUTES LATER...
THEY WERE 15 PLAYERS AND I'M 14th PLACE...
ET MOI ... 15 ... LAST PLACE!
SWEAT-DRENCHED

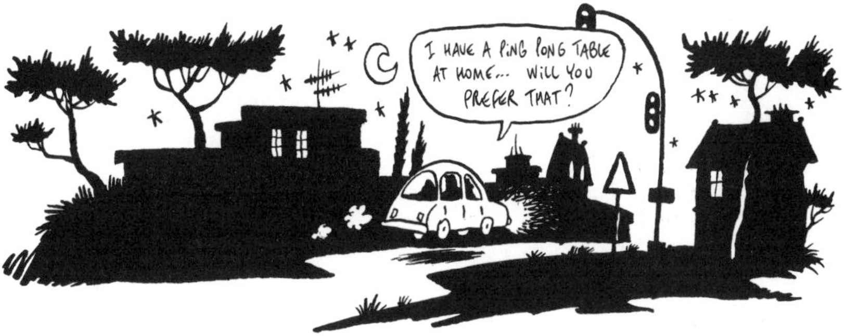
I HAVE A PING PONG TABLE AT HOME... WILL YOU PREFER THAT?

HAPPENED 26 AVRIL – DRAWN 27 AVRIL

So Lewis being the comics celebrity that he is was invited by a magazine devoted to paintball and "laser-tag" to participate in a session at a new local facility. He brought along Nicolas & I & his other buddy Christophe, and we dorked out like 12 year old boys.

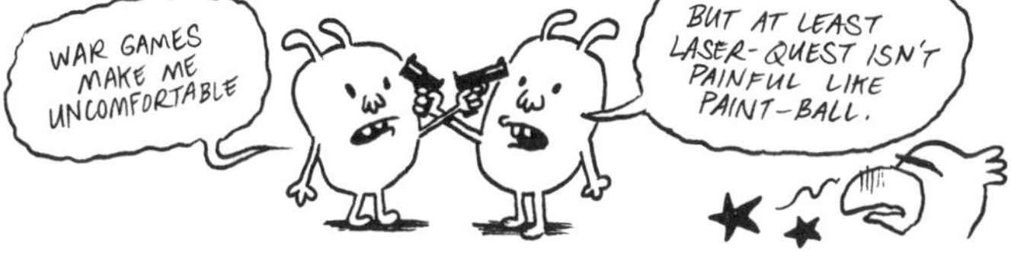
WAR GAMES MAKE ME UNCOMFORTABLE
BUT AT LEAST LASER-QUEST ISN'T PAINFUL LIKE PAINT-BALL.

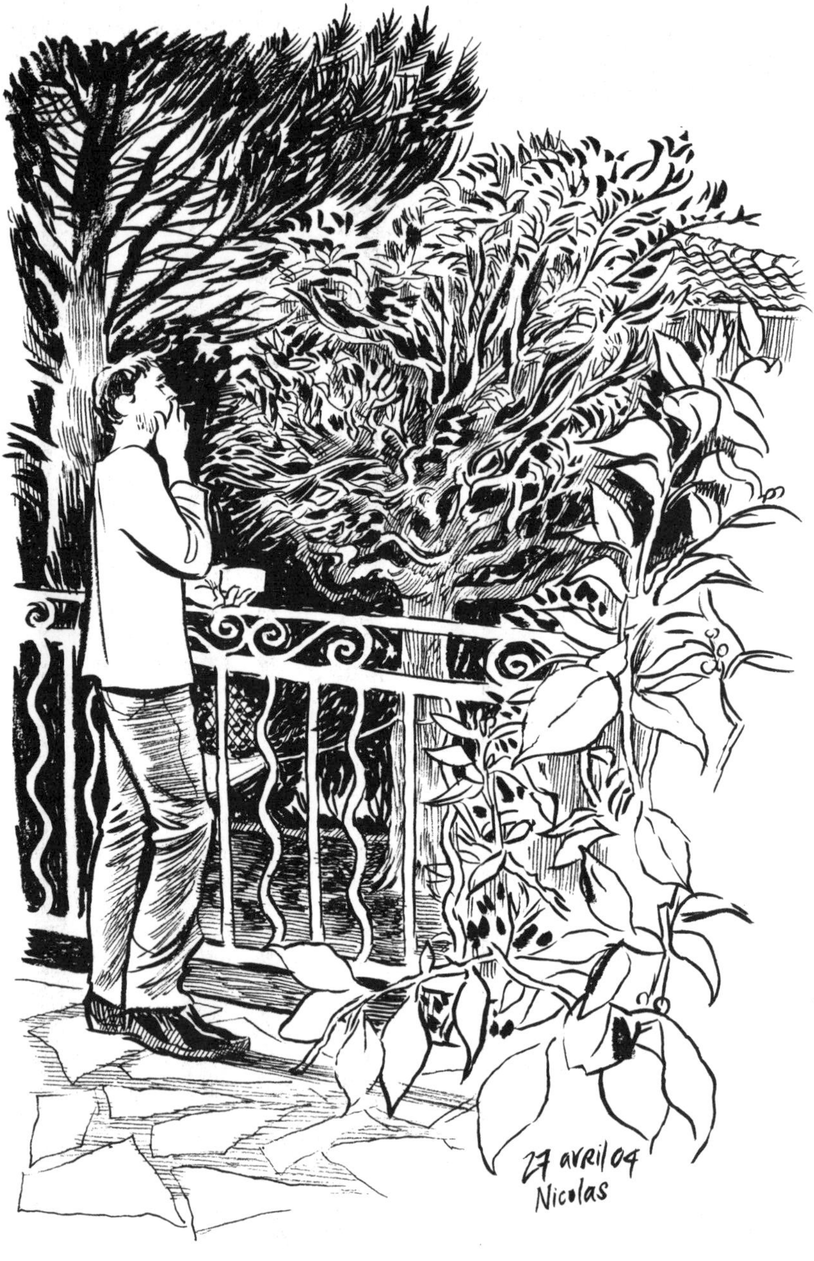
27 avril 04
Nicolas

27 avril 04

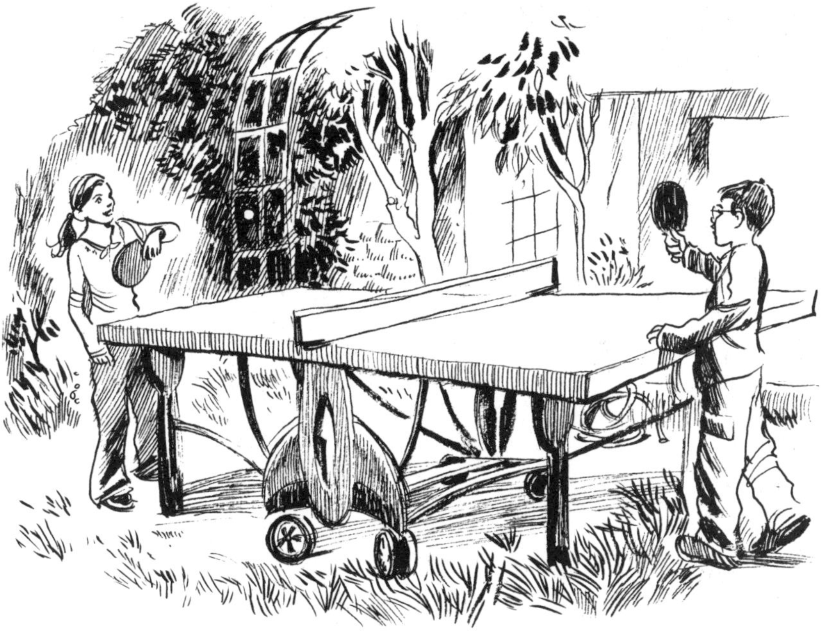

And - of course - today, the ping-pong table was hauled out to the sunny backyard. Here's Jeanne & Pierre playing. The day was an extension of yesterday -- more sun, lazy walks, ping-pong galore, zero responsibilities -- slacker-style summer vacation. In the evening, Lewis took me out to eat at a four-star restaurant.

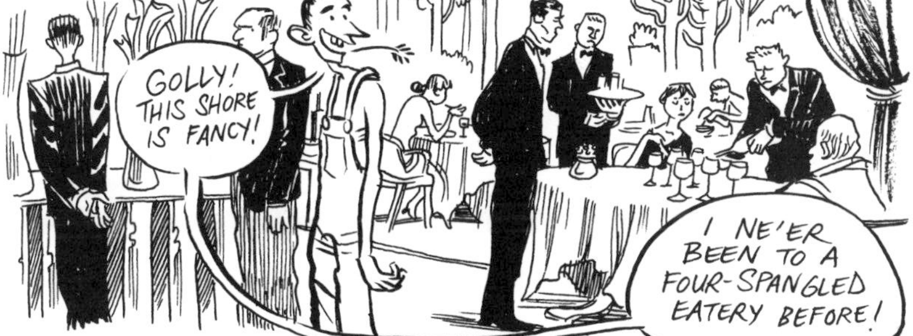
GOLLY! THIS SHORE IS FANCY!
I NE'ER BEEN TO A FOUR-SPANGLED EATERY BEFORE!

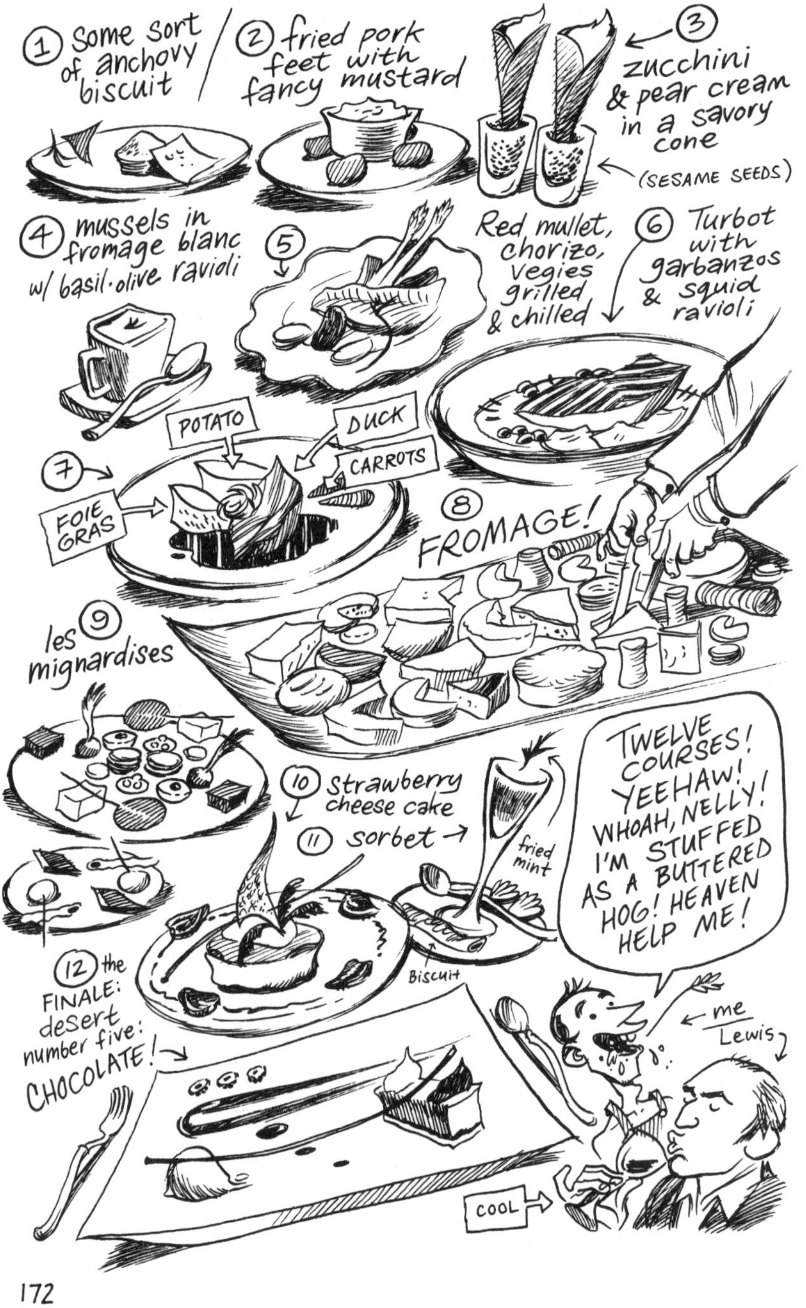
1 Some sort of anchovy biscuit
2 fried pork feet with fancy mustard
3 zucchini & pear cream in a savory cone
(SESAME SEEDS)
4 mussels in fromage blanc w/ basil·olive ravioli
5
Red mullet, chorizo, vegies grilled & chilled
6 Turbot with garbanzos & squid ravioli
POTATO
DUCK
CARROTS
7
FOIE GRAS
8 FROMAGE!
les 9 mignardises
10 strawberry cheese cake
11 sorbet
fried mint
Biscuit
TWELVE COURSES! YEEHAW! WHOAH, NELLY! I'M STUFFED AS A BUTTERED HOG! HEAVEN HELP ME!
12 the FINALE: desert number five: CHOCOLATE!
me
Lewis
COOL

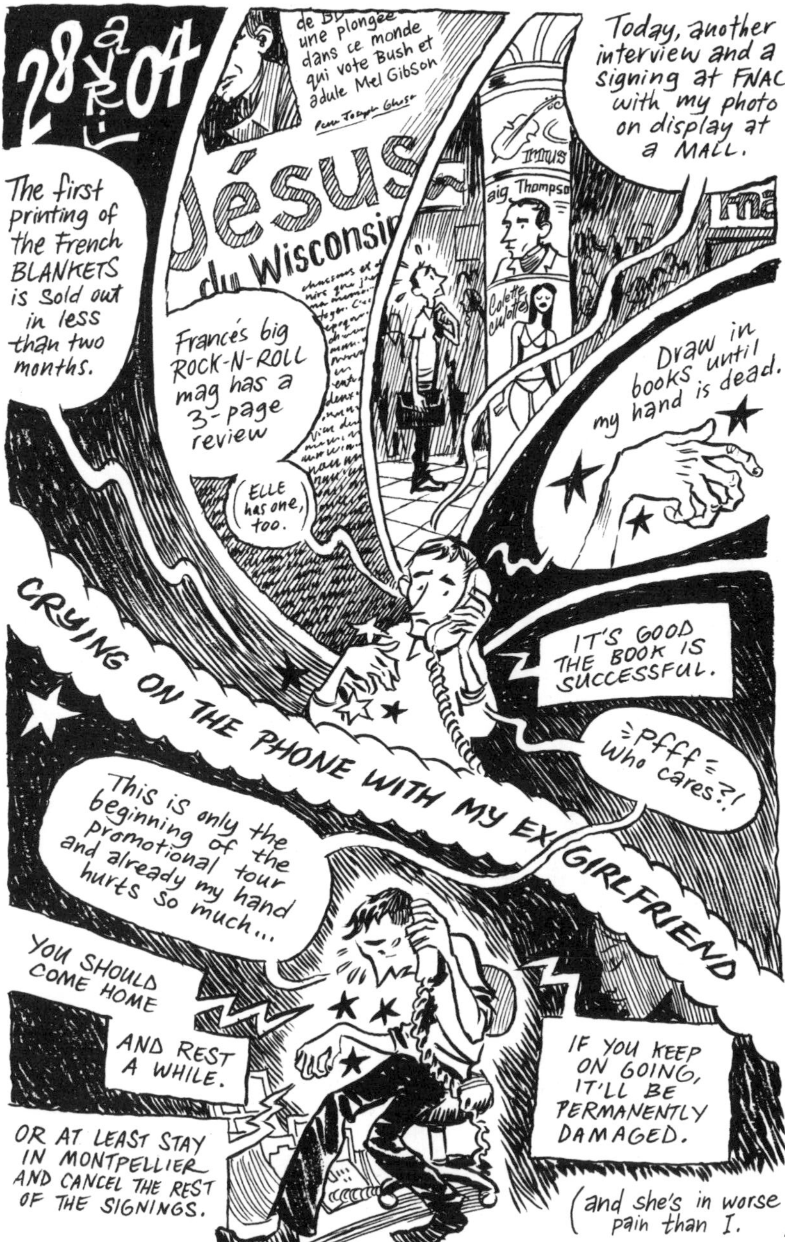
28 avril 04
The first printing of the French BLANKETS is sold out in less than two months.
de BD une plongée dans ce monde qui vote Bush et adule Mel Gibson
Jésus du Wisconsin
France's big ROCK-N-ROLL mag has a 3-page review
(ELLE has one, too.
Today, another interview and a signing at FNAC with my photo on display at a MALL.
Craig Thompson
Draw in books until my hand is dead.
CRYING ON THE PHONE WITH MY EX-GIRLFRIEND
IT'S GOOD THE BOOK IS SUCCESSFUL.
Pfff Who cares?!
This is only the beginning of the promotional tour and already my hand hurts so much...
YOU SHOULD COME HOME
AND REST A WHILE.
OR AT LEAST STAY IN MONTPELLIER AND CANCEL THE REST OF THE SIGNINGS.
IF YOU KEEP ON GOING, IT'LL BE PERMANENTLY DAMAGED.
(and she's in worse pain than I.)

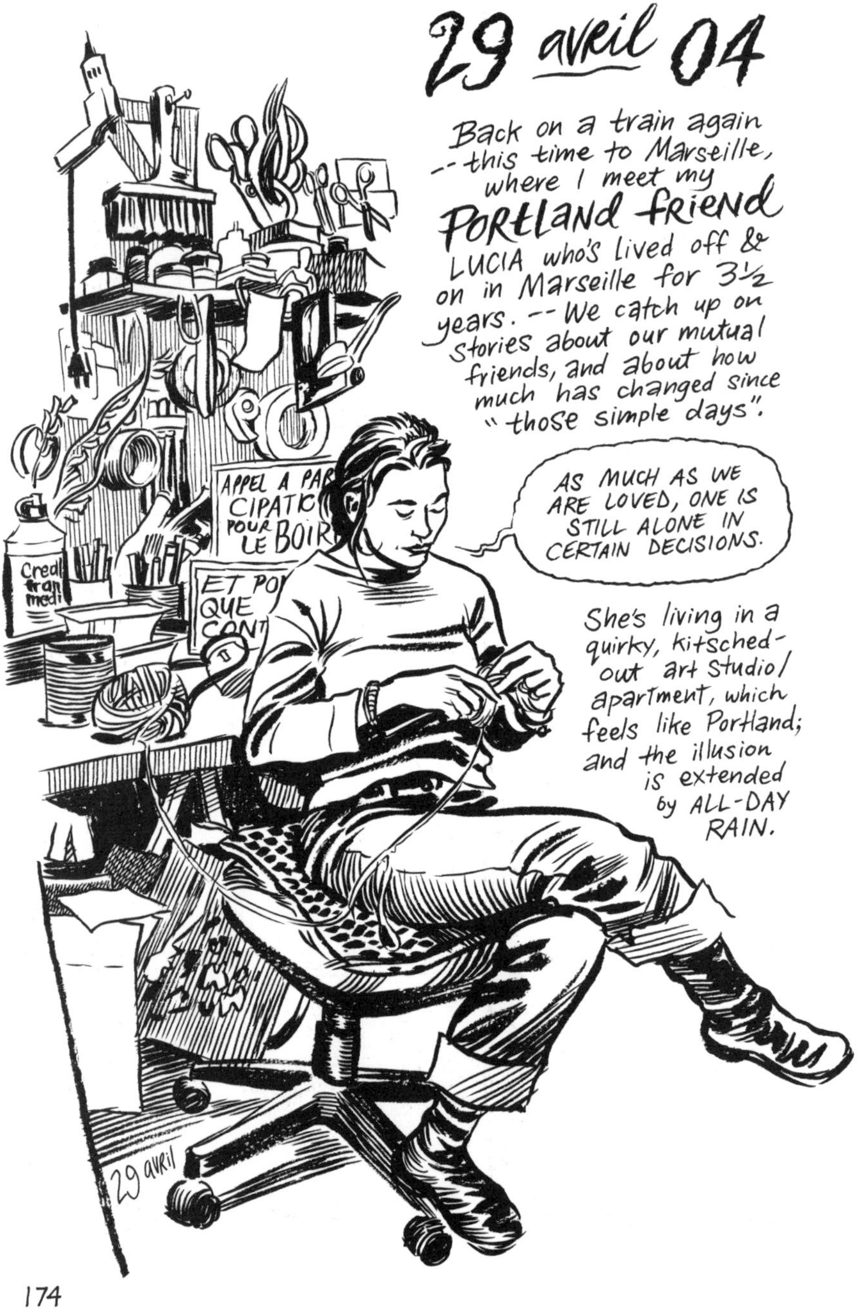
29 avril 04
Back on a train again -- this time to Marseille, where I meet my PORTLAND FRIEND LUCIA who's lived off & on in Marseille for 3½ years. -- We catch up on stories about our mutual friends, and about how much has changed since "those simple days".
AS MUCH AS WE ARE LOVED, ONE IS STILL ALONE IN CERTAIN DECISIONS.
She's living in a quirky, kitsched-out art studio/apartment, which feels like Portland; and the illusion is extended by ALL-DAY RAIN.
29 avril

We visit some cartoonist friends of Lucia's at their studio, and then go to acupuncture together. To work on my hand pain, the acupuncturist hooks me up to electrotherapy -- electricity pulsating through my arm Frankenstein-style -- an android plugged in to reboot.

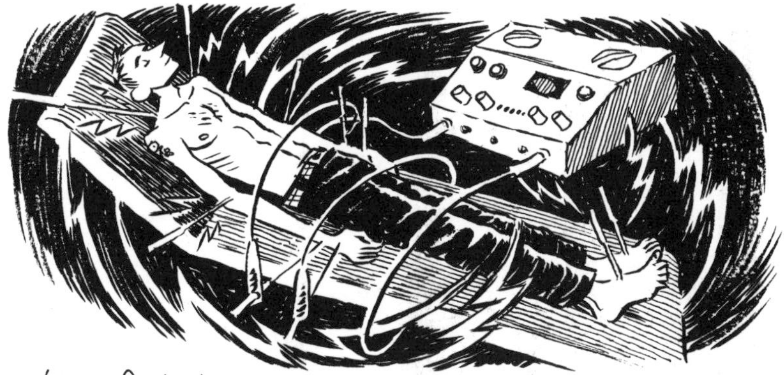

I can feel the energy circulating through my body, buzzing through the spots I've tensed up or closed off (I keep popping boners!).

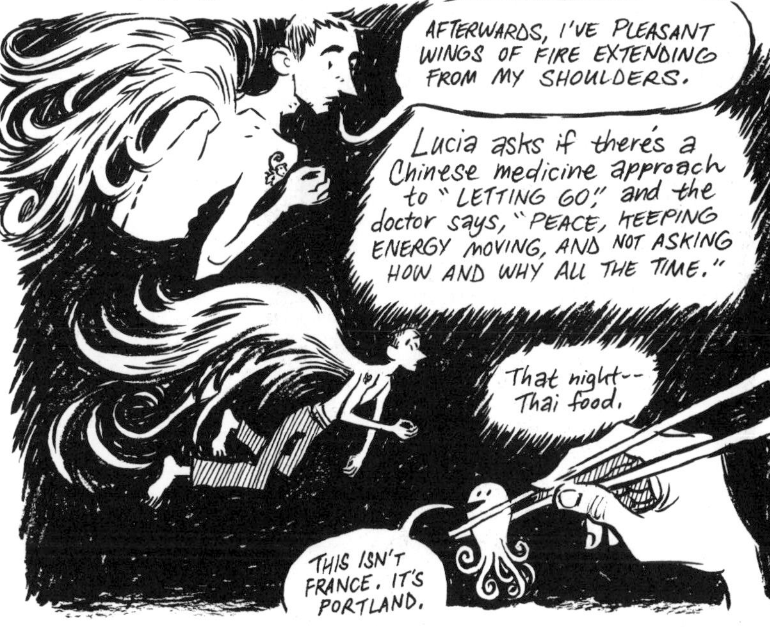
AFTERWARDS, I'VE PLEASANT WINGS OF FIRE EXTENDING FROM MY SHOULDERS.
Lucia asks if there's a Chinese medicine approach to "LETTING GO," and the doctor says, "PEACE, KEEPING ENERGY MOVING, AND NOT ASKING HOW AND WHY ALL THE TIME."
That night-- Thai food.
THIS ISN'T FRANCE. IT'S PORTLAND.

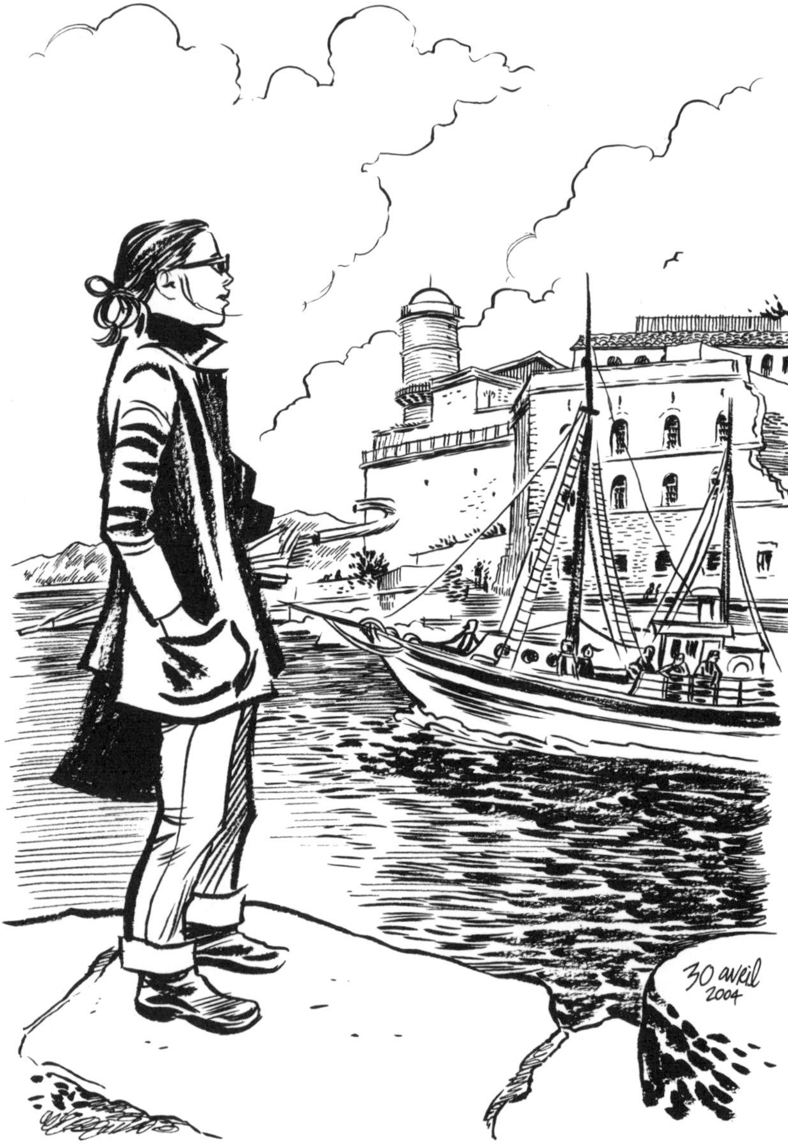
30 avril
2004

30 avril 04

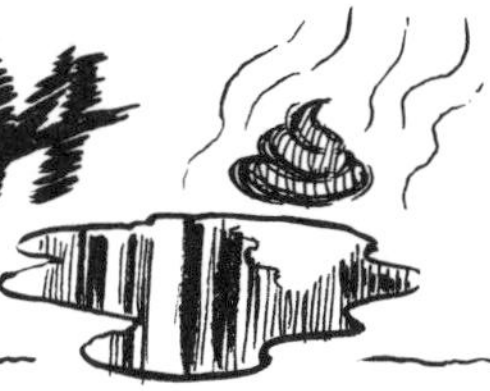

It rained all morning, but then the sun came out, evaporated the puddles, and baked the dog crap on the street.

Lucia and I were walking along the Mediterranean, when suddenly it looked quite enticing -- So we climbed down to the rocks and stripped to our underwear in front of a restaurant.

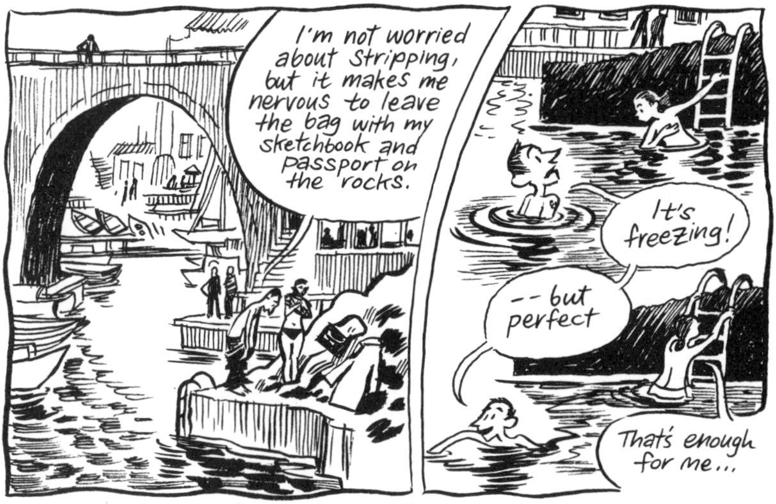
I'm not worried about stripping, but it makes me nervous to leave the bag with my sketchbook and passport on the rocks.
It's freezing!
-- but perfect
That's enough for me...

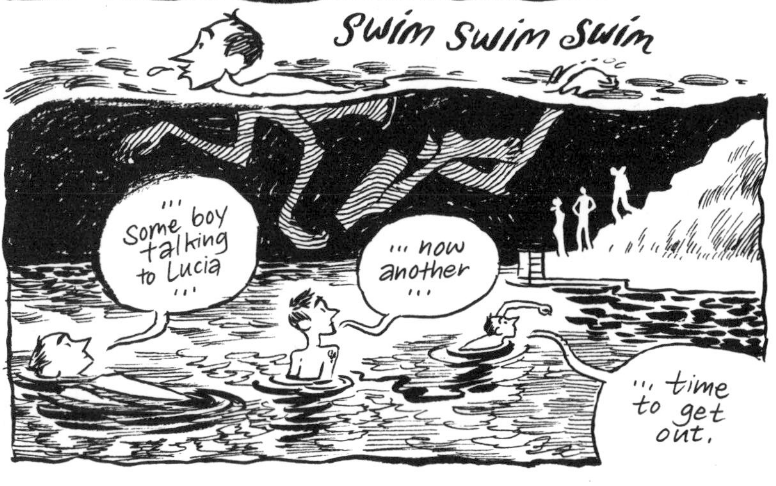
Swim Swim Swim
... Some boy talking to Lucia ...
... now another ...
... time to get out.

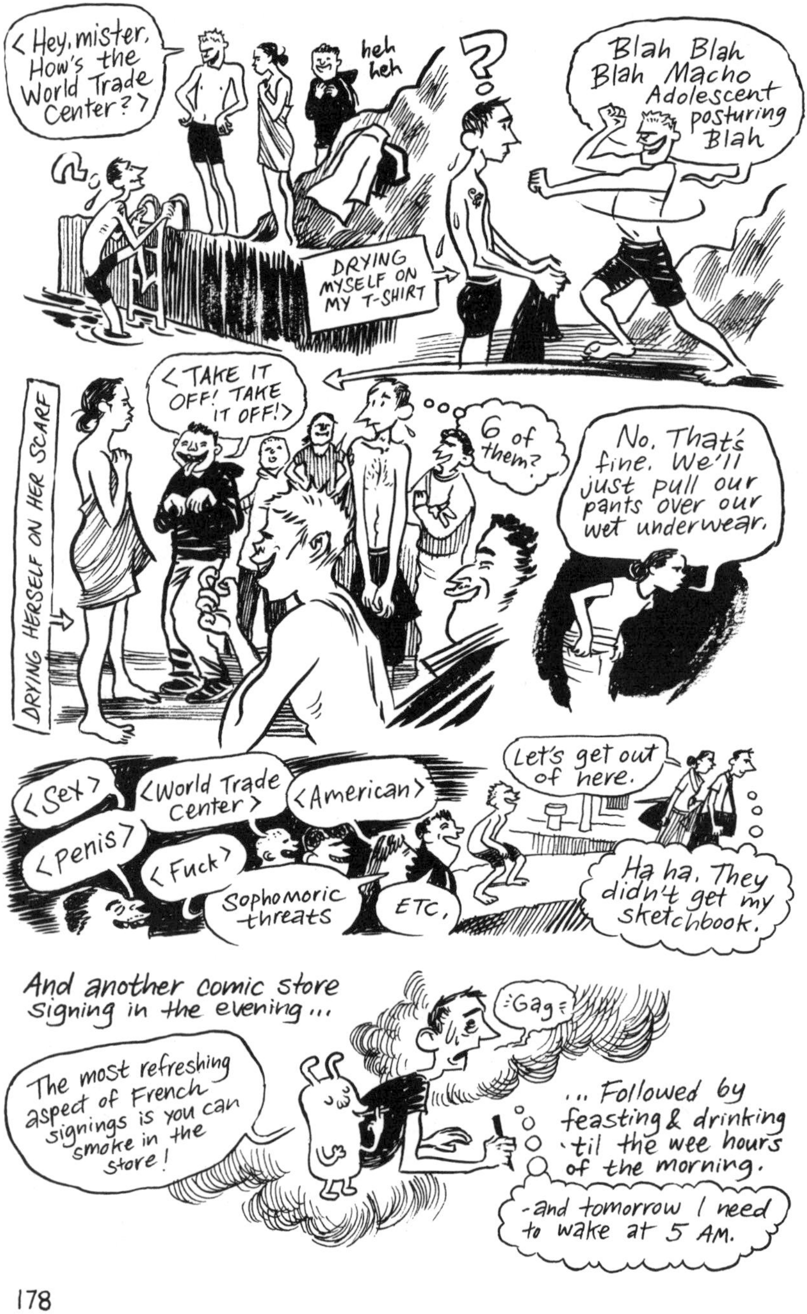
<Hey, mister, How's the World Trade Center?>
heh heh
?
Blah Blah Blah Macho Adolescent posturing Blah
DRYING MYSELF ON MY T-SHIRT
DRYING HERSELF ON HER SCARF
<TAKE IT OFF! TAKE IT OFF!>
6 of them?
No. That's fine. We'll just pull our pants over our wet underwear.
<Sex>
<World Trade Center>
<American>
<Penis>
<Fuck>
Sophomoric threats
ETC.
Let's get out of here.
Ha ha. They didn't get my sketchbook.
And another comic store signing in the evening...
Gag
The most refreshing aspect of French signings is you can smoke in the store!
...Followed by feasting & drinking 'til the wee hours of the morning.
-and tomorrow I need to wake at 5 AM.

01 MAI 04

Three hours of sleep, then I'm back at the train station – bound this time for Geneva, Switzerland.

I sleep on the first train; and on the second, I clear out an entire car. That is,,. an attendant comes aboard and asks aloud a question. Groggy, and listening only for the name of my stop, I ignore him. Suddenly, they're kicking everyone out of the car. I go to grab my suitcase, and three attendants are handling it. Finally my French comprehension kicks in-- they'd been inquiring about the unattended luggage I'd stored in the luggage rack just outside the door. I explained & apologized, and they allowed the passengers back in the car. Thus ended my first self-instigated TERRORIST THREAT.

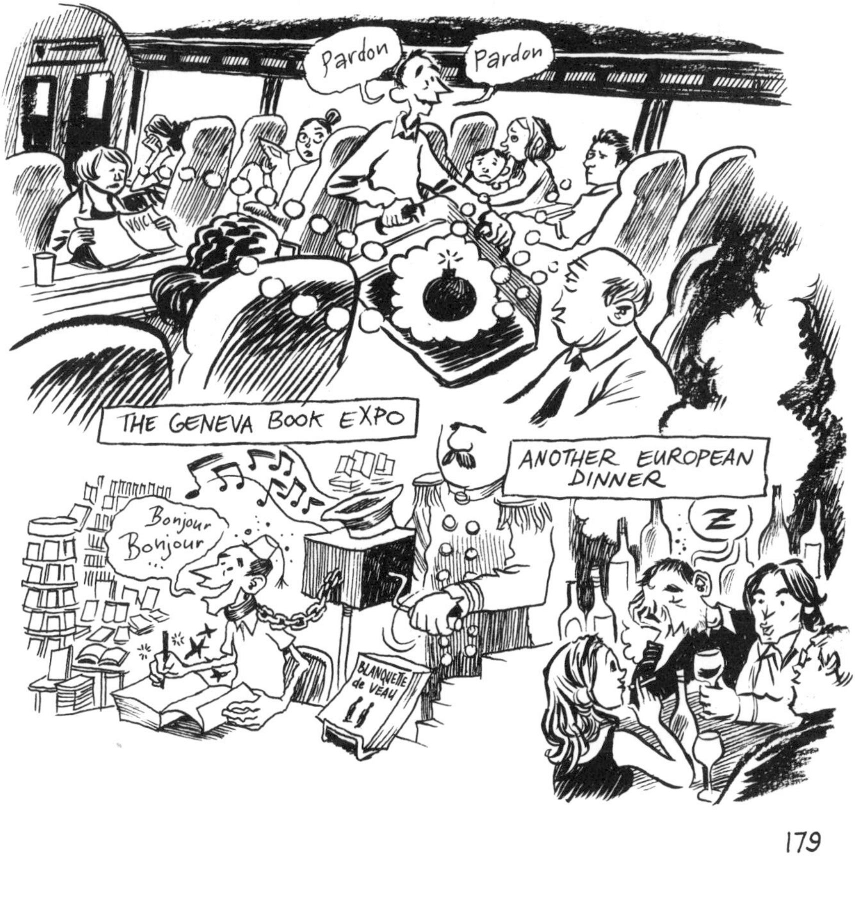

Pardon
Pardon
VOICI
THE GENEVA BOOK EXPO
ANOTHER EUROPEAN DINNER
Bonjour Bonjour ...
BLANQUETTE de VEAU
Z

GENEVA · BOOK · EXPO

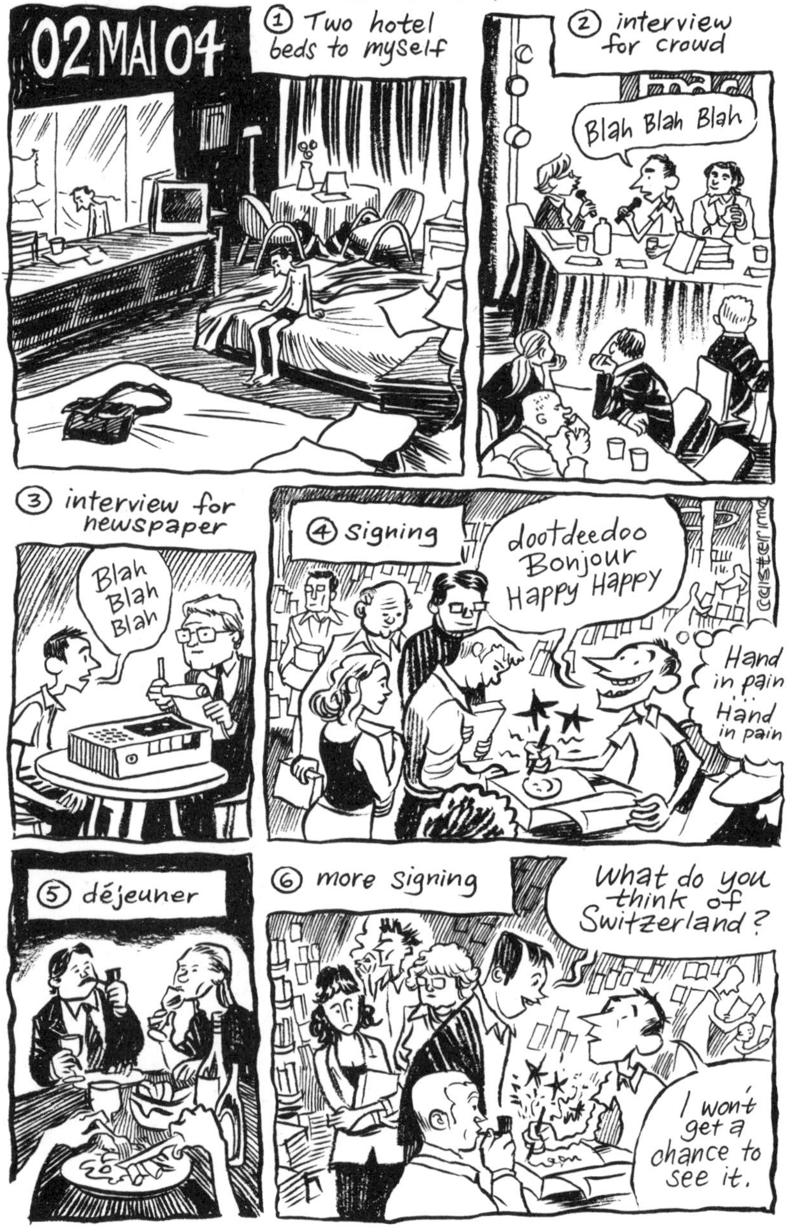
02 MAI 04
① Two hotel beds to myself
② interview for crowd
Blah Blah Blah
③ interview for newspaper
Blah Blah Blah
④ signing
dootdeedoo Bonjour Happy Happy
Hand in pain... Hand in pain
⑤ déjeuner
⑥ more signing
What do you think of Switzerland?
I won't get a chance to see it.

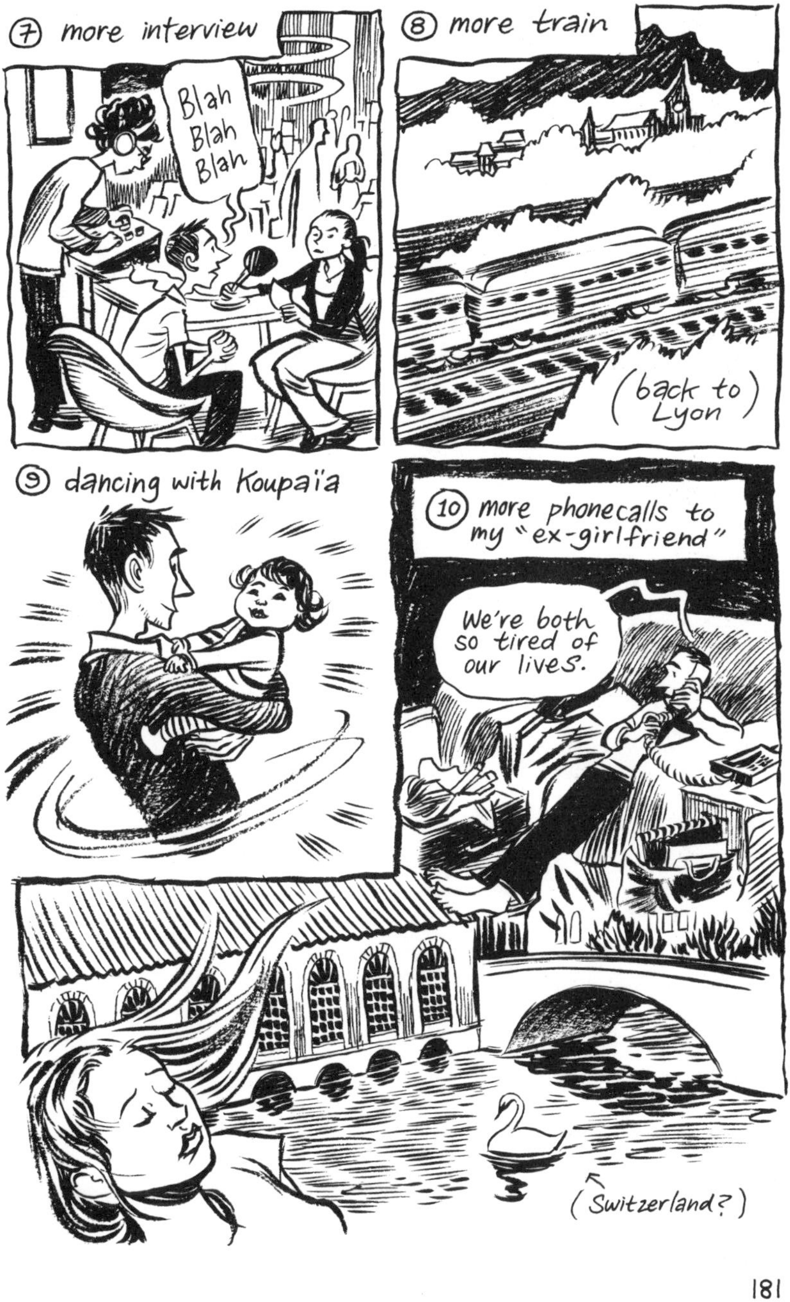

⑦ more interview
Blah Blah Blah
⑧ more train
(back to Lyon)
⑨ dancing with Koupaïa
⑩ more phonecalls to my "ex-girlfriend"
We're both so tired of our lives.
(Switzerland?)

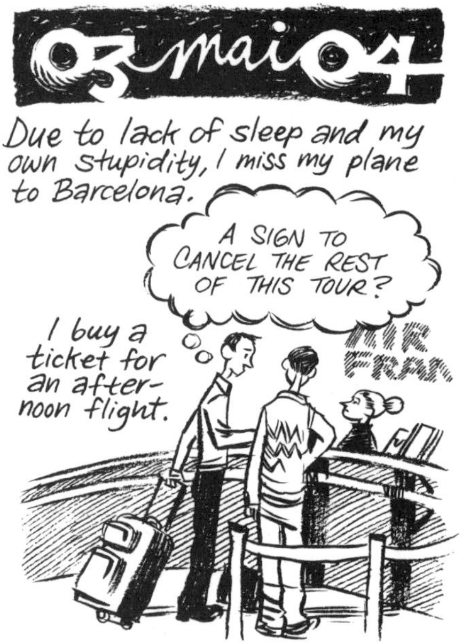
03 mai 04
Due to lack of sleep and my own stupidity, I miss my plane to Barcelona.
A SIGN TO CANCEL THE REST OF THIS TOUR?
I buy a ticket for an after-noon flight.

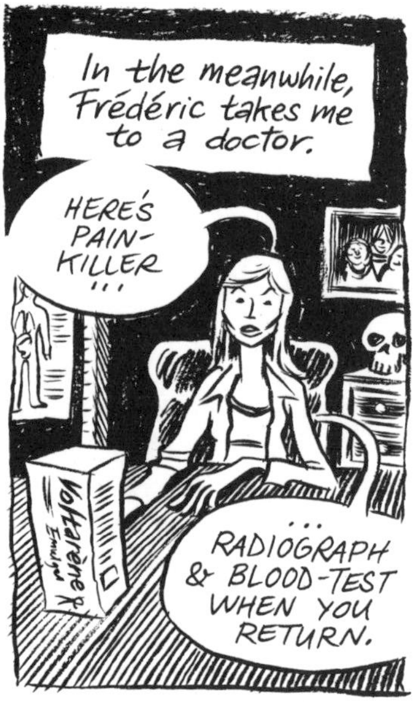
In the meanwhile, Frédéric takes me to a doctor.
HERE'S PAIN-KILLER ...
Voltarène
... RADIOGRAPH & BLOOD-TEST WHEN YOU RETURN.

Laëtitia & Frédéric & I spend part of the day together, then I'm back to the airport and off to Spain.

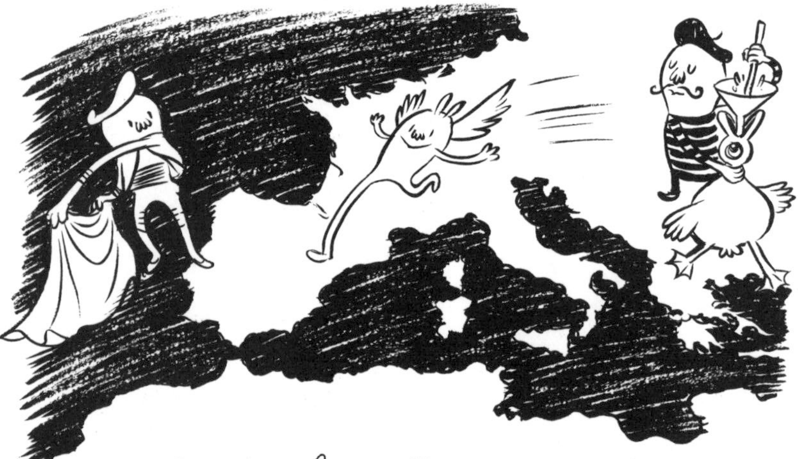

The Barcelona Comics Expo has invited me as a guest. David Macho - a principal organizer - greets me at the airport & deposits me at a hotel.

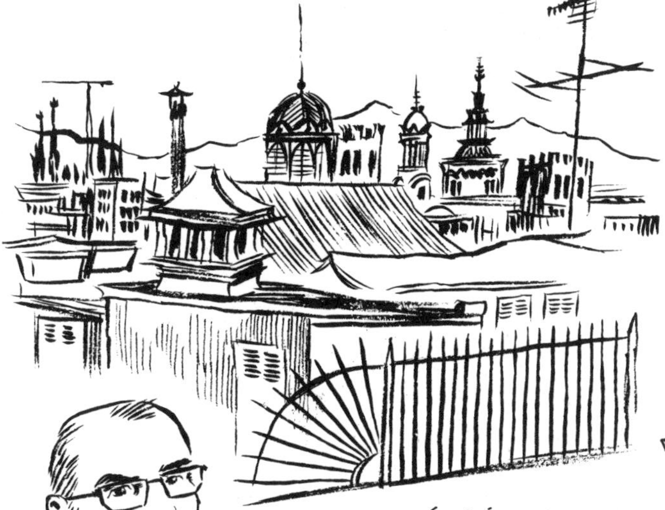

(GLIMPSE FROM HOTEL ROOM WINDOW)

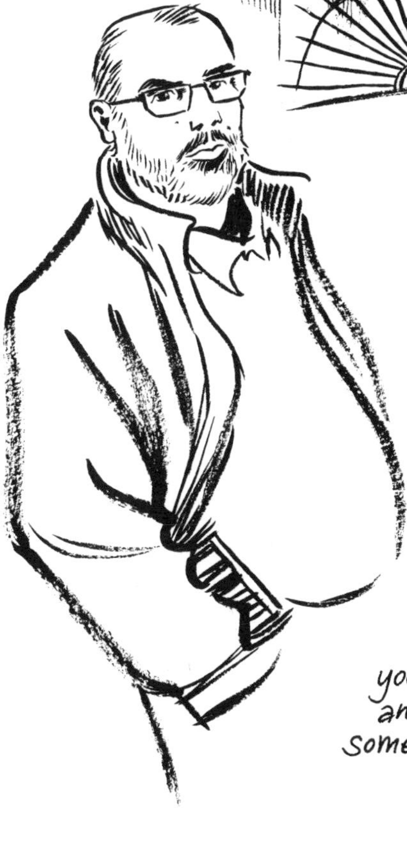

After a moment's rest, I call Laureano, my representative at ASTIBERRI — the publisher who's debuting the Spanish edition of BLANKETS at the festival.

Laureano and I share some important things in common, including a young fixation on religion, and being in love with someone seriously ill.

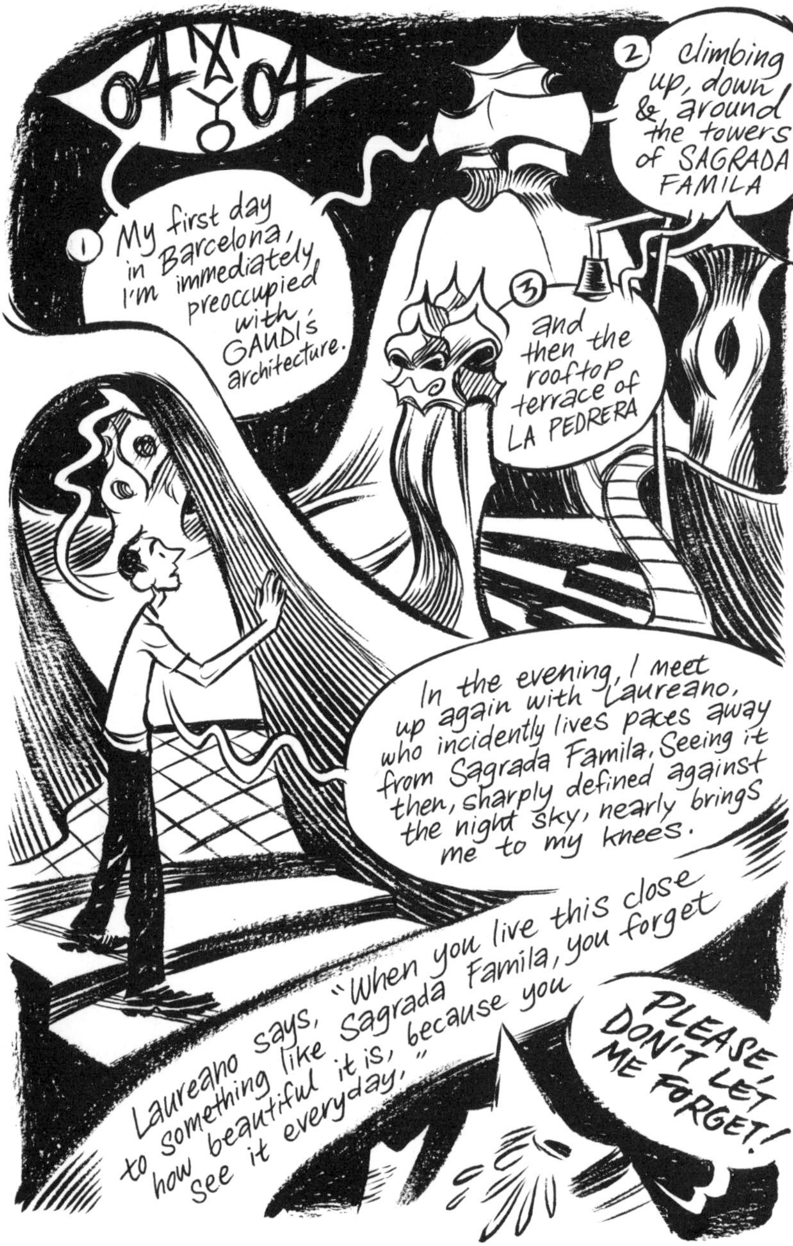
04 04
1 My first day in Barcelona, I'm immediately preoccupied with GAUDI's architecture.
2 climbing up, down & around the towers of SAGRADA FAMILA
3 and then the rooftop terrace of LA PEDRERA
In the evening, I meet up again with Laureano, who incidently lives paces away from Sagrada Famila. Seeing it then, sharply defined against the night sky, nearly brings me to my knees.
Laureano says, "When you live this close to something like Sagrada Famila, you forget how beautiful it is, because you see it everyday."
PLEASE, DON'T LET ME FORGET!

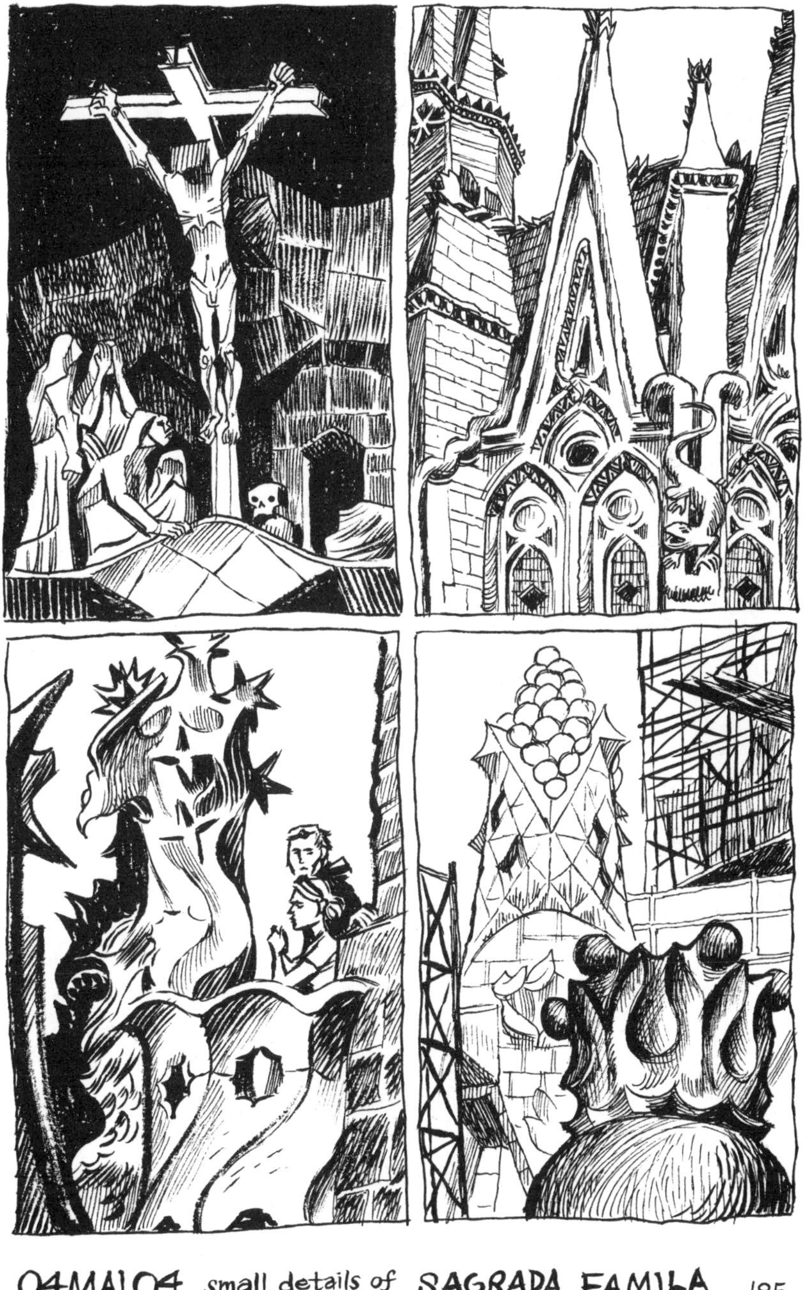

04MAI04 small details of SAGRADA FAMILA

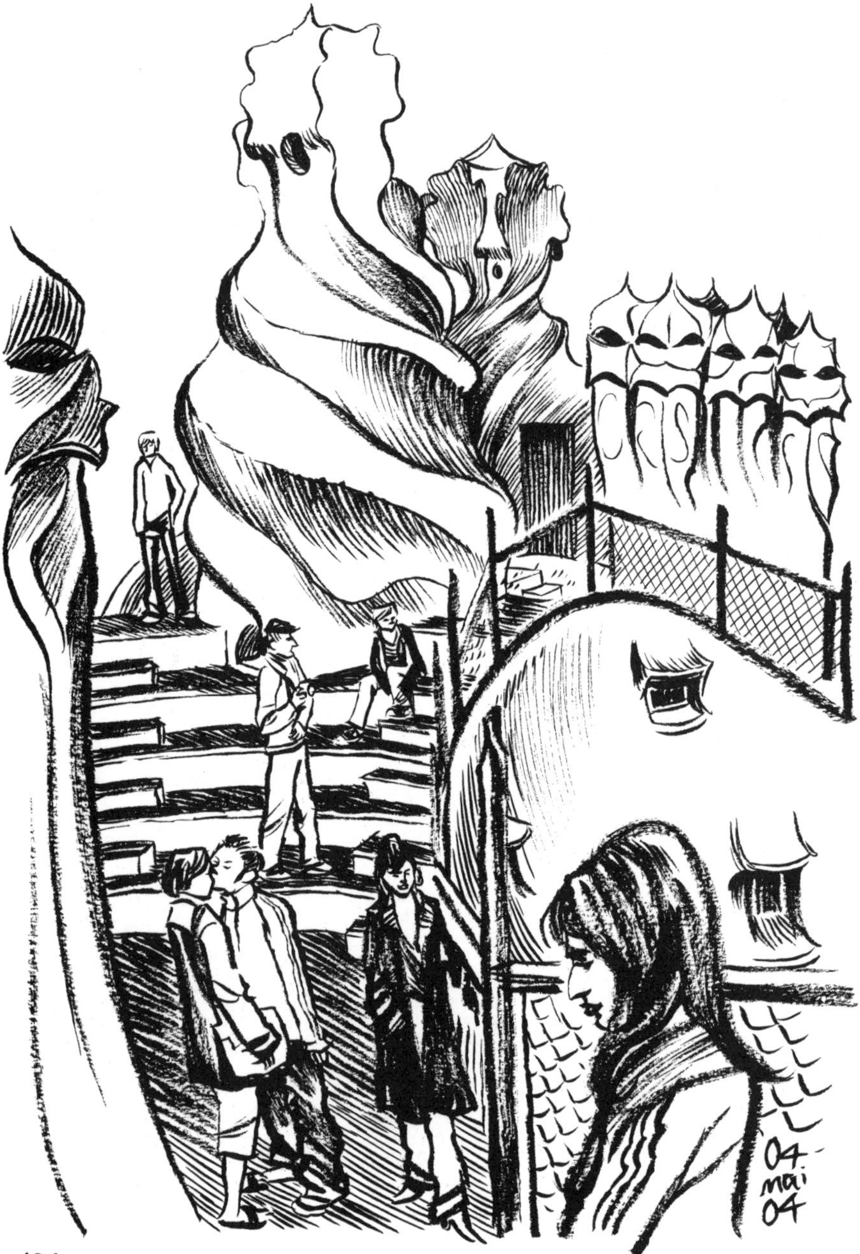
04
mai
04

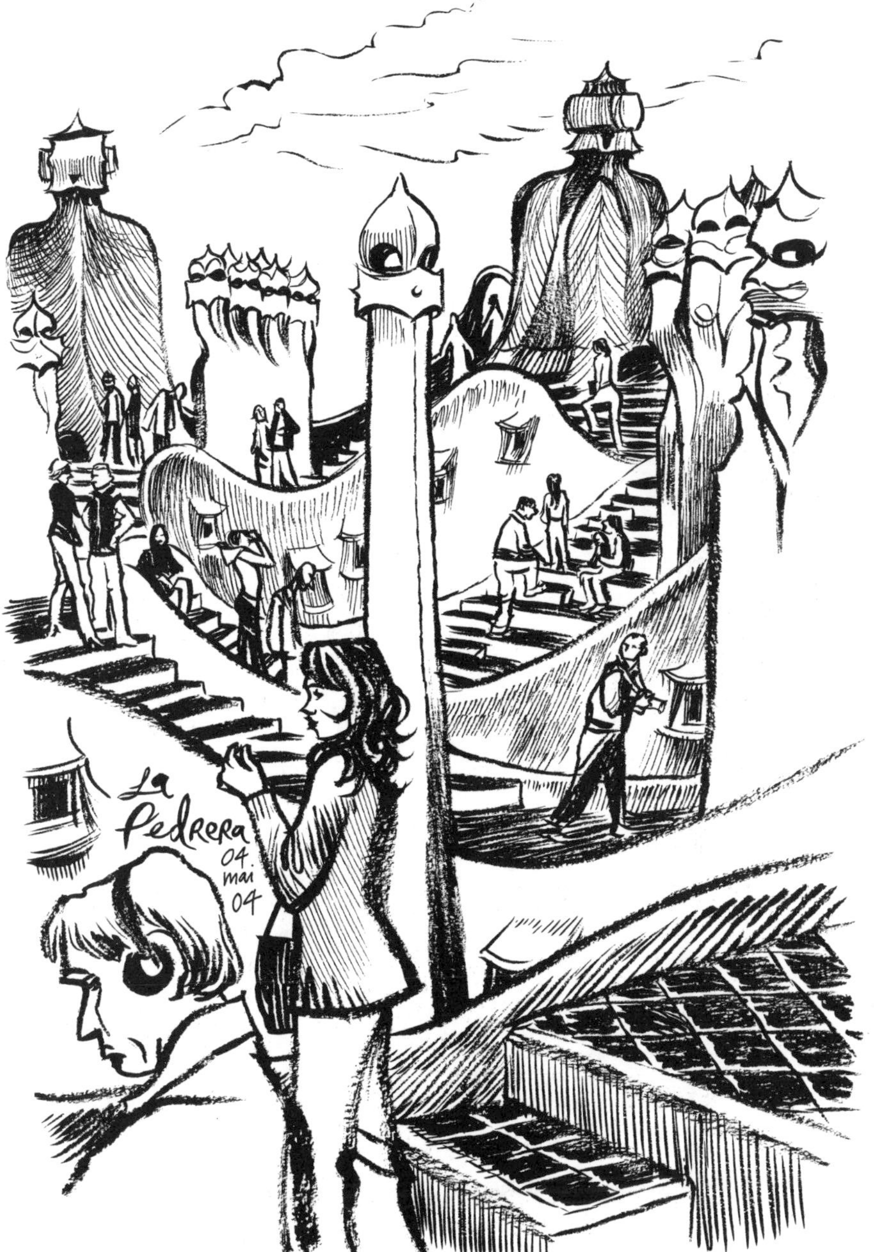
La Pedrera
04 mai 04

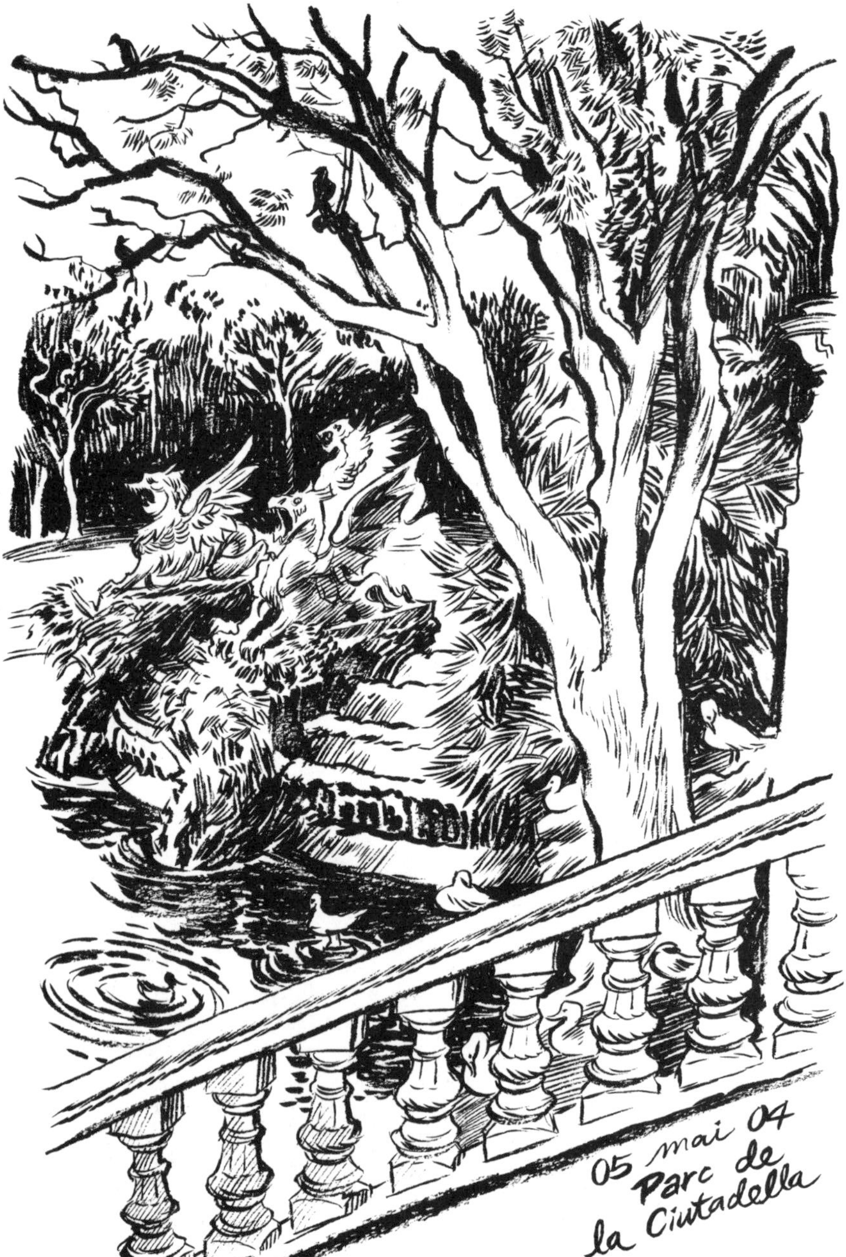
05 mai 04
Parc de
la Ciutadella

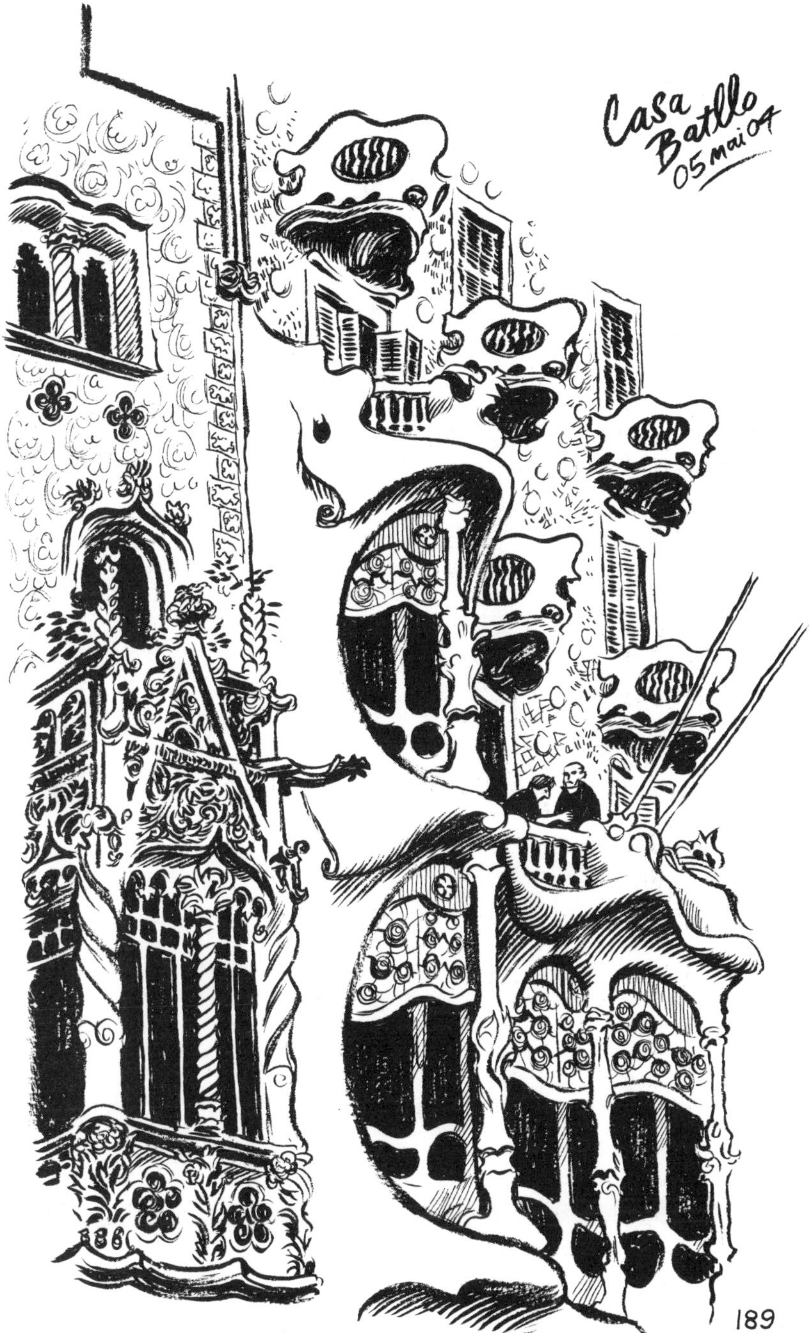
Casa Batllo
05 mai 04

05 MAY 04

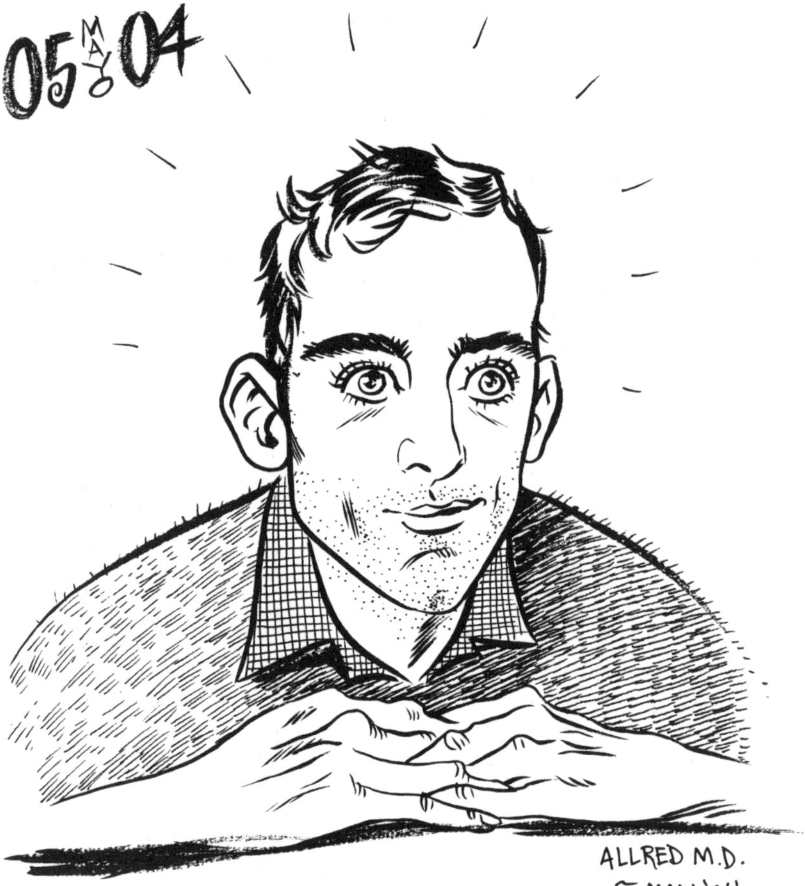

ALLRED M.D.
5 MAY '04

It rained in the morning & got bitter-chilly in the afternoon, but it was still frickin' amazing to walk the streets of Barcelona. At mid-day, many of the other guests arrived, including Charles Berberian & Charles Burns, Peter Milligan, Mark Waid, my Oregon buddies Joe Sacco and Mike Allred along with their loved ones. We shared lunch and dinner in a massive group. While waiting for food, Mike drew me.
(I was too lazy to return the favor.)

After two months of travel, I could observe Americans from an almost European standpoint, and I can confirm that to our credit and our fault, we Americans are very casual critters. Mike summed it up while ordering desert, **"BRING ON THE CHEESECAKE!"**

06 MAYO 04

Ah, sweet, glorious Barcelona! Brushing my teeth on the hotel balcony!

First, an expedition to another Gaudí site -- Parc Güell — accompanied by Doreen — a toy designer & fiancée of a Marvel editor, and an ex-Marvel-employee herself. Our visit was limited by another scheduled lunch with our fellow guests.

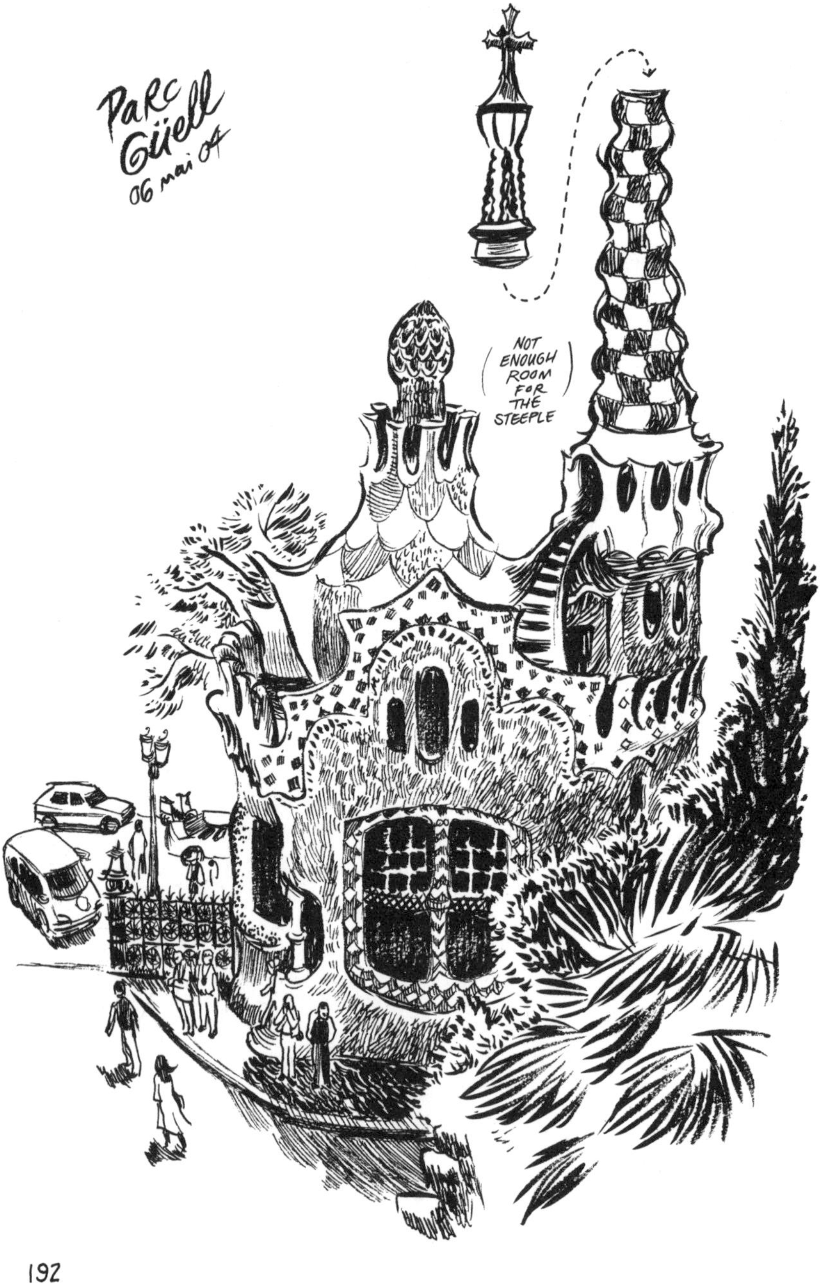
ParC Güell
06 mai 04
(NOT ENOUGH ROOM FOR THE STEEPLE)

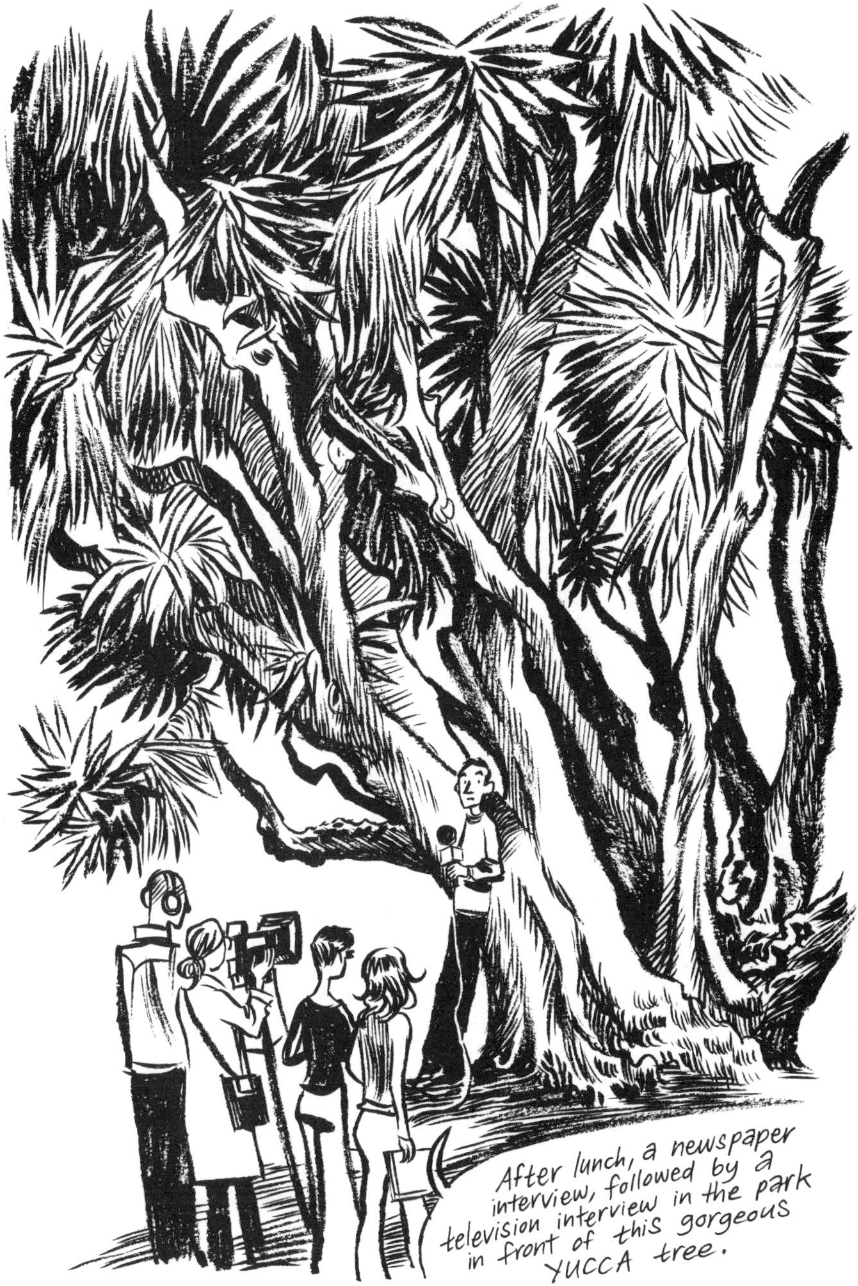
After lunch, a newspaper interview, followed by a television interview in the park in front of this gorgeous YUCCA tree.

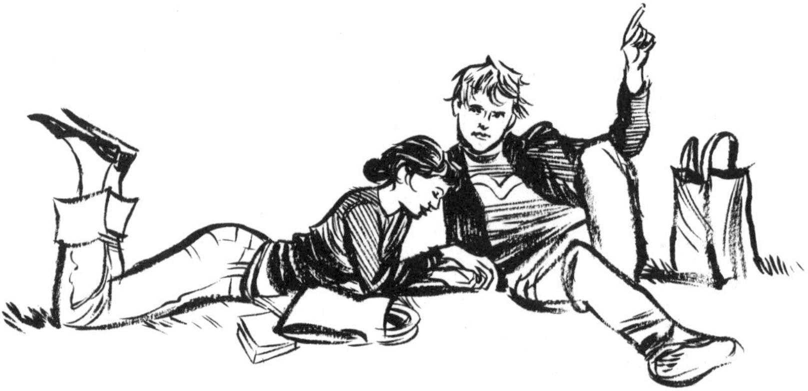

After the interview, I draw the yucca tree, then sit next to two strangers in the park. We immediately begin discussing sex --- orgasms, durations of celibacy, good sex, bad sex... After a while, we make introductions.

She's a Swedish girl named Hillevi. He's an Israeli boy named Chicky. I ask if they're lovers. -No- He's leaving for Israel that night; She invites me to a party. I need to dash for dinner with my Spanish publisher, & suddenly I'm obsessed...

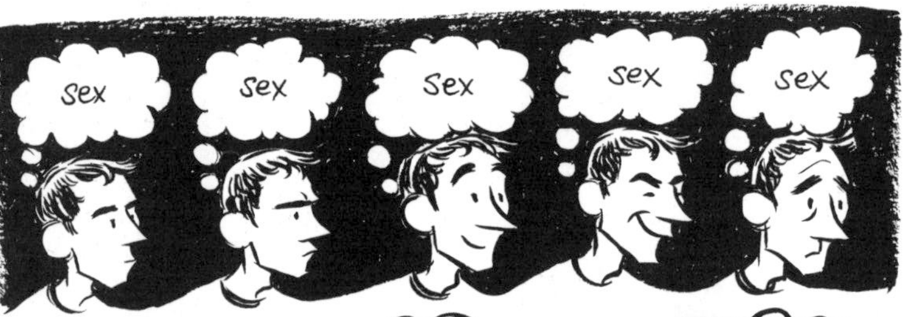
sex
sex
sex
sex
sex

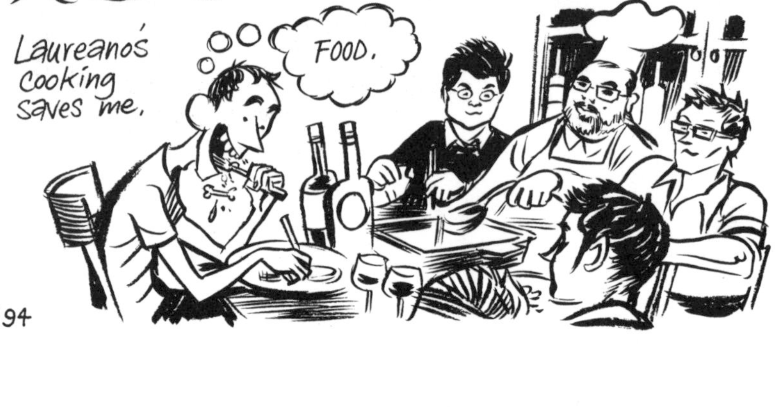
Laureano's cooking saves me.
FOOD.

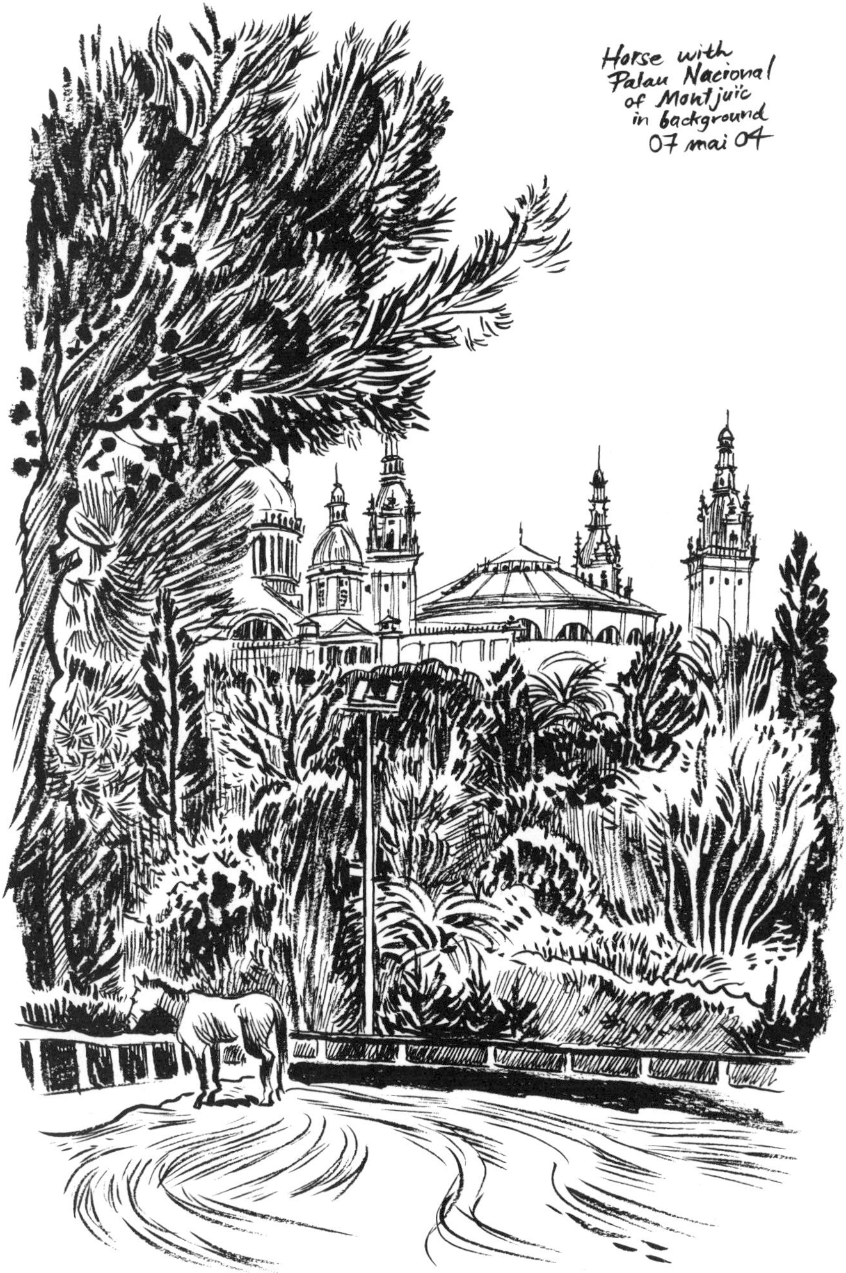

Horse with
Palau Nacional
of Montjuïc
in background
07 mai 04

07 MAYO 04

Wandered in the morning -- off the streets, down quiet wooded paths, found a litter of wild kittens, and then emerged at this horse stable (pictured on the previous page). --Rushed back to group lunch, and afterwards strolled to the beach with Kelby Allred. A perfectly mellow start to the day, but then I entered again the frickin' fray of "comic book promotion".

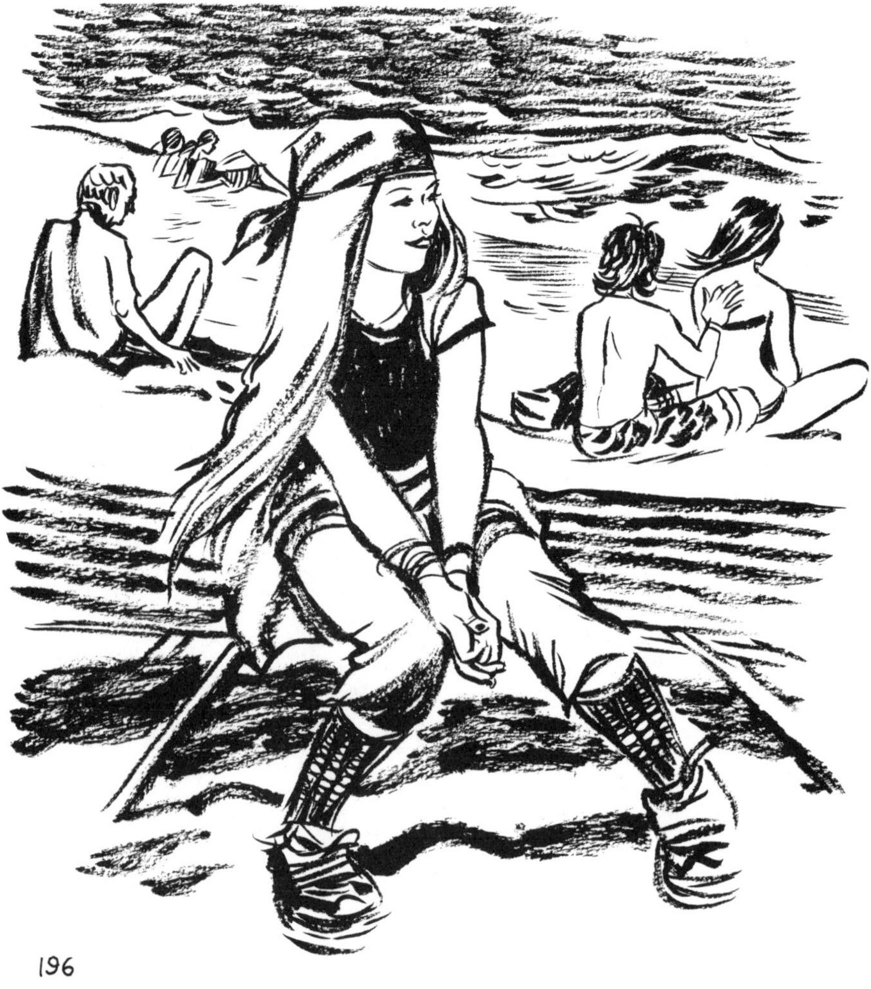

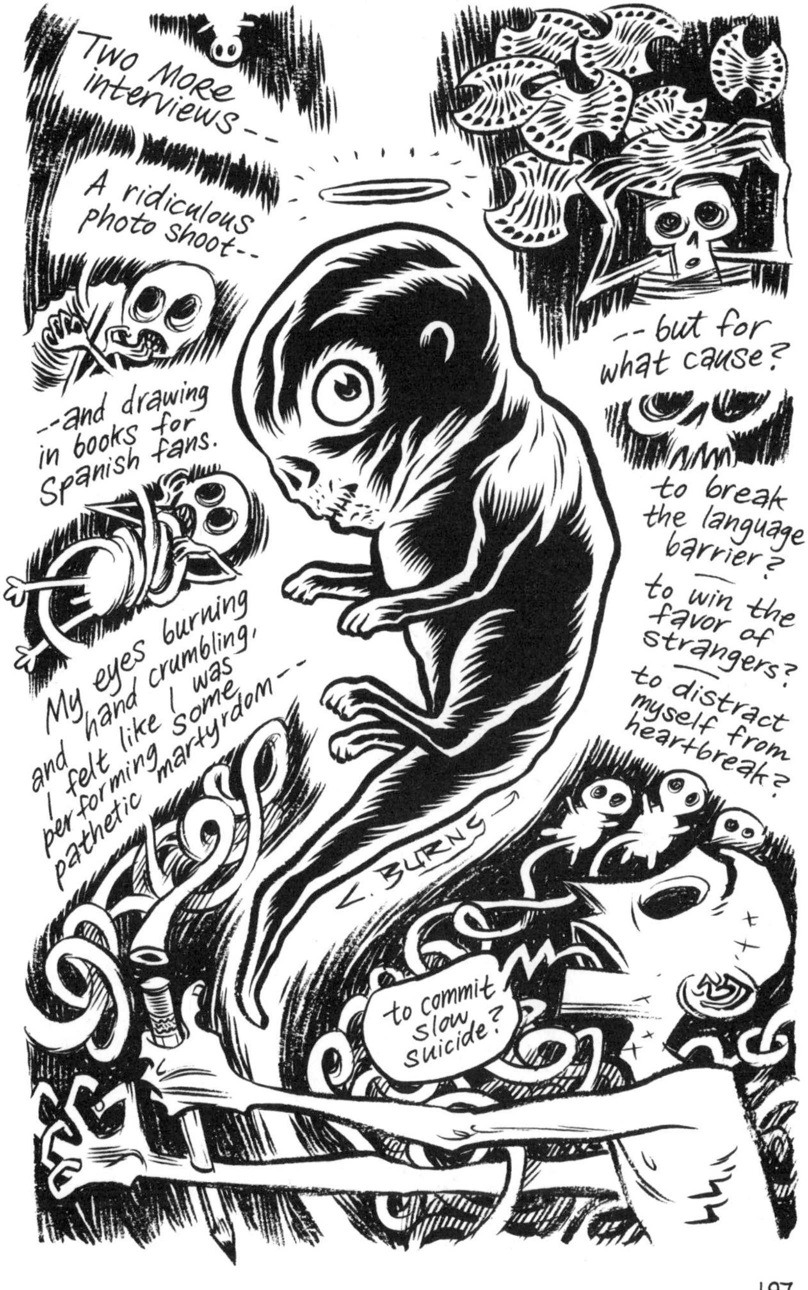
Two More interviews---
A ridiculous photo shoot--
--and drawing in books for Spanish fans.
My eyes burning and hand crumbling, I felt like some performing pathetic martyrdom---
--but for what cause?
to break the language barrier?
to win the favor of strangers?
to distract myself from heartbreak?
to commit slow suicide?
C. BURNS

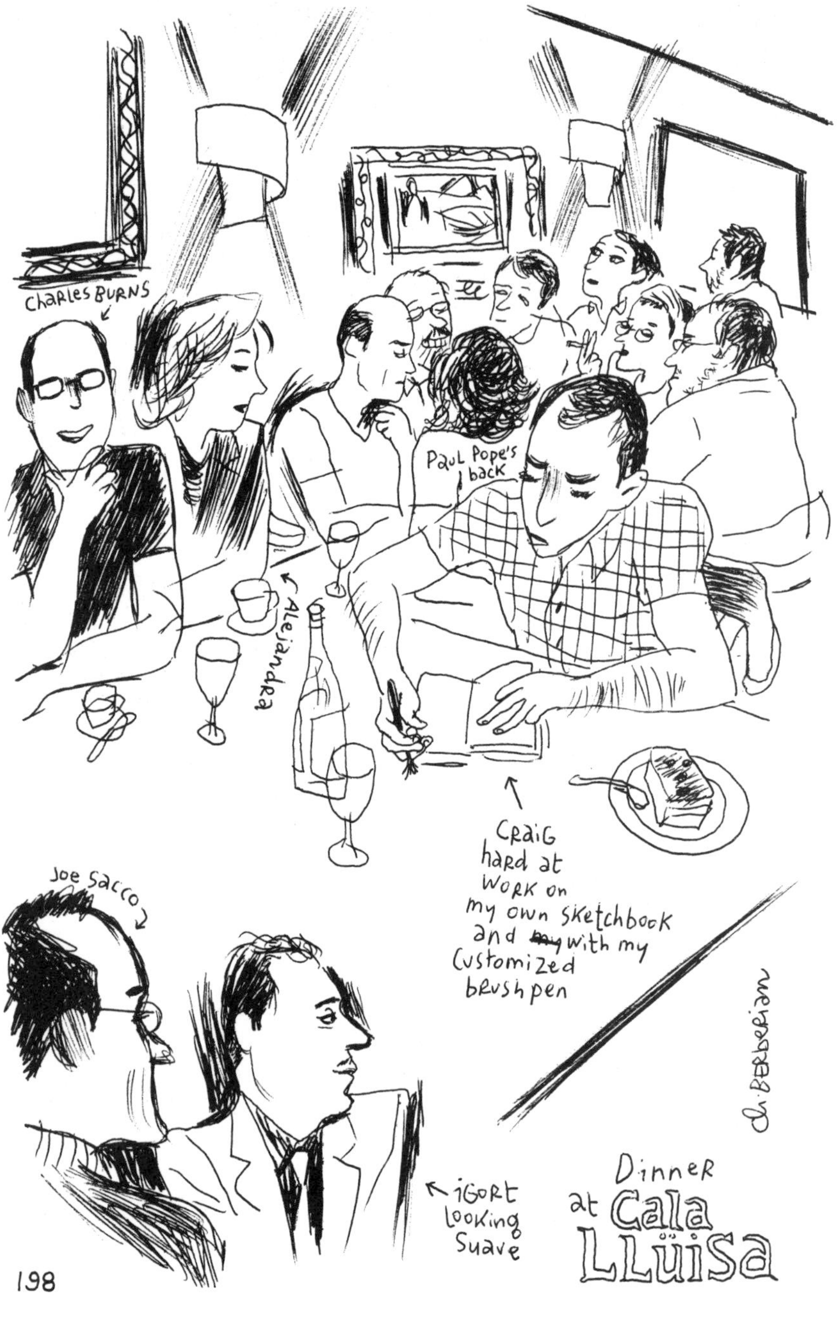
Charles Burns
Alejandra
Paul Pope's back
Craig hard at work on my own sketchbook and ~~my~~ with my customized brushpen
Joe Sacco
iGort looking suave
Ch. Berberian
Dinner at Cala Llüisa

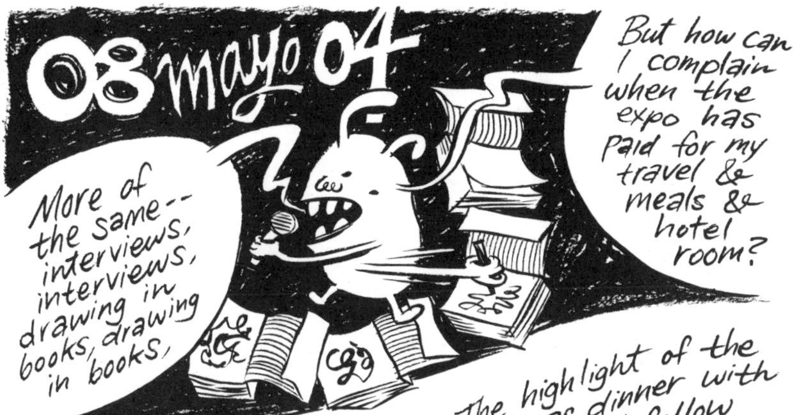

08 mayo 04
More of the same-- the same-- interviews, interviews, drawing in books, drawing in books,
But how can I complain when the expo has paid for my travel & meals & hotel room?

In the afternoon, growing sick, I bought medicine and took a siesta. Later, everyone was concerned and checking up on me.

The highlight of the day was dinner with friends and fellow cartoonists. Charles Berberian documents to compensate for my sketchbook neglect.

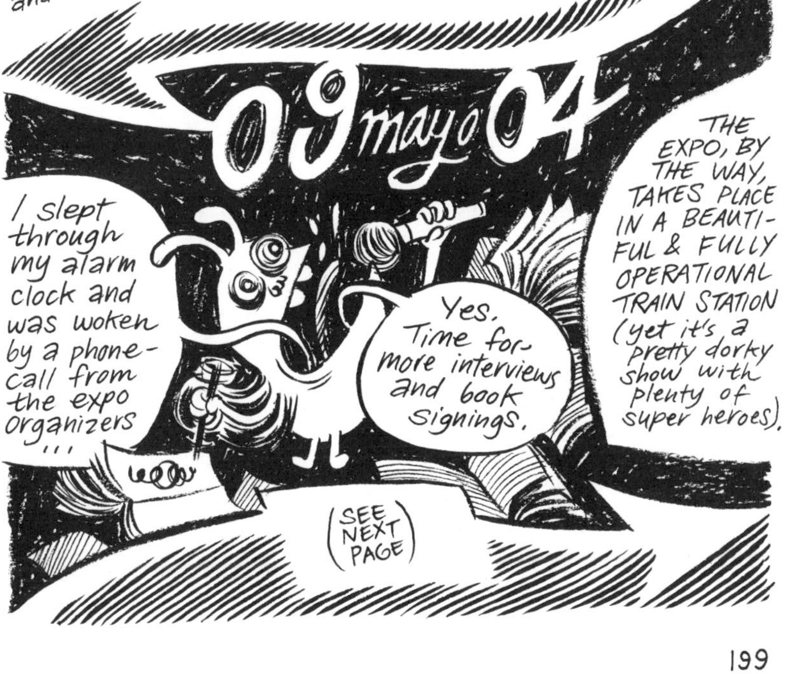

09 mayo 04
I slept through my alarm clock and was woken by a phone-call from the expo organizers ...
Yes. Time for more interviews and book signings.
THE EXPO, BY THE WAY, TAKES PLACE IN A BEAUTIFUL & FULLY OPERATIONAL TRAIN STATION (yet it's a pretty dorky show with plenty of super heroes).
(SEE NEXT PAGE)

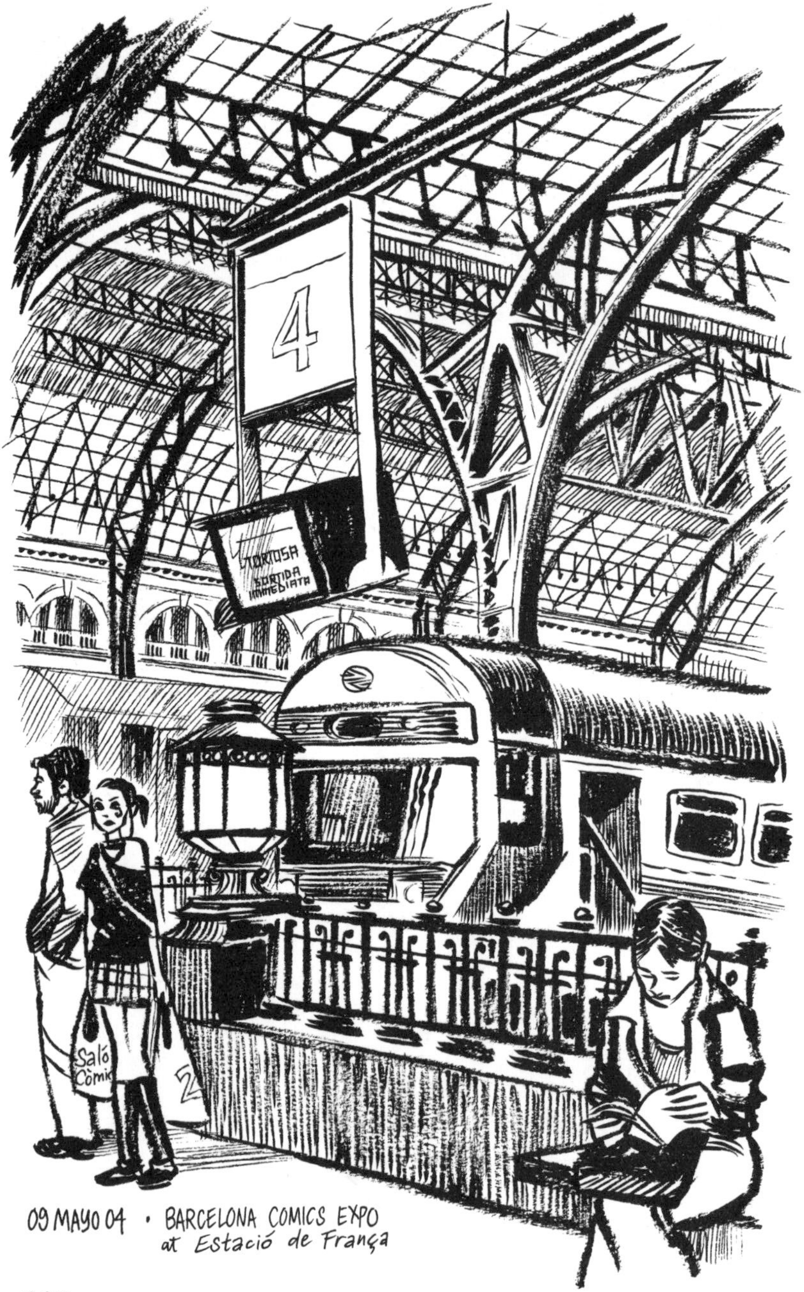
4
TORTOSA
SORTIDA
IMMEDIATA
Saló
Còmic

09 MAYO 04 • BARCELONA COMICS EXPO
at *Estació de França*

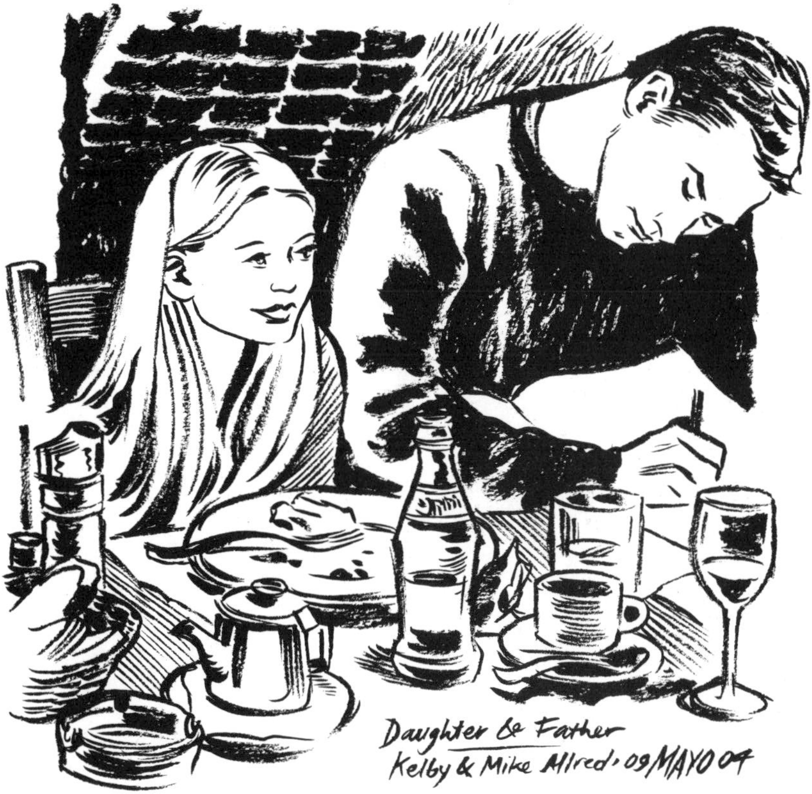
Daughter & Father
Kelby & Mike Allred · 09 MAYO 04

José Muñoz is a living comics legend – It's an honor to sit across from him at dinner. How does he feel after the four-day show?

three times tired = I-I-I = the pain of being somebody.

We're all exhausted, and we've all bonded in the commotion just like summer camp. Paul Pope and I tromped through the streets with arms around each other-- BROTHERS! He talks of moving to Barcelona, and Charles Berberian starts planning a summer visit. We all want to return.
In the middle of the night, I look over the city with the Allreds from their ample hotel room terrace.

10 MAYO 04

The show was over and the gigantic SPIDERMAN banners came down from the regal façade of Estació de França. Appropriately, it was raining and dreary. I transferred out of the hotel to Laureano's apartment, and for a bit, he and I just decompressed--camped on the couch, looking at pictures.
I called Hillevi, the Swedish girl I'd met in the park, and we joined up for lunch along with her friend Ari. The rain let up and suddenly it was summer. Hillevi went house-hunting with a friend, and I drew Ari in front of the orange and lime trees.
In the evening, I tried a hundred times to get a hold of Paul Pope on his last night in town, but to no avail. Instead, Laureano and I went out for pizza.

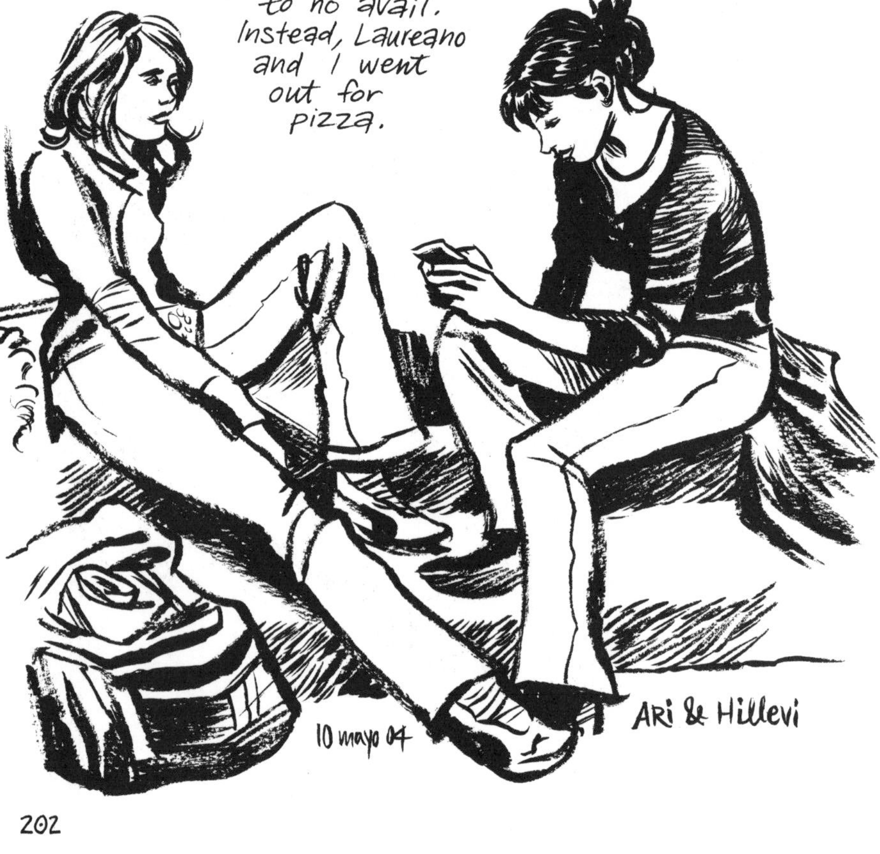

10 mayo 04
Ari & Hillevi

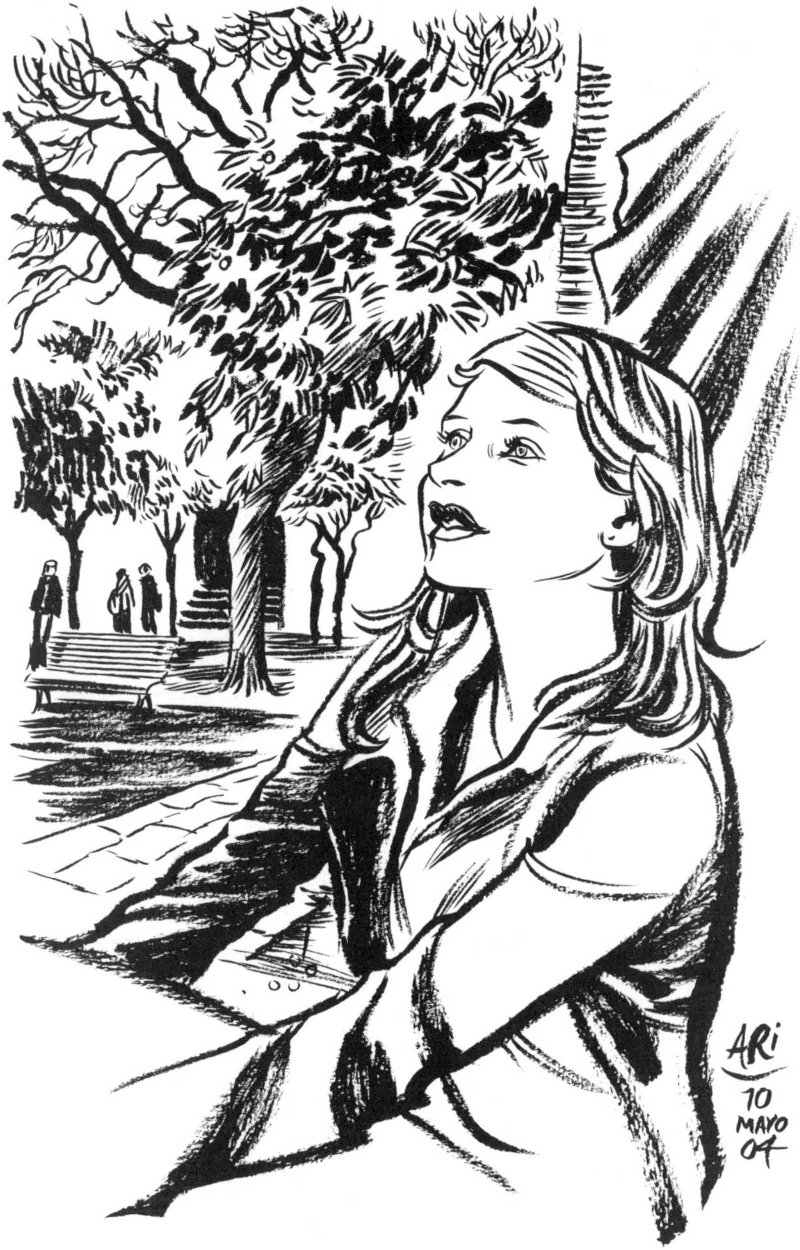
ARi
10
MAYO
04

11 MAYO 04 Laureano departs from Barcelona in the morning, leaving the apartment to me for the rest of the week. My own apartment... no more expo... I'm free to do what I like in GLORIOUS BARCELONA, but the weather is miserable-cold, rainy, uninviting. I collapse on the couch with the most intense homesickness I've suffered on this entire trip.

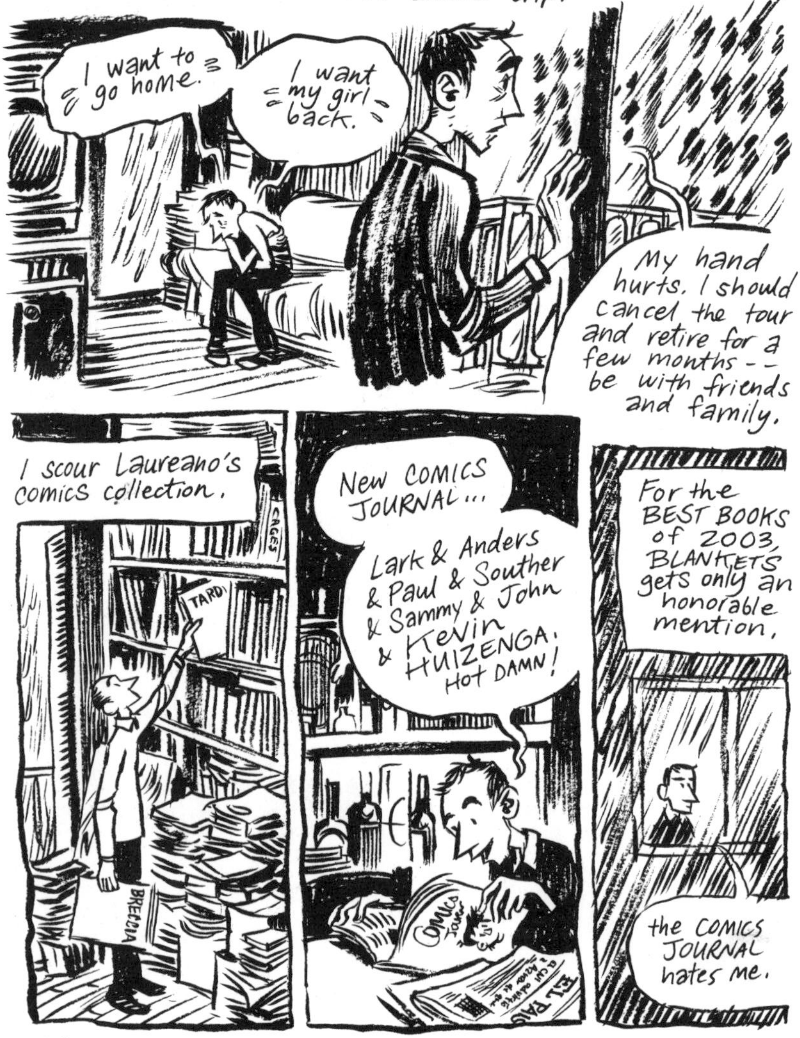
I want to go home.
I want my girl back.
My hand hurts. I should cancel the tour and retire for a few months -- be with friends and family.
I scour Laureano's comics collection.
CAGES
TARD
BRECCIA
New COMICS JOURNAL...
Lark & Anders & Paul & Souther & Sammy & John & Kevin HUIZENGA. Hot DAMN!
For the BEST BOOKS of 2003, BLANKETS gets only an honorable mention.
the COMICS JOURNAL hates me.

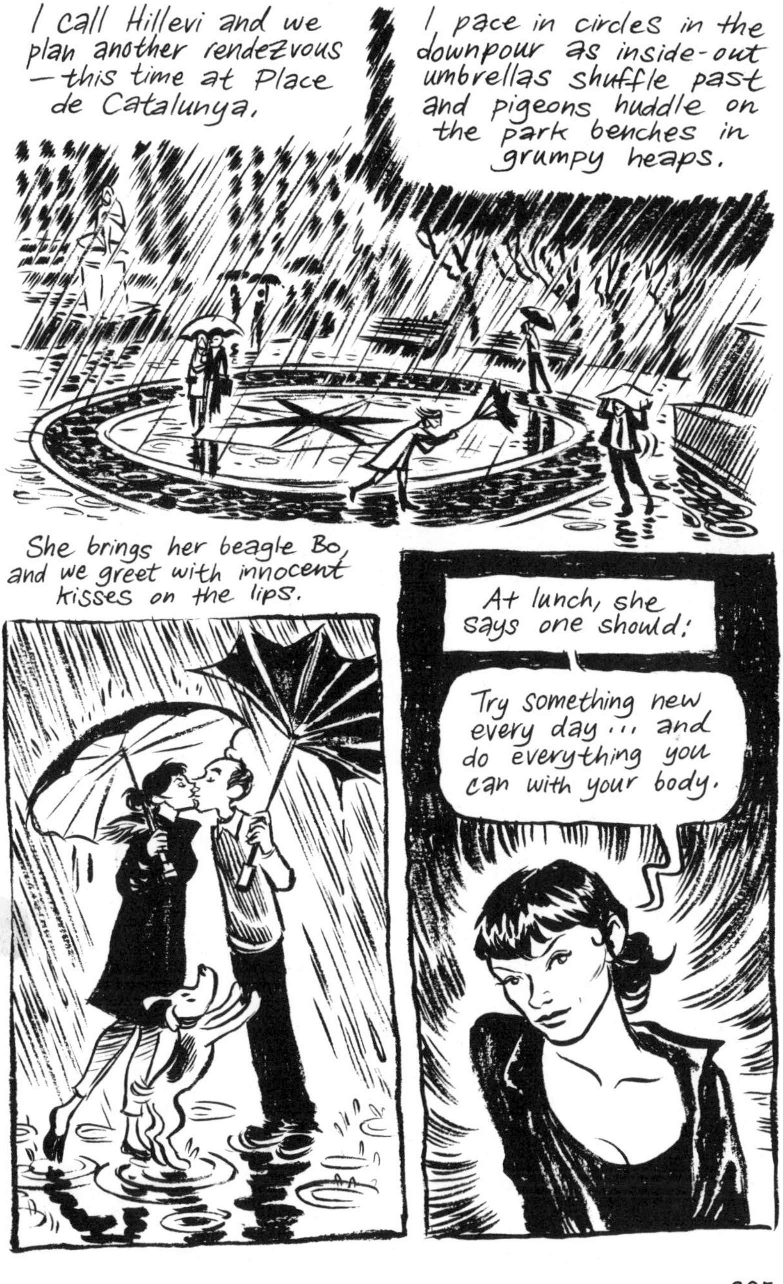
I call Hillevi and we plan another rendezvous —this time at Place de Catalunya.
I pace in circles in the downpour as inside-out umbrellas shuffle past and pigeons huddle on the park benches in grumpy heaps.
She brings her beagle Bo, and we greet with innocent kisses on the lips.
At lunch, she says one should:
Try something new every day... and do everything you can with your body.

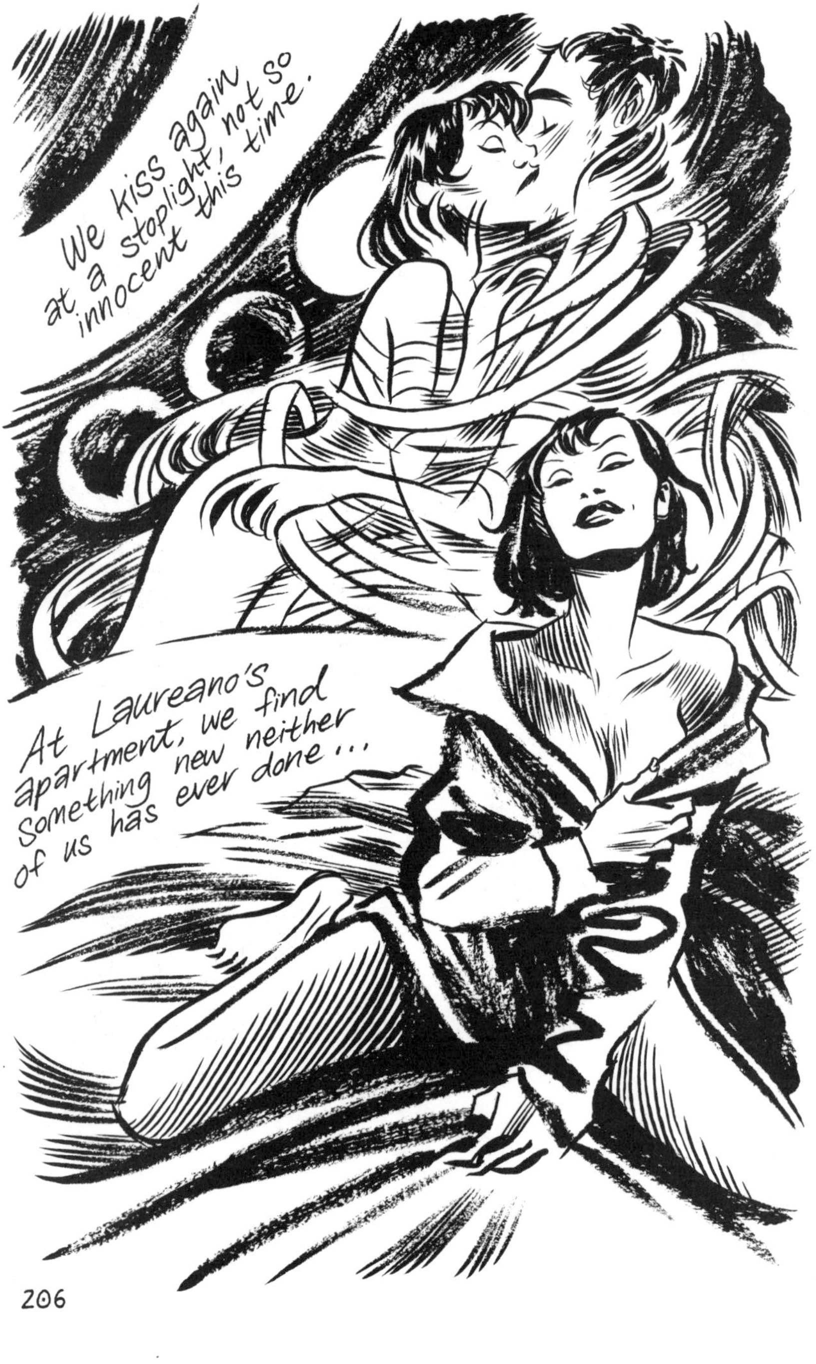
We kiss again at a stoplight, not so innocent this time.
At Laureano's apartment, we find something new neither of us has ever done...

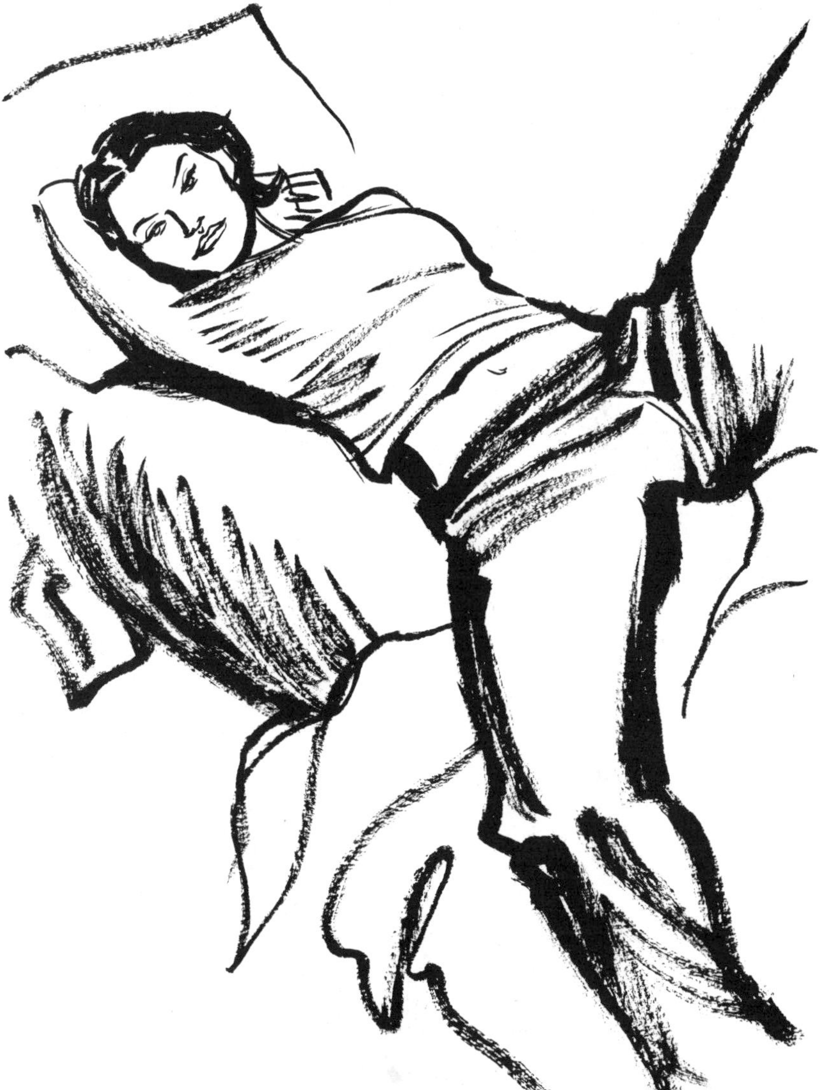

11 mayo 04
hillevi

208

We stay awake until dawn, walk Bo, then finally collapse for a few hours before an afternoon lunch. While eating, Hillevi repeats, "Try Something new every day... What are we going to do today, Sweetie?"

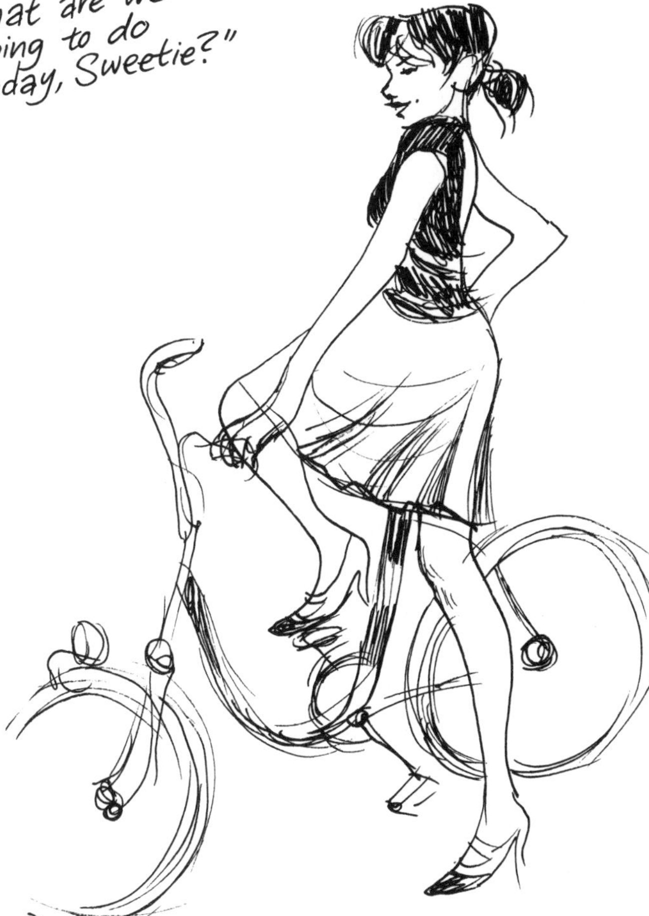

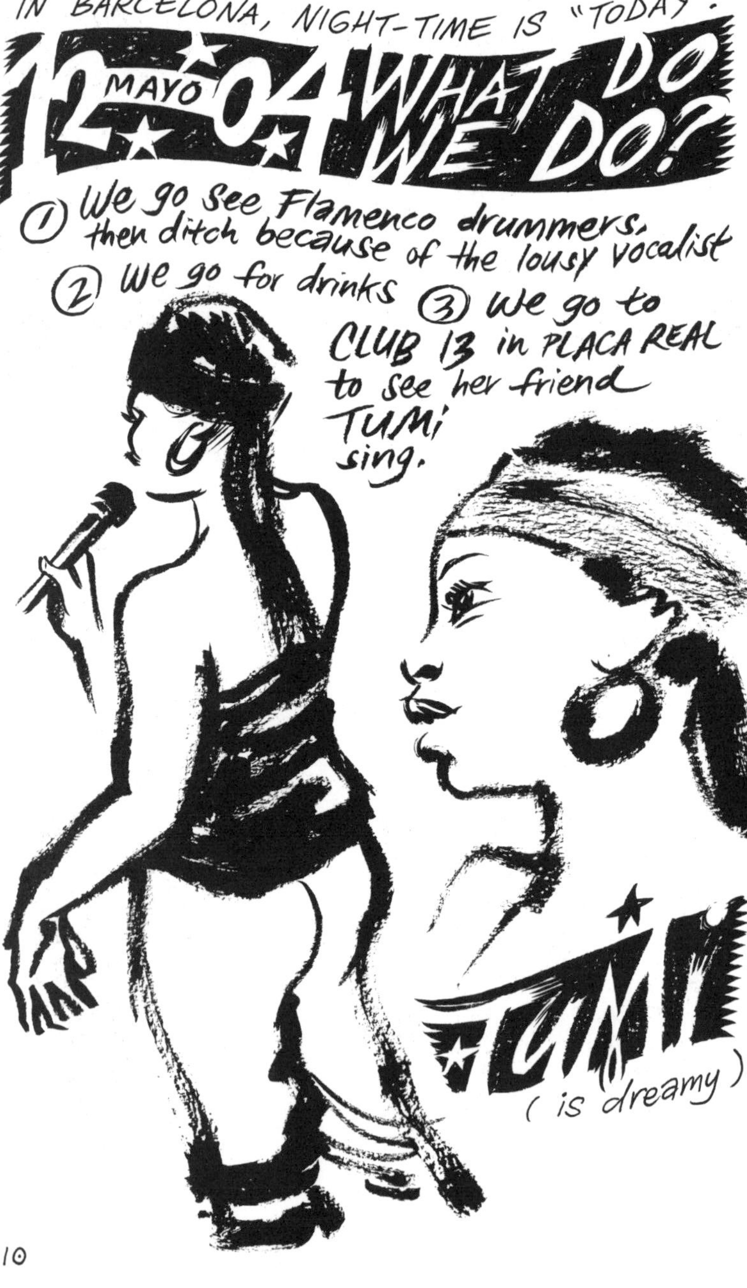
IN BARCELONA, NIGHT-TIME IS "TODAY".
12 MAYO 04 WHAT DO WE DO?
① We go see Flamenco drummers. then ditch because of the lousy vocalist
② We go for drinks
③ We go to CLUB 13 in PLACA REAL to see her friend TUMI sing.
TUMI
(is dreamy)

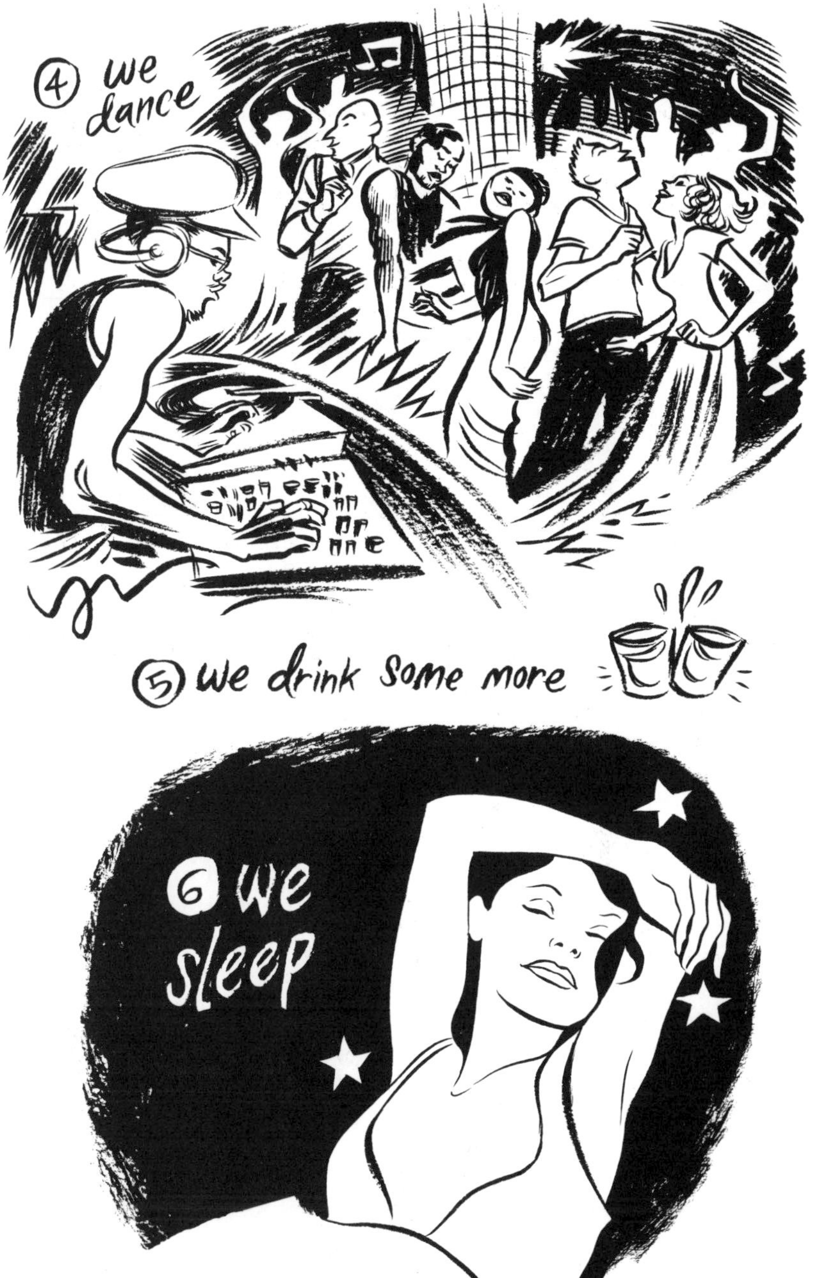
④ we dance
⑤ we drink some more
⑥ we sleep

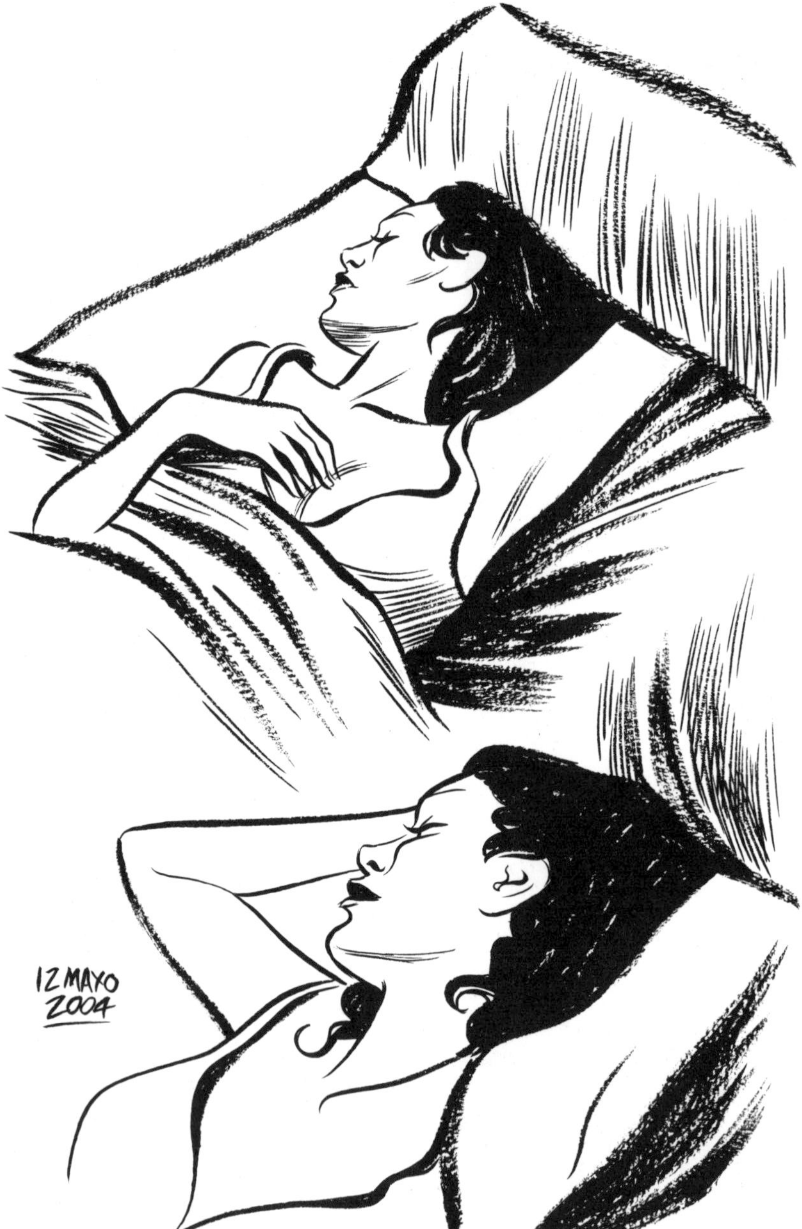
12 MAYO
2004

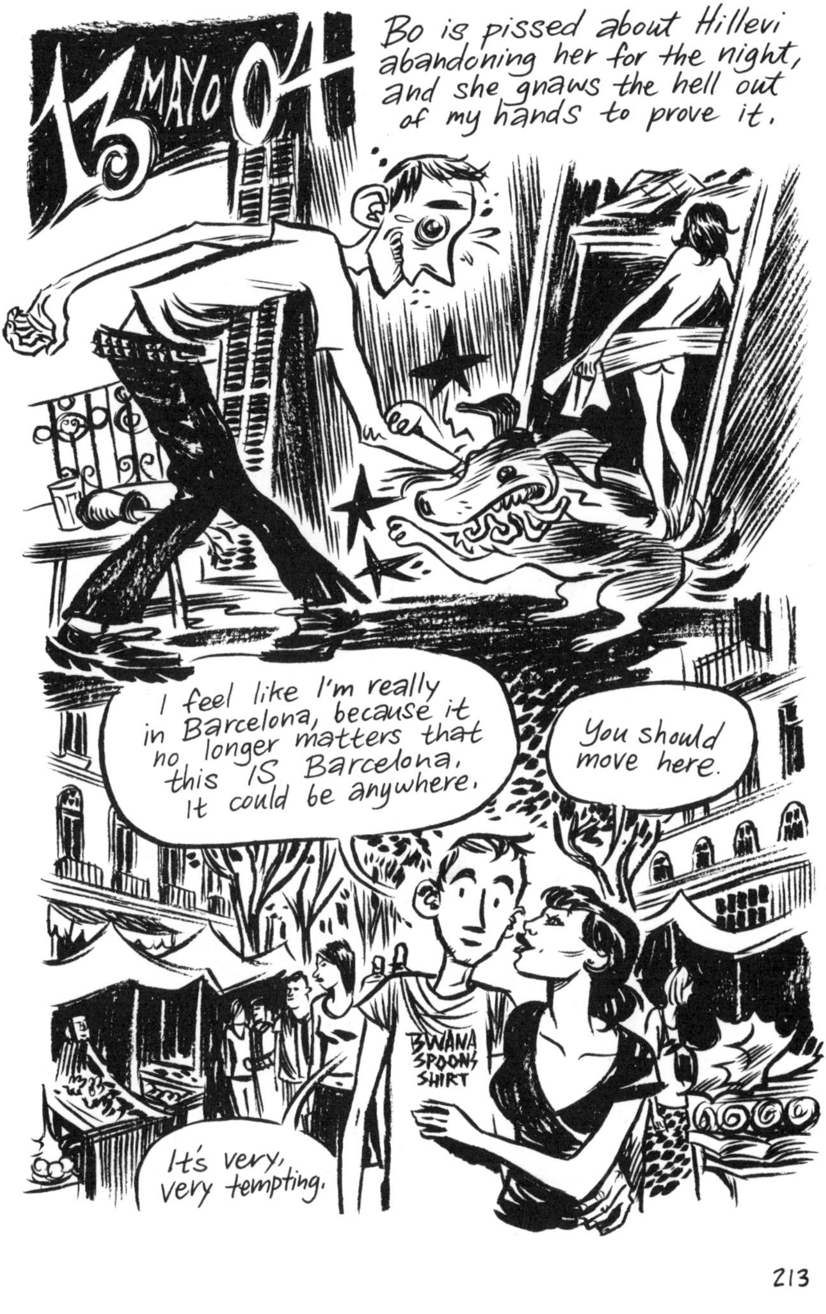
13 MAYO 04
Bo is pissed about Hillevi abandoning her for the night, and she gnaws the hell out of my hands to prove it.
I feel like I'm really in Barcelona, because it no longer matters that this IS Barcelona. It could be anywhere.
You should move here.
BWANA SPOONS SHIRT
It's very, very tempting.

13 MAYO 2004
katie & hillevi

Of course, I'm no longer drawing the city -- only girls.

Hillevi with her friend Katie in the morning outside the Modern Art Museum.

Hillevi in the middle of the day smoking from the balcony.

Hillevi with her friend Ari -- we meet for a picnic at Parc de la Ciutadella in front of that same Yucca tree.

214

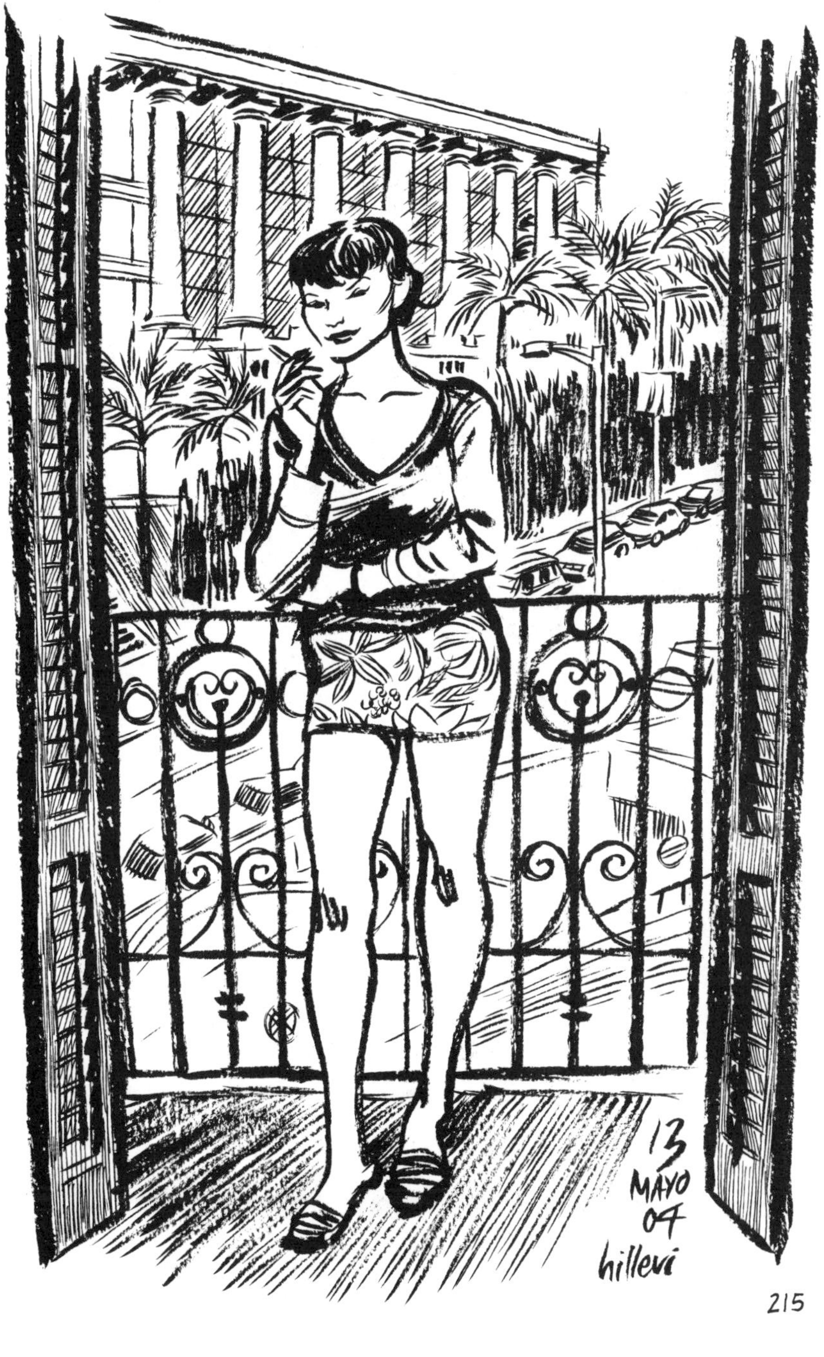
13
MAYO
04
hilleri

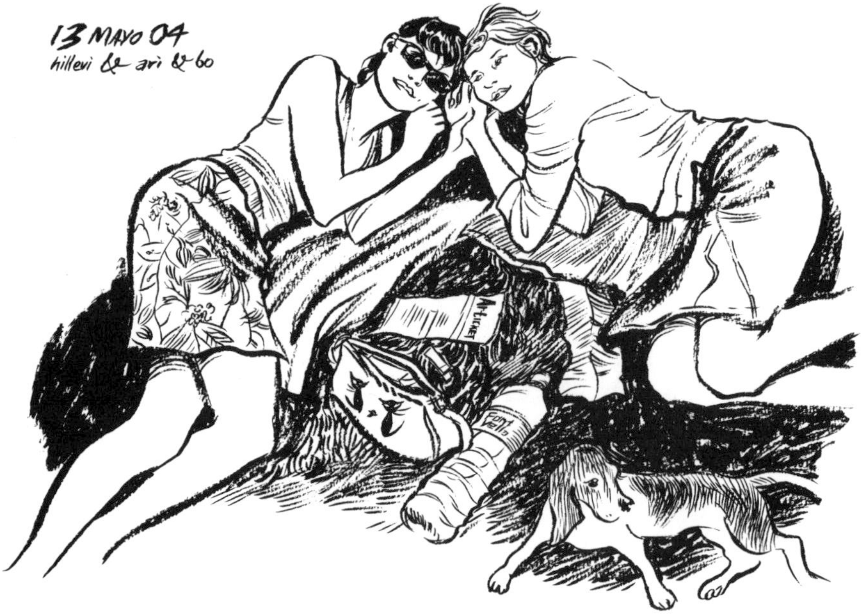
13 MAYO 04
hillevi & ari & bo

In the evening, free movie at an art pad, dinner, more drinks, Katie's "boyfriend" DJs.

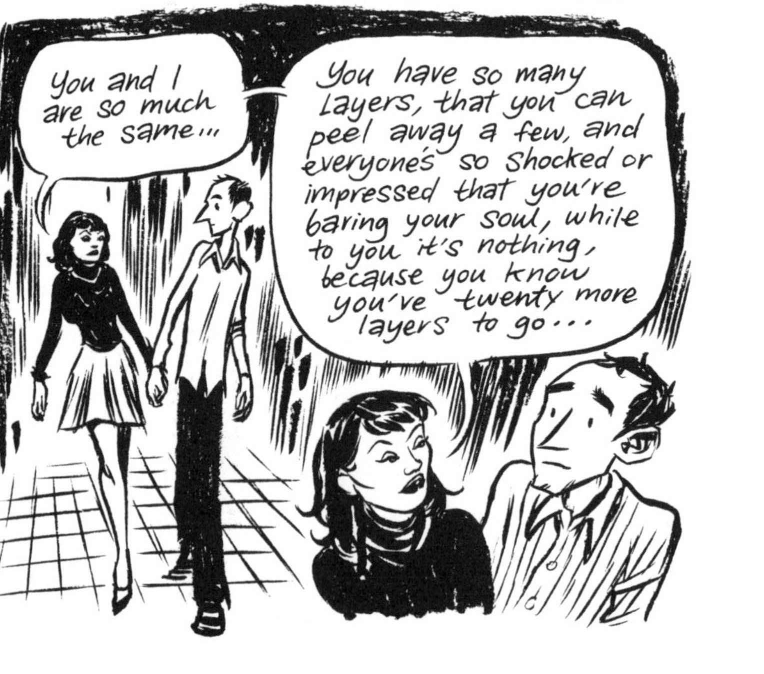
You and I are so much the same...
You have so many layers, that you can peel away a few, and everyone's so shocked or impressed that you're baring your soul, while to you it's nothing, because you know you've twenty more layers to go...

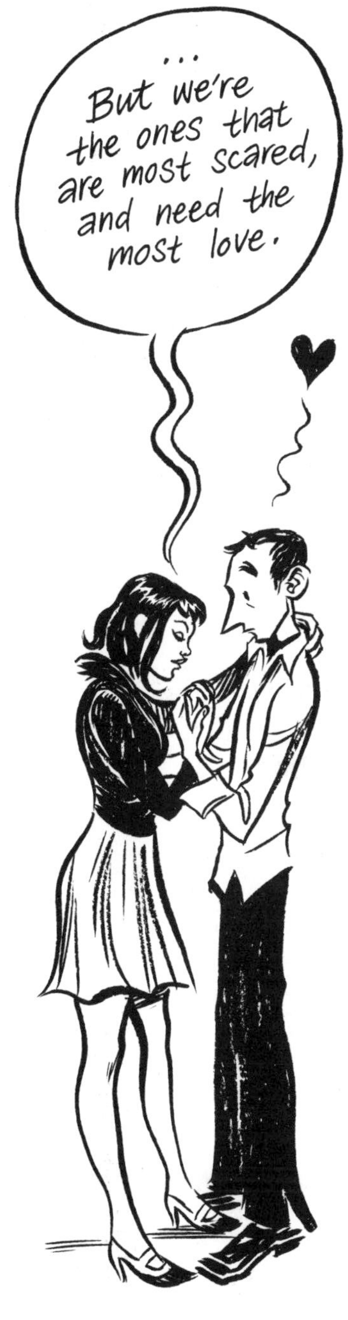
... But we're the ones that are most scared, and need the most love.

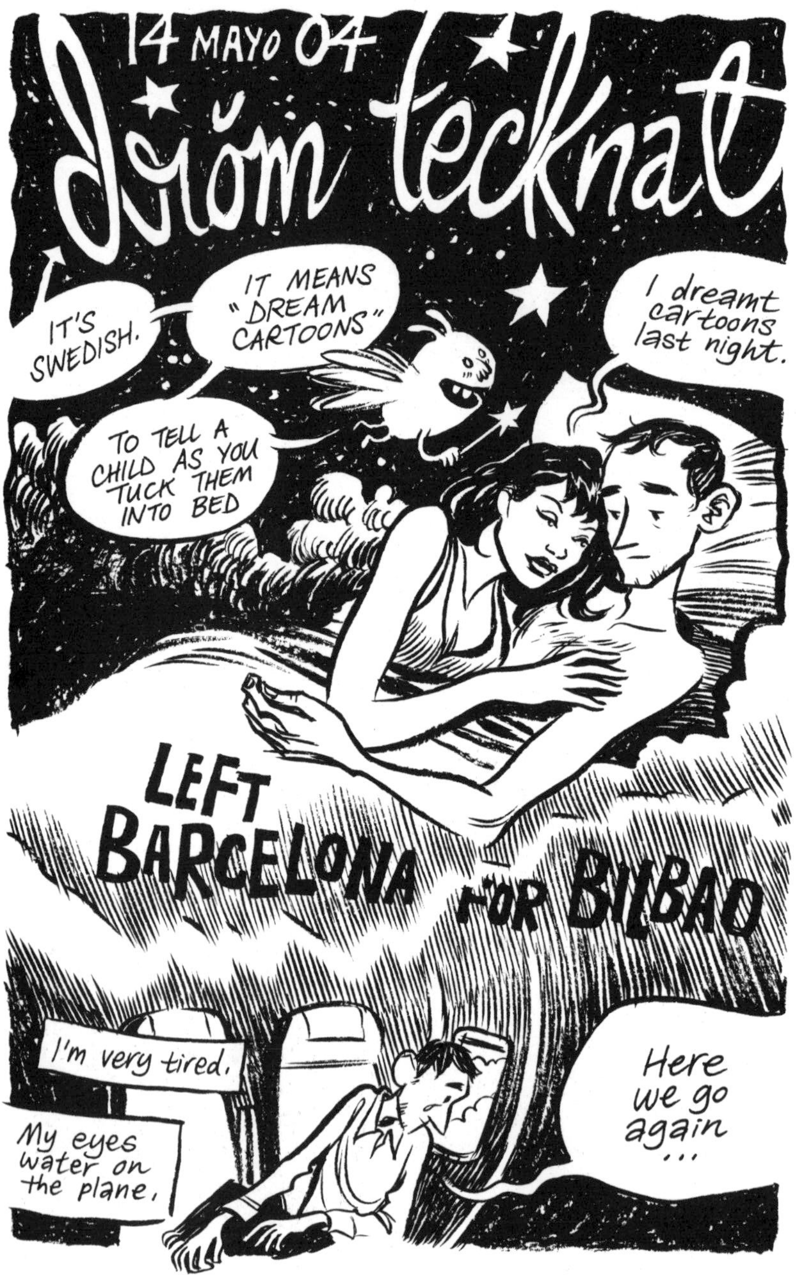
14 MAYO 04
Drŏm tecknat
IT'S SWEDISH.
IT MEANS "DREAM CARTOONS"
TO TELL A CHILD AS YOU TUCK THEM INTO BED
I dreamt cartoons last night.
LEFT BARCELONA FOR BILBAO
I'm very tired.
My eyes water on the plane.
Here we go again...

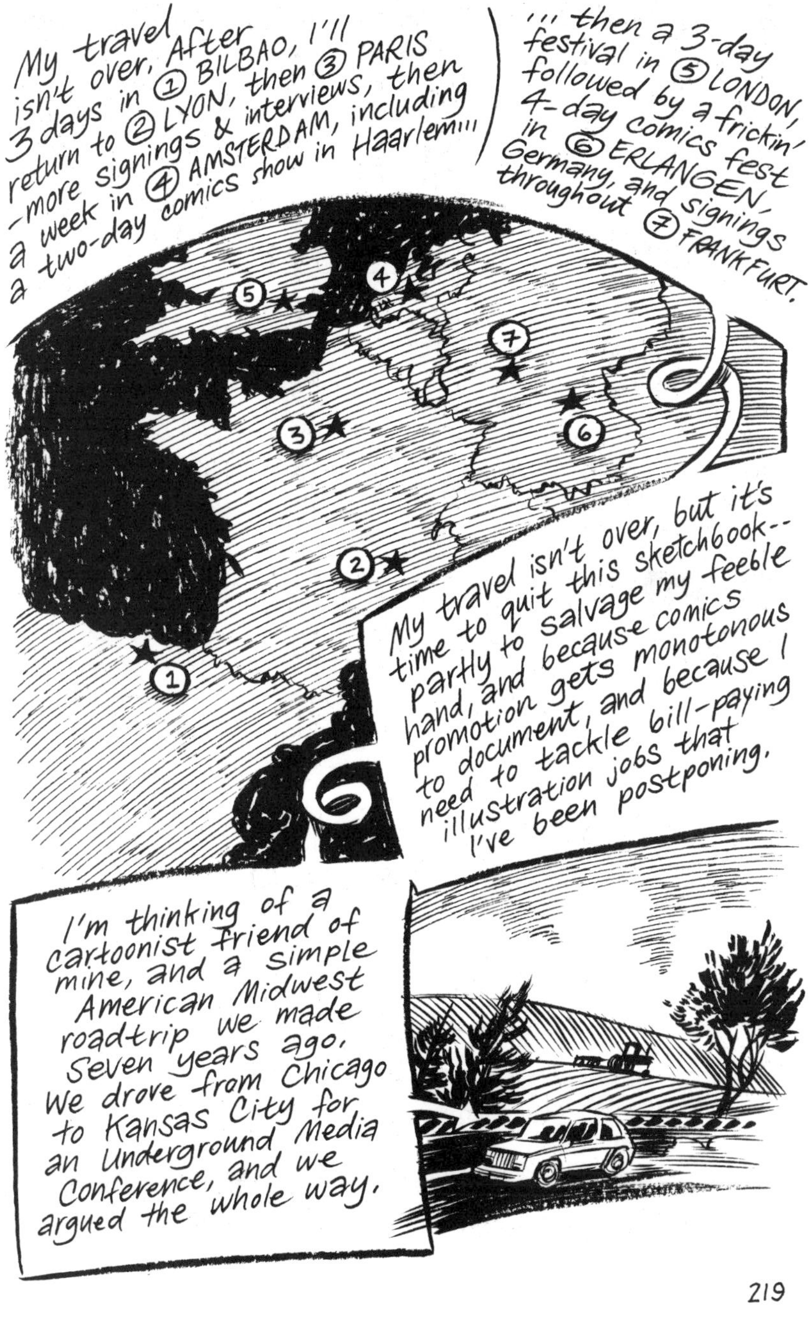
My travel isn't over. After 3 days in ① BILBAO, I'll return to ② LYON, then ③ PARIS --more signings & interviews, then a week in ④ AMSTERDAM, including a two-day comics show in Haarlem...
...then a 3-day festival in ⑤ LONDON, followed by a frickin' 4-day comics fest in ⑥ ERLANGEN, Germany, and signings throughout ⑦ FRANKFURT.
5
4
7
3
6
2
1
My travel isn't over, but it's time to quit this sketchbook-- partly to salvage my feeble hand, and because comics promotion gets monotonous to document, and because I need to tackle bill-paying illustration jobs that I've been postponing.
I'm thinking of a cartoonist friend of mine, and a simple American Midwest roadtrip we made seven years ago. We drove from Chicago to Kansas City for an Underground Media Conference, and we argued the whole way.

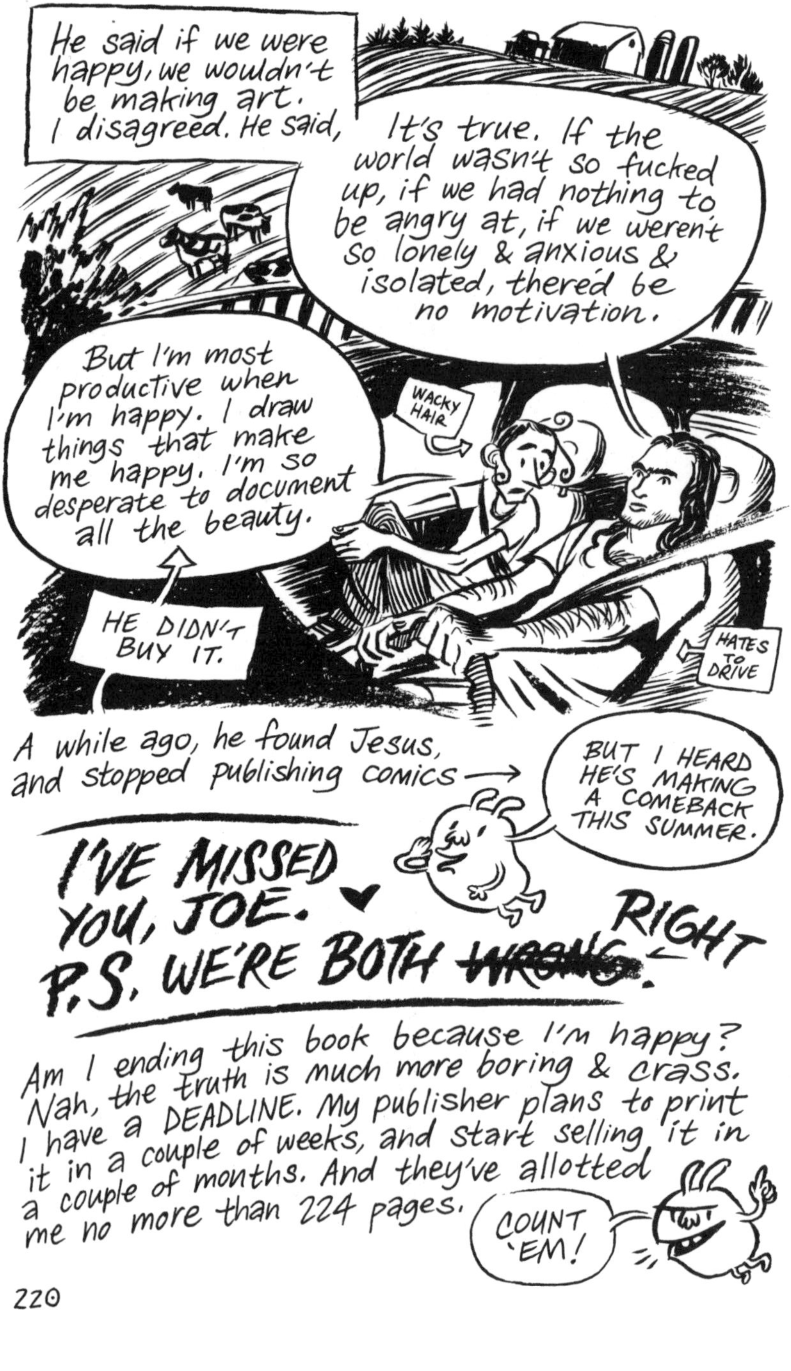
He said if we were happy, we wouldn't be making art. I disagreed. He said,
It's true. If the world wasn't so fucked up, if we had nothing to be angry at, if we weren't so lonely & anxious & isolated, there'd be no motivation.
But I'm most productive when I'm happy. I draw things that make me happy. I'm so desperate to document all the beauty.
WACKY HAIR
HE DIDN'T BUY IT.
HATES TO DRIVE
A while ago, he found Jesus, and stopped publishing comics →
BUT I HEARD HE'S MAKING A COMEBACK THIS SUMMER.
I'VE MISSED YOU, JOE. ♥
P.S. WE'RE BOTH ~~WRONG~~. ← RIGHT
Am I ending this book because I'm happy? Nah, the truth is much more boring & crass. I have a DEADLINE. My publisher plans to print it in a couple of weeks, and start selling it in a couple of months. And they've allotted me no more than 224 pages.
COUNT 'EM!

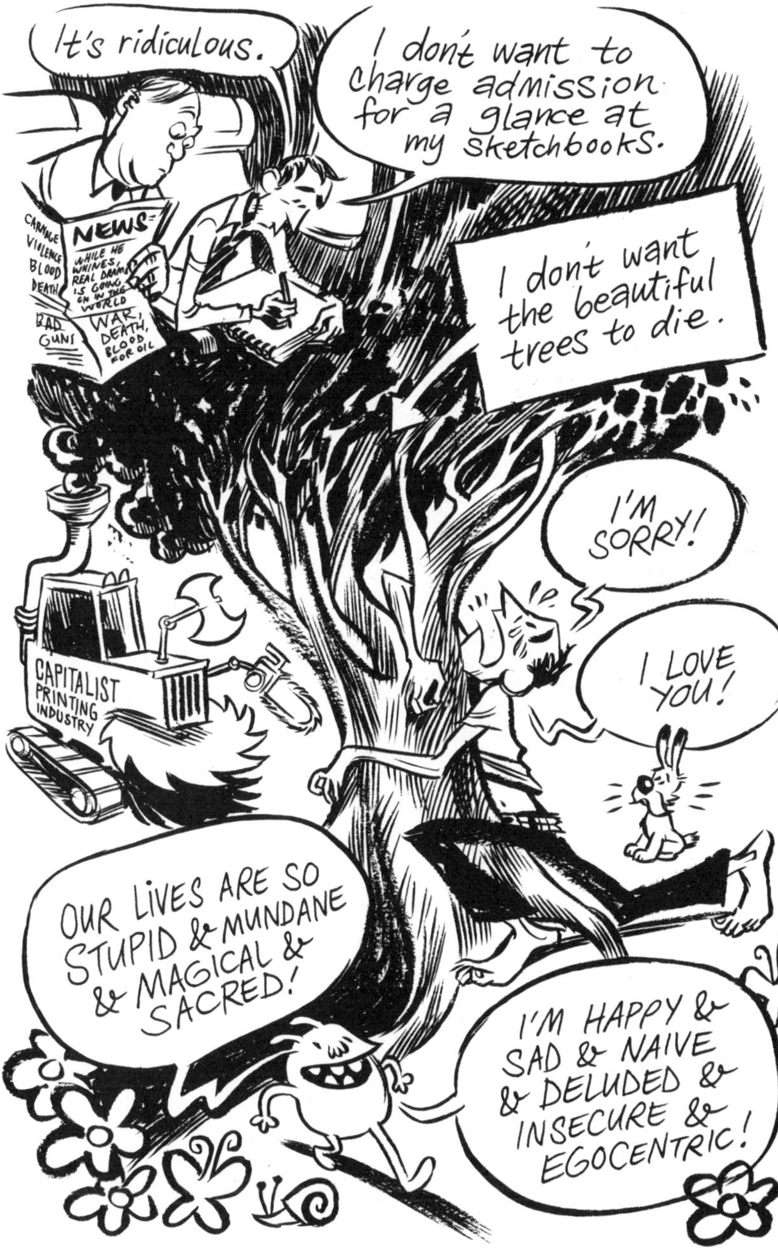
It's ridiculous.
I don't want to charge admission for a glance at my sketchbooks.
NEWS
WHILE HE WHINES, REAL DRAMA IS GOING ON IN THE WORLD
CARNAGE VIOLENCE BLOOD DEATH
BAD GUNS
WAR, DEATH, BLOOD FOR OIL
I don't want the beautiful trees to die.
CAPITALIST PRINTING INDUSTRY
I'M SORRY!
I LOVE YOU!
OUR LIVES ARE SO STUPID & MUNDANE & MAGICAL & SACRED!
I'M HAPPY & SAD & NAIVE & DELUDED & INSECURE & EGOCENTRIC!

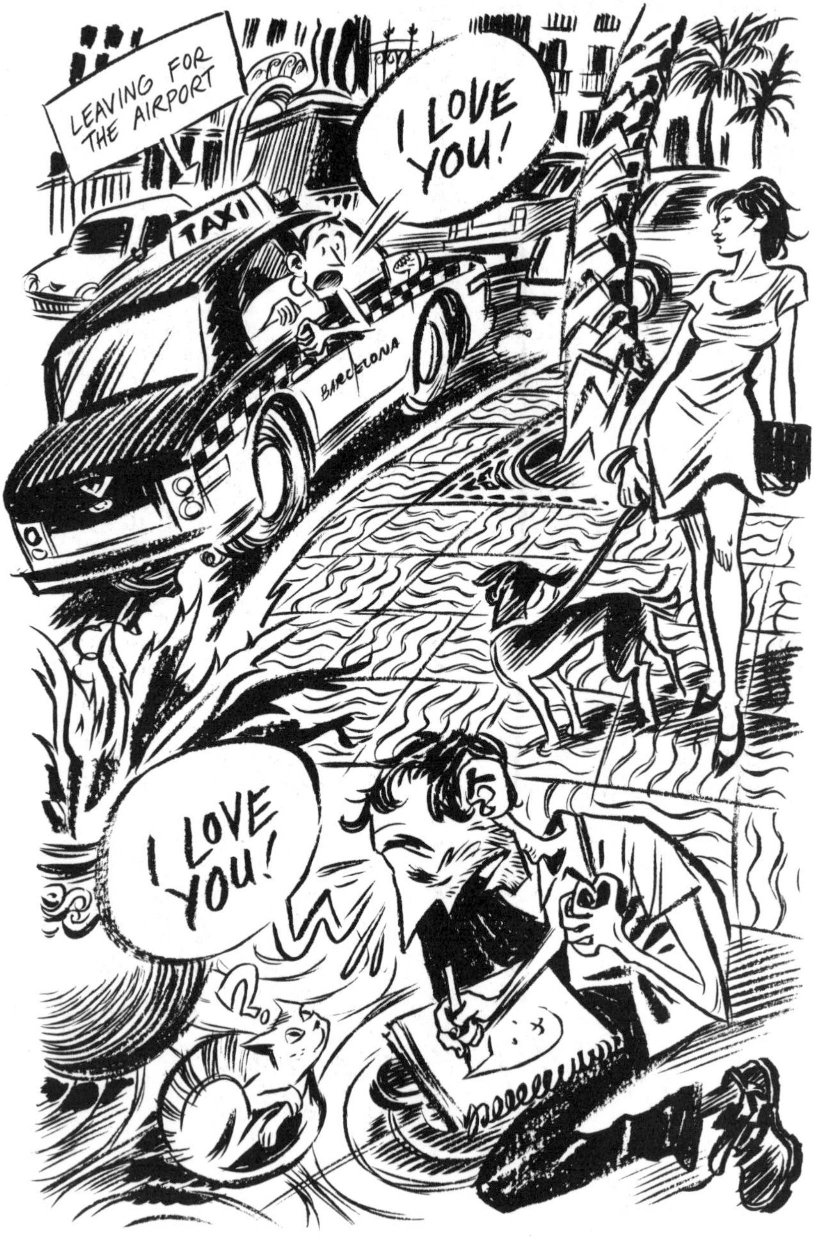
LEAVING FOR THE AIRPORT
TAXI
I LOVE YOU!
BARCELONA
I LOVE YOU!

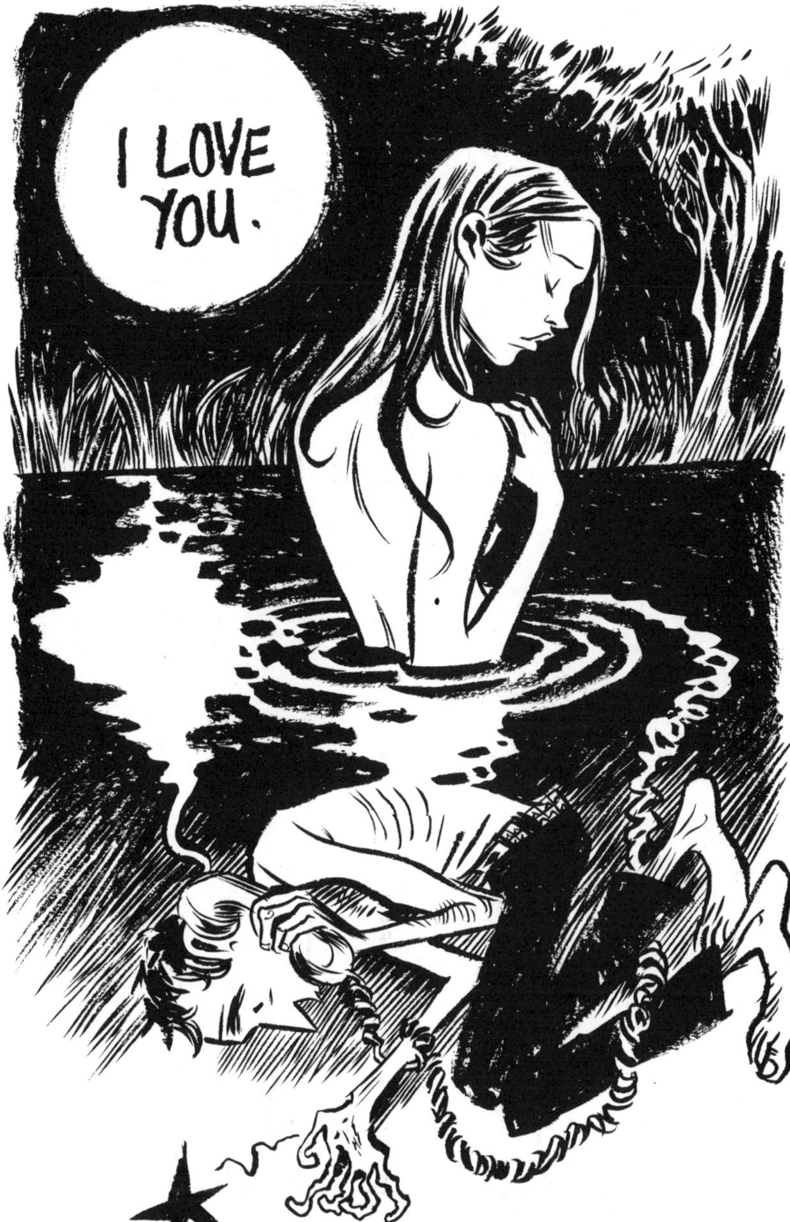
I LOVE YOU.

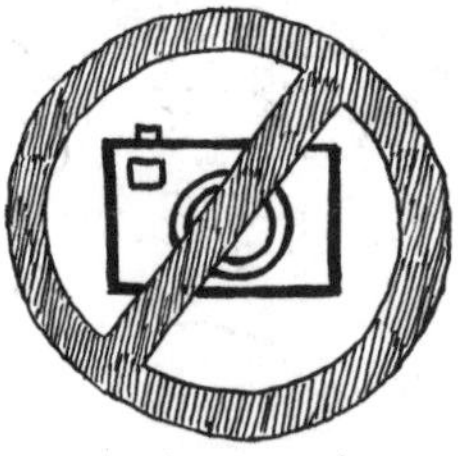

To my credit, no cameras were used in the making of this travelogue -- just my frickin' eyes & brush pens. The exceptions are page 126 - referenced from old photos of AIMÉ - and pages 138 & 142, where the mountains were borrowed from digital photos à la Frédéric - C'est tout!

Mille Mercis

to Frédéric & Laëtitia, who made the raw scans from my sketchbooks. Thanks to them, the book will make it to press in less than a week. Thanks to them, the book exists.

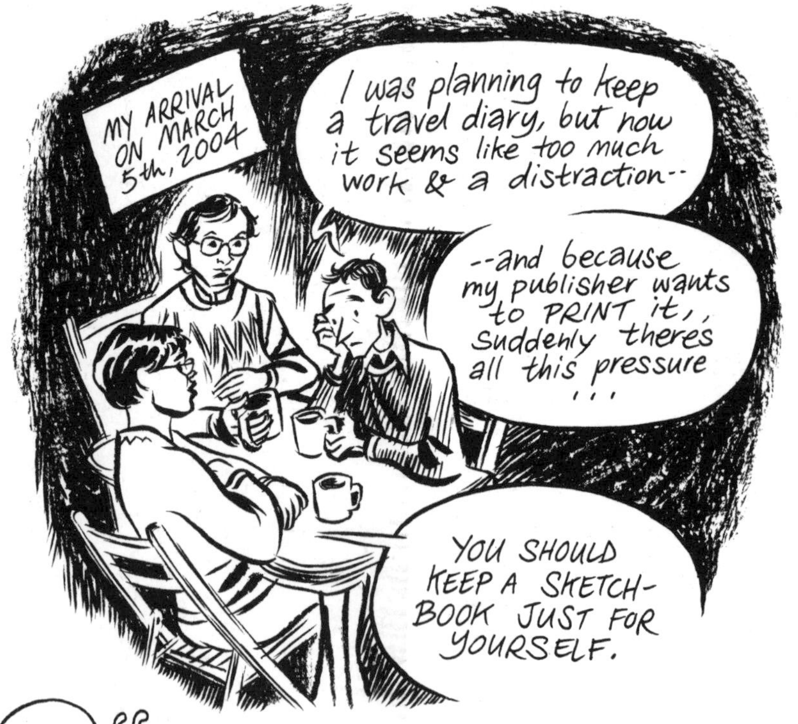
MY ARRIVAL ON MARCH 5th, 2004
I was planning to keep a travel diary, but now it seems like too much work & a distraction..
--and because my publisher wants to PRINT it,, suddenly there's all this pressure ...
YOU SHOULD KEEP A SKETCH-BOOK JUST FOR YOURSELF.

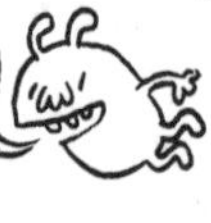